D0699982

DAVID J. LAWLESS

*Associate Professor of Psychology
and Associate Dean of Arts*

University of Manitoba

EFFECTIVE
MANAGEMENT
SOCIAL
PSYCHOLOGICAL
APPROACH

PRENTICE-HALL, INC., *Englewood Cliffs, New Jersey*

ISBN: 0-13-244319-8

Library of Congress Catalog Card No.: 72-38413

10 9 8 7 6 5 4 3 2 1

PRENTICE-HALL INTERNATIONAL, INC., *London*
PRENTICE-HALL OF AUSTRALIA, PTY. LTD., *Sydney*
PRENTICE-HALL OF CANADA, LTD., *Toronto*
PRENTICE-HALL OF INDIA PRIVATE LIMITED, *New Delhi*
PRENTICE-HALL OF JAPAN, INC., *Tokyo*

This Book Is Dedicated to My Mother and Father.

CONTENTS

PREFACE

This book has been undertaken only because of the encouragement I have received over the years from graduate and undergraduate students and from all levels of practicing managers to put some of my ideas on paper.

The main reason for writing it is my feeling about the ever-widening gap between research findings in social psychology and their application to the daily problems of supervision and management. In every type of organization—industrial, commercial, educational, hospital, union and professional society, recreational, governmental and the rest—the person who has supervision over others is dealing constantly with social psychology. There are various legitimate reasons which the professional social psychologist has for staying in his university laboratory to work on theoretical problems; but the result of his not bringing behavior science into the "real world" has meant an appalling lack of application of known principles to known problems. This is wasteful of resources at the individual level, group level, organizational level, national level, and global level.

Because we can't bring the scientist out, then my solution is to bring the manager in. In other words, make him a manager-scientist. Science is not magic nor is it mysterious, and a good part of this book is devoted to trying to show how the practicing manager can be a practicing behavioral scientist with little effort but with greatly improved results in his work. This is the theme you will find running through the book, and which I refer to as theory Z management.

There are other reasons for writing, of course. Among them is my hope that the reader will feel more courageous in undertaking more complex tasks in our highly complex world. Also that the world of work will become a happier and growth-healthier place for all members of the organization. Needless to say, I also feel the benefit will be evident in improved work performance.

Throughout many chapters there will be reference to researchers and theorists who hold that the views and philosophies of science as expounded by others are not reconcilable with their own. Perhaps researchers have to be that way before they can be great researchers—

dogmatically convinced that they are right and that those opposed to them are stupidly or perversely wrong.

But I have never been primarily a researcher. I have done research and I enjoy it. However, I have acceded more to demands to be a teacher and an administrator. As teacher it has been of paramount importance to sift through *all* theories and to try to present them without bias to mature students. (To present them without bias is probably impossible but it is the ideal and does not preclude the teacher's voicing his personal preferences and value judgements provided he identifies these to his students). As an administrator I have always held that one must test all reasonable and relevant theories if they promise to make the organization more effective, and even when such ideas are not in accord with one's previous practices.

Because of these things, I feel a certain smug advantage over the authors of many of those books on my desk and bookshelves. I admire these researchers greatly and, over the years, they have become my heroes. But I am not blind to their prejudices for I love and respect the work of their rivals also. Only by listening openly to the arguments of their opposition can I assess the greatness of their findings and their contributions to knowledge. I don't think I have read or studied any of them without having learned something about how people interact in organizations.

To these writers and researchers, especially the pioneers in social psychology and in organizational psychology, I must acknowledge my debt. This book would have been impossible without them.

I would also like to thank the Research Grants Committee of the Department of Graduate Studies, University of Manitoba for financial assistance, particularly for help in preparing Chapter 21.

My thanks go to Professor Joseph L. Massie, Associate Dean, Director of Graduate Studies, College of Business and Economics, The University of Kentucky, and to Professor Robert H. Doktor of the Wharton School of Finance and Commerce, Philadelphia, and the International Institute of Management, Berlin, for reviewing my manuscript and offering sound advice.

To Mrs. Margaret Glew, my faithful amanuensis at St. John's College, University of Manitoba, I owe a special appreciation.

1

SOCIAL BEHAVIOR

Everything that people do is behavior. (Indeed, to psychologists, everything that any creature does is behavior.) For the psychologist the closest synonym for behavior, then, is probably "activity" or "performance" rather than "conduct" or "deportment" which the term "behavior" implies to the nonpsychologist.

The psychologist, being a scientist, considers as behavior only those things which he can observe and measure. Throughout the years he has developed rather sophisticated techniques for measuring personality, motivation, thinking, attitudes, memory, and other private behaviors as well as the more obvious activity of our reactions, muscles, skeleton, and nerves.

As man is constantly interacting with other men, the far greater part of his activity is social behavior. This is why man is referred to as a "social animal." (In fact, very little of our behavior makes sense outside of the social context.) Almost everything the average person does in work or work-oriented activities (e.g., driving to work, training for work, looking for work) is social behavior and constitutes a substantial and important part of his life.

The manager cannot hope to be effective unless he understands social behavior. For this reason the introductory part of the book is devoted to social psychology, its meaning and implications for management; to a discussion of work as social behavior; to the perception of (or way that we see) other people and the consequent way that people react to one another; to an introduction of the study of personality (including our own); and, finally, to motivation or what makes people "tick" the way they do and what can be done about it.

1

AN INTRODUCTION TO SOCIAL PSYCHOLOGY

The objective of this chapter is to find out what psychology is and what psychologists do. How can psychology be used by the manager? Why do not managers make more use of this science? Social psychology is a specialized area of general psychology. What do social psychologists do and why do they, specifically, have so much to offer managers? What can the organizational psychologist give management to help cope with sweeping social changes affecting work? Not only information but, more important, a tool.

Social psychology has many immediate applications to management not only because it can help people to manage organizations better but also because it can make both manager and worker more fully grown individuals. As a manager your main interest in reading a book on the subject is probably the possibility it holds out to you of self-improvement. The series of lectures and seminars this book is based on have been highly regarded by thousands of managers and supervisors and it is because of their encouragement that I am trying to put them into written form.

Social psychology has been among the most active branches of research in human behavior over recent years. The researchers themselves may be classified as psychologists, sociologists, anthropologists, psychiatrists, and so forth, but their primary focus is the same—people interacting. More and more we are coming to realize that a major part of life is concerned with just that—people interacting. Parent with child; teacher with student; nurse with patient; neighbor with neighbor; friend with friend; salesman with customer; and all the rest. In this book we are interested in the interaction of people as workers and managers—a cardinal relationship in which a greater part of the adult population participates. The outcome of the interaction may be highly effective in terms of a task accomplished or a goal achieved or it may be unprofitable in terms of quantity and quality of ideas, products, and services. The outcome may also be highly effective in terms of satisfied and psychologically healthy owners, employees, and clients or it may result in frustration, anger, and even twisted personal lives.

Everyone who has a position of authority in the management of people has a responsibility to understand how people interact. In this late twentieth century mankind stands poised before the possibilities of either a fabulous future or the degradation of humanity. We stand on the shoulders of thousands of generations of forebears and if we dare open our eyes at this dizzy height the perspective is such as none of our fathers has glimpsed. Those entrusted with authority in these exciting times have a responsibility to both those they serve and those they supervise to use the total array of resources available to accomplish the purposes of their group. Mediocre managers, like mediocre golfers, keep practicing the same bad swing. It never improves unless someone points out the mistake and shows us the correct way. From then on it is a matter of more practice, patience, and perseverance.

The reports of social psychological researchers run into the thousands annually. No manager, or even social psychologist, would be able to scan them all as they are produced. Moreover, the field is such an interesting and pioneering one that few social psychologists venture out of their university laboratories to apply their findings to the problems of management. There is more than enough basic research to keep them happy and occupied in their university labs for many years to come. Attempts at application have been made, of course, but perhaps the manager is considered less important or more capable of looking after himself than are the children, the sick, the delinquent, the troubled, and the student on whom much more applied research is done.

Although there have been some worthwhile attempts, only a small fraction of the findings of social psychologists have been put into practice by administrators of organizations. I feel the time is overdue for the social psychologist to take seriously his responsibility to the society which supports him, especially that segment of society caught up in the daily work of managing or being managed in the modern complex organization, including the leaders and organizers of unions and officials in the public service.

This book tries to set out some of the underlying causes of organizational effectiveness through a study of social psychology. Effectiveness will be defined later as containing elements of productivity, morale, adaptiveness, and meeting with general objectives. It is sought for a number of reasons. Among them are the possibilities for making this vale of tears a better place to live in—better organizations, better managers, better workers, more satisfied customers and clients, and happier and more fully developed human beings who work in these organizations or who are served by them. The organization must be used as a tool to pursue the dignity and fullness of humanity; humanity must not be used to accomplish the efficiency of the organization. True organizational effectiveness is also a little bit like the Holy Grail—never quite reachable, but always challenging, and promising the researcher by its beauty and its technical possibility.

Social psychology is a science. It advances by the rigorous application of experimental methodology and highly controlled field research. Anything the psychologist says or writes must be open to replication and verification to his fellows before it will be fully accepted. Even then it may not satisfy all the demanding criteria of critical colleagues.

Science and its findings are open to anyone willing to use them. Unfortunately, two things militate against the practicing manager using the findings of psychology. First, he is often not trained as a scientist so that interpretation of research results and their application is difficult. Second, there is such a glut of information and research constantly pouring from our universities that the nonpsychologist simply cannot find or sort out what may be relevant to him. (It is encouraging to see all this research, but rather discouraging to see how little of it is used to help in management and administration.) This book intends to attack both of these problems and thereby improve the manager's position. First, he will be encouraged to bring the principles of social psychology into his office, factory, or store, turning his work situation into a natural laboratory. This can be done with minimal expenditure of energy. It is mainly knowledge he needs for this, not extra time or complex equipment. Second, the book will outline some major areas for his research and application and point the direction to further information which could be useful to him.

WHAT IS PSYCHOLOGY?

The most commonly accepted definition of psychology today is that it is the study of behavior. This covers a huge range of events from the activity of a one-celled microscopic organism through animal and human actions to the categorization and prediction of national habits and to the interaction of nations. On another plane it ranges from a study of brain cell activity to total body fatigue. On still another it ranges from the chemistry involved in memorization to the complexity of attitude and value systems. There are probably many such dimensions to a study of behavior.

Psychologists categorize themselves under many headings: learning psychologists, physiological psychologists, educational psychologists, clinical psychologists, personality theorists, counseling psychologists, sensory process researchers, linguistic psychologists, organizational psychologists, and, among others still, social psychologists. What they all tend to have in common is a similar basic training, a reliance on the scientific method of inquiry, graduate training and research, and membership in the same professional societies.

The difference between psychology and psychiatry is that the latter is a branch of medicine. There are many occasions for psychologists and psychiatrists to work closely together both in research and in care of sick people. But with a medical base to his training the psychiatrist is primarily a healer. The psychologist is primarily a researcher although his daily duties may involve a given psychologist more in healing and counseling than in research.

Sometimes a distinction is made between experimental and applied psychologists. The division is somewhat artificial for the applied psychologist is experimental and the experimenter is interested in seeing his findings applied. A working distinction is apparent between the psychologists who definitely apply their findings to improving supervisory practices or classroom teaching and the ones who conduct laboratory experiments with rats or who build mathematical models of brain cells. A glance at a general psychology textbook with its chapters on the nervous system, sensory organs, statistics, nonsense syllables, rats and pigeons, and experimental hardware might make the practicing manager conclude there is nothing of value for him in psychology. This would be a serious error. There is a great deal of value in general psychology. The problem is that it requires a trained psychologist with special types of interests to interpret it to the nonpsychologist manager.

This book will borrow freely from the findings of many branches of psychology and even psychiatry although its major sources are in the works of social psychologists.

SOCIAL PSYCHOLOGY

Psychology as a branch of philosophy has existed for many centuries. It was only in the late nineteenth century that it became distinguishable as a branch of science and in the twentieth that it became firmly established as such. Social psychology is a relatively modern area of specialization which remained almost indistinguishable from general psychology until the middle of this century. In the past twenty years it has mushroomed in terms of research findings, their application, the number of its students and researchers, and public awareness of its importance. In recent years it has become one of, if not *the,* most popular university courses above the freshman year. Because of this, by far the major occupational orientation of Ph.D.s in social psychology has been employment by the universities.

As implied earlier, social psychology also has depended for its growth on sociology. Many social psychologists classify themselves as sociologists rather than psychologists. This reflects a different background of training and often a somewhat different interest in the same phenomena. As against the psychologist's focus on the individual, the sociologist focuses on the social system in which the individual fills his role. Although the two different approaches sometimes lead their protagonists to cross swords about priorities and emphases, they quote freely from one another's findings, more frequently collaborate than quarrel, and often among "their own kind" can be heard to say, "Oh X, is he a sociologist (psychologist)? I always thought he was a psychologist (sociologist)."

The applied social psychologist usually devotes his attention to "social problems" such as crime, mental disorders, divorce, intergroup conflict, prejudice, and so on and his work is of interest to legislators, judges, clinicians, nurses, policemen, and jailers. But more and more he is turning the application of his findings to education, to work and leisure, and to personal development. Leaning heavily on other social sciences such as economics and political studies and finding their base in psychology and sociology, a growing number of researchers are becoming interested in the theoretical and applied study of man in organizations. These organizational psychologists have already gathered a tremendous body of information which is becoming of greater and greater value to the administrator and the manager, no matter what type of organization he may be with. The main difference between the "applied" and the "pure" social psychologist is that the former takes into account the particular people and the specific social context of his research questions while the latter deals with social behavior in general terms.

FIELDS OF SOCIAL PSYCHOLOGY

Depending on a number of personal factors, each social psychologist might divide the area of study into five or ten major problem areas. Some of these areas will be of more relevance in this book than others. To give the reader an acquaintance with the content of social psychology and the interests of social psychologists, these will be discussed under the following headings: animal social psychology, socialization and personality, social and person perception, attitudes, social interaction, groups and group dynamics, society and culture, speech and linguistics, work and organization, and methodological problems.

Animal social psychology is perhaps the smallest research area. It is related to zoology, biology, and animal psychology and got its major impetus from the study of social insects and animal groups. Today we do not feel that ant and bee societies, complex as they are, provide much guidance in understanding human behavior. However, some recent interest has been shown in the social behavior of baboons and apes and in comparing it to human groups.

Related to many other areas of psychology is a study of *socialization* processes. Such research is concerned with how children or others acquire the patterns of behavior which are acceptable or nonacceptable to other members of their groups. The formation of *personality* is important in socialization, as are learning processes, education, and the development of maturity in the child. The learning of new patterns of social behavior among adults is part of socialization and so it becomes a relevant area to management why or why not employees develop work habits which contribute to organizational effectiveness.

A bias in my own approach to social psychology is a heavy emphasis on how and why people see the world the way they do. This is called *social perception* and much of it deals with *person perception*. People act toward others in very different ways depending on how they view the world and the people around them. This raises the fundamental issue of how information from the social environment is picked up, processed, stored, and used. According to how well we perceive things, our best and our worst judgments are made and our most appropriate and inappropriate behaviors are carried out. Only when perceptual processes are effective can the human being be an effective person and only then can he effectively fulfill his role of manager, worker, husband, friend, neighbor, or whatever.

The study of *attitudes* occupies the attention of many social psychologists. It takes us to a higher level of analysis of social behavior than perception because attitudes contain elements of feeling or emotion and of action tendencies as well as of information. A man's system of attitudes is quite closely related to what we call his personality. How are these social attitudes formed? How do they influence behavior? How can they be changed? These tie in with many other questions of communication, personality, motivation, learning, and so forth. Job attitudes have been an important area of study. Unfortunately, they have often been studied outside the context of other social psychological problems from which they cannot be divorced. We shall have much to say about the formation, change, and results of attitudes throughout this book.

Social interaction is another basic area of research. Why do people interact in the first place? Why do they keep interacting? What principles govern their interaction? These questions run through much of our concern in management psychology. The practicing manager deals with these basic social processes every day. His own interaction with his workers and theirs with one another and with clients are the foundation of organizational effectiveness.

Group study and the sometimes maligned study of *group dynamics* is another active area of research. Building on social interaction, attitudes, and social perception, psychologists try to find out what really goes on when a formal group is constituted to accomplish some task. Among the things they observe happening and that they conduct research on are the attraction of people to one another and group cohesiveness, power, social status, conformity to group rules or norms, and the roles and conflicts people have because they are members of more than one group. This is a very large area of social psychological research and there will be a great deal more to say about it throughout the text. The whole study of leadership falls under this heading because leadership makes sense only when studied in the context of the group.

Society and culture cannot be neglected because of their·influence on socialization, attitude formation, and development of social motivation, and because every group or organization is embedded in a larger social context. This is one of the areas in which psychologists come together with sociologists, anthropologists, and other social scientists in trying to determine what influence the individual has on the larger world around him and what forces from that larger world influence his individual behavior.

Speech, linguistics, and *communication* is another important area of social psychology because words are the symbols we use in interaction. It is communication that ties all social behavior together. Although an attempt to reduce all management problems to "a failure to communicate" is an oversimplification, it has a grain of truth in it. Effective management without effective communication is inconceivable. Yet communication involves far more for the psychologist than the mere speaking of words to one another. Communication is the cement of socialization, perception, attitudes, social interaction, group dynamics, and society itself. Without it all social behavior falls apart.

The psychology of *work and organization* is a relative newcomer as a specialization in social psychology. The realization that the social situation of his job is one of the most important of man's life has forced social psychologists to focus research in this specific area of social behavior where general and laboratory findings are often modified by the specific demands of the situation. This is a meeting ground for all principles and specializations, some more than others. It is here that a distillation of ideas from other areas can serve the manager, the worker, and the organization. Although the psychologist by his training and professional preference is mainly interested in theoretical and "pure" findings, the organizational psychologist is more willing and capable of stepping across the line to apply his findings and interpret them to nonpsychologists. This is the area of greatest fallout for practicing managers.

Not to be forgotten among all the foregoing is the specialized problem of *methodological study*. Social psychology presents the researcher with somewhat peculiar difficulties both in the laboratory and in the field. The very fact that the researcher interacts with the subjects of his research influences their behavior and sometimes distorts the findings of his study. As we are all in some ways researchers in social behavior by the fact of being social creatures the methodologist is very important to us. Sometimes he points out that "common sense" has led us to incorrect conclusions, sometimes he helps us understand ambiguous findings, and always he warns us of built-in errors in our attempts to predict behavior.

The differences in these specialties are more apparent than real. Social psychologists speak and write the same jargon (sometimes a stumbling block to the interested public), sympathize with one another's objectives, and co-operate. All are interested in providing the world with a better understanding of and a better means of predicting social behaviors. With these objectives they have a great deal in common with the manager.

ORGANIZATIONAL PSYCHOLOGY

If the last century was the age of individualism this is the century of the age of the individual-as-a-member-of-the-organization. As organizations grow bigger and become more interconnected, they influence more and more of our lives. Most of us, at least occasionally, are consciously aware of living in a world in which we both organize and are organized, manage and are managed. Although they have a structure, the very life of these organizations and of their activities consists of the social behavior of their members and clients. Thus some of the most important questions for the health, sanity, and future of contemporary man fall right into the focus of social psychology.

The organization is a group. Indeed, it is a group of groups interacting as a whole. The principles of group behavior apply to it. But to these principles something extra must be added. In general psychology, researchers can be classified according to the way they approach problems as *molecular* (dealing with the nervous system, sensation, reflexive responses, etc.) or as *molar* (dealing with personality, social learning, clinical problems, etc.) depending on whether they deal with small units of behavior or larger ones. Equally the social psychologist may deal with molecular units like the interaction of two people, the behavior of small groups, and so on, or with molar units like organizations.

According to Kelly's[1] description, the formal organization is one which has been deliberately established for a particular purpose,

[1] Joe Kelly, *Organizational Behavior* (Homewood, Ill.: Irwin-Dorsey Ltd., 1969).

the goals or objectives of which have been clearly defined;

the rules or norms which its members must follow have been specified;

it has a structure which has not occurred by chance but, rather, has been built into it through the conscious effort of some organizational architect;

and it operates, not in a vacuum, but in the context of many interlocking organizations and groups with which it may have formal or informal relationships.

To this description may be added that the objective of the organization has been subdivided for the work of individual members, subordinate groups, and interlocking organizations.

Obviously, such a description encompasses a wide range of formal organizations: retail chains, marketing agencies, service organizations, the church, the military, educational institutes, government agencies, school systems, fraternal societies, hospitals, universities, labor unions, political parties, and all the rest.

MANAGING SOCIAL CHANGE

Although there is a tendency for management to treat it as such, static is one thing society is not. Of course, no healthy organization treats it as static in the sense that there is no adjustment to meet social needs or no attempt to forecast buying preferences, and so on. But, in spite of this, the unexpressed attitude of management is usually that human nature remains the same. The social psychologist is aware that human social needs, motivations, and personality patterns are changing and evolving. People are *not* the same today as they have always been, nor as they were one hundred years ago, nor fifty years ago, nor twenty-five years ago.

We are all familiar with the analogy of technological evolution in which the age of man on earth is reduced to a twenty-four-hour period during which the wheel was invented a few hours ago, the alphabet a matter of minutes ago, and the jet airplane, the television set, and the computer split seconds ago. Although we readily accept the analogy, it sometimes does not cross our minds that social evolution has been going on at the same pace as technological evolution. A little bit of reflection on our personal experience will tell us that the needs of today's worker in North America are not the needs of the worker in the 1930s or 1940s.

Yet today's successful manager can always fall back on the irrefutable argument that he got to the top by holding such-and-such a philosophy of work and the worker. True, yes, but the chances of his going from bottom to top today with the same philosophy are nil. Years of practice of management techniques which were successful in the 1940s will not make you an effective manager today. Even some of the great researchers and writers who pioneered the study of management psychology and organizational effectiveness during the forties and fifties have not realized this lesson. In mock seriousness, I sometimes tell my students they should treat all research and writing in management and organizational psychology done before 1960 as "of historical interest only." This is not wholly true, but it puts the student on guard so that he can interpret earlier findings in the light of later ones.

The manager who achieves a little success in his promotion up the organizational ladder is sometimes convinced that his way of looking at the world is the best one and the key to success. He also thinks sometimes, misguidedly, that his own "cognitive world" is the same as everyone else's. The senior worker also falls into the same trap. The use of yesterday's techniques today often results in an appalling and unhealthy dullness about the job. Life does not have to be dull and stultifying—no part of it, whether at leisure or at work. Those forces in manager, organization, and worker which militate against making working and living an exciting adventure must be resisted and denied. We must throw off those myths of management and of work which make jobs humdrum and negative things. All men, both managers and workers, should be able to find psychological growth and maturity through their jobs. Any objective which opposes this is a relic of the past and has no place today and in the future.

No organization is exempt from change. Go back to your home town, or to the street where you were born. The change (or your changed conception of it) is startling. But the same is true of the organization in which you started to work only a few short years ago—it has changed, the people have changed, and you have changed in those intervening years. With average observational abilities these changes in time are apparent. What is more difficult to observe are the changes *as they are going on.* Yet that is what the good manager should be able to do and what he should be able to predict. He must not merely be able to adjust to things which have obviously happened. He must take the lead and "be with it." This calls for a diagnostician and not a mere treater of symptoms, and here is the value of understanding social psychology. As the manager unavoidably deals with people, he must be able to diagnose and predict social events.

More and more, the business of management is becoming that of providing for impending change and of trying to steer inevitable change in the direction of effectiveness. This is the difference between progress and retrogression. At the same time that forces and knowledge become available to help the work group go ahead, forces are building up which threaten to impede its progress. Depending on how he deals with these forces, the manager is effective or noneffective.

Planned change must take into account not only the forces of that environment which the economist, the politician, and the business analyst study, but those forces which influence the dynamics of the work group. The mix of technological development, of national and international context in which the organization is set, and of changing worker involvement must all be considered and predicted if change is to take place in the right direction. For some combination of reasons this last factor, the human factor, has not been given the attention it deserves. Perhaps because—although it was considered that everything else was undergoing change—man himself was erroneously considered immutable.

The agent for guiding planned change is the new manager, a thoroughly professionalized management technician, and not merely a professional from another discipline upon whom has been plunked a few years of managerial experience. Looking back on my own management experience, I can see how often I carried through with the false assumptions of my predecessors and of the faulty system which I entered. The manager of today and of the future cannot afford that—nor can the organization he works for or the people it serves.

But how can he be a diagnostic technician if he does not understand social behavior? No one in his right mind would propose that we make social psychologists into managers. On the other hand, it poses no great problem to teach managers some basic principles of social psychology. Here we come back to one of the major purposes of this book—to bring social psychology, its findings and methods, out of the lab and into practical management. More is involved in this than simply applying social psychology to the organization in a blind technological way. The management setting can become a *source* of knowledge which in some ways will be even more useful than the lab because the artificiality of experiments will be minimized.

2

WORK IS SOCIAL

This chapter raises a number of issues. Why do people work? (There is certainly more at stake than money.) What social changes have been and are continuing to take place in regard to work? How do different individuals react to the changing nature of work? What are the pressures on managers? Can we do anything about the extremes of a demanding rat race and work-produced monotony? Do attitudes toward certain occupations affect people who work in those categories?

Imagine you suddenly and unexpectedly won or inherited a fortune. Would you quit your job? The vast majority of people who are asked a question like this (a number of researchers including myself have made this kind of survey) reply that they would continue working, even those near retirement. A tradesman I knew when working in the shipyards in 1951 hit the jackpot in the Irish Sweepstakes—$156,000 when that really meant something. He was in his late fifties and wouldn't make one third of that money by continuing to his retirement, but he did not miss a day of work. He bought a new car but that was the only noticeable change in his life pattern.

Yet so many people *say* or *act as if* work were an onerous burden that one might wonder why they are so enamored by it. Well, imagine yourself again as being preretirement age and *not* having a job. What would you feel when people asked you, "What do you do?" or "Who are you?" or asked your wife, "What is your husband?" or when you fill out the inevitable form which asks, "Occupation?" You would probably get a funny twinge in your stomach at the expression on people's faces when you replied, "Nothing."

The fact is that our occupation "ties" us to society. It tells people about our background, our present situation, and our future. In other words, when the TV interviewer accosts you on the street to ask your opinion on the latest civic developments and asks, "Who are you, sir?" it is much more meaningful to reply "I am an accountant" than to say "I am John Jones." Knowing a person's occupation allows us to make many predictions about his behavior. Predictability of other people's behavior is the basis of social interaction and that is why we might look askance at a nonworker. His behavior is less predictable. Among the reasons we work, then, is that healthy adult males in our society are expected to work.

Our occupation also provides a handy social categorization and we use it to classify people even as among "the unemployed," "the unemployable," "the retired," "the pre-employment student," and so on. But there are other social reasons for working, some of them more obvious. To satisfy our social needs (not merely needs for food and shelter), such as need for social contact, prestige, love, and respect and common social symbols for them such as a good car, nice clothes, our own house, we need the income from an occupation. The job itself may also represent a contact point with friends, colleagues, and like-minded persons. Without these contacts we may have very little to talk about to our wives during TV commercials. As the job ties us to our past and present, so also are our dreams and aspirations intertwined with it.

THE CHANGING NATURE OF WORK

As work is social and as society and people are changing, then work itself must change. I have often wondered what happened to a very pleasant and hardworking chap I met while working on private house construction jobs during the 1940s. He dug holes for septic tanks at twenty dollars each—by hand. As roofers we rather looked down on his humble occupation but he explained that he could dig a hole in less than an eight-hour day and that made him a higher paid worker than any tradesman in the city at the time. But no one digs holes with a spade any more, it seems. Hole digging has long been "professionalized" with the digger using a very expensive piece of machinery that only he and a few others know how to operate and to care for. The same has happened and continues to happen in so many other jobs. I am acutely aware of this each time I spend the weekend at the office trying to catch up. Duplicators and other office machinery that the girls can handle as easily as I can use the lawn mower do not seem to function properly for me.

There are also many managers working in organizations composed predominantly of professionally trained personnel (e.g., hospitals, universities, school systems, research institutes, etc.) who are not trained in those professions themselves. This means they will not always be aware of technical changes and new orientations in the professions with which they must intimately interact. Indeed, computerization and large-scale automation sometimes leaves the manager almost completely at the mercy of his technocrats.

There is more to it than technology. The workers themselves have changed. They have a more extensive informal education and more formal schooling. Their attitudes toward machines, toward jobs, toward their elders, toward leisure, and toward the function and goals of life are in some ways different than those of their parents. This is not always obvious because there are more similarities than differences but occasionally the difference in outlook locates us very definitely in the older generation.

From an examination of writings and research concerning work and workers carried out in the past seventy-five years, there seems to be evidence of a shift in the purposes a worker has for working and in the kind of needs a job can satisfy. The shift follows a pattern which we shall discuss later but, briefly, the emphasis has moved away from working for sheer economic necessity to a stage of working to satisfy social needs, and now stands poised for a further shift toward working to achieve a level of self-esteem and autonomy.

Not that economic necessity has been forgotten but there are, among other things, many other forces in today's society which ensure we do not starve to death or die of exposure. This change in the pattern of need satisfaction achieved through work parallels the job attitude change from one generation to another.

It would be foolish to think that jobs and job attitudes have stabilized and will not evolve even further—most of us have another generation worth of working life in us. Today's manager who will survive as an effective manager in the stream of evolution for another generation is better off with an understanding of social psychology than he is with a crystal ball.

Noting these changes, Herzberg[1] concludes that a burning issue facing modern man is to discover the basic "myths" and preconceptions of work and its purpose as they are expressed by society's dominant institutions—the large organizations. Man himself, and what he does and why he does it, makes sense only when examined in the context of his history and social evolution. What man was, did, and why he did it in various historical ages is understandable only in the light of the dominant institutions of his time.

[1] Frederick Herzberg, *Work and the Nature of Man* (Cleveland: World Publishing Co., 1966).

Take medieval Europe, for example. The artistic and architectural remnants of thousands of anonymous workers stand as mute evidence of the fact that life was oriented to a dominant institution of religion expressed through the Church. Without understanding this social-historical fact, a tour through medieval European cathedrals, cloisters, fortresses, bridges, and civic monuments might leave one thinking that they are the result of an amazingly stupid frivolity.

Somehow we must be astute enough to understand ourselves in the context of today's society as clearly as we can understand in retrospect the Europe of centuries ago. Not only is society, its products, and its purposes changing but, as Erich Fromm points out,[2] so is the personality of man himself. This greatly complicates the analysis we want to perform for we are simultaneously observer and observed. Pointless contemplation of our belly-button should not be our purpose, yet we must have some glimmer of what we are really about before we can be expected to serve our life's purpose meaningfully by spending the greater part of our working day and the best years of our life working as members of the organization, no matter how noble its social purposes may appear to be.

This makes the difference of feeling ourselves to be a peg in a hole or a purposeful human. As a manager, the former can carry out only a holding operation while the latter can find the willingness to spend himself for an achievable goal.

The meaningfulness of work is an obvious next question. Maslow [3] has some wise words on the subject when he says, "Real achievement means inevitably a worthy and virtuous task. To do some idiotic job very well is certainly *not* real achievement. I like my phrasing, 'what is not worth doing is not worth doing well.'"

Some modern writers decry the fact that so much work has been broken down into meaningless and humdrum bits. I am not quite convinced that is an important point about modern work. As long as the humdrum and meaningless bits can be seen in the context of something important, what does it matter. Rocking a baby to sleep is quite a dull task, so is teaching a child how to say the alphabet or how to write his name, and so is peeling a potato or sorting out nails from a rusty heap on the workbench, or even emptying bedpans or changing sheets for a cancer patient, but all of these things can be considered as part of something both valuable and interesting.

Among the important tasks of a manager is to bring out the real value

[2] Erich Fromm, *The Sane Society* (New York: Holt, Rinehart & Winston, 1955).

[3] A. H. Maslow, *Eupsychian Management* (Homewood, Ill.: Irwin & Dorsey, 1965).

and meaning in his subordinates' work. This has the effect not only of making healthier and more mature workers but also of ensuring that a better job will be done in reaching organizational goals.

Although its importance cannot be downgraded without serious consequences for the organization, man does not work for bread alone. Through his job man identifies himself both for his own sanity and for the sake of all society with which he interacts.

EFFECTS OF RAPID CHANGE

Suppose your daily job involved sorting eggs. Suppose your farm factory was somewhat old-fashioned and your work required you to stand in front of a moving belt down which the eggs came. As each egg passed you, you had to make an estimate of its size and push a button determining whether it would continue on a side track for large-size eggs.

Now industrial psychologists can tell us that, if the belt moves at an optimal speed, you will not make too many errors in judgment. If the belt moves too slowly, in fact, your rate of error will go up, not down. But also the more we speed up the belt beyond an optimal pace, the more your performance will deteriorate for you will make errors, become confused and indecisive. If you are kept at this speeded-up job over a long period of hours and days you will become tense and irritable. Ultimately, you may decide to quit the job because trying to meet environmental demands is too frustrating.

The same is true of management decisions and choices as it is of selecting eggs. The quickened pace of today's work life puts the same demanding pressure on the manager, threatening the efficiency of his behavior, frustrating him, confusing him, and making him irritable.

But let us go back to the egg sorter. Let us suppose that we now require him to choose from a battery of buttons whether each egg is to be classified "large," "medium," "small," "seconds," "discards," or "extra large." Predictably, his error rate will increase. If we further require him to push a button for "large," pull a lever for "medium," depress a floor pedal for "small," flick a switch for "seconds," tug a cord for "discards," and move a dial for "extra large," we know he will not last long on the job. When at the same time we increase the speed of the belt and then change the rules every now and then so that it is no longer "button" for large but "lever," we will be able to reduce him to a neurotic wreck before lunch time if he is not smart enough to quit.

We have to take a step backward to understand what is really happening in this sadistic little example. A basic tenet in psychology is that humans, to survive either as individuals or as a species, must adapt to their environment. As the environment is not static, this survival depends on ability to adapt to an environment which is changing physically through technology and socially through historical evolution.

There is no question that the current social environment of Western society is undergoing rapid change. Without really understanding what we are doing and without really understanding its impact on us, our Western society seems to be on a fantastic spiral of change. This change affects all aspects of our life at home, at work, at leisure, and all our waking hours.

The very *pace* of life itself undergoes change and seems to be on the same frantic spiral. People today find themselves being forced to confront novel situations more frequently, and to master them in ever shorter intervals. We are forced to choose among options which multiply at some logarithmic rate, processing information at a far more rapid pace than was necessary in the society of centuries past or even, indeed, of a few years past. Some of these demands and their effect on us are outlined in Toffler's book, *Future Shock*.[4]

We know that thinking creatures must be able to predict with reasonable success the outcome of their actions and decisions. Our stability as humans is dependent upon it. When faced with an irregularly changing situation or a novelty-loaded situation which demands fast and irregular prediction and decision making, our ability to predict declines and our adaptability to the demanding environment decreases. Depending on the level of our individual adaptability and the demands of our peculiar environment, our ability to function normally may deteriorate to the extent that we behave erratically, neurotically, or even psychotically.

What can we expect to happen, then, when the manager or supervisor or anyone else involved in administration is plagued with rapid, complex, and never-ceasing novel decisions? The results of information overload are many short-circuited managers.

Some people can tolerate more novelty than others; some are able to process information more rapidly than others. The contemporary problem, though, appears to be the compounding of novelty with the information explosion and the demand for quick decision at a relentless rate. There is a paradox here with which we must deal constantly, for the new pace requires a quicker decision while the novelty and the new information requires a more careful decision. It is not surprising that many managers and executives feel that they are constantly pressed to the limit of tolerance, that they are perpetually harried by the demands of others, that they are obsessed by fears of futility and inability. When the ulcer begins to act up they may start to feel that the rat race is too tough, that things have gotten out of control, that the world has become a somewhat unreal one, as might be seen by the mentally disturbed person suffering from an "es-

[4] Alvin Toffler, *Future Shock* (New York: Random House, Inc., 1970).

trangement" (i.e., a person who has the uneasy feeling that the world is unreal and disintegrating and that people do not appear to understand one another when they talk, etc.). In such a context the individual is overwhelmed by powerlessness.

This all has in it an element of Alice in Wonderland where poor Alice never knew whether she was growing upward or downward. What does a manager do in this situation? Perhaps he clings to reality by blocking any input of new and unwelcome information. He falls back on the cliché and clings obsessively to formerly successful adaptations or managerial tricks that are quite irrelevant to today's problems. He glories in the good old days and holds a backward-viewing social outlook. If he is a technician or a professionally trained person, he may manage to keep up with all the latest developments in his narrow specialty but remains increasingly closed to any broader social, political, or economic developments. He may dream nostalgically of his youth in a small town or speculate about the slower pace of life in the past—and collect antiques. He may even think of how he could retire early and buy a small farm, raise chickens or beef cattle or flowers.

The more desperately he employs these attempted solutions the more erratic does his behavior become in the ever increasing complexity of his world. Anxiety and instability give way to neurosis which in turn gives way to psychosis which in turn gives way to death or self-destruction.

When he was Chief White House Adviser on Urban Affairs, Daniel Patrick Moynihan stated that the United States increasingly exhibits the qualities of an individual going through a nervous breakdown. It is common to refer to the world as a madhouse. The theme of insanity runs through much of our contemporary literature and art. Hallucinogenic drugs allow an escape from reality, astrology and occultism allow an escape from personal decision making, antiscience is prevalent among university students who search for "gut experience" as against rational thinking. The belief that reason has failed reflects the experience of millions, including bright young students, who find it increasingly difficult to cope with change. Youth turns to drugs, adults turn to television and alcohol, the elderly vegetate in loneliness, being bypassed in a world that changes too quickly for them.

Has all this anything to do with social psychology and management? Yes, it does. I started out by saying that man either as an individual or as a species must adapt to his environment if he wishes to survive in it. That environment is becoming more complex and demanding. One aspect of this complexity is the contemporary development of the modern organization in which we are all caught up and in which we are likely to be even further enmeshed in the future. Unless we can understand it and control it, we will be consumed and destroyed by it or at least rendered apathetic robots. I have the sneaky feeling that few people are even aware of the dangerous possibilities of species extinction that the development of the contemporary organization makes possible.

I also feel that many of those involved in the study of organizations are so involved because they wish to make the organization an even more effective machine than it is now. I have no quarrel with them over this.

The development of a more effective organization and system of interlocking organizations is one of the keys to positive development of human society. As Teilhard de Chardin, the famous philosopher of our times, says, the human race is evolving in a manner which is impossible for us to understand. But like Teilhard I think there is the possibility for a glorious future development. To reach it, we must avoid developing a highly efficient organization or system of organizations which is merely some sort of perpetual motion gadget composed of human elements with no greater purpose than to increase its efficiency and to which end its molecular parts have become subservient. Effectiveness, good management, and the whole function of man's most complex invention, the organization, surely has a better and more meaningful future than that.

JOB SATISFACTION AND SKILL LEVEL

Moving up from bottom- to top-level worker, we normally find that jobs require more skill. This reflects more formal training, seniority through investment in time, often a higher education level, more maturity in personal development, and so forth. We also find higher level jobs less repetitious, calling for less routine and allowing for more personal discretion and choice. As might be expected, managers and upper-level workers experience a greater sense of fulfillment, self-actualization, and individuality through their jobs. The higher the level, the more do workers show patterns of intrinsic work motivation than they do external pressures to work, and the more positive and healthy a picture do they have of themselves and their job.[5]

Lower level personnel may not achieve the same sense of fulfillment and importance in their work and their motivation patterns tend to reflect more extrinsic pressures than do those of their managers. Because his job may not allow the same opportunity to realize his potential and to provide satisfaction, a worker at the bottom of the hierarchical pyramid can experience serious frustrations. Low-skill assembly line workers are an ex-

---

[5] D. J. Lawless, "Employee Attitudes Toward Self and Job According to Time at Work and Status Achievement" (unpublished Ph.D thesis), University of London, 1969.

ample of this, according to a number of researchers.[6] White-collar clerical workers doing repetitious jobs also have the same difficulty and the difference in satisfaction has been shown to be related to use of skill rather than to pay differentials.[7]

It is not simply a matter of tending to find technicians, tradesmen, supervisors, and managers more "gung ho" about their jobs than general workers. More important for us, there is a danger that low-skill and monotonous jobs will contribute toward group and organizational ineffectiveness. Lack of interesting work often means costly labor turnover, absenteeism, tardiness, lack of care for equipment, wastage of material, neglect of patients, accidents, and all the rest. Obviously, the effective manager wants to minimize these outcomes.

Monotonous jobs, especially when they tend to be only partly repetitious thereby requiring the worker to pay constant attention to an endless cycle, produce boredom and weariness. Such tedium is magnified when the job to be done is below the worker's ability and represents no challenge to him. Monotony has been shown as a prime factor in job quitting in some industries and lack of challenge or dullness is a complaint frequently heard in exit interviews with clerical workers.

Monotony depends on more than repetitiveness. It also relates to the amount of attention demanded by the work, as well as the skill level, the diversity of activity, the physical surroundings, and whether individual or team work is involved. There are great individual differences in whether work produces boredom. In one study [8] of women doing light repetitive work, tedium was reported more by younger women, by those who also said they were generally restless during the nonworkday and less satisfied with home and personal life. Less bored were those who preferred regularity in daily routine and spent less active leisure time.

Level of general intelligence is a factor found to be related to turnover in many jobs—clerical, policemen, taxi drivers, bus drivers, bank workers are among those in which this has been found. More important than general intelligence may be level of formal education (to which intelligence is often related). The pattern is usually that those above some intelligence level or below it are more likely to quit the job. For one group, the job does not challenge abilities or meet aspiration levels; for the other group, they find they cannot do the work well enough to achieve satisfaction from

[6] E.g., C. R. Walker and R. H. Guest, *The Man on the Assembly Line* (Cambridge, Mass.: Harvard University Press, 1952).

[7] N. C. Morse, *Satisfactions in the White-Collar Job* (Ann Arbor: Institute for Social Research, University of Michigan, 1953).

[8] P. C. Smith, "The Prediction of Individual Differences in Susceptibility to Industrial Monotony," *Journal of Applied Psychology*, XXXIX (1955), 322–329.

it. The complexity of or difficulty of even repetitious work also influences the reaction of more intelligent workers to reduce job quitting.

Argyris [9] notes that mentally retarded workers have been found more satisfactory from a management point of view on low-skill repetitive jobs than were normal workers. He refers to a study by Brennan in which management had very high praise for the work of retarded girls, noting how they were obedient, well behaved, honest, trustworthy, and so on, so much so that "we were surprised they were classified as subnormals for their age." It is a questionable managerial attitude which finds retarded workers superior to normal workers. If all work could be reduced to sufficiently repetitive small bits, all morons[*] and many other of the retarded could be ensured permanent employment. An argument to support this practice could be made, although perhaps it would not be fully supported. However, the insidious corollary is that breaking down and arranging work in a repetitive form to achieve one type of efficiency tends to reduce the intelligence level of normal workers by requiring them to adjust to behavior patterns beneath their ability. Using morons may be supportable practice; making them is wasteful of human resources and on those grounds alone represents ineffective management. Effective management calls for maximum use of all resources, including human, and maximum development of all resource potential. Anything less is retrogressive.

OVERCOMING BOREDOM

As monotony in work leads to ineffectiveness both in terms of productivity and in terms of worker development and morale, the manager's responsibility is to try to reduce it in the work group. Bass [10] makes a number of proposals how this might be done. According to the given characteristics of the work and the workers, one or another or none of these techniques may be useful. Or, indeed, as implied in the previous section, boredom may be tolerable or desirable to the particular workers and hence to try to relieve it could have disruptive effects.

First, one might attempt to make the work itself more interesting by helping workers to understand the service and product more fully (e.g., giving assembly line workers an occasional tour of the total plant or related units) or enabling them to see the significance of the overall organization's contributions to the larger society. This works better with some employees than with others. One may feel proud to know his company's

[9] C. Argyris, *Personality and Organization* (New York: Harper, 1957).
[*] In Chapter 4 "moron" will be defined as the highest level of mental retardation.
[10] B. M. Bass, *Organizational Psychology* (Boston: Allyn and Bacon, Inc., 1965).

product is marketed in Timbuctoo, another could not care less. Bass feels that increased information could hardly maintain unflagging interest over the years. However, I have seen cases of low-level employees (e.g., security guards, cleaning ladies, janitors) whose personal involvement, pride in the company's or institution's achievements, and so on, had become one of the focal points in their lives. The organization may have come to mean so much, for example, to the school janitor during his thirty years of service that retirement is a traumatic and shattering personal blow like the loss of a close friend or relative. I have known low-skill retired people who would have worked for their organization gladly for a nominal supplement to their pension or for the mere recognition that they were still members.

A second suggestion is to improve the general interests and leisure time activities of workers. With higher interest off-job activities, workers may better be able to bear the monotony of routine work. Becoming interested and involved in outside activities such as discussion groups, clubs, community affairs, municipal politics, church activities, the civic band or orchestra, the drama group, and so forth, the worker finds life a pleasant enough experience so that he can put up with a bit of monotony. Also it makes the coffee breaks, lunch hour, and car pool to and from work among the most interesting parts of the day as he recounts experiences, sells tickets, and lays out plans to companions, and generally feels that the world of work is an interesting place in spite of the monotony of the work itself. What does this outside activity have to do with the manager? It would be an interesting experiment to see whether there were any relationship between degree of outside involvement and contentment with a dull job. If such did exist, the manager might encourage community activities among those for whom work is boring.

Another suggestion is work rotation. By switching the job around throughout the day, or from day to day, productivity has seemed to improve in some assembly work. It may not have much effect if the various jobs are too similar and also if too much start-up time is required for each new task.

Batching has been attempted with some types of assembly or repetitious clerical work. Here the employee is given a batch of work to complete in a given time, usually an hour or so, before he starts a new batch. Experiments indicate this system may be of limited value in certain types of jobs.

There are a number of highly technical psychological-physiological reasons why short rest periods or coffee breaks of a few minutes may help relieve fatigue or boredom and increase productivity, especially in highly repetitive jobs.

Job enlargement is a popular proposal of recent years. Some studies have shown it reduces monotony, raises product quality, and increases productivity. (For example, see IBM's experience.) [11] In practice, it may not be easy to introduce in some work situations; it may give rise to side problems (e.g., demands for promotion or higher pay for doing a higher level job); and, further, it makes no sense if a job is enlarged only to contain further elements of meaningless and unrelated work. Also, the worker currently achieving close to his potential may find the new complexity of enlargement too difficult to cope with. We shall have more to say about this in later chapters.

Social psychologists have their own preferred suggestion to add to the foregoing ones. Starting with the premise that work is social, the manager should do what he can to ensure that social needs are satisfied. Under the guidance of the capable manager the group can become an effective one. An effective group can be an effective work team (equally, it can become an effective leisure group if not guided to its task by the manager). Where work is repetitious and monotonous, employees should be made to feel part of a mature, responsible, and coordinated group rather than to feel isolated victims of a blind, impersonal, and mysterious organizational system. Isolation, fear, and boredom give way to camaraderie, confidence, and interest when one belongs to a healthy work team. Individual differences in skill level and work satisfaction among members will become less pronounced if the group is cohesive. More will be said about the cohesiveness of groups in later chapters.

Optimal team size probably varies with the task to be accomplished. Also, the degree to which group activity is satisfying varies somewhat among workers (e.g., women feel more strongly about working in groups where they can socialize than do men). But the true "loner" is not common among normal people and when the average person is made to feel alone by psychological isolation, environmental isolation (e.g., noise or other factors preventing smooth interaction), or the nature of his job, productivity and work satisfaction may then suffer.

Think of a monotony-producing work situation with which you are familiar. Which of the above suggestions might improve it? Are there other solutions that could be attempted?

ATTITUDE TOWARD JOB BY OTHERS

Different occupations are variously ranked and viewed by the general public. One ranking of fifty-two industries by college students [12] put

[11] C. R. Walker, "The Problem of the Repetitive Job," *Harvard Business Review*, No. 28 (1950), pp. 54–58.

[12] R. E. Campbell, "The Prestige of Industries," *Journal of Applied Psychology*, XLIV (1960), 1–5.

medical-university-research-banking-teaching at the top and meatpacking-labor organizations-laundries-local bus driving-coal mining at the bottom with various services, manufacturing, and military toward the middle.

A study we shall refer to again in the next chapter [13] found that factory workers tend to be regarded by students as lacking in intelligence. Experience in counseling high school students and college students supports a generally negative attitude toward manual occupations (even the skilled trades) and toward low-skill clerical and sales work. This may reflect the different background and aspiration level of such students, but the point is that if a job is not highly regarded by a large segment of the population this might be reflected in the satisfaction that those in such occupations get out of their work.

There is probably a relationship between job status in the eyes of the general public and level of satisfaction of workers in those occupations. Findings of some early surveys support this opinion by showing a relatively small number of professionals would choose another occupation if they could while a substantial percentage of factory workers would do so. More recently, Blauner [14] found that the percentage among professionals who would choose the same kind of work if they were beginning their career again ran from 80 to 90 percent. In some skilled trades it was about 50 percent and in some unskilled work, considerably lower (e.g., among unskilled auto workers, only 16 percent said they would choose the same kind of work).

Income range likely enters into the formation of these attitudes although in my personal experience it was some years after receiving a graduate degree before I was able to match income levels I had achieved earlier as a tradesman in construction and shipyard work, or even in unskilled jobs like stevedoring. Certainly, during my preuniversity working career I earned far better money than school chums who went into white-collar jobs.

These points are mentioned here to show that public attitudes toward work may be one of the factors complicating the manager's task of trying to overcome negative job attitudes of his workers. How he might deal with these problems belongs to later discussion.

One last point about the attitudes toward various occupations concerns the *nonperson*. By the very nature of their work, some people are

[13] M. Haire and W. F. Grunes, "Perceptual Defenses: Processes Protecting an Original Perception of Another Personality," *Human Relations*, No. 3 (1950), pp. 403–412.
[14] R. Blauner, "Work Satisfaction and Industrial Trends in Modern Society," in *Labour and Trade Unionism*, eds. W. Galenson and S. M. Lipset (New York: John Wiley & Sons, Inc., 1960).

completely disregarded by other members of the work team or by the general public. The recording secretary at the board meeting, the translator at a political or international meeting, recording photographers, TV crewmen, waiters, and other "servants" are often treated as if they did not exist, or as if they were simply a part of the mechanical background. In some such occupations, nonpersons' supervisors might have to take this into consideration.

SUMMARY

Work is social. It is through his job that the average person relates himself to the society in which he lives. We use his occupation to categorize him—or we classify him among "the unemployed," "the unemployable," and so on. The job itself also provides a means of satisfying our many social needs such as prestige, companionship, and so on.

But society is changing and this means that the nature of work is changing with it. For one thing, work is becoming more technological; for another, workers today have different experience, education, and attitudes; and, for a third, working people work to satisfy a different package of needs than they did a generation ago. One of the objectives of this book is to help managers discover what some of these changes are so that management strategies will not remain based on outmoded preconceptions of work and its purposes. This requires us to discover what work actually means to the worker.

The rapid changes taking place throughout all society put the manager, in particular, on an ever upward, ever tightening spiral of new demands and new adjustments. Unless he can adapt to the fast pace of social evolution, the rat race may become his own dance of death in both a figurative and a literal sense.

There is a great deal of evidence that the amount of satisfaction achieved in a job depends on its skill level. Low complexity and repetition produces monotony and frustration for many workers although others can bear it. Intelligence, education level, and other individual differences and life circumstances (e.g., dissatisfied with home life) are related to the level of repetition and monotony people will bear before quitting a job. Retarded workers are better for some jobs than are normal persons, which raises questions about how such work is designed to be done and how much of a normal person's potential is sapped by dull work.

As monotonous work can be ineffective in terms of both productivity and morale, some suggestions were made on how it might be changed. Getting workers to understand more fully the product or services to which they contribute; developing general off-job interests; work rotation; batching; correct spacing of coffee and rest periods; job enlargement; and development of a positive and healthy work team are some of the suggestions. Perhaps the last holds out best promise for most situations.

It was suggested that attitudes of students and general public toward different occupations may influence the level of satisfaction achieved in the job.

3

SOCIAL PERCEPTION
OF PEOPLE

Because the way in which we see and understand people and social situations underlies the way we act toward them, this chapter provides some basic ideas on the perceptual processes. What is perceptual selectivity? How does it influence the way we see people? What happens to information when it becomes part of a cognitive system? How do forms of perceptual economizing help us deal with a complex world? And how do they get us into trouble? Which cues do you use when you perceive a person? Do you know why you so often think you are right in judging other people? What perceptual processes are likely to be most important to managers?

One of my favorite books on social psychology was written more than four hundred and fifty years ago. It is the story of Don Quixote, Gentleman of la Mancha, written by Cervantes. I say it is a book on social psychology with tongue in cheek because we all know it is a narrative of the witty adventures of that deranged gentleman, his man Sancho Panza, and his nag Rocinante. The story I think of now while discussing perception is about Mambrino's helmet. You may recall that Don Quixote, with Sancho beside him, was riding along searching for good deeds to do when he spied a man riding across a field with a shiny "helmet" on his head. He pointed this out to Sancho saying this was obviously a roguish knight who had stolen the great Mambrino's helmet and announcing his intention of engaging the villain in combat and recovering the helmet. In spite of Sancho's observation that it looked to him like someone on a donkey with a basin on his head, the brave Quixote charged off, lance lowered, to impale the evildoer. Sancho was right, of course, for the "rogue" was a barber from the next village who had put his basin on his head when a few drops of rain began to fall. When the poor fellow looked up to see a madman charging at him, he jumped from his donkey and scrambled off leaving his basin behind. When his master had recovered it, Sancho observed again that it was simply a barber's basin. But the Gentleman from la Mancha pointed out that it was truly Mambrino's helmet which the villainous knight had "obviously" melted down, removing the precious metals and stones from it and having the remaining base metal shaped like a barber's basin so no one would recognize it. Reverently placing it on his head, he announced that he would stop at the next blacksmith's to have the basin beaten into the shape of a helmet again, and off he rode.

I have before me a beautifully worked leather box, a gift of Spanish friends, on which Quixote rides, Sancho at his heels, his proud head held high balancing Mambrino's helmet. The point of the story is that we tend to perceive (or see) the world around us as we want to perceive it. And, just as Don Quixote did, we can put up almost irrefutable arguments to support our point in defiance of the common sense of all the Sancho Panzas in the world.

To emphasize this, let us move ahead four and a half centuries to a well-known research by Mason Haire [1] on labor and management's perception of one another. He chose seventy-six members of a Central Labour Council and 108 industrial relations or personnel men from plants or employers' organizations. Two photographs of "ordinary people" with no particular expression on their faces plus four different descriptions of the two men in the photographs were his experimental equipment. The descriptions of the men in the photos were identical except that in half the cases the man pictured was described as "local manager of a small plant which is a branch of a large manufacturing concern" and in the other half as "secretary-treasurer of his union." The labor and management people were given one minute to study a picture and description, then checked through a list of 290 adjectives relating to personality to describe the person pictured. Although the details of the study make interesting reading, it is Haire's conclusions which concern us here. He found that the general impression of a person is radically different when he is seen as a member of management and then as a representative of labor; that this difference in member-

---

[1] M. Haire, "Role Perceptions in Labour Management Relations: An Experimental Approach," *Industrial and Labour Relations Review*, VIII (1955), 204–216.

ship depends on whether the picture is seen by management or by labor; that management and labor persons each see the others as less appreciative of the other's position than they are themselves; and that they tend to see the others as deficient in thinking, emotional characteristics, and interpersonal relations as compared with themselves. Haire concludes that management and labor are not talking to the same people when they confer with one another and that, although there may be only two people in the room, in fact, four people seem involved in the conversation. Obviously, such misinterpretations interfere with the resolution of whatever differences exist as each member pursues his private Mambrino's helmet.

A discussion of social perception is important to managers and psychologists, then, because first we must have a realistic picture of *what* is there before we start worrying about *why* it is there or *how* it works.

BASIS OF PERCEPTION

Although the man-machine analogy is one we must employ with great caution, the human brain is like a huge data processing center. From the body's extremities and from all sensory organs millions of bits of information are constantly being fed. They are processed in the brain, brain stem, and spinal cord and appropriate messages are sent to relevant parts of the body when action is called for. The sheer volume of these bits of information makes it impossible for all to get through to the highest centers of the nervous system, much less to be recorded, processed, and acted upon. Some psychologists are convinced that a number of behavior disorders are the result of too much of this data getting through to the brain when it should not.

A process of selectivity appears to operate at several unconscious levels to prevent superfluous, irrelevant, or interference-producing information from disrupting the person's task at hand. I recall a hockey game during which a fantastic series of charges and breakaways failed to produce a goal when a fellow player and I skated to the bench gasping while our reliefs jumped onto the ice. We both slumped down on the bench panting; then I noticed my companion's leg. He was dripping blood at the shin from a deep gash; he did not even notice it until I called his attention to it. It required several stitches to close it. Here is a case on the physical level where concentration on the task at hand blocks out relatively important interfering information.

At the level of social information processing, the problem is even more complex because of the range of possible interpretations of the data received. On the physical level a pinprick is always ultimately revealed as a pinprick; on the social level the gestures, words, and actions of people may be as difficult to interpret as in Franz Kafka's novel *The Castle*, in which the entire social world around K., the hero, was bizarre and distorted.

The origins of social behavior lie in the perceptual-cognitive processes —that is, in those human processes through which we pick up data from the world we come into contact with and form ideas or impressions of that world. Through these perceptual-cognitive processes, human beings form frames of reference common to all. Because of this they are able to communicate, setting up rules for interaction and for reaction to events around themselves, and hence to share socialized behavior upon which a society can be built.

As you may have gathered from the reference to Mambrino's helmet, to Haire's managers and union men, and to Kafka's Castle, traditionally, the study of perception has concerned itself with the problem of how the world "out there" (in reality) corresponds or does not correspond with the world "in here" (my personal experience). How does the manager know that the worker "out there" really has the characteristics he attributes to him in his personal evaluation? How does he know that the entire group "out there" is really reacting to him as he thinks it is? Either he can be like the brakeman and fireman quoted in Carl Sandburg's autobiography— "What do you know today—for SURE?" and the fireman answered honestly the only thing he knew for SURE was "not a damn thing!"—or he can be like Don Quixote with his unswerving certainty about Mambrino's helmet. The good manager cannot afford to be like either the fireman or the knight errant.

PERCEPTUAL PROCESSES

Let us start with some basic problems of person perception. Why is it that people are perceived to have those qualities which we are quite ready to attribute to them with minimal or *no* information provided by the subject person? I may perceive a subordinate as being "hard working," for instance, and then go on from there to perceive him as "honest" even though I have absolutely no evidence of his honesty. But because I consider him honest, I treat him differently than another worker I perceive as "lazy" and hence not as honest. Yet some hard-working people may be dishonest and some of the worst loafers may be honest.

Now what is it about people that leads us to make such rapid judgments and predictions about their behavior with such slight substantiating evidence? Is it the lines of their face? their mouth? their eyes? the tilt of their head? their general grooming? or some combination of these many things?

It is surprising, really, to think of what complex cognitions we are willing to form instantaneously on sketchy evidence. And it is really surprising how often we regard such perceptions and cognitions as essentially correct after we have tested them out.

Let us say you are having a luncheon meeting with a couple of managers from another organization to discuss matters of mutual interest. You know these two only by name and by sight. You meet in the bar at the Chamber of Commerce and start off with some casual banter before going to your table for lunch and serious talk. As you do not know these two well, you will need to pick up a lot of information about them very quickly. In order to have a successful meeting, it will be necessary to locate their exact power and role position in their organization. If one says, "Jim here runs our computer department and I'm in charge of accounts," exactly what does this imply? "Runs" and "in charge of" are ambiguous. Under whose authority does Jim run the department? How much control does he have over decisions? Is today's discussion the idea of these two? Or have they been sent to sound you out? Does their organizational level equate with yours? What type of persons are they? Warm? Cold? Efficient? Intelligent? Many such questions run through your mind both consciously and unconsciously. At the same time you must talk intelligently, be quick with your light repartee, figure out their level of interest in sports and politics, decide whether it would be considered offensive or even childish to tell your favorite off-color joke, and determine whether you are "coming across" favorably to them, all the time making sure that you do not spill rye whisky on your new silk tie. While all these questions are being answered—as it were, instantaneously—you are making appropriate statements, nodding when you are supposed to nod, laughing when you are supposed to laugh, and expressing half a dozen other emotions at the correct split second. One mistake—one simple error like laughing when you are supposed to express sympathy—would show you up to be either an idiot or a madman.

Now all this requires that human data processing center to carry out a fantastic number of operations simultaneously without allowing one message to get crossed or misinterpreted. How? The key word is selectivity. We shall say there are two types of selectivity: the first we shall call *stimulus selectivity* and the second *personal selectivity*. By stimulus selectivity is meant those things that intrude into our perception even when we do not want them to—for example, bright lights, loud sounds, startling colors, taps on the shoulder, the telephone ringing on our desk, sharp contrasts, extraordinary size, unusual occurrences, a shout for help, sudden movements seen from the corner of the eye are all things which we normally cannot help but notice. Personal selectivity depends on our own preferences and expectations of what is to be seen and upon our own previous experiences in perceiving and reacting to things. In short, then, we could say that personal selectivity refers to our readiness to react to things in a certain way in a given set of circumstances. As well as a predisposition to act in a certain way, then, personal selectivity involves our state of motivation and the frequency with which we have reacted in that way before.

As the significance of stimulus selectivity can be understood readily, it is more important to examine personal selectivity in some detail. For our purposes, a further distinction can be drawn in personal selectivity between *selective sensitization* and *selective distortion* (in practice, they may be difficult to distinguish but both terms are useful). Selective sensitization refers to that readiness we have to see the things we want to see or expect to see even when they are barely perceptible. Thus in meeting the two other managers at the Chamber of Commerce bar I might be selectively sensitive to cues indicating that they have confidence in me, that I am getting across to them, that I can be frank with them. Selective distortion would operate either to block out the perception of information we do not want to see or to distort such information so that it supports what we want to see or expect to see. Thus I interpret the smile on the man's face as he shakes my hand at the bar as an indicator of friendliness. Still, if the same man with the same smile, a stranger, parks so close to me in the parking lot that his car door could chip mine if opened, I will interpret his smile as a shallow cover-up for what even he recognizes as bad parking. In the first instance, I expect the same man with the same smile to be friendly; in the second, I suspect his stupidity will chip the door of my new car. Yet, after a successful business luncheon at the chamber, I go out to the parking lot with my two new friends, bantering and planning for the future. Arriving at my car, I find we are parked side by side and he has pulled in too close to me so that the other manager, in opening his door, has made a little chip on the driver's door of my brand new car! Perceptual distortion suppresses this to the extent that I treat it lightly (and privately) or distort it by telling myself, "I guess I can't keep it new forever."

Given the fact that we all have different backgrounds of experience, different aspirations for the future, different feelings toward the world around us, and different motives and intentions, we may well ask the epistemological question (epistemologists are those philosophers concerned with whether or not reality is real): Are there such things as impartial facts? In the identical set of circumstances each observer sees something slightly different, reaches a different conclusion, and forms different ideas or cognitions. This brings us to our next major consideration: What happens to this new information when we store it?

Before examining that question, here is a little research [2] to support what has been said above. A group of twenty-three executives employed by a large manufacturing firm were enrolled in a company-sponsored executive training program. They were given a ten-thousand word case history dealing with the organization and activities of an industrial com-

[2] DeWitt C. Dearborn and Herbert A. Simon, "Selective Perception: A Note on the Departmental Identifications of Executives," *Sociometry*, XXI (1958), 140–144.

pany; they were to examine it and then indicate what they considered the most important problem facing the firm. Six of the executives were in Sales, five in Production, four in Accounting, and eight in miscellaneaus departments. All but one sales person felt the major company problem was in the sales area. Four of the five production people said the problem was to "clarify the organization." Three of the four accounting people had close contacts with Sales and stated that Sales was the most important problem. The researchers concluded that, although the case history called for looking at the problem from a company-wide perspective rather than from a departmental viewpoint, the criterion for seeing the problem was from a departmental point of view.

Our point is that departmental experience and motivation provides the expectation and background experience to see things in terms of personal selectivity.

ORGANIZING PERCEIVED INFORMATION

One of my favorite epistemological stories is told by Hadley Cantril, who has made personal experiences his study. It is about three baseball umpires discussing their profession. The first says, "Some's balls and some's strikes and I calls 'em as they is." The second says, "Some's balls and some's strikes and I calls 'em as I sees 'em." The third says, "Some's balls and some's strikes but they ain't nothin' till I calls 'em."

The same is true for many of the things, events, and experiences "out there." They ain't nothin' till we calls 'em and we only calls 'em as we sees 'em. Once we pick up some information "out there" and make it "ours" it becomes neatly organized into a *cognitive system*. This is to say that no "fact" stands on its own but exists only in relationship to other "facts." And, depending on our personal selectivity, fact *a* may be organized into system *X* in one person but into system *Y* in another person. Regardless of where it is incorporated, it becomes something slightly different than it was "out there." An old analogy of this is the geometric pattern shown in Figure 3-1.

The use of cognitive systems enables us to put a person into a category even when we have little information about him. For example, if we know a worker is older than average and little else about him, we may put him into a category involving ideas of greater responsibility, more patience, less energetic, and so on.

It is because we perceive the world in this way that it is easy to see that the general office clerk sitting back in his chair with his eyes closed is "goofing off" while the senior manager leaning back at his desk with his eyes closed is quite obviously trying to work out a complex problem. The research on perception and social perception is filled with examples of things being perceived differently, depending on what cognitive system

FIGURE 3-1

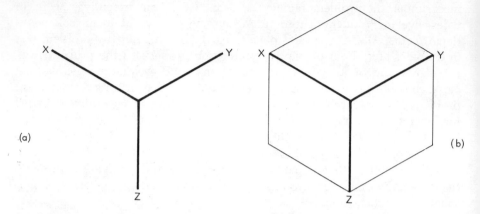

The angles formed by lines XYZ in Figure 3-1(a) are obtuse angles. In Figure 3-1(b) the same angles are seen as right angles because they are incorporated into a system of other lines.

they are incorporated into. It is also easy to call examples to mind through our own experience: workers make stupid mistakes, managers make miscalculations; professors are absent-minded, students do not remember because they have not learned well.

This type of perceiving involves us as much in "not perceiving" as it does in perceiving in certain ways. If perceiving behavior x in a person leads us to conclude that he is lazy while perceiving behavior x in another person does *not* lead us to this conclusion, something has to be "not perceived" or suppressed in the second case (or the first case). On reflection, most of us can think of a number of instances in which we have engaged in an unenjoyable conversation with another person, yet every hint that we wanted to terminate the conversation was ignored and our attempts to get away or change the subject were futile. The reason for this is the tendency to avoid seeing unpleasant and disturbing things which enables the other person to be a contented bore. In fact, the same principles appear to operate in all conversations, although in a less exaggerated form. The function of not perceiving that the other person does not like us or is not interested in our conversation is to keep social interaction smooth.

This leads to the fascinating theoretical discussion of "perceptual defense." The experimenters have concluded that defense (i.e., not seeing things which are there because we do not want to see them) consists of three things:

1. Emotionally disturbing information has a higher threshold for recognition (i.e., we do not perceive it readily) than neutral or nondisturb-

ing information. This is why a chain of events may be seen differently by those who are not personally involved than by those who are involved, so that warning signs of trouble are often not seen by those who will be most affected by the trouble.

2. Disturbing information and stimuli are likely to bring about substitute perceptions which are distorted to prevent recognition of the disturbing elements. In this way the manager can perceive that his workers are happy when actually they are disgruntled. Then when a grievance committee is formed or a strike takes place, he cannot perceive his "happy" workers participating willingly and concludes that it is because they have fallen victim to some agitator and that things in the shop are still basically fine.

3. Emotionally arousing information actually does arouse emotion even though the emotion is distorted and directed elsewhere. Kicking the cat, snarling at the wife and kids, cutting someone off for trying to pass you on the right while driving home, or browbeating an underling all offer a sense of relief and a good substitute for perceiving that the people "upstairs" think you are an idiot.

Unfortunately, the research on perceptual defense has not yielded clear results. There is some suggestion that when *some* emotionally disturbing information is presented we do not recognize it clearly; yet when *strongly* emotionally disturbing information is presented we recognize it even more readily than neutral information. Only further research will show the nature of the true relationship.

People sometimes have what we call a "blind spot" in the sense that they consistently not-see or misinterpret a particular type of event or set of circumstances. Such a blind spot is not uncommon in managers who deal with a lot of people. Can you think of any manager in your experience who has a blind spot? Have you ever wondered if you have any yourself?

The fact of the matter is that, just as we treat emotion-arousing information in a special way and as the information we perceive must be perceived in such a way that it fits into preexisting cognitive systems, all information we pick up from our social environment has to be treated in special ways. There is no such thing as open-mindedness in the sense that all information is fully perceived and weighed objectively. This is impossible. Even if we wanted to do it we could not. As has been seen, even the sheer volume of physical incoming data cannot be dealt with in total.

Being able to fit new information into existing systems requires an economizing process enabling us to deal instantaneously with large bits of constantly incoming data. Seeing the dozing clerk, I can immediately put that bit of information together with other bits I have about clerks, their work habits, job attitudes, and so on and conclude that he is goofing off without having to gather any more data or asking him questions or ensuring that my analysis of the situation is objective. On the other hand, similarly, when I see the meditating manager, I can immediately conclude that he is working out some grave question and wants no distractions.

By so economizing with incoming information the human being becomes a much more efficient social data processor.

When, added to this, are techniques like perceptual defense to keep the anxiety level low or give early warning of serious social dangers, man is effectively equipped to deal with a highly complex social environment.

Although these techniques enable us to carry out smooth and effective interaction, they sometimes get us into trouble by leading us to make erroneous judgments. For this reason we want to take a closer look at the economizing processes of perception, sometimes referred to as *cognitive economics.*

COGNITIVE ECONOMICS

A detailed examination of how we make maximum use of minimal incoming data is a very interesting aspect of social and person perception. We are going to look only at the major techniques here. This should enable the manager to get a clearer picture of human interaction.

First, let us take the concept of *adaptation level.* This adaptation level is the point, as it were, on the range or continuum of opinion which is the neutral point for the individual. Let us say, for instance, that all opinions about unions could be arranged on a line from very pro-union to very antiunion. We could do it like this:

FIGURE 3-2

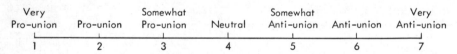

Very Pro-union	Pro-union	Somewhat Pro-union	Neutral	Somewhat Anti-union	Anti-union	Very Anti-union
1	2	3	4	5	6	7

A range or continuum of opinion from very pro- to very antiunion used to measure a person's thinking about unions.

In Figure 3-2 notice each of these points has been given a number. Our range from 1–7 is supposed to be objective and is supposed to represent the complete range of possible opinions. Now Mr. X could hold an opinion at point 5. We would thereby judge him as being somewhat antiunion. However, Mr. X does not judge himself as antiunion. He judges himself as smack in the middle—those to one side of him are antiunion and those to the other side are pro-union. This is Mr. X's adaptation level and, theoretically, his adaptation level could be anywhere along the continuum.

The economizing advantage of this is that other people, statements, events, information, can all be immediately placed by Mr. X as pro or con, even though this judgment is personal to Mr. X and not objectively valid.

We all like to feel that we are good guys at heart, that we are broad-minded and willing to give a fair hearing to any just cause. We do not consider ourselves extremists on issues unless we are trying to make an important point thereby. It is the other guys who, mistakenly or perversely, cannot see all the facts or cannot grasp their significance.

The *first impression* is a familiar economizing process which many people employ. The experimental evidence is that we carry our first impression of people forward into subsequent interactions with them. We also modify further information about them because of the information we have about them from the first impression. This economizing proccess means that we have to make only one major judgment of a person and not judge him over and over again.

Our first impression may be wrong, of course, and this is where the economizing process can get us into trouble. All first impressions can and frequently do change as further information and experience with the person cause us to revise it. Also, when a person has been forewarned that a first impression might be erroneous this tends to eliminate its disproportionate influence.

Related to first impression is a person perception process known as *temporal extension*. This indicates that a momentarily observed characteristic of a person is regarded as permanent. Thus the worker observing the manager expressing a sincere personal concern for another worker may employ temporal extension many months later when he says to his fellows, "Mr. Jones is always personally concerned about the men in his unit," even though he has never witnessed another expressed concern from Mr. Jones.

Related to both of the above economizing processes is the tendency to see persons as constant and unchanging entities. This is false, of course. All persons change both physically and psychologically over time. Our motivations, ambitions, aspirations, level of tolerance, willingness to commit ourselves to a cause, flexibility, and so on tend to change over time. However, the economy of seeing a person as constant eliminates the necessity of perceiving those of his behaviors which deviate from his assumed character. Just think back to what your plans and ambitions were five or ten years ago and see how much they have changed.

Another economizing bias is the tendency to see a person as the orgin of action rather than to see the situational circumstances in which social acts take place. For example, when a fellow member on an important committee refuses to agree with the majority in spite of overwhelming evidence that he should change, it is easier to perceive him simply as a perversely obstinate person than it is to perceive him as someone tangled in a highly complex web of social conflicts (see Chapter 15). Later, we shall look at some aspects of communication where the research has demonstrated that, depending on a person's position in the organization, he will be seen as internally motivated (self-motivated) or forced to comply. This question of *locus of cause* (i.e., does the motivational origin of the activity lie within the person or in some external pressure?) makes us perceive people either as interested in their work or working from necessity of having a job; as responsible for their own actions or doing what is required; as choosing to act through free will or having to do something they would not like to do were the circumstances different. Our perception of the locus of cause for a person's action also determines the degree to which we see his acts as justifiable, how responsible we hold him for these acts, and how honorable we judge his intentions.

An economizing technique we shall refer to again in a later chapter is the *implicit personality theory*. This is the idea that the perceiver, without realizing it, has a "theory" about what other people are like and that this theory influences all his judgments of people. We are all familiar with "the trusting soul," "the lemon," "the perpetual grouch," and others who have a relatively fixed bias in judging people and their behaviors.

A number of psychologists doing research on implicit personality theory have found tendencies of some people, for example, to judge all people they perceive as higher in honesty, sincerity, responsibility, and so on than most people judge them. Others always judge people low on these traits. Other biases are evident when a person perceives that certain personality characteristics are always found together. For example, friendliness is always perceived by some people as going with honesty; or intelligence, honesty, and personal appearance always go together; and so forth. A person with such a bias who perceives a person as honest, for instance, will also perceive him as intelligent and of good appearance, even though he has no evidence of these last two traits. Or a person who is seen as not good looking may be judged dishonest and unintelligent, even though there is no evidence about his level of honesty or intelligence. In short, we tend to assume a relationship between those traits and characteristics we use in perceiving and judging other people.

Similar to this theory is the *halo effect*. This is the tendency, in forming an impression or judgment of a particular characteristic of a person, to be influenced by our general impression of him. Thus, if we judge him favorably, there is the tendency to overrate him on characteristics for which no evidence is available; or if we judge him unfavorably, he is underrated on specific characteristics. If, for instance, we perceive a person unfavorably, we may judge him as not getting along with fellow workers, not being committed to the company, and having no ambition to improve himself, even when there is no evidence for these latter judgments.

All these economizing processes serve us well, as stated. More often, they lead us to the correct conclusion than to the false one. (If they did not, the cost of incorrect decisions based on them might bring us to re-examine what we are doing or to change our techniques of economizing.) Nonetheless, people can allow biases in person perception to distort the accuracy of their judgment over the course of their entire lives. It is these biases, leading to ineffective management, for which we must be on the lookout.

We can all understand how the multiplication of such biases can lead to wrong decisions. One dangerous place they can come into effect is on the personnel assessment form. (Many of these forms are badly designed— but that is another story.) It can be seen that, depending on the information already recorded on the form by other supervisors, the influence of first impression, locus of cause, implicit personality theory, halo effect, and other economizing processes may lead us to make a favorable judgment of a poor candidate or an unfavorable judgment of a deserving candidate. This is certainly a strong argument in support of discussing the assessment with the candidate and allowing him to comment on it openly.

PHYSICAL FACTORS IN PERSON PERCEPTION

When we have little information, no opportunity for interaction, or an ambiguous interaction to use in judging another person, we then may make maximum use of nonverbal information such as facial features, general appearance, body build, expressive movements, and so forth. Use of photographs is an example of this. As a management trainee, I was astounded one day when an old-timer was showing me the ropes on how to deal with application forms received through the mail. All forms submitted were required to have an attached photograph. On the desk of my trainer (the chief of a small division) was a large desk magnifying glass which was placed over each photo so that the details of eyes, mouth, nose, hair, skin color, cheekbones could be seen in blown-up form. In stunned disbelief, I heard the interpretations of facial features that belonged to an earlier century. I asked my trainer if he had ever heard of Lombroso.* The explanation for my question seemed to strike him as confused irrelevance and I tuned out his further instructions on the interpretation of physiognomy.

Actually, there is evidence of general agreement among people in linking certain facial characteristics with certain personality characteristics. However, there is no evidence that the perceived relationships exist.

---

* Lombroso was a nineteenth-century criminologist who set forth theories about facial features and criminal types. His theories have been thoroughly discredited.

For thousands of years theories have been put forward which related general body type with certain personality characteristics. (More will be said of this in the next chapter.) All schoolboys are familiar with Shakespeare's Julius Caesar making this statement:

Yon Cassius has a lean and hungry look,
He thinks too much: such men are dangerous.

Even modern attempts to discover a relationship between body build and personality have failed, although body build is often used by people in the formation of personality impressions, whether such impressions, are correct or not.

Gestures, posture, voice qualities, and expressive movements are all used in judging the perceived person. There is some agreement among people about the interpretation of these various cues but, again, little evidence that those in agreement are correct. Some exceptions are the use of body posture as a cue to whether a person is tense or relaxed and the use of voice qualities in judging social class.

Inference through analogy is another form of using physical information to reach conclusions about the psychological characteristics of the person. This type of inference is based on the fact that we use terms which are primarily for describing physical events when in fact we are describing people. There are many examples of these in English as well as in other languages. We describe people as deep, cold, rigid, bright, slow, sharp, loud, and so on. From here it is only a short step to suggest that physical qualities imply psychological characteristics. Indeed, studies have shown that people with thin compressed lips are rated low on "talkativeness"; people wearing glasses tend to be seen as more intelligent, dependable, and industrious; a man with a loud voice may be seen as more persuasive; a woman with full lips may be seen as more sexy because lips are used for kissing; and many other inferences through analogy.

As with all these uses of physical cues, a person may make a perceptual judgment without being aware of the information he used in reaching his conclusion. Many are based on cultural stereotypes (fat people are jolly like Santa Claus, redheads have fiery tempers). A great deal more research must be done to determine exactly what cues we use in sizing up people so confidently. Also, more research is needed on how valuable this type of perception is to us as against how often it leads us to make judgmental errors.

STEREOTYPING

Perhaps the most widely used and accepted method of economizing on our perceptions involves *stereotypes*. This is the assigning of attributes to a person solely on the basis of the class or category to which he belongs. This form of economizing differs from the ones mentioned previously in that there is some culture-wide or society-wide agreement on the relationship between certain categories and certain traits.

According to Secord and Backman,[3] stereotyping has three characteristics:

1. The categorization of persons.
2. Consensus on the traits attributed to a category.
3. A discrepancy between attributed traits and actual traits.

First, the categorization of people requires a classification based on some distinguishable characteristics. These characteristics may be physical —for example, age, sex, skin color, facial features, presence of a beard and long hair. Or they may be based on membership in a group or society —for example, church, city, nation, civil service, military, labor union, Chamber of Commerce. It could also be based on occupational grouping— for example, middle management, foremen, construction workers, paramedical personnel, office workers, professors, dentists. It could even be based on distinctive behavior patterns—for example, sportscar drivers, cigar smokers, shoppers, commuters, sports fishermen, men who carry rolled umbrellas. In other words, a stereotyping involves membership in a category which evokes the perception that such a person has all the characteristics that go with that category.

Second, the common consensus is that people who are identified as belonging to these categories share certain personal attributes. For example, all poorly groomed long-haired and bearded young men are lumped together into a category called "hippies" and it is believed that they use drugs, have loose sexual morals, are not interested in permanent employment, hold antiestablishment values, and drift all over the country. Or people who rush around hospitals dressed in white but not wearing stethoscopes around their necks are all lumped together as paramedical personnel; they are thought to have better than average education, the ability to keep calm during emergencies, a sense of responsibility and dependability, and a tendency to speak down their noses to nonmembers of their group who are not medical doctors. Sportscar drivers can also be put into a class: they dress jauntily, are extroverted, exceed the speed limit, weave in and out in heavy traffic, are aggressive, spend as much time pampering their cars as their girls, and thoroughly enjoy life.

Most research on the degree of consensus involved in stereotypes has been done on racial and national groups. Consensus on the stereotype of

[3] P. F. Secord and C. W. Backman, *Social Psychology* (New York: McGraw-Hill Book Company, 1964).

Americans and Russians is quite prevalent in many countries, according to a UNESCO-sponsored research, and there is some international stereotyping of other nationalities. Many studies extending to the present from back in the early 1930s have found racial and national stereotyping quite evident in the U.S.A.

Consensus, then, means that the majority of people in a society believe that there is some validity or some basis to such stereotypes. Stereotypes which will be of detailed concern to us in Chapter 8 are those which management and workers have of one another.

The third aspect of stereotyping is that there is some degree of discrepancy between the attributed and actual traits of the category. Almost always, then, stereotypes are considered at least partially false. When the perceiver believes some of the agreed characteristics are possessed by the *average* member of a class of persons and at the same time recognizes a range of differences among *some* members of that class, his stereotyping can then be an effective form of cognitive economics. However, when he perceives *all* members of the category to *always* have *all* the attributed characteristics of that category, it is false economizing and leads to errors of perception. Thus there are many bearded and long-haired young men who dress casually but are highly responsible, disdain drug usage, are moralistic, and would like permanent gainful employment. Equally, there are paramedical people who lose their heads in an emergency or who are very polite and sociable to strangers asking which direction they must go to get out of the hospital. Or introverted sportscar drivers who do not even know how many horses are under the hood.

Stereotypes do not necessarily consist of unfavorable traits. Categories can be perceived as hard working, progressive, dependable, honest, brave, and so forth.

As with all other forms of economizing with our perceptions, face-to-face confrontation and interaction with a specific individual who is a member of a category makes us aware of his unique characteristics and enables us to see how he differs from the consensus on his category. "Categorical" responses diminish during personal interaction. The better we get to know a person, the less likely are we to fall back on stereotyping and other perceptual economies.

SELF-FULFILLING PROPHECIES

A research story that appeals to me concerns an early study which tried to discover why children stutter. The researchers started off by advertising for experimental subjects between the ages of two to ten years who were stutterers. A large number of parents volunteered their children and extensive medical, psychiatric, and psychological tests of both children and parents were carried out. Then an equivalent large number of volunteers whose children did not stutter were subjected to the identical tests. When the results of the tests from the two groups were compared, the researchers were astounded to find that the only substantial difference between the two groups was that one set of parents said their children stuttered and the other group said their children did not stutter.

The actual reason that children stutter probably results from the interaction of a number of factors. But the perceived expectation of the parents that their child stammers is most certainly a complicating factor. The facts are that *all* children "stutter" during that period of life when they are acquiring a mastery of speech. Coordinated thinking, remembering, and speaking requires a fantastically complex control over millions of delicate muscles and sensitive nerves in the brain, face, head, throat, tongue, and upper body. Considerable time and practice are required to gain a controlled coordination and young children make many errors. Those parents who are overly conscious of children stammering focus the child's attention and their own too closely on these many errors, making him self-conscious and increasing his error-proneness.

Wittingly or unwittingly, we tend to do many such things with children. Parents who state openly to friends and relatives in the presence of their children that three-year-old Johnny "is our problem child" are thereby giving Johnny a sort of license to misbehave because he sees that this is what they really expect of him. On the other hand, parents who describe their four-year-old Jillian as "Mommy's little helper" implant in her perception a set of parental expectations about her household behavior. Parents, of course, can use these little tricks knowingly but at times they provide cues for subtle expectations unknown to both themselves and their children.

I once toured through a factory with its manager who stopped where one of the men was working at his lathe and said, "Bill Jones here is one of the best machinists we've ever had. Look how neat he keeps his equipment and work space, and his production record is tops for quality and quantity." Bill Jones looked up from his work only to give a nod and a smile but I thought that I perceived the man glow with pride and thought sure that his feet felt a few inches off the ground. I could just imagine with what satisfaction Bill Jones would tell the story to his wife that night and I would be willing to wager that his production record continued high.

I also remember working in a large office where I was told, "If you want a girl from the pool to take any dictation try to get Miss A, Miss B, or Miss C. Don't give anything important to Miss M, she's sloppy and she's slow, I don't know why they keep her here." Over the following weeks and months I had occasion to give work to Miss M, the sloppy typist. One day she confided to me, "That was kind of fun to do. I don't get many interesting things to type around here. I've been here almost a year but the work I do is really dull, not like my old job. I can't get excited about it." In ensuing weeks I fed Miss M more and more demanding work, complimenting her for work well done and correcting her when she made mistakes. Within a few months it seemed as if I was the only junior man in the office with a private secretary. Miss M was quick, neat, bright, and dependable. How she had ever got tagged with the "sloppy typist" image I never found out; perhaps it was because she did not bathe as often as she should have or because she dressed rather carelessly. However, the image of her as sloppy typist had certainly been fulfilled, for the duller the work she was given the more she responded with carelessness.

The point of all these anecdotes is to illustrate the importance of the self-fulfilling prophecy. It is so simple to make our own perceptions (and misperceptions) become true that I could give endless examples of how it takes place among psychologists, researchers, and managers. Indeed, Chapter 8 has a great deal more to say about how managers make such perceptions come true and Chapter 20 points out the same thing for researchers.

To emphasize how insidious this self-fulfilling expectation can be to parents, teachers, managers, medical doctors, and scientists, let me tell you one more tale. I can take litters of rats from my departmental laboratory, divide them into two groups so that both groups are perfectly matched for heredity and training background, then give one group to some students hinting to them that these are a rather dull strain of rats, and hinting to some other students that they have a bright strain of rats. I can then instruct both groups of students to give the rats identical training in, let us say, solving a maze-running problem. I will now find that the "bright" rats require a much shorter average training time than the "dull" rats even though the rats, the instructions, and the tasks are identical. Similar experiments have been replicated many times.

As even rats learn better when they are expected to be bright and capable, what about our subordinates!

There are limitations to everyone's capabilities on every task, of course, but we are often closer to the lower limit than the upper limit. Time and again, experiments have shown that people with low self-esteem fulfill their own low self-expectations while those with high self-esteem fulfill higher expectations.

I will not labor the point any further. Every reader can think for himself of the implications of the perception and interaction involved in this social psychological process. Later in the book some of the graver implications of this process will be spelled out in detail.

IMPLICATIONS OF PERSON PERCEPTION
FOR MANAGEMENT

Because the people we interact with during the course of our work are so important to us in facilitating or blocking the achievement of our goals, it is very useful for us to be able to predict their behavior. To make such predictions requires generalizations about their future behavior on the basis of the scattered bits of their past behavior which we observe, on their general appearance, on our knowledge of other persons in similar categories, and on the impressions they make on us. We constantly make assumptions that people will behave in the future as we have perceived them to behave in the past or, at least, in some manner systematically related to how they or other people like them have behaved. Without such predictions, interaction with other persons would be most disturbing.

The greater our success in assigning persons to categories with predictable behavior patterns, or the better we are able to fit them under clearly descriptive labels, the better are we able both to predict and to organize the many separate bits of information we have about them. Accuracy in perceiving others is not a single skill that some people have and others do not have. Nor is it something acquired by studying psychology texts, although these may help. One study showed that university students who had never taken a course in psychology were just as good at perceiving the personality of people as were those students who had taken psychology courses. Indeed, it has been suggested that one might learn as much about accurate perception of character by studying Shakespeare as by studying psychology. The important thing appears to be how sensitive we are to the differences among the people we are perceiving and judging.

The manager whose perception of himself is positive and accepting is more likely to see the favorable aspects of people around him than the manager who cannot accept himself for what he is. This means as well that the more accurately we know ourselves, the more accurately are we likely to perceive others. Certainly, our own characteristics affect the characteristics we are more likely to see in others. As an example, let us consider a process psychologists call *projection*. If a person receives new information about his own personality, feelings, or motives, his perception of others may change as a result. If he perceives himself to have more of a certain characteristic than he had previously, he tends to see those around him as having more and sometimes having less of that characteristic than he previously thought. Thus, if he becomes aware of some fault for which he feels ashamed or guilty, it could reduce his feelings of discomfort to focus his attention on similar faults in others. It may comfort him to think that many others possess the same fault for that means he is not so much of a deviant. Guilt associated with padding his expense accounts can be relieved by perceiving many subtle cues that "everyone else" does it too.

But we have seen that errors, distortions, and some of the other things we do in person perception can make our predictions and behaviors ineffective. Experimental evidence shows[4] that if a supervisor finds it convenient to drop in and check the work of subordinate A every now and then but rarely has the opportunity of checking on subordinate B, if both A and B turn in equally good work the supervisor then tends to perceive B as more trustworthy and more capable of working independently than he perceives A to be. As a consequence, he tends to spend more of his time scrutinizing A's work than B's even when subsequently it becomes equally convenient to drop in and check the work of either. This is not really a case of misperception on the manager's part but, rather, represents the way that perceptual processes take place. It is "tricks" of perception like this that cut down on a manager's efficiency.

In a study by Haire and Grunes,[5] a group of college students were given a list of seven words and phrases describing "a man who works in a factory." A similar group of students were given the same list to which had been added the descriptive word *intelligent*. Both groups of students then had the task of describing in a paragraph what sort of person they thought the man was. The differences were striking. The first group unanimously described the man as an unintelligent typical American Joe. The second group of students had trouble with their descriptions because the addition of the word intelligent did not fit their stereotype of a factory worker. Some denied he was intelligent—for example, "intelligence not notable even though it is stated," or "he is intelligent, but not too much so, since he works in a factory." Other students distorted this item to render it harmless—for example, "he is intelligent but doesn't possess the initiative to rise above his group." Some promoted the worker to foreman to get rid of the inconsistency.

The students have an unfortunate stereotype of a man who works in a factory. But the research is mentioned here because it illustrates what we are capable of doing when our stereotype is challenged. The first reaction, then, is *not* to give up the stereotype but to question or distort the information which threatens it. We all tend to do this whether we are managers or not. But it is the type of perceptual process against which the manager must guard.

Being required to make complex perceptual judgments, we some-

[4] L. H. Strickland, *Surveillance and Trust*, Journal of Personality, XXVI (1958), 200–215.
[5] M. Haire and W. F. Grunes, "Perceptual Defences: Processes Protecting an Original Perception of Another Personality," *Human Relations*, III (1950) 403–412.

times fall back on irrelevant cues—for example, smiling or not smiling is used as a cue in judging honesty. When the judgments are abstract or intellectual, we tend to perceive on the basis of what we like and dislike. And we put more weight on perceptual evidence coming from a respected or favored source than on a neutral or nonfavored one.

Although each of us faces the same problem of never being able to identify all the unique factors we use in perceiving people and events, this book is designed to sharpen an awareness of the problem we face in becoming effective managers and to prevent us from trotting around like Don Quixote with Mambrino's helmet perched on his head. He took himself very seriously (but no one else did); he was very brave, energetic, and ambitious (but he accomplished nothing); his head was full of ideas from all his reading and studying (but it was mainly nonsense).

In the perceptual processes, in the ways we use for organizing our perceived information into unique cognitive systems, and in our various methods of economizing on the data constantly coming in from our social environment lie the origin of our ideas about people and their motivation; the basis of communication problems in the organization; our entire management style; the willingness to change our mind; and all the dynamics of the group interacting. These factors must be examined in detail throughout this book but they make sense only in the context of social perception.

SUMMARY

The possibility of misperception of events in his social environment and of people with whom he interacts has serious implications for the manager. To deal adequately with his world and to predict events in it he must first have an accurate picture of it.

The basic perceptual processes whereby we take what is "out there" and make it part of our world "in here" were examined. It is not possible to use all the given data. The prime process of trimming it down to a usable quantity is selectivity. This selectivity may be based on the qualities of the stimulus object or on our personal selectivity, based on our unique experience, preference, and expectation. Using data selectively allows us to make maximum use of minimal perceptual cues.

Unfortunately, selectivity may cause us to ignore data or to distort it to meet our unique package of motives. This misperception takes place without our awareness and sometimes gets us into trouble.

Facts "in here" can be considered truly objective only in the broad sense. Each of us stores his facts in unique cognitive systems where they are flavored or modified by information, experience, and feelings we already possess. We can use our private perceptual defenses to keep information from disturbing us.

In a general sense, these processes involve cognitive or perceptual economics. There are many such processes. We looked at adaptation levels which we use as our base line for judgment, at first impressions where we found folklore justified through experimental evidence, and at temporal extension. The tendency to see persons as unchanging entities is obviously false but perceptually useful, as is seeing persons as the originators of interpersonal interactions rather than roles, and other events of group dynamics. Locus of cause, halo effect, and implicit personality theory were other processes we considered.

Next, we turned to some of the physical factors commonly used in judging the psychological characteristics of people. Facial features, body type, expressive movements, and voice qualities are all used with various levels of effectiveness in perceiving people. Often they are deceptive or useless for prediction, but when no other cues are available we tend to fall back on them.

Stereotyping, its advantages and disadvantages, came next. It involves three factors: a category into which people can fit; a general consensus on what attributes go with people in this category; and a recognition that there is a discrepancy between true and attributed characteristics of the category. Stereotyping represents a useful form of perceptual economics but nonrecognition of the exceptions leads to distorted perception and poor prediction.

All these economizing processes are modified by interaction with or further knowledge of the person involved, with errors and distortions decreasing the more we interact with the specific individual.

Perhaps the most dangerous aspect of perceptual economics is that we can make our economized picture or stereotype or our prediction come true. Some examples of this were presented and implications for more detailed examination were mentioned.

The distorting effect of the perceptual processes depends on the personal characteristics of the manager doing the perceiving. The more accurate his self-picture, the more accurate his social perception will be. Unfortunately, there is no simple set of rules which can be applied to bring about objective perception. Sensitivity to individual differences is something which cannot be acquired by reading a textbook. An awareness of the complexity of the problem of seeing our social world correctly and of predicting it accurately is the first step in the right direction.

4

PERSONALITY

*The purpose of this chapter on personality is to help the manager
understand the people he must deal with. What are some of the major
theories of personality and their main concepts? What concepts can be
useful to management? What issues in personality study can influence the
way we think about the control people have over their own behavior? Is
there any value in typing personalities? How does the concept we have
of ourself influence our behavior? What is meant by "abnormal" personality
and what are some forms of it encountered by the manager? Do psychological tests deserve the importance we give them?*

The field of psychology which has always held the greatest fascination
for the layman and the nonpsychologist is that of personality. Perhaps it is
because with the overt intent of trying to understand people we disguise
the covert intent of trying to understand that most fascinating and most
important of all God's creatures—ourself.

As well as the self-understanding we all crave, the study of personality
appears to offer some hope of interpreting the mystery of what motivates
people to do the things they do, especially when these things are different
from what we would have done. It also offers us a system of categorization for the astronomical range of behaviors of people. Finally, but impor-
tantly, it involves the possibility of predicting people's behavior.

Unfortunately, most students are disappointed in these expectations.

The study of personality is fraught with antagonistic and seemingly irreconcilable theories. Basic questions which appear more of a philosophical or theological nature than of a psychological one remain unanswered or unanswerable, yet upon their answers depend other major conclusions. The despairing student is usually either content with a superficial treatment of personality study, or latches on to a favored theory and ignores all others, or becomes interested solely in personality tests and bizarre personality disorders.

Personality study makes sense only in the setting of social behavior, yet a direct study of it tells the average student far less about what makes people tick than does a broader approach of general social psychology. Still, there are many useful things the manager can learn from even a cursory glance as this chapter can provide.

Rather than try to present a fair but miniature review of the field of personality, I shall attempt to outline a biased but useful sample of what the manager can learn from this area.

THE MAJOR THEORIES

A sketch of some major personality theories provides both descriptive jargon and a background against which a few of the major relevant issues can be discussed intelligently.

Psychoanalysis (Freud)

The psychoanalytic theory as outlined by Sigmund Freud (d. 1939) has dominated the study of personality for the past fifty years and will probably always be a major influence, in spite of the controversies and bitter attacks it evokes from psychologists and nonpsychologists alike. Hardly a contemporary psychiatrist, clinical psychologist, counselor, or psychiatric nurse has not read some of Freud (he was a prolific writer) and been influenced by his ideas. Scarcely an artist, novelist, dramatist, or advertiser has not felt the impact of his theories. The psychoanalytic "movement" is undoubtedly one of the most all-pervasive cultural forces of the twentieth-century Western world. Whether you agree or disagree with the theory it cannot be avoided.

The major points in this highly complex theory are, first, that all behavior has a psychological cause. This means that there is some psychological reason for even such things as dreams (over which we have no control), forgetting of names, slips of the tongue, many forms of accidents, and our gestures, as well as all of our other daily behaviors. As all behaviors have a psychological cause and as we honestly could not know the true psychological cause for all of them, the second major point of the theory is that most motivation is unconscious—that is, the true reasons we do things remain unknown to us. Unconscious behavior is more important to the psychoanalyst than conscious behavior. As human beings primarily seek to avoid unpleasantness and pain and as the true reason for many of our behaviors would be embarrassing, guilt-provoking, or bring retaliation from others, then painful, embarrassing, and potentially dangerous thoughts, motives, feelings, and behaviors must be *repressed* into the unconscious mind. This is the third major point and the fourth follows from it. Namely, repressed hostilities, frustrations, and emotions can be held in check only at a cost to some other aspect of the personality and there are many ways of the repressed feelings "sneaking out," as it were, and finding expression in disguised or symbolic forms. Finally, sexual motivation is of extreme importance. Seemingly, Freud uses the ideas of sexual motivation in the broadest sense (e.g., physical stimulation of any part of the body, such as scratching an itchy back, is sexual) and the narrowest sense simultaneously. Sexual experience starts in infancy with the physical contact a child has with his mother and progresses through a number of critical stages in the first five or six years of life. As the child learns to resolve these sexual crises in the first years, the base for all future personality development and motivation is established.

The mind is divided into three major provinces: the id, the ego, and the superego. The *id* is the oldest and most primitive part of the mind. It contains everything biological, animal, instinctive, and inherited. Because it is not rational it is often brutish, greedy, destructive of self and others, childish, eternally demanding, and never satisfied. The *ego* is that part of the mind that developed as the child learned to distinguish reality from unreality. It is rational and logical but always self-interested. It is the executive of the mind, keeping the id under control yet providing for the biological needs of the person in the best way according to the circumstances of the environment. The *superego* is a cultural imposition on the mind, a remnant of parental and social control when the child needed help in controlling the voracious id. It is often harsh and strict and operates on the basis of what is "right and correct" rather than on the basis of reason, logic, beauty, and so on. Because the superego is committed to the destruction of the id and the denial of all pleasures, and because the id wants nothing but complete riotous control of the person, the ego is constantly embattled by both. Depending on how well it manages this difficult task, the person is either sick or healthy. When too much energy is sapped from the ego by the difficulty of its task, little is left for personal development or any type of constructive work. If either id or superego gains control of the personality or exerts too much influence, a personality disorder ("nervous breakdown") or a twisted personality is the result.

The id-dominated character will always do what is expedient. The superego-dominated character will always do what is moralistically correct. The ego-dominated character will steer a path between expediency and morality.

Freud and his followers had much more to say about personality but we shall content ourselves with two more points. First, the more repression of biological drives a society imposes on its members, the more will psychological energy find an outlet through creativity or constructive activity (this is called *sublimation*). So the more repression, the higher the civilization. Unfortunately, also, the more repression, the greater is the likelihood that the ego will lose control and the person will become psychologically sick or neurotic. This means that an increase in psychological disturbances will be the unfortunate by-product of a society becoming more and more civilized.

Second, in order to relieve the pressures of repressed energy and to protect itself from the forces of the id and superego, the ego resorts to a series of adjustive techniques called *ego defense mechanisms*. There are many defense mechanisms and a person's character will consist of those he favors. *Projection* is an example of one we have seen in the last chapter. It consists of relieving guilt feelings (pressures from the superego) by considering others as guilty and not merely ourselves as guilty. Another favorite is *rationalization*. This consists of deceiving ourselves about the true intentions or motives of our actions, even though these excuses do not stand up to logical reasoning. For example, a man may say, "I never had a chance to get ahead in life because I had to go to the army just at a critical time in my development." The statement may be partially true but would probably be difficult to defend objectively. However, both the rationalizer and those who hear him accept it at face value.

Carl Jung

Carl Jung (pronounced 'young') was an early colleague of Freud but broke relations with him and his school in 1912. He founded his own school of analysis, often referred to as the Zurich School, as against Freud's Viennese School. He died in 1961. Like Freud, he was a prolific writer but his work has not had the same popularity. His theory of personality cannot be reduced to as simple terms as Freud's but there are a few concepts which are worth considering.

The best known of his ideas refer to the *introvert* and the *extrovert* as the two basic personality types. His actual classification of personality is more complex than the two basic types. The life of the extrovert is dominated by things outside of himself and he is characterized by the flowing of psychic energy to the world outside of himself. The introvert is the opposite. His psychic energy is directed inward. In North America extroversion is often regarded as a desirable characteristic in many types of managers. This, apparently, is not true in all societies and perhaps we should be cautious about underselling the value of introversion in managers.

Jung did not place great value on sexual motivation. His writings show great concern for the positive development of personality and not merely the correction or cure of psychic illness. He felt that if men were to devote as much energy to the development of their own personalities as they did to harnessing physical forces and to producing things the world would be a more beautiful place. Themes of self-actualization run through much of Jung's work.

Alfred Adler

Adler was another colleague of Freud who broke with the psychoanalysts in 1911. He died in 1937. Some people consider his writings folksy and shallow but he advanced a number of useful ideas.

Much of his writing focused on the idea of the *inferiority complex.* He felt that this is present in all children because they are obviously disadvantaged in dealing with an adult world. Feelings of inferiority can be carried forward into adulthood as well. Children as well as adults learn methods of *compensation* for inferiority by striving for mastery or *superiority* over everything and everyone in their world. The ideas of inferiority complex–superiority complex, of compensation-overcompensation run through much of Adler's writings. Remnants of these childhood conflicts are evident in the adult.

Adler felt that we each develop a *style of life* as our typical approach to solving the difficulties of early life and our striving for life goals. Understanding a person's life style was the key to understanding and predicting his future behavior.

Because he thought we are capable of determining our own future and our own life style, Adler recommended *courage* against adversity and fear. Full personality development could come only when cowardice was left behind and when the person had developed a social interest in the world around himself. Adler was one of the first to realize that personality can be fulfilled only in a social context.

Organismic and Existential Theories

Many theorists and writers on personality who are connected with the philosophical question of man's existence and its psychological implications can be fitted more or less comfortably under the above awkward title. In general, they tend to share the idea that the growth of personality comes from within the person rather than from forces outside of him.

Forces outside of the person largely provide the climate in which man can develop, but he is not their victim.

The environment is obviously important to most organismic and existentialist theories of personality, but the force for growth is always inherent in the person and can take place even against almost overwhelming opposition. Many of these theorists feel that the primary responsibility for personality growth rests with the person himself.

Perhaps the best known to management people among these theorists is Abram Maslow (b. 1908). His ideas on the hierarchy of need motivation are widely known and will be discussed in the next chapter. We shall also discuss his ideas on Eupsychia (a psychological utopia of 1,000 families) and Eupsychic management. Maslow feels there is much more to be gained from studying the lives of healthy, successful, creative people than the lives of sick people (as Freud had done). He feels that man is good by nature and not aggressive and destructive as some theorists assume. Man becomes aggressive and destructive only when his inner nature is twisted, denied, or frustrated. The most important message Maslow has for managers is that they should not repress the humanity of their subordinates (or their own) but should work to establish the climate for optimal growth. The development of the individual need not be at the expense of the organization or his job but should enhance them.

Responsibility for our personal growth and behavior is a concern for many existentialists. Among the best known of such theorists is Carl Rogers (b. 1902) who has made great contributions to the practice of counseling, interviewing, and therapy. He feels that as a person is intelligent enough to get himself into a psychological problem he should be intelligent enough to get himself out of it with the aid of a counselor. Every manager engaged in counseling or interviewing should be familiar with his work.

Field Theorists of Personality

Field theorists take their major analogy from physics. To understand the behavior of a particle in a magnetic field and to predict its future behavior, it is necessary to understand the true nature of the particle as it is *right now* and to understand all the forces acting upon it *right now*.

In personality theory this means that it is not as important to understand a person's past life, childhood problems, how he got along with parents and siblings and so on as it is to understand what he thinks, feels, and wants *right now*. A person's behavior is a function of the field of psychological facts which exists at the time the behavior occurs. All the coexisting facts of this field are mutually interdependent.

Kurt Lewin is the best-known field theorist of personality. He died in 1947 soon after setting up the research center for group dynamics at MIT. The principles of his personality theory and their emphasis on the totality of coexisting facts were more readily applied to understanding the work group and the behavior of its members than they were to understanding personality in the traditional sense. On his death, his associates moved to the University of Michigan where they established the Research Center for Group Dynamics. Many of them have been very influential in the area of personnel, organizational, industrial, and management psychology research.

Learning Theories of Personality

Researchers in the psychology of learning have contributed many useful ideas to understanding personality but few of them have attempted to develop a full-blown theory of personality. Among these few are John Dollard (b. 1900) and Neal Miller (b. 1909). They attempted to combine the facts of culture and society with the rigor of scientific methodology and the dynamic force of psychoanalytic theory.

Their conclusions were that external forces in the form of parents and society strengthened certain biological drives and weakened others and favored certain methods of responding to the environment and solving the problems of life. Like Freud, they felt that the early formative years of childhood were of extreme importance in the shaping of personality. Their theory could be called a "habit" theory of psychology in that habitual methods of responding to our environment and of solving problems are strengthened with practice and give personality its final form.

The main emphasis of all learning theorists is on the forces in the environment (social or physical) which shape or condition one manner of responding to that environment as against others. These forces act to reward or reinforce a set of responses that will then be repeated under future similar circumstances. Learning theories have a natural conflict with organismic or existentialist theories which emphasize that the force for change comes from within the person rather than from outside of him. The conflict is probably reconcilable but few of the protagonists on either side are willing to talk the same language to one another.

Factor Theories of Personality

Factor analytic theories attempt to do the opposite of what many of the theories already mentioned attempt to do. Instead of starting off with basic ideas and gradually building up theories of human behavior, they start with as full as possible descriptions of behavior and try to boil them all down to basic psychological factors. Because of their preoccupation with the measurement of observable behaviors, one of the useful by-products for management has been the development of psychological tests which are both descriptive and predictive of behavior. More will be said of such tests soon.

Perhaps the best known to managers of the factor analytic theorists is Raymond B. Cattell (b. 1905). His theory is a highly complex one. The tests he has devised for measuring personality and motivation are perhaps among the most popular administered to supervisory and management candidates. As early as 1936, Cattell published his *A Guide to Mental Testing for Psychological Clinics, Schools and Industrial Psychologists*. His most important concept is that of the personality *trait* inferred from behavior to account for regularity or consistency in this form of behavior.

The seven personality theories discussed above are not exhaustive. There are many more. Their differences give the layman some idea of the range of opinions and diversity in a most complex branch of psychology. Those selected for mention here were chosen because of their direct interest or value to management people. The superficial treatment of their ideas called for in a book of this nature does little more than identify them and their main concepts.

MAJOR ISSUES IN PERSONALITY STUDY

In discussion, any two personality psychologists soon become caught up in one of the major issues of their discipline. Most of these issues are not of direct concern to the manager. A few are, and I have singled out two for attention: the nature-nurture controversy and the determinism–self-determination argument.

The *nature-nurture controversy* deals with the question of whether a man's personality is the result of what is inherited and has developed from the organism he was given at birth or conception or whether it is the result of the type of upbringing, experience, and background he has had up to this point.

Some psychologists quote studies which show that there is a greater chance of mental illness developing in a person whose parents or other family members have suffered personality disorders than in people with no family history of disorder. Studies on intelligence show a closer relationship in level of intelligence between true parents and adoptive parents. Reports and studies of this type support the nature side of the controversy —that is, the major determinations of a man's personality are to be found in his constitutional makeup.

The *nurture* (upbringing) side of the controversy questions the results of studies like these and attempts to put different interpretations on the same conclusions. For instance, children of psychologically inadequate parents are less likely to learn from such parents how to cope with life's problems and hence are more likely to suffer behavior disorders and personality defects. Also, many studies show how environmental conditions are related to intelligence and school achievement and how environmental enrichment improves performance on intelligence tests.

The best approach to the controversy is not to be caught up in the antagonistic question, Which has more influence—heredity or background? The question is probably deceptive and not answerable. A better question might be: *How* do heredity and background experience interact with one another to produce personality? No one has the definitive answer to this, but we are likely to get better answers than by asking the question of *which*.

The second issue is the *determinism versus self-determination* argument. It asks whether forces outside the person control him (determinism) or whether the person has a choice in shaping his own personality.

The determinists argue that all human behaviors are caused by events which preceded them. Freud was a determinist as are learning theorists. Thus Freud felt that the causes of distorted personality in adults were to be found in childhood conflict. Learning theorists feel that every observable behavior is brought about by some antecedent condition.

The self-determination theorists feel man is more than an empty organism at the mercy of the rewards and punishments of his environment, and more than a robot programmed by the toilet-training experiences of his infancy. They feel that the private inner life of man is the source of major decisions and aspirations. They argue that such an inner life is the most relevant part of man's existence and, whether or not it can be measured by the standard tools of science, the fact is that we all experience it as real.

The extremes of determinism make man into a machine, a highly sophisticated one but still a machine. The extremes of self-determination would have man capable of pulling himself up by his own bootstraps under any circumstances through the force of "mind over matter." The arguments are further compounded by issues of responsibility, culpability, free choice, willpower, and theological beliefs about sin and the human soul.

Although some psychologists argue the issue fiercely, they usually generate more heat than light. In personality theory it is possible to accept and to integrate both viewpoints without compromise. To the reader who is astounded by such a possibility and would like to know more about it, I would recommend that he read Joseph Rychlak on the subject.[1]

PERSONALITY TYPOLOGIES

From at least the time of the ancient Greeks, men have been trying to describe sets of psychological types into one of which each personality

---

[1] Joseph F. Rychlak, A *Philosophy of Science for Personality Theory* (Boston: Houghton Mifflin Company, 1968). See especially Chap. 8.

could be fitted. The reason the game is still going on is that no typology has ever been completely satisfactory (nor is it likely that a satisfactory one will ever be devised). The earliest known proponent of such a theory was Hippocrates with his famous four temperaments: choleric, sanguine, melancholic, and phlegmatic. One still hears his terms applied descriptively. The twentieth-century successor to Hippocrates is William Sheldon whose monumental work was based on a study of thousands of photographs of college students. He found high correlations between certain types of body structure and certain components of temperament. These are summarized as follows:

Body Type	Primary Temperament Components
Endomorphy—softness and spherical appearance, underdevelopment of bone and muscle, floats high in water, highly developed viscera.	Visceratonia—has a general love of comfort, sociability, gluttony for food, people, and affection. Is relaxed in posture, reads slowly, is even-tempered, tolerant to others, and easy to get along with.
Mesomorphy—hard and rectangular physique with a predominance of bone and muscle; strong, tough, and injury-resistant body, well equipped for strenuous physical demands.	Somatotonia—often loves physical adventure and risk-taking. Needs muscular and vigorous physical activity. Is aggressive, callous toward others, overmature in appearance, noisy, courageous, given to claustrophobia; action, power, and domination are important to him.
Ectomorphy—linear and fragile, flatness of chest and delicacy of body; usually thin and lightly muscled.	Cerebrotonia—displays restraint, inhibition, and the desire for concealment. Is self-conscious, secretive, youthful in appearance, afraid of people, happiest in small enclosed areas. Reacts overquickly, sleeps poorly, prefers solitude when troubled. Does not like to attract attention to himself.

Briefly, these three types could be described as fat, muscular, and linear. Santa Claus would be a good representative of the endomorph; most football players, boxers, and other athletes are mesomorphs; Shakespeare's Cassius from the play *Julius Caesar* ("Yon Cassius has a lean and hungry look. He thinks too much") would be a good example of the ectomorph.

In spite of the prodigious amount of work which went into his research, Sheldon's conclusions have been seriously questioned and his theories are not as widely applied as are those of other personality psychologists. They are summarized here mainly because of the descriptive value of the terminology and because they represent the best of the attempts to relate body type and personality.

Most other typologies differ from Sheldon's in that they make no reference to body types. We have already referred to Jung's typology of introvert-extrovert. The other best-known one is psychoanalytic and is based on Freud's theory of the psychosexual stages of childhood development. The idea is that the adult personality reflects the childhood behavior patterns of these early stages of growth. First, there is the *oral character*. This is the earliest developmental stage in which the mouth is the principal region of activity. There are two types of oral character. The one takes pleasure from incorporating things (knowledge, food, drink, possessions) and sucking things (thumbs, pencils, cigars, or kissing). They are often gullible people (will swallow anything they are told). They are dependent on others, particularly when anxious. The other oral character originates in the stage when the infant gets his teeth. His character centers around biting and chewing. Sarcasm (biting words) and argumentativeness are common in this person. As a manager he may enjoy "chewing out" his subordinates. All oral characters feel insecure.

The *anal character* is next. It is related to toilet training. Strict toilet training is supposed to relate to a retentive character. He is obstinate and stingy (constipated). Often, he is punctual to the second, extremely neat about his person and possessions (e.g., desk, the way his pencils are sharpened), and demanding. On the other hand, strict toilet training may produce the opposite of these characteristics stemming from the actions of the child who resists such repressive measures by expelling at inappropriate times. This becomes the prototype for all kinds of expulsive traits in adulthood: cruelty, senseless destructiveness, temper tantrums, messy disorderliness, aggressiveness, vengeance, and so on. Finally, when a mother pleads with her child to have a bowel movement, praises him extravagantly when he does, and rewards him, the child may get the idea that productivity is extremely important. This is supposed to be the origin of creativity and productivity in the adult.

The *phallic character* develops from the child's sexual and aggressive feelings associated with the genitals. Fantasy, competitiveness, boldness, fear of failure, showing off, loudness, and hostility are some of the traits of the phallic character.

Finally, the *genital character* is the mature, realistic, sociable, self-controlled, helpful, and well-rounded person.

The biggest problem with these, as all other personality types, is that the "pure type" is so rare that one never knows how to categorize the average person. The vast majority of people have *some* characteristics of all the supposed types.

THE SELF

Each of us has a concept or a picture of our self that we use as a central point of reference for our thoughts, emotions, and behaviors. Such self-pictures have varying degrees of accuracy and different levels of awareness. Regardless of such accuracy or awareness, the concept we have becomes the focal point in our behavior and motivation. If a man thinks himself robust, he willingly takes on vigorous exercises; if he thinks he is knowledgeable, he will speak up on an issue; if he thinks himself fragile, he avoids strenuous activities; if he thinks he is not capable of it, he will not apply for a senior position; and the person who thinks he is "no good" will not resist temptation as well as the person who pictures himself as "good."

The concept of self is also the basis for our relationship to other people, to occupation, and to property. It is only because I am able to identify myself that I can refer to *my* wife, *my* job, *my* car, *my* idea, *my* experience, *my* plans for the future, and so on. My self, then, is the mechanism I use to bind me to society, to the present, past, and future, and to anything else to which I can relate.

There are varying degrees of distortion in our self-picture for a number of reasons. We may start off with a distorted body image, for one thing. A person may think that he looks either more or less youthful, handsome, tall, graceful, distinguished than he actually is. Usually, people don't recognize their own voice when they hear it recorded or recognize their own gait when they see it from behind on a film and sometimes we fail to recognize our own handwriting. The major distortions, though, come because our perception of our self is dependent on what we perceive (first possible distortion on basis of perceptual processes discussed in the last chapter) other people perceive (basis of second distortion) us to be. In other words, we react to other people's reaction to us. This is the so-called "looking-glass self." Sometimes the results are similar to looking into a funhouse mirror while wearing badly fitted glasses.

Our self-concept corresponds quite closely to what we believe other men in general think we are rather than to what we think those in our immediate presence think of us. Also, the manner in which we conceive of our self tends to fit rather well into the cultural or social definition of the particular role we fill in society. For example, top executives tend to conceptualize themselves as having a lot of drive, a desire for achievement, a sympathetic view of authority, decisiveness, ability to organize, and a realistic orientation. Their subordinates tend to attribute quite similar traits to them.

Our self-concept is a relatively enduring thing. Even studies done on children (who are quite changeable during development) show considerable consistency of self-concept over periods of several years. Not that we do not change; we do. But significant changes rarely take place overnight. When they do, we recognize them as exceptions and refer to them as "conversions" (religious or otherwise).

The self-image we have each developed could be a positive, healthy, and growth-oriented one or it could be a wretched and miserable one. Part of it consists of those general and specific aspirations we have set for ourselves. It may contain an insightful "cognitive map" as Gordon Allport, a great personality psychologist, called it. Such a map, geared closely to the reality of his capacities, can be used by the person to plot a sound course of personal development. Allport illustrates his theory by referring to the life of Amundsen, the polar explorer, whose dominant passion from youth to explore the Pole enabled him to withstand fatigue, hunger, ridicule, and danger.

Everyone is capable of self-development. A realistic cognitive map helps even when it has to be revised periodically. Those without any map at all soon get lost in the human jungle.

THE ACHIEVING PERSONALITY

Among the many personality traits isolated by psychologists is the need for achievement. It is defined by personologist H. A. Murray as follows: "To accomplish something difficult. To master, manipulate, or organize physical objects, human beings, or ideas. To do this as rapidly and independently as possible. To overcome obstacles and attain a high standard. To excel oneself. To rival and surpass others. To increase self regard by the successful exercise of talent."

A little reflection will tell you that persons who are high in this personality trait will be good managers. Indeed, that has been amply demonstrated. The vast majority of successful entrepreneurs and managers rank high on this characteristic, no matter what their country of work is and no matter what social strata they come from. It is as true in North America as it is in Eastern Europe or any part of the world where it has been investigated.

Most of the research on the need for achievement has been done by psychologist David McClelland, whose book, *The Achieving Society*, summarizes his theories and speculations on achievement motivation.[2] Contrary to what Karl Marx assumed, and contrary to what today's youthful radicals assert, and even contrary to what businessmen themselves have

[2] David C. McClelland, *The Achieving Society* (Princeton, N.J.: Van Nostrand Co., Inc., 1961). See also, by the same author, "Business Drive and National Achievement," *Harvard Business Review*, XL (July-August 1962), 99–112.

come to believe, the successful businessman and executive is *not* motivated by greed and self-interest. His success, prestige, and income are due more to his high need for achievement.

Specialists and professionals of comparable education and background do not score as highly on tests of need for achievement. Achievement scores for managers and executives in state-operated businesses in Poland, in private enterprises in the U.S.A., or in government service are about equal. More successful managers tend to score higher than less successful managers (except in government service where promotion depends more on seniority).

The main characteristics of the high achiever are, first, a liking for situations in which he is personally responsible for finding solutions to problems. In this way he can gain satisfaction from the successful outcome. On the other hand, gambling or winning by chance have no appeal to him as he prefers success through personal effort. Second, he tends to set moderate achievement goals and to take "calculated risks." Overcoming an easy or routine problem provides little satisfaction to him and an extremely difficult problem may cut him off from satisfaction for he may not succeed with it. Between the two extremes lies the best chance of gaining maximum personal achievement. He is always a little over-extended, complains of overworking, has more problems than he knows how to deal with, and is threatened with ulcers. However, this is a condition of his own making because it is precisely in overcoming these difficulties that he gets his achievement satisfaction. Indeed, if problems did not exist he might very well create them for the sake of challenge. Third, he wants concrete feedback of his success for this provides him with a gauge of how well he is doing. Figures on sales, costs, production, and profits are a good source of such feedback for him. The daily movement of a highly visible line on a wall chart makes excellent concrete feedback for him. Money, of course, is an ideal form of feedback because in a society like ours it provides a widely acknowledged symbol of success. But this does *not* mean that money is valued for its own sake and this is where the stereotype of the money-motivated capitalist is erroneous. In Communist countries, other forms of concrete feedback are provided to the high-achievement manager. The meeting and excelling of regular quotas is one of the most favored of these.

McClelland concludes,

> A businessman knows . . . that in the final analysis it is the spirit in the company that counts most—the entrepreneurial drive of the executives, the feeling of all that they are working together to achieve a common goal; it is not 'hardware' that counts in the long run—the size and slickness of the plant, or the money in the bank. These assets will melt away like snow in a hot sun without the proper achievement orientation in the

company. Knowing this, the wise executive acts accordingly. He is concerned to keep the achievement orientation of the company alive by talking about its aims, by setting moderate but realizable goals for himself
and his associates, by assigning personal responsibility, by making sure
that people know how well they are doing, by selecting executives with
high n Achievement or by developing it in those who need it.[3]

ABNORMAL PERSONALITY

No one likes to be categorized as having a behavior disorder, no
matter how innocent or mild. There is something threatening about mental
illness; it implies that the person does not have the control over his world
and himself that we all desire. Nonetheless, the rate of behavior disorder is
relatively high in civilized society. Estimates vary, but a reasonably conservative one is that one person in ten will at some stage of his life require
help for a behavioral problem. The odds are that most managers will
encounter behavior disorders directly or indirectly several times in the
course of an average managerial career and should know something about
such problems.

The full range of psychological disorders is too extensive for even a
summary here. Most managers rarely encounter serious disorders among
colleagues and subordinates. Those who do encounter mental illness
regularly have some training in recognizing it. Contrary to popular belief,
most severe disorders do *not* break out suddenly and dramatically. Most
develop slowly over days, weeks, or months, gradually worsening and
sometimes temporarily disappearing. Also, it often happens that the sick
person can carry on almost regularly during some segments of the day
(e.g., at work) while showing greater deterioration when away from the
supportive routine of the job.

The term *neurotic* is most commonly used to refer to those people
suffering from behavioral problems severe enough to interfere with daily
working and living yet not severe enough to require institutionalization.
The term *psychosis* generally refers to those with more severe disorders.

The common criteria in determining whether or not a person's behavior is normal are whether it is socially acceptable (some examples of
nonacceptable behavior in our society would be: hearing voices, being too
terrified to ride in an elevator, and being unable to eat or drink from non-
sterilized plates and silverware) and whether it involves impairment or
injury (extreme fatigue from anxiety, loss of coordination in driving, loss
of memory or of calculative ability, washing hands so frequently and
harshly that they become skinned).

Many types of disorder are preceded a few days, weeks, or months

[3] David C. McClelland, "Business Drive and National Achievement," *Harvard Business Review*, XL (July-August 1962), 99–112.

by such things as a grave loss of love (broken marriage, death of someone close, broken romance), seriously disturbed plans (business failure, flunking out of university, loss of job, loss of health, pregnancy), or sudden new responsibilities (major promotion, marriage, motherhood).

A British government study reported significant increase in neurosis among workers who:

1. Worked more than seventy-five hours per week.
2. Had frequent changes of work.
3. Lived alone or in overcrowded conditions.
4. Were separated or widowed.
5. Had heavy domestic responsibilities or stress.
6. Had poor social contacts.
7. Disliked their job or found it boring.
8. Were doing work too high or too low for their intelligence.

There is no implication that any of these conditions *caused* neurosis but simply that they went hand in hand with it. It can be seen that most of these conditions relate to social adjustment, which underlines again the importance for the manager of understanding social psychology. Some of the major, readily recognizable neuroses are outlined here.

Paranoia can be very severe. Often, it takes the form of extreme, even bizarre, suspicion of everyone and every event, strange interpretations put on normal events (check numbers are considered to have some mysterious significance, the angle of parked cars is a warning of some forthcoming event, etc.). The paranoid can trust no one and lives in a world no one can understand but himself. Often, he is more intelligent than the average person and knows how far he can go with a point without being sued, fired, or put into jail. It is very difficult to maintain him in a group situation because friction and noncooperation result, yet to put him to work in isolation will probably make him more paranoid. He is among the most difficult of disturbed people the manager will come across.

Another extremely difficult person to deal with is the *sociopath* (sometimes called *psychopath*). Often, this person is also very clever and has been known to do beautiful "con jobs," for he can be a smooth talker. He has absolutely no respect for the rights, feelings, or property of others. He lives for the moment only and seems not to heed the consequences of his own acts. These persons appear to have no conscience, no feelings of remorse, no depth to their affections. Robbing by deceit his own grandmother who would willingly have given him the money on request comes easily to a sociopath. I have dealt with a few, and I hope you never have the same experience.

The *alcoholic* and the *drug user* are both addicted. Alcohol is used as a form of escape from frustration, anxiety, and tension by many people.

It is habit-forming in the sense that it can be used to escape emotional problems or to increase sociability. But some people cannot leave it alone even when it threatens to destroy everything they have and are, and even when it destroys the lives of those around them. The cause seems to lie in a combination of biological and social psychological factors. Overcoming the problem is never easy. For the manager the problem is often compounded by the fact that the alcoholic is sometimes a likeable and sociable person whose friends cover for him whenever they can. Yet it is a behavior disorder and must not be ignored. Drug addiction has become an increasing problem in recent years. "Hard" drugs (e.g., heroin) are highly addictive and are usually associated with severe behavorial problems. Other drugs are either less addictive or nonaddictive (e.g., marijuana) but are disruptive of normal behavior and can endanger the life and health of workers. All drug users, as all alcoholics, need professional counseling.

The term *anxiety neurosis* is sometimes used to refer to those neurotic conditions which involve such symptoms as palpitation of the heart, high blood pressure, loss of breath, sweating, nausea, feelings of imminent doom, as well as many other pains, aches, loss of energy, doubts, fitful sleep, nightmares, sleep-walking, fears, and worries. By themselves a group of symptoms like this usually constitute an anxiety neurosis but, in fact, such symptoms also accompany the other common forms of neuroses. Indeed, no true neurosis develops without being accompanied by such complaints and symptoms.

We refer here to a severe form of anxiety, of course. Slight anxieties are relatively common and can have the effect of putting the person on general alert, increasing his sensitivity to his social environment, and calling for an integration of his behavior. A more severe but still moderate anxiety causes the person to be somewhat rigid, narrows his social perception, and makes him less spontaneous. The severe anxiety that we find in all forms of neurosis brings with it impaired thinking and learning; irritability; and a breakdown in personality in the sense that behavior patterns are not well organized, do not lead to effective goal achievement, and display immature judgment.

There are many different types of *phobias*, which are often given exotic-sounding Greek names such as claustrophobia (fear of closed places, like elevators, airplanes, tunnels), acrophobia (fear of heights), zoophobia (fear of various animals and insects), nyctophobia (fear of darkness), agoraphobia (fear of crowds), and many more. The phobic reaction could be attached to any object or situation and takes the form of an anxiety or panic attack when the phobic object is present and the person cannot escape from it. The person who has a phobia knows that it is a silly and unreasonable thing and is generally ashamed of it but, as he says, he "can't help it."

Obsessive-compulsive reactions involve the person in a repetitive behavior which he is unable to control. Obsessions are repetitive ideas or thoughts (a recurring image that he is killing his fellow workers, robbing the company safe, or burning down the office); while compulsions involve repetitive acts which must be carried out to avoid anxiety (tapping three times before using the telephone, having to be the last person to leave the room, or not being able to pass a door without knocking on it). There is an element of ritual magic in the compulsion and anxiety follows when the neurotic is not able to perform it. Some of these rituals are elaborate and bizarre. Obsessions and compulsions frequently accompany one another. They often involve washing, eating, and environmental cleanliness which are so severe and demanding that the neurotic person is not able to eat or work with other people. Kleptomania (uncontrollable impulses to steal things, even though they are not needed) and pyromania (impulse to set things on fire) are obsessive-compulsive.

The various forms of *hysteria* are also debilitating. They are physical symptoms with no physical basis. Examples are partial paralysis, loss of bodily sensitivity, blindness, deafness, muteness. Very often the affected part of the body or the loss of sensitivity is a very critical one for the person in carrying out his job (paralyzed fingers in a typist, partial blindness in a precision machinist), which would suggest that the hysteria is a means of escaping difficult or frustrating work. Although there may be similarities between some forms of hysteria and malingering or "swinging the lead," hysterias are serious behavior disorders and need treatment.

In the *depressive reactions* we find the neurotic retreating from normal contact with all other persons. His anxieties and physical symptoms are accompanied by fits of despair and gloominess; rumination about suicide and his own worthlessness; crying, sobbing, and self-recriminating; inattention to personal grooming and eating and loss of interest in everything around him. It seems impossible to cheer him up as he withdraws completely into his shell. Although a person can recover spontaneously from neurotic depression, it can also worsen and become very severe. The danger of suicide is always present and the popular myth that people who talk about committing suicide never do commit suicide is not true. Early recognition and treatment is very important for a good recovery.

There are many other forms of disorder but those above represent the major classifications the manager is likely to come across. All such persons should be steered as soon as possible to psychiatric or other medical help. Treatment is usually more effective if provided in the early stages.

The manager's task, of course, is not to be a diagnostician or a therapist—there are professionals to do that. But the effective manager, oriented both to people and to productivity, should be sensitive to the onset of neurosis or other behavior disorders. Particularly, he should be wary of the personal tragedy followed either by the development of bizarre and "peculiar" behaviors or by the change in character and habits so often accompanying the development of a behavior disorder. He should also be prepared to do something positive about it in its early stages (not merely fire the person). In this way he serves his subordinates, his group, and his organization.

PSYCHOSOMATIC DISORDERS

Psychosomatic disorders are physical disorders which either have their origin in or are aggravated by emotional difficulties (hence the term *psychosomatic,* i.e., psyche—mind; soma—body; implying that both factors are implicated). They occur against a background of prolonged frustration in which the person develops a chronic emotional tension. Such a condition produces changes in the delicate balance of the biochemistry of the endocrine glands.

One common outcome of the stress and glandular change is the development of gastric or peptic ulcers. This is not to say that all ulcers in humans are the result of emotional stress, but there is no question that they occur more frequently among people undergoing prolonged anxiety. Financial difficulties, family conflict, constant pressure to make decisions when good prediction is impossible, real or imaginary fears about job security, illness, and so on provide the background setting for ulcers. Some theorists feel the function of the ulcer is to take the person out of the position of frustration (i.e., into hospital) or to bring him the special care a sick person normally receives thus relieving his anxiety.

Many other disorders have been attributed either in whole or in part to emotional stress. Among them are high blood pressure, coronary thrombosis, angina pectoris, mucous colitis, sinus disorders, asthma, some forms of skin rashes, allergies, and obesity.

Also often linked with psychosomatic disorders is *accident-proneness.* Estimates of causes for industrial accidents in the United States have ranged as high as 80 percent due to accident-prone workers. Dr. Flanders Dunbar, a controversial but important figure among psychosomatic theorists, estimates about 80 percent of those who have one serious accident tend to have more and that such persons tend to have special personalities. People with a history of minor accidents are more likely to have a serious accident. In the previous history of accident patients, accidents account for more total illness than in the history of other types of patients. Accident-prone people often have unusually good health records. They are men of action and are quick-witted; they are *not* dull and clumsy. They tend to be impulsive and have short-term goals; they often resent authority and have a high rate of voluntary absenteeism.

Once again, the manager must resist the temptation to be a diagnostician unless his field is medicine. Emotional stress does not necessarily produce psychosomatic disorders. Indeed, as we have seen, the high-need-for-achievement executive may thrive on it. Also, not every case of hay fever, angina pectoris, or skin disease has its origin in psychic causes. Many are straightforward physical disabilities.

Nor can it be assumed that the higher the organizational level, the higher the stress, and hence the higher the rate of psychosomatic disorder. A six-year study at duPont found annual heart attack rates for vice-presidents and other senior managers to be 2.2 per one thousand; middle management had 2.5 per one thousand; foremen, clerical supervisors, and low-level managers had a rate of 4 per one thousand; semiskilled and unskilled had a rate of 3.2 per one thousand; lowest salaried clerical workers had a rate of 3.7 per one thousand.

PSYCHOLOGICAL TESTS

There are several different categories of psychological tests and within each category are hundreds of specific tests. Even the trained professional is not familiar with all of them. There are a few ideas about tests in general and about some specific types of tests that may be useful to the manager.

First, tests are better for measuring present and past behavior than for predicting behavior, although some tests make quite good predictors.

Second, no psychological test is foolproof, although some are highly sophisticated and would be difficult to beat.

Thirdly, no psychologist can give a person such an extensive battery of tests that he "knows everything about him." One of the problems of test use is employing tests when they are not necessary. I am always suspicious about those of my psychological colleagues who give people every test they have in their office.

Some of the major categories of tests are intelligence tests, personality tests, aptitude or skill tests, and achievement tests.

There are many intelligence tests and their use depends on the person to be tested and the test situation. Often they yield a score called the IQ (Intelligence Quotient). Actually, such a quotient is rarely employed these days although we still refer to IQ-equivalent scores. Intelligence tests yield a similar score when the person is measured with more than one. Yet there can be some fluctuations and the psychologist should always take this into account; this is one reason psychologists are reluctant to divulge actual IQ scores. Another reason is that such scores are often misunderstood and misinterpreted. About 50 percent of the total

population are around average in IQ measurement (90–109 IQ); 25 percent are below average (less than 89 IQ); and 25 percent are above
average (110+ IQ). About 2 percent of the population are of very superior
intelligence (above 130 IQ). Those within an IQ score range of 80–90
are often referred to as dull-normal or low-normal. With a score below 80,
persons are capable of performing only simple or repetitive tasks and
require considerable supervision.

There are two common misunderstandings about intelligence and intelligence tests. First, many people think that all psychological tests are
intelligence or IQ tests. This is not so. A relatively small proportion of
psychological tests give any indication of a person's intelligence. Second,
no one *has* an IQ; an IQ is not a thing. We can have an IQ *score* or an
IQ-equivalent score only if we take an intelligence test and it is our score
for that specific test.

Again, there are a wide variety of personality tests, more than of
intelligence tests. Many are devoted wholly or partly to discovering ab-
normalities. Some of the best known which deal with diagnosing ab-
normalities are the Rorschach Test (using the famous Rorschach ink
blots in highly complex scoring patterns), the Thematic Apperception
Test, (TAT) which uses pictures and stories in a highly complex scoring
system, and the Minnesota Multiphasic Personality Inventory (MMPI),
which asks for a yes or no answer to 550 questions. Others, like the Allport-
Vernon-Lindzey Study of Values, measure the weight given to his values
by the normal personality. Although these tests can be useful for selection,
guidance, and placement, other personality-type tests are more useful for
these purposes. Among many are the California Psychological Inventory
(CPI), the Motivation Analysis Test (MAT), the 16 Personality Factor
Questionnaire, and the Edwards Personal Preference Scale. These latter
types of tests measure such personality characteristics as aggressiveness,
sociability, tolerance, achievement, autonomy, exhibitionism, flexibility, and
so on. They are called "pencil and paper" tests because that is all the
material they involve. Computerization has been a boon to test users because it is now possible to obtain extensive personality profiles quickly.

Aptitude or skill tests are available for almost every conceivable
skill from artistic and musical ability to finger dexterity and mechanical
reasoning. Also, the industrial psychologist is trained in designing such
aptitude tests to meet specific training and placement problems.

Related to such aptitude tests are a number of useful measurements
of vocational interest and preference. Used in conjunction with personality,
intelligence, and aptitude tests, these vocational tests are very useful for
counseling people both into or out of certain occupations, training programs, and educational programs. Among the best known of such tests

are the Kuder Preference Record (scored with pinpricks) and the Strong Vocational Interest Blank (SVIB), a sophisticated test, simple to administer and scored by computer.

Finally, we may mention achievement tests, given to schoolchildren, university students, and management trainees to determine their course progress. Such tests are designed by their instructors in various forms to measure a specific content of learning or progress. Certain intelligence-type tests or aptitude-type tests can also be used to measure progress or achievement rather than to predict future performance or ability. When such is the case, they are called achievement tests rather than intelligence or aptitude tests.

A GLOSSARY OF COMMON PERSONALITY TERMS

The study of personality is so specialized that its own jargon has developed over the years. Frequently, the manager comes across such jargon in reading personnel records and reports from psychologists, psychiatrists, social workers, or medical officers. Many such terms have already been defined in this chapter and many have been used in a context that helps us to understand them. Others are so common that they need no clarification (exhibitionism, aggressiveness, autonomy). Our intention in this section is to define only those major terms not already mentioned that the manager might come across from time to time.

ABASEMENT (need for)—passive submissiveness to external force; willing acceptance of injury, blame, criticism, punishment; self-blame, surrender, resignation to fate, admission of inferiority.

AFFILIATION (need for)—enjoyable cooperation with others; please and win affection from others; loyalty to friends.

APHASIA—speech disorder which may involve such things as loss of ability to understand what is read or heard.

ASTHENIC—thin, slender ectomorph.

ATAXIA—muscular incoordination.

BELITTLING—form of compensation by which a person increases his own self-esteem by disparaging what others do or have done. It indicates a reaction against one's own feelings of insecurity or lack of self-esteem.

CASTRATION COMPLEX—anxiety associated with fear that the penis might be cut off. Freudians made much of this childhood fear because it is supposed to be carried forward into adulthood in a disguised form. Sometimes women with masculine characteristics are referred to as *castrated*, that is, like a man, except without a penis.

CATATONIC—severe abnormality which sometimes involves maintaining frozen statue-like positions and total lack of reaction to the environment.

COMPLEX—organized group or constellation of feelings, thoughts, perceptions, and memories of which we are normally not conscious (e.g., a mother complex is organized around feelings toward one's mother).

CONGENITAL—present from birth but not necessarily inherited.

DEFERENCE (need for)—admire and support superiors; praise, honor, emulate, conform; yield easily to the influence of allies.

DISPLACEMENT—emotional displacement involves focusing anxiety on something not its real cause—for example, taking out displaced anger or frustration on one's wife or subordinates.

EGO IDEAL—idealized picture of the self toward which one aspires; a self-portrait of the person "at his future best."

EGO INVOLVEMENT—being "wrapped up" in a person, situation, or job so that what happens to the person or situation is felt to be keenly personal—for example, being ego involved with one's organization brings a sense of pride when the company is singled out for some honor.

(EEG) ELECTROENCEPHALOGRAM—record of electrical rhythms in the brain; often used in diagnosis of brain damage.

(ECT) ELECTROCONVULSIVE THERAPY—sometimes called *shock therapy*. It involves passing an electric charge through the brain of the unconscious patient. Mainly used in depressive disorders. Its effects are controversial but it is still widely used.

ERG—innate dynamic source trait allowing its possessor to experience a specific emotion more readily than others and leading to certain types of satisfaction.

FIXATION—inflexibility in some habitual behavior. Psychoanalytically, it refers to retention of an infantile trait into adulthood.

FUNCTIONAL DISORDERS—disorders which have no known physical basis and are thereby assumed to be psychologically based.

GENIUS—person with exceptionally high intelligence, having an IQ level of 140 or more.

GROUP THERAPY—procedure for therapeutic treatment of more than one neurotic at the same time. Usually, the patients have similar disorders.

IDENTIFICATION—incorporation of the characteristics of another and adoption of that other's ego ideals—for example, the son of his father; the adolescent of his football coach; the trainee of an idealized supervisor.

IDIOT—person in the lowest intelligence bracket (less than 25 IQ).

IMBECILE—middle range of feeblemindedness (IQ 25–50).

INDIVIDUATION—psychological growth into a healthy and indivisible wholeness of person.

INHIBITION—complete or partial arrest or holding back of some activity, process, emotion, wish.

INSANITY—legal term for severe mental illness in which the person cannot be held responsible for his acts. Equivalent to the psychiatric term *psychosis.*

MANIA—exceptionally, sometimes wildly, excited state which occurs in some psychoses.

METAERG—environmental source trait, similar to the erg but resulting from factors of experience or society rather than from physiological makeup.

MORON—highest range of feeblemindedness (IQ 50–70).

MULTIPLE PERSONALITY (dual personality)—form of neurosis in which more than one distinct personality appears operative on different occasions. Although popularized by fiction and myth, it is extremely rare.

NEURASTHENIA—form of neurosis characterized by abnormal fatigue and bodily complaints.

NONDIRECTIVE THERAPY (COUNSELING)—form of counseling designed so that insights come from the person seeking counseling rather than from the counselor. C. R. Rogers is its main theoretical supporter.

NURTURANCE (need for)—gives sympathy and assistance to anyone weak, disabled, tired, inexperienced, lonely, defeated, humiliated, confused.

NYSTAGMUS—oscillating movements of the eyes.

OCCUPATIONAL THERAPY—attempts to alleviate behavior disorders by having the person engage in interesting work. In other words, the work is considered to have remedial effects.

OEDIPUS COMPLEX—psychoanalytic term referring to the attachment (sexual) of a son to his mother and the consequent jealousy toward his father. The sexuality takes a disguised form and the jealous aggression is often repressed.

ORGANIC BEHAVIOR DISORDERS—as against functional disorders, many behavior disorders have an organic basis—for example, epilepsy, feeblemindedness, drug addiction, senility.

PARESIS—organic behavior disorder usually originating in syphilitic infection. Sometimes called *general paralysis (or paresis) of the insane.*

PHRENOLOGY—attempts to discern personality or character by the bumpy shapes on the head. A thoroughly discredited ancient technique of personality measurement.

PHYSIOGNOMY—attempts to discover personality traits, characteristics, and aptitudes from facial conformations (shape of nose, mouth, or jaw). A highly dubious practice.

PRECONSCIOUS—anything which may readily become conscious—for example, something "on the tip of the tongue."

PROJECTIVE TEST—type of personality test requiring the person to "project" his private interpretation of ambiguous situations to the psychologist. The Rorschach ink blots are an example of this technique.

PSYCHE—ancient Greek word for the soul or mind.

PSYCHONEUROSIS—neurosis.

REGRESSION so called reversion to earlier, childhood behavior patterns in the face of frustration or anxiety. Examples would be crying, temper tantrums, stamping one's feet.

RELIABILITY OF PSYCHOLOGICAL TESTS—dependability of a test to measure exactly the same thing each time it is used.

SCAPEGOATING—like displacement, this involves finding a person or group upon which to take out some real or imaginary wrong on a regular basis.

SCHIZOID—personality characteristic noted for withdrawal, introversion, and limited emotional response to others.

SCHIZOPHRENIA—severe form of psychosis characterized by withdrawal from reality. It takes many forms, some worse than others.

STRESS INTERVIEW—interview designed to determine an individual's ability "to take it."

SUBCONSCIOUS—what is below the level of awareness. The term *unconscious* is more commonly used.

SUCCORANCE (need for)—to have one's needs satisfied by others; to be nursed, supported, protected, loved, guided, forgiven; to remain close to a devoted protector.

THERAPY—any procedure designed to cure or alleviate a disorder.

UNDOING—form of ego-defensive magic by which what has been done can be undone. Doing penance and apologizing are common forms. In its magical form, it tries to make what has already happened not to have happened. A good example is the mother "kissing away" the child's hurt. Managers also use techniques to undo their errors to save face with themselves.

USES TEST BATTERY—aptitude battery used by the U.S. Employment Service to screen applicants for jobs.

VALIDITY OF TESTS—a test has validity when it measures the things it is supposed to measure.

WECHSLER SCALES—well-known intelligence test.

SUMMARY

This chapter outlines some of the general theories, ideas, and applications of psychology of personality which could be valuable to the manager. They could be useful in enabling him to understand motivation, to describe people or understand descriptions of people, to recognize some of the major personality disorders and their origins, and to understand the potential for self-fulfillment of himself and his subordinates.

A few major theories of personality were outlined, starting with psychoanalysis. A number of Freud's ideas and terms have been incorporated into our language, art forms, and culture. Carl Jung, Alfred Adler, and the organismic and existentialist theorists have emphasized the necessity of personality growth and the responsibility of the individual himself in achieving it. Field theorists emphasize the importance of understanding the here-and-now forces on the personality rather than the pseudocauses in the individual's past history. Learning theories, on the other hand, emphasize the forces in society and family which shape the direction of personality growth. Although personality theorists seem to thrive on disagreement with other personality theorists, some of their differences are not as irreconcilable as they imagine.

The major and pervasive issues of the nature-nurture controversy and determinism as against free choice were discussed. The difficulty is that the issues tend to be phrased as "either . . . or" whereas it would be more profitable to consider both sides of the issues as reconcilable.

Personality typologies were considered. The body types (or somatypes) of Sheldon were outlined, as were the major Freudian types. Whether body type or psychic type, all typologies suffer from the same drawback of the impossibility of categorizing people accurately.

The concept of self was examined. The self is pivotal in all our behavior and hence is important in understanding motivation and aspiration. The self-concept always carries some distorted perceptions with it. Depending on the amount of distortion, the person may behave realistically or unrealistically. Occupational role and organizational level are related to differences in self-perception.

David McClelland's research on achievement motivation was considered. Successful managers, executives, and entrepreneurs are persons with high-achievement need in their personality. This is true across cultures. Such persons like responsibility for their own actions, are moderate risk takers, are realistic about their abilities, and like concrete feedback of success. Although they tend to be among the highest salaried workers, money is not a major motive for them; it is, rather, that money represents recognition of the success of their efforts.

Some major personality disorders were described so that managers might recognize them and refer people for treatment. The paranoid, the sociopath, the alcoholic, and the drug addict are among the most difficult subordinates with which to deal. The various neurotic reactions tend to occur in the context of a grave personal loss or a new responsibility and are often discernible by relatively abrupt (over days, weeks, or months) changes in basic interests and behavior patterns.

Psychosomatic disorders are physical disorders with a psychic origin. Strong experimental evidence has been presented of emotional causes for gastric ulcers. The degree of emotional cause in various other psychosomatic disorders is more controversial. Not every ulcer is psychosomatic nor does everyone experiencing emotional stress develop psychosomatic symptoms.

Our last discussion was on psychological tests. Four major categories, with some popular tests in each category, were mentioned. These are intelligence tests, personality tests, aptitude tests, and achievement tests. Their uses and some misconceptions about them were discussed.

The final section of this chapter was devoted to a glossary of commonly used terms frequently found in reports on personality, personal, medical and personnel assessment.

5

MOTIVATION
AND INCENTIVES

This chapter sets out both some broad theoretical approaches to motivation as well as some specific theories relevant to managers. What does the average person think motivates behavior? What is meant by drive, incentive, aspiration? What is a need hierarchy and what is meant by the need for self-actualization? How does a person's level of aspiration influence his work? And how does his work influence a person's level of aspiration? Is competition an effective incentive? What about money? How does the motivation-hygiene theory deal with some of the conflicting findings on motivation?

Some discussion of motivation has been unavoidable in the past two chapters. Motivation and perception are at times difficult to separate and personality theorists almost invariably have something to say on the subject either directly or by implication. Some personality theories cannot really be separated from motivational theories. The concept of self, the need for achievement, the issues of determinism versus free will and nature-nurture could easily have been discussed in a chapter on motivation.

Motivation is a popular subject among managers and it is often the first choice of topics among people arranging management seminars. Yet most psychologists are probably a bit like myself. When asked to speak on motivation or arrange a seminar around it, I begin to get that uneasy feeling that I am skating on thin ice even though I have done research in these areas. University colleagues who have taught courses in motivation have told me it is a most difficult subject to teach because they never know where to begin and where to end, for motivation pervades all human behavior. Whenever we ask the question "why" about behavior (ours or someone else's) we are asking about motives. Some psychologists have reached such a point of despair in studying motivation that they have claimed it is not a fit topic for psychologists to deal with, but should be left to philosophers and theologians. Yet the philosopher, the theologian, the layman, and the manager consider it a perfectly natural question to ask the psychologist, "Why did so-and-so do such-and-such?" Whether we like it or not, we are stuck with the question and many psychologists have risen to the challenge, making brave efforts to answer it and conducting extensive research to guide us.

A wise statement on the subject comes from Maslow[1]—"Typically an act has *more* than one motivation"—and there are usually various cultural paths available to the same goal.

The intent of this chapter is to examine some basic ideas about motivation and some ways in which these theories can be applied as incentives by the modern manager.

THEORIES OF MOTIVATION

It has been proposed that every theory of motivation falls under one or another of four headings,[2] although some theories may fall under more than one heading simultaneously. These four types of motivational theory are as follows:

1. *Cognitive theories.* A cognitive theory of motivation is so called because the cognition or the thought or the idea is supposed to underlie the observed behavior. Thus, if a person *thinks* that he should compete in a promotional competition, he proceeds to do so; if he *thinks he should not*, he does not.

As a simple type of theory, it has a certain appeal to the man in the street, for often enough he feels that this is the way he is motivated: that any man in his right senses can take thought, weigh the consequences, and proceed to act.

It was far and away the most popular theory of motivation until Sigmund Freud came along and raised the issue of unconscious motivation. Now it is universally recognized that some people (psychotics and neurotics) do things without knowing why, and it is quite generally agreed

[1] A. H. Maslow, "A Theory of Human Motivation," *Psychological Review,* (1943), 370–373.
[2] Edward J. Murray, *Motivation and Emotion* (Englewood Cliffs, N. J.: Prentice-Hall, Inc., 1964).

that we often do not know the reasons (or, at least, the true reasons) why we carry out certain behaviors.

Cognitive theories almost inevitably involve us in the question of free will, which we have seen caused difficulty for psychologists. It is as if, having taken thought, the person *wills* to carry out a certain behavior.

Cognition and free choice are the whole basis of the social, legal, judicial, governmental, managerial, and educational systems of our culture. Without this keystone we would have to build a new society. Yet the concepts of "thought" and "free will" cannot be adequately measured by psychologists. Psychologists, more than others perhaps, have felt the sting of this truth because one of their basic tenets is that anything a person does can be measured.

In spite of these problems, many highly respected psychologists are convicted cognitive theorists of motivation. Indeed, elements of such theorizing pervade Freud, Jung, Adler, Lewin, Maslow, Rogers, and many others who are currently concerned about human motivation.

2. *Hedonism.* Hedonism is an ancient philosophy of motivation and is not irreconcilable with cognitive theories of motivation. Basically hedonism says that a person always acts to achieve satisfaction and avoid pain (or nonsatisfaction). This concept pervades many contemporary theories, and its basic assumptions underlie Part 3 of this book just as the basic assumptions of Part 2 involve cognitive theories of motivation.

Many an undergraduate evening has been spent over a case of beer arguing whether or not man can be completely altruistic (not self-interested) as against whether man is always ultimately self-interested. The prospect of such a debate still whets my appetite although I know the question is not resolvable (or, at least, it has not been resolved by the cumulative debates of undergraduate students these past several hundred years).

What is one man's meat is another man's poison. Pleasure for one person is lying in bed with the Sunday paper while another, who would consider this prison, prefers to spend his weekend scaling dangerous mountain crags. Even death is desired by the suicide and the marytr. And the sadist gets his kicks out of seeing others in pain. An objective measurement of pleasure, then, seems impossible and, without an objective measurement which we can apply to all people, pleasure and pain cannot form the foundation of a scientific theory of motivation.

Yet, in spite of the difficulty of working with such a theory, it is difficult for psychologist and layman alike to avoid the common sense and simplicity of the idea that people do things because they like to and do not do things that they do not like to. And even though we psychologists can demonstrate quite easily that a person may be conditioned to perform certain types of responses *when we want* him to, regardless of how strongly determined he is *not to* respond, and even though we can demonstrate that hypnotic suggestions and posthypnotic suggestions make a person do things he would not normally do, these things do not seem like "real life" to the man in the street.

So difficult is it to explain behavior without recourse to hedonism that every theory of personality or motivation I am aware of contains some element of it. A few modern psychologists have taken the bull by the horns in recent years and are trying to build a theory of motivation on experimental hedonism, starting from measurable differences in sensations of heat, sound, touch, and so on.

3. *Instinct theories.* Instinct theories of motivation are old, popular, and thoroughly ingrained in the thinking of Western civilization. The instinct is an identical behavior pattern found among all men and is inborn rather than learned. The maternal instinct and the social (or herd) instinct are perhaps the most common, but a host of other behaviors are acceptably explained by saying, "I instinctively felt (thought, reacted, moved, chose) that he was friendly (that it was correct, that we needed it)."

Even more instincts are claimed for animals. It has often been stated that animal behavior is totally instinctive while man's behavior is at least partly instinctive. However, it is quite difficult to explain Fido bringing the master's newspaper to him by instinct or the cat and dog playing together as good friends. Also, some psychologists can put up a very convincing argument that even such instinctive behaviors as the chick pecking its way out of its egg are *learned* rather than instinctive.

Early in this century instinct theories of behavior became quite popular among psychologists who, seeing man as a social animal, described a number of human social instincts such as the instinct of gregariousness. Over the years this list of instincts grew so long that people began to be dubious about the whole concept of instinct as applicable to humans. They began to realize that calling some behavior "instinctive" did not help to explain it but rather hindered understanding. Classifying behavior as instinctive meant "sweeping it under the carpet" in the sense that it was no longer subjected to experimental investigation. With the list of instincts becoming so long and so silly, most psychologists abandoned instinct theories of motivation.

However, instinct theories have enjoyed a comeback in recent years, perhaps in part due to the research and writing of people like Conrad Lorenz with his studies on various animals and birds. Less scientifically rigorous but popular writers like Desmond Morris (*The Naked Ape*) and Lionel Tiger (*Men in Groups*) have tried to show that much of human social behavior resembles primate (apes, baboons, chimpanzees) instinctive behavior although it is overlaid with a great deal of human cultural learning. Again, psychologists have become open-minded but cautious about the possibility of some instinctive influences on human behavior.

4. *Drive theories.* Similar to instinct but on a firmer basis of ex-

perimental evidence, psychologists slowly began to build up a theory of *drives*. The drive is a physiological condition which causes an organism to become active. Initially, it has no definite direction but becomes directed to specific objects and patterns of behavior depending on environmental conditions. Thus we can talk of a hunger drive becoming activated when the content of sugar in the blood decreases below a certain level. The person or animal then begins to feel hungry, initiates behavior designed to locate food, and, depending on what kind of food is available, may become motivated to eat it, cook it, or go and buy some different food.

On the basis of such drives as hunger, thirst, sex, stimulation (need for stimulation of the senses, for exploring and manipulating things, for contact and affection), and pain and pleasure (based on stimulation of areas of the brain), it is possible to build up a complex theory of motivation. From these *primary* physiological drives we can demonstrate the development of *secondary* or learned drives. For example, with the hunger drive different cultures, even different social classes or families, learn to prefer one kind of food as against another as a means of satisfying the drive. In Hong Kong a banquet may center around various dishes of snake. Most of us would not enjoy snake but might enjoy half a dozen raw oysters which would be repugnant to the Chinese.

Some rather clever demonstrations have been carried out by psychologists to show how a chimpanzee can learn to carry out simple mechanical tasks for which he receives periodic payments of poker chips. When he has gathered enough poker chips, he can trade them for grapes to eat. The parallel of the factory worker converting his paycheck into groceries for the family is striking, of course.

The majority of today's psychologists are drive theorists of one sort or another, yet they tend to feel rather uncomfortable about drives as the sole basis for human behavior. Serious philosophical and scientific issues underlying drive theory make psychologists reluctant to give it total support. Although he may use drive theory in his experimental lab, in his more speculative moments during coffee break or while trapped in a traffic jam, the psychologist muses about the possibility of other theories of motivation or ruminates on his doubts about drive theory.

WANTS, NEEDS, MOTIVES, INCENTIVES, AND THE LIKE

We have been using a number of different terms to describe why people do things and we have yet to consider a few more. It is best that we clarify their meanings before going further.

A *need* is a requirement of a person for optimal adjustment to his environment. He may have a need for food, for shelter, for feeling secure, or for many other things to keep functioning in society.

A *drive*, as has been implied, is a physiological condition which moves the person to satisfy his needs. It is not specifically directed to some object. The hunger drive, for example, moves us to satisfy a need for food.

A *motive* is our urge to attain some goal or objective such as food when we are hungry or the desire for advancement in the organization. A motive has a clearly defined goal.

An *incentive* is the object or end of the motivated behavior. It is a thing we want to achieve, accomplish, or avoid—like food, money, a promotion, or being left behind.

A *reward* is similar to an incentive but it implies that the incentive is a positive thing (we could work to avoid punishment, a negative incentive). For psychologists reward refers to a satisfying outcome which follows from a behavior thereby inducing the person to carry out that behavior again to receive the same outcome. For example, the manager giving approval to the worker for a good job is rewarding him and reinforcing his desire to continue doing a good job.

Wants is a term social psychologists use to refer to positive forces impelling a person toward certain objects or conditions. Wants are similar to needs but imply that the object is social and not merely physiological. In a sense they are similar to secondary drives. Thus we speak of affiliation, acquisitive, prestige, and power wants. These wants are also similar to what used to be referred to as social instincts.

Goals are the objects (or the activities associated with those objects) which fulfill or satisfy the relevant want, need, or drive. *Intermediate goals* refer to the subgoals set up for achievement on the path toward a final goal which is remote in time. Intermediate goals may help to maintain morale and long-term effort toward more distant ones.

Aspiration refers to the plans and strivings involved in reaching a certain goal or level of performance.

Thus an *aspiration* to achieve the *goal* object of president of the company may be *motivated* by a *want* for prestige rather than by a *drive* to satisfy the *need* for shelter or even the *secondary need* for a colonial-style mansion for shelter, and on the way to achieve this goal the various *intermediate goals* of manager, general manager, and vice-president will be the *incentives* of sufficient *reward* value to keep the person aspiring toward his goal.

Out of this, the manager's concern is what incentives he should use to motivate his subordinates to most fully achieve company objectives. Although the answer to this problem will not be forthcoming in this chapter, rest assured that it is among the major considerations of this book. Undoubtedly, this is the reason many of you picked up this book in the first place. But anyone who tries to give you an answer in ten easy steps or in one easy chapter is deceiving both you and himself. This is the reason I prefer to stir up and muddy the waters so they may be seen as they really are before trying to lead you to the knowledge which will make them settled and clear. Often, the manager in the muddy waters of people inter-acting will have to grasp at a straw. What I would like to teach him is how to distinguish straws which have roots from those broken ones with their ends buried in the mud. Have patience, you men of action! Managers are good managers because they want to get down to the basic issues, to the nitty-gritty, and because they want to do it fast. They prefer a digest to a book and dislike reading introductions and prefaces. This impatience works both to their advantage and disadvantage. The good manager and the good academic approach a book differently. The manager is anxious to read the conclusions and applications which the writer presents; the academic may never bother to read them but never fails to scan the introduction and the preface.

THE HIERARCHY OF NEEDS

Almost every modern manager has heard of Maslow's hierarchy of motives.[3] Over the past few years the theory has won very wide acceptance among managers and is so frequently mentioned in seminars, training pro-grams, and management literature that it will be presented sketchily here to refresh the reader's knowledge.

As mentioned in the last chapter, Maslow's personality theory is organismic and hence assumes that the potential for growth is contained within each person. Maslow is also more interested in growth and growing than in stunted or twisted growth. Just as there are degrees of disordered personality, he felt that there were degrees of healthy growing personality. These healthy people differ from the sick ones mainly in their general patterns of motivation. Those who are self-actualizing are growth-motivated; the fulfillment and achievement of potentials and talents is their dominat-ing motivation.

The underlying needs for all human motivation can be organized on five general levels from lowest to highest. Within these levels there could be many specific needs.

The lowest level of needs is *physiological*. The need for food, drink, shelter, and relief from pain would be among these. Very primitive societies would classify these as major needs, or they might become dominant during wars, floods, famines, or other catastrophes. If one needs food badly enough, he will risk his life for it or even sell himself into slavery or bind himself to serfdom. In North America and Europe today people are rarely threat-

---

[3] A. H. Maslow, *Motivation and Personality* (New York: Harper & Row, Publishers, 1954).

ened by starvation or death by exposure and hence incentives based on these needs are not as important as others. In some countries these threats are still real and emerge every now and then making their satisfaction a major motivating factor.

The next lowest set of needs is for *safety and security*. Once the physical needs of the moment are satisfied, the human begins to concern himself about whether these needs will be satisfied in the future. It is only with satisfaction of the first needs that man becomes interested in planning and in the future. In Europe and North America this type of security is quite widely provided for by the socialism of both "capitalist" and "socialist" states and even by the "capitalists" themselves. To some members of the older generation, with bitter memories of the depression and a relatively brief enrollment in the company pension scheme, such needs are still real.

The third need level is for *belongingness, social, and love needs*. These are probably the dominant needs in Western society. As the first two need levels are widely satisfied, people can feel concerned about their relationship to others. It is because such needs are dominant that it is appropriate to write a book on social psychology for management. The major needs, the effective incentives, the important motivation for today's worker are these *social needs*. The strong need of the average person of today to feel part of his group and to be a full-fledged, accepted member of society means the manager must understand social perception, attitudes, group structure and dynamics, power, status and role. A generation ago such knowledge may not have been as important. Earlier studies in psychology showed that the dominant needs of workers centered around security. The picture has changed today and the effective manager must change with it. New attitudes, knowledge, and management skills are needed. If my son writes a book on management, hopefully he will be able to say, "A generation ago the dominant needs of our society were social. Today these have largely been filled."

The fourth level of needs is for *autonomy and self-esteem*. Feeling secure and accepted, the person now wants to be accepted for what he is rather than for what he can offer others. Love and social needs are good but, when they carry with them a dependency upon others for approval of one's thinking and behavior, true personal growth can be stunted. This calls for autonomy in one's behavior, freedom to exercise independence in thinking, and a desire to be respected for one's true self, not merely to receive respect as a symbol of organizational authority or because one has a high income. Related to autonomy are needs for feelings of adequacy, mastery, and power. Related to self-esteem are needs for recognition, status, and appreciation. This fourth level of needs is of increasing importance today. It is especially prominent among successful managers, professionals, highly skilled workers, and those with a high need for achievement. Advancing up the organizational hierarchy, from lowest to highest status worker, it becomes of increasing significance.

The highest level is the need for *self-actualization*. Even with the four lower need levels filled, man craves total fulfillment of the self, the fullest achievement of his capacity, and the realization of his potential. We talk of self-actualiz*ing* people and not of self-actualiz*ed* people because there is always room for more development. This level represents the full flowering of psychological health. With all lower needs satisfied, there is the possibility of a degree of existential freedom in which man, though still fully human and earthbound and not even wanting to renege on the animal aspect of his existence, reaches to the stars as master of himself and in the fullness of his humanity.

Diagrammatically, the hierarchy can be described as in Figure 5-1. Here we see that all the needs overlap. The lowest needs never disappear: we must always eat, sleep, and take refuge from the weather. And no one can worry much about self-actualization if he is busy worrying about tomorrow or about whether he is a full-fledged member of society. As Maslow points out, *behaviors always have more than one motivation*, and this becomes clear in a close look at Figure 5-1.

The implication of this hierarchy of motives is that the organization must present the *climate* within which the person can grow. Depending on the climate provided, the organization could be instrumental in keeping the individual worker fixated at any level. The disadvantage to the organization would be that it would get only half a man for its efforts as the full man would not be able to develop. Half a man may be easier to control, in one sense (in another sense, he is less predictable), but may be more costly because his better half is lost. Also, the organismic pressure to grow may find a climate for growth off the job, to the detriment of the organization. How many organizations today cut off their nose to spite their face! How many people under your supervision take evening courses at the YMCA, the community club, the community college, the university, or elsewhere —in oriental expression, pottery and ceramics, oil painting, dressmaking, judo, ancient religions, flower arrangement, history of the occult arts, foreign languages, history of art, medieval architecture, and a host of other subjects. They pay good money for these courses and often they participate more willingly than they do with their employers. I know. I have given such courses. Not that taking them should be disparaged—on the contrary, it should be encouraged, especially when work is unavoidably dull. The growing and self-actualizing personality is hungry for knowledge and experience from all sources.

Following an extensive examination of a group of self-actualizing people (truly self-actualizing people are quite rare), Maslow concluded that they are described as follows:

FIGURE 5-1

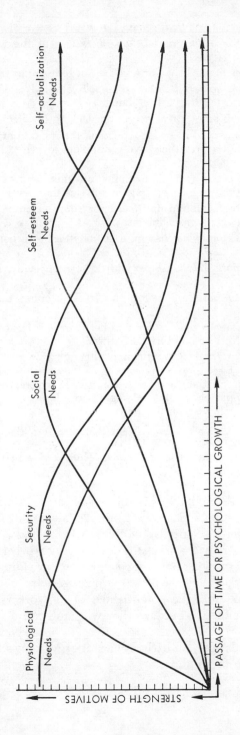

It can be seen from the diagram that all of the needs are always present, but at different stages of psychological growth higher ones dominate the need hierarchy and the basic ones decline in importance.

They are *realistically oriented,* seeing the world as it really is.

They are highly *accepting of self, of others* and of the world without prejudice or hypocrisy.

They are *spontaneous* in behavior and are not hidebound by convention.

They are *problem centered* rather than self-centered and with a wide frame of reference for the task at hand.

They are *detached,* enjoy privacy, yet not lacking in affection.

They are *autonomous* and independent of their environment, gaining maximum satisfaction from their own continuing growth rather than from the opinions of others.

Lack of stereotyping in their appreciation of others and of things. They can enjoy good things again and again without their ever getting stale.

Most of them have profound *mystical or spiritual experiences,* although not necessarily religious in character.

They *identify with mankind,* having a genuine desire to help the human race.

They have *intimate relationships* with a few specially loved people rather than many casual ties.

They *discriminate between means and ends,* keeping their sights on ends.

Their *sense of humor is philosophical* rather than hostile; it is not smutty or based on the hurt or inferiority of others.

They have a great *fund of creativeness* although this may not take the form of objects of creation. It is more that they see creatively and express creativity in all their activities. Not all highly creative people are self-actualizing. Special creative talents can reside even in severely disturbed people (such as, Van Gogh).

They *resist conformity* but try to improve society from within rather than to fight it or reject it from without.

They may have many *lesser imperfections.* They can be boring, stubborn, vain, lose their tempers.

The emphasis throughout this theory of a need hierarchy is on the motivation of healthy and growing people. Management which bases its incentives on lower-level needs is in danger of doing a number of ineffective things. First, it will attract the less healthy workers and drive off the more healthy and growing ones. Second, by not providing a rich growth environment it will not allow healthy personal growth to take place and thus will cut itself off from the potentialities of its workers. Third, its incentives will not be effective because they will motivate a narrower range of employees.

As Douglas McGregor, an early applicant of Maslow's theory to management, summed up in an address:

Man is a wanting animal—as soon as one of his needs is satisfied, another appears in its place. This process is unending. It continues from birth to death—man lives for bread alone, when there is no bread . . . *a satisfied need is not a motivator of behavior!* This is a fact of profound significance that is regularly ignored in the conventional approach to the management of people. . . . management, fearing hostility to its own objectives, often goes to considerable lengths to control and direct human efforts in ways that are inimical to the nature of 'groupiness' of human beings . . . The typical industrial organization offers few opportunities for the satisfaction of these egoistic needs to people at lower levels in the hierarchy.

What about your organization or ones you are familiar with? What chance do they provide for self-actualization? At what level would their incentive systems belong? What is the general motivation of most employees?

Maslow estimates that the average man in the street has physiological needs 85 percent satisfied, security needs 70 percent satisfied, belongingness needs 50 percent satisfied, ego needs 40 percent satisfied, and self-actualization needs 10 percent satisfied.

LEVEL OF ASPIRATION

Success and failure are forms of reward and punishment and hence can either satisfy and encourage continuing effort or, through failure, discourage the further expenditure of effort. But when we looked at hedonism we saw that reward and punishment (pleasure and pain) are subjective factors and depend on the ideas and experiences of the person who receives them. To make sense out of the feelings of success and failure, the psychologist places them in the context of the person's level of aspiration. The degree of satisfaction received from a reward depends on both the person's level of aspiration and the nature of the reward. Also, it depends on the level of skill or intellectual demand of the person's job.

Kurt Lewin did some of the early major research on level of aspiration and described it as the degree of goal difficulty a person sets for himself.[4] He pointed out that it was influenced both by the individual's stability, as he measures it through his past successes and failures, and *by the standards of the group* to which he belongs. Success and failure of the individual's efforts result in raising or lowering the level of aspiration accordingly, but this is not dependent on the achievement itself as much as upon the *relationship between the achievement and the person's expectations.*

A person's level of aspiration on a particular task is also related to his

[4] Kurt Lewin, *Field Theory in Social Science: Selected Theoretical Papers,* ed. D. Cartwright (New York: Harper, 1960).

self-esteem (which, we have seen, depends on his perception of how others perceive him). This is a fundamental relationship. We all witness (even practice) the ego defense mechanism of projection when in the face of failure an inadequate tool, lack of full cooperation, or an accident is blamed for the nonachievement. (This is a true ego defense for it defends the self or ego from loss of esteem.) To experience actual success or failure, the person must attribute the outcome of an action to himself so that it is perceived as "my success" or "my failure." The feeling of failure can be removed at least partially by cutting the tie of ownership between the self and the result, thereby rejecting responsibility for the outcome. Raising the level of aspiration is also directly related to self-esteem and particularly to feelings of status in the group. As well as his own ability to reach the goal, the level of achievement prevailing in his group influences the aspiration level. This is true not merely of his immediate work group but others such as clubs, friendship groups, neighbors, members of the same graduating class, and so on. These groups have a very strong influence on keeping the level of aspiration either too low or too high for one's ability. (See Chapter 14.)

Success on a task does not always lead to a raised level of aspiration (one series of experiments showed it was raised 69 percent of the time; 7 percent of the time it remained the same; 24 percent of the time activity ceased); nor does failure always bring a decrease (in the same studies it was lowered 50 percent of the time; 21 percent of the time it remained the same; 27 percent of the time activity ceased). Part of this is probably due to the fact that often there is no *clear* failure or success. This is certainly the case with most managerial tasks and perhaps for most of the tasks the average manager supervises. However, it is quite obvious that people more readily raise their aspiration level after success and more readily lower it after failure. And it is important to note that many people simply cease the activity. There appears to be a clear difference in individuals as to whether they are easily influenced to lower their aspiration levels and, equally, as to whether they leave off trying entirely rather than lower their aspiration. Also, some show surprising persistence at a task but at the unfortunate price of constantly lowering their level of aspiration.

Many work tasks have no level on their maximum achievement. As well as an ideal goal, then, there are a series of intermediate goals and each success narrows the gap between these intermediate goals and the ideal goal, bringing the ideal closer to a level of reality. Failure has the opposite effect; it makes previously real goals vanish into the thin air of fantasy. When an ideal goal is reached, a new goal arises. The young trainee who aspires to become divisional director may reach this ideal goal over a series of promotions representing his intermediate goals. Still, before achieving his ideal goal, he has probably set new ideal goals for himself—such as general manager, vice-president, and president. He might have considered this last goal as fantasy in the early stages of his career. One early study in this area[5] stated, "It is interesting to note that those who were already at the top of the occupational ladder were most interested in further advancement, and those at the bottom were least interested in advancement . . . high school students . . . considered advancement less important than most occupational groups."

Stop reading for a moment and reflect on the changes (if any) in your own level of aspiration over the past few years. What do they indicate when taken in this context?

If the task set is of too high a degree of difficulty, then no feeling of failure results from nonaccomplishment. Equally, no feeling of success arises when the task is below some degree of difficulty. There is a tendency to keep the level of aspiration down out of fear that failure would bring a drop in self-esteem, yet a simultaneous tendency is to raise the aspiration as high as possible because of the potential satisfactions it can give. This is where the manager's role is so important (see Chapter 18) for many people start cautiously with a relatively low level of aspiration and, only after succeeding, raise their level in short steps. This is contrary to the assumption of some managers that the way to motivate people is to keep success always somewhat out of their grasp. Constantly dangling the carrot before the donkey does not work. Rather, the old maxim "You can catch more flies with honey than with vinegar" has been experimentally proven.

Feedback in terms of clear knowledge of results (of success or failure) is used by the individual in establishing or altering his level of aspiration for future output. Normal feedback brings a stabilization of self-set goals and levels of aspiration at an adequately high level realistically related to performance. Regular feedback of failure brings a first sharp drop in level of aspiration followed by a relatively stable low level of aspiration. Performance as well as level of aspiration suffers from constant negative feedback (knowledge that the goal has not been achieved) but both recover to a high stable rate when success is regularly experienced. Thus the manager who thinks his subordinates will be challenged more by always having goals they cannot quite reach is in error. Also, the manager who thinks that letting the employee feel successful might make him go soft and want to rest on his laurels is in error. Success produces higher striving and more success; failure leads to discouragement and a tendency to take it easy. This means that the employee who has been sitting around for years and going nowhere is probably really going downhill (although he may have acquired a certain skill at concealing that fact). Rather than getting

[5] C. E. Jurgensen, "What Job Applicants Look For in a Company," *Personnel Psychology*, I, No. 4 (1948), pp. 443–445.

rid of him as "dead wood," a more positive approach would be to try to raise his level of aspiration.

Stouffer's study of the American Soldier [6] will be mentioned again. Among its findings was that the men most dissatisfied with the promotional system were in the branch with the highest rate of promotion (air-force) while those most satisfied were in the branch with the lowest rate of promotion (military police). It was suggested that failure to be promoted was frustrating or not frustrating depending on whether one's colleagues expected one to be promoted. It was not the *fact* of being deprived of promotional opportunity but the *expectation* of promotion in the eyes of one's fellows that brought satisfaction or dissatisfaction. Subsequent laboratory experiments have demonstrated this principle.

Our conclusions, then, are that success and failure are forms of reward and punishment because they satisfy or deny certain social and ego needs. But such satisfaction depends on the person's perception of the outcome of his efforts and this, in turn, is closely related to the way other members of his group perceive such efforts and outcomes. Raising or lowering levels of aspiration depends on past successes and expectations. The mature person will eventually work out a realistic balance between his abilities and his level of aspiration.

COMPETITION AS AN INCENTIVE

Although it is sometimes assumed that competitiveness among humans is an inborn characteristic, it is likely that much of our competitive spirit is learned and at least one society of people regard competitiveness as an abnormality. These are the Zuñi Indians of the American Southwest who consider themselves social outcasts if they demonstrate a competitive spirit. Even in a footrace, a person who has already won once will not win a second time and it is difficult to get schoolchildren to take examinations seriously.

However, in our society people will compete for rewards when they are limited in number and will also compete just for the sake of winning. When the competition is for the sake of winning it is likely providing the reward of status, self-esteem, or some other ego need satisfaction. But in an actual competition there are losers as well as winners and if one gains social need satisfaction, others must lose it. There is a danger, then, that competition will produce not only need satisfaction and raised levels of aspiration, but also need deprivation and lowered levels of aspiration.

This is quite easy to demonstrate in the school classroom; a popular

[6] S. A. Stouffer et al., *The American Soldier: Adjustment During Army Life,* Vol. I (Princeton, N. J.: Princeton University Press, 1949).

incentive of teachers used to be to divide the class into teams and have them compete for various types of scores. Many little classrooms had a blackboard graph where the weekly progress of "the Rockets," "the Angels," "the Astronauts," and "the Jets" could be read by all who entered the room. On a random assignment of students to their groups the chances are reasonable that competitive ability will be about equal. But, by a simple manipulation, the teacher could put all of the brightest students into one group and all of the dullest into another. Now let them compete. After a few abortive attempts of the dullards to respond to Teacher's prodding to match the clever group, the game will be over. Not only do the dullards lower their level of aspiration and stop competing but, equally, the more mature members of the brighter group will lose interest as it is no challenge for them. In fact, various studies have demonstrated that co-operative groups are likely to achieve higher productivity on various problem-solving tasks than are competitive groups.

What about competition in games? Is it not fierce and does it not cause expenditure of great energy? Yes, it does. But play differs from work in a number of ways. It is carried out in a friendly spirit and no hard feelings are caused because understanding of the game calls for certain attitudes of sportsmanship. When there is a difference in skill level, a handicap or a "spot" is given to the less skilled. Disgrace for losing is seldom present and all players readily provide face savers to losers. Losers are praised and credited with putting up a good fight, often they are physically embraced by the winners, and everyone acknowledges what good sportsmanship they show. People cheer for the underdog against the champion as a matter of course and excuse his bad showing by blaming Lady Luck or the fact that he is having an "off" day. In many games, then, a person can lose without feeling inferior.

When winning is strictly a matter of skill, experience, or ability, interest in the competition among winners, losers, and spectators begins to decline as soon as one party begins to win consistently. Incentive to try harder can be present only as long as an element of uncertainty exists. Games and sports maintain interest by matching equals and not permitting competition between unequals.

Giving first, second, and third prizes in sales campaigns is a popular type of competition but it has been criticized on the grounds that it motivates only a few.[7] Competition between groups for safety records has equally been criticized because *winning* rather than *safety* becomes the objective, with the result that accidents go unreported and injured men are kept on the job to maintain the record. Also, many managers fear that their

[7] Norman R. F. Maier, *Psychology in Industry,* 3rd ed. (Boston: Houghton Mifflin Company, 1965).

men will consider a competition a management trick to exploit them, or that it will put the unions on their backs. Competition does represent a threat to the inferior worker and often the others will resist a threat to any member of their group. This will become clearer when group cohesiveness is examined in Chapter 11.

Spontaneous competitions among workers are quite common. In such situations the competition is treated like a game and often takes place when no supervisory people are present. In many jobs I have worked at, roofers, shinglers, marine laggers, stevedores, and shoe salesmen often engaged in this type of game as a relief from boredom. If the experience of winning is spread out among groups or individuals these competitions raise interest. In such instances supervisors who become involved should ensure that records or scores do not become a part of the production record and, although some pressure is necessary to make the game enjoyable, the atmosphere should always be relaxed. Even minor games in a small office involving wastage of paper, punctuality, suggestions, and general housekeeping can be fun, tension-relieving, and improve effectiveness when handled properly. But the least sign of threat, managerial pressure, or loss of esteem to the loser will turn all players sour.

Caution also has to be employed that high productivity scores do not lessen quality. When productivity alone is the criterion of the game or competition service or quality then suffers. In the roofers' and shinglers' competitions the accusation was sometimes made (often on good grounds) that the winner put in only three nails when five were called for; I remember as a boy competing in sales campaigns for newspaper subscribers assuring potential customers that they had to sign for only one month after which they were quite free to drop the subscription (which many did); I have also been on stevedore crews competing with other crews to fill a ship's hold with *sacked* wheat when as much *unsacked* wheat was buried in the corners and under the sacked piles; and as a warehouseman I have seen dolly loads of sugar or detergents accidentally destroyed in heated competitions.

This pinpoints the problem of competition, for the *score* rather than the production the score was supposed to represent becomes the goal. Scores are important in any game. Indeed, many sports maintain a variety of scores for each team and each individual member. One complaint about managers is that they tend to use the various scores of their work groups as means of criticizing or questioning the results of their subordinates rather than as means of encouraging them further.

MONEY AS AN INCENTIVE

Every man has his price, the saying goes. Maybe it is true. But the payoff may not be in money, as is so often assumed.

The exact role of money as an incentive at any job level is almost impossible to measure accurately. Money can symbolize so many things and can be used as the means to attain many things. We pay for food, clothing, and shelter with it (Maslow's physiological level); we can buy insurance and accumulate savings with it (to satisfy security needs); we can afford to get married, to live an active social life, to join a club, and so on if we have it (social need satisfaction); we can gain power, prestige, and independence with it (self-esteem and autonomy need satisfaction); and we can use it in innumerable ways for self-improvement (toward self-actualization). It would be foolish, then, to assume that money is not a good motivator.

Yet money as motivator is a far more complex thing than used to be assumed. In Chapter 8 we shall discuss what happens in the organization which assumes that man is economically motivated. As Whyte reminds us in *Money and Motivation*[8] man is not born loving money; he has to learn to love it. The attitude he acquires about money and the possibility of making more of it varies throughout the world. Western businessmen in underdeveloped countries have often been dismayed to find local citizens who prefer to work a lesser number of days to earn their customary income and who do not accept the opportunity to earn more money by working longer hours or more days. The desire for money appears to have a direct relationship to the desire for goods and services. Whyte claims that Americans have a stronger interest in making more money and in the things that money will buy them than is found in most other parts of the world. Yet even among United States factory workers there are great variations in response to money. Certainly, money is not the only reward nor lack of money the only punishment in terms of the worker.

The major trouble with money is that it is never received solely as a reward but always contains an element of punishment. To earn money a person has to sacrifice something and to earn more money he has to make a greater sacrifice. Rarely are we faced with the choice of making more money uncomplicated by other conflicting considerations (such as being branded a rate-buster by fellow workers or risking job security or doing less pleasant work or giving up more free time).

Money as an incentive cannot be considered on its own but only in terms of some other context, such as status (see Chapter 13), where it is not the money itself but its level of comparison with the income of those around us which really counts. A raise symbolizes recognition and thus adds an important reward to the receipt of more money by itself. Tying money directly to production by means of a piece rate has long been abandoned as the sure way to maximize productivity because of the many com-

[8] W. F. Whyte, *Money and Motivation: An Analysis of Incentives in Industry* (New York: Harper & Row, Publishers, 1955).

plications it introduces. Such a system appears to work only in limited circumstances. Nor can high money assure high job satisfaction.

Man does not live by bread alone. But in our society if the employer stops giving him money or even threatens to do so, a man immediately starts looking for another job. Even in those countries where major social revolutions have taken place, money is extremely important to the individual, so it is likely to be an incentive for a long time. Yet exactly what its incentive value is remains an unknown variable in the vast majority of instances.

THE MOTIVATION-HYGIENE THEORY

A theory of work satisfaction and motivation which has aroused a good deal of comment, support, and controversy in recent years is the motivation-hygiene theory of Frederick Herzberg.[9] He buttresses the conclusions reached after several studies and after replications of his work by others with a philosophy of the dual nature of man. This idea is an ancient one which underlies many historical philosophies and religions. The first aspect of man's nature is the animal, instinctive, sweat-of-the-brow half. Herzberg calls it the Adam nature of man. It can be held in check by hard work and perseverance. The other half contains man's potential, higher nature, capable of rising to a spiritual fulfillment. He calls it the Abraham nature of man. This Adam-Abraham dualism underlies the Judaeo-Christian tradition.

The original major research underlying the theory was reported in 1959.[10] Two hundred engineers and accountants were interviewed about events at work which had brought them marked job satisfaction or marked loss of satisfaction. There was a noticeable difference between factors which make people happy, contented, or satisfied with their work and factors which produced dissatisfaction on the job. A number of similar studies have given general support to these findings among supervisory and nonsupervisory workers; male and female workers; skilled, unskilled, and professional workers—both in the United States and in other countries.

Herzberg concludes that the opposite to job satisfaction is *not* job dissatisfaction but, rather, the *lack of job satisfaction*. The opposite to job dissatisfaction is *not* job satisfaction but, rather, a *lack of job dissatisfaction*. In other words, job satisfaction and job dissatisfaction do not represent the opposite ends of a continuum or scale but, rather, must be considered as separate measurements or scales. This is where we get back to the

[9] Frederick Herzberg, *Work and the Nature of Man* (Cleveland: World Publishing Company, 1966).

[10] F. Herzberg et al., *The Motivation to Work* (New York: John Wiley & Sons, Inc., 1959).

Adam-Abraham duality of man again. On one dimension we have the animal-Adam nature of man represented by the avoidance of anything painful or unpleasant. When unpleasant factors cannot be avoided they produce job dissatisfaction. These dissatisfactions isolated by Herzberg's research are

- —company policy and administration
- —supervision
- —salary
- —interpersonal relations
- —working conditions

Essentially, as can be seen, these dissatisfiers describe the environment of the worker (physical and social). They are called the *hygiene* factors of the job because they can be controlled and prevented from interfering with the "health" of the worker. The organization can modify these environmental factors for their workers, thereby preventing dissatisfaction in the same way that we can practice dental hygiene to prevent cavities, gum disease, and so on.

On the other dimension are those factors which produce job satisfaction for the human-Abraham nature of man. Although all the hygiene factors may be present there may still be little job satisfaction. The things which provide satisfaction have been termed by Herzberg as the *motivators* and have been isolated as

- —achievement
- —recognition for work well done
- —work itself
- —responsibility
- —advancement

So, as many psychologists have come to reject the thinking that would put mental health and mental illness at opposite ends of the same scale, this theory posits that there are two, not one, separate scales of "working health." Just because a person is not mentally sick does not mean that he is necessarily mentally healthy; and just because a person is not dissatisfied with his job does not mean that he has job satisfaction.

The hygiene factors, then, are preventive. If the organization provides them, it will prevent the workers from getting sick of work (being job dissatisfied). But to help them do creative, satisfying, responsible work the organization must provide them with the motivators; the hygiene factors contribute little towards this.

The truly healthy person has to have a balance of both hygiene and motivator factors. He likes to enjoy life, to play, to have a pleasant environment, but at the same time he has a strong desire to accomplish and create. He may well have a reputation in his organization for being a griper or a maverick and have good grounds for his complaints and frustrations. For in the organization which concentrates its attention on providing the hygiene factors to its workers and in which the workers themselves tend to be mainly hygiene seekers, there will be a general complacency. But complacency and good hygiene are not enough for the motivator seeker. He wants the chance to grow, and to feel strong and healthy in his work. If these opportunities are not available, he will demand and complain. By implication some of the greatest complainers, demanders, and agitators in the organization may be among its potentially healthiest members.

Before jumping to the conclusion that the company's great troublemakers represent its greatest potential, though, let us consider those who are constantly demanding things in the list of hygiene factors—better hours, lighting, air conditioning, and cafeteria meals, more fringe benefits and social interaction, less demands, and so on. These people are hygiene seekers and crave the hygiene effects in the same way that an addict needs his drugs or an alcoholic needs his liquor. The more they get, the more they want, and the less satisfying and valuable the drugs become the more they use them.

This is a very important point which we will take up again in Chapter 18. If the organization concentrates on supplying hygiene factors to its workers (padded furniture, air conditioning, fringe benefits, folksy company newsletters, office picnics, and all the human relations paraphernalia) and neglects the motivators (interesting work, responsibility, on-the-job growth, self-improvement opportunities, advanced training in both technical and theoretical areas, educational support, recognition), then evermore workers are going to seek the hygiene factors.

If management operates on the implicit assumption that these are the types of things people *want* in their work (the types of things they work for), supplies them, and then sees that the workers want more of them and continues to supply them (all the time neglecting the motivator factors), the management assumption will come true, a self-fulfilling prophecy. The result is that the organization is caught in a vicious circle largely of its own making, and it does not even realize this. Rather, senior management employs the same type of projection as the worker who blames his tools, finding the cause of the problem in the insatiable appetites of the "good-for-nothing" workers.

Oh for the day that the union will decide by vote to go out for self-actualization! Then we will be able to speculate about a rosy future.

The way out of the dilemma is not easy; neither is it so difficult. It requires a new attitude toward the reason men work at all; much more will be said about this in Chapter 8. Certainly, it would be foolish to suggest that hygiene factors are not important. They are important. Salary, company policy, and good administration and working conditions must not be neglected, but they must be held in proper perspective. It always has been —and probably always will be—easier to understand, to measure, to control, and to manipulate the hygiene factors. The motivators are more complex, more subjective, and elusive to measure. Hence the easy way out is to focus attention on the hygiene factors and neglect the others. The end result is the management tendency to deal with one half a man. Let us say, for instance, that an employee comes to his manager feeling discouraged and frustrated with his job and thinking about quitting to try another type of work. As he is a good worker, the manager does not want to lose him and begins to hold out the prospects of better salary and working conditions to encourage him to stay. It would probably be more effective, however, to try to provide him with more interesting work, more responsibility, and the opportunity for achievement.

If your organization has allowed itself to slip into the trap of being a hygiene provider and a motivator neglecter, the future prospects for you may then involve meeting greater and greater demands for higher salaries, better working conditions, more fringe benefits, shorter hours, and so on. It is time to start working your way out of this trap.

CONCLUSION

Having examined some of the major theories and ideas about motivation and work, we are still far from being in a position to set out ten easy rules for motivating workers. What are some of the problems?

First, there is the basic problem of being able to understand what motivation is. We cannot really come to grips with it unless we know how to hold it down and measure it. One possibility is that we are looking for answers in the wrong places—that there is no such thing as "motivation" in the sense that there is some generalizable force underlying the behavior of all workers. To be a useful concept to us, perhaps motivation has to be *operationally defined* as the experimental psychologist would define it (i.e., by describing what the person does before he could be referred to as "motivated"). However, it is difficult to make clear operational definitions of motivation to work because of the very complexity of work behavior. Another thing we might do to make motivation a useful concept is to be cautious about some of the common assumptions and implications contained in many of today's incentive practices and try to understand motivation more in the context of the total social psychological activity of the complex organization. This is our approach in this book. Finally, we need more experimentation on motivation to work. At first sight, this may not appear to be such a good idea for the thousands of studies to date on worker motivation have not provided many useful results. But many of these studies are simplistic and rather naïve in terms of what we know today and some of their implicit assumptions and lack of clear definitions and measurements make them almost certain to yield results which could not be applied.

The major problem of motivation was pinpointed by Kurt Lewin many years ago when he was working out his field theory: Once we establish a general theory of behavior or of motivation, how do we move from the generalization to make a prediction in the case of the unique individual? Once we have formulated a general rule, it becomes necessary to treat all individuals as identical, which is simply not true. We must carefully reexamine some of the useless generalizations about motivation that we still carry around with us. Man is complex and no one is likely to ever come forward with a simple explanation of his motivation.

Some organizations are doing exploration in motivation and incentive systems. There are the Scanlon-type plans and other types of profit sharing or cost-reduction sharing. There are awards for ideas and schemes and other types of prizes for groups and individual incentives. Most seem to have their merits and most also have their critics who point out problems with each of them. It does not appear that there is one type of incentive scheme which would be applicable to all organizations.

SUMMARY

We have come full circle in this chapter, starting with the confession that psychologists do not really know much which is unequivocal about motivation and ending by stating that we cannot give much unambiguous advice on incentive systems. Yet in between these admissions an attempt was made to show what the main problems of understanding motivation are and how a few psychologists have attempted to put forth useful theories of motives and job satisfaction.

We sketched out the four major categories of motivation theory, with a few words about their strengths and weaknesses. These were, first, cognitive theories which assume that man always thinks out or plans what he is to do. Such theories cannot account for unconscious motivation nor can they provide a useful means of predicting behavior. Second are the hedonistic theories based on the concept of pleasure and pain (or satisfaction and dissatisfaction). Although hedonism runs through all theories, it fails to deal with the problem that pleasure and pain are subjective experiences. Third, the instinct theories tend to offer descriptions and predictions. Their descriptions are not explanations and their predictions are unreliable because of the interference of learned behaviors. Last, the drive theories, although offering the most rigorous and useful approach, leave many problems unsolved. The concept of learned or secondary drives is a useful one, but drive theory is better for explaining animal behavior than human behavior.

As so many terms are used in a discussion of motivation, a list of psychological definitions was provided for terms such as wants, needs, motives, incentives, and so on.

The theory of motivation best known to management people is Maslow's need hierarchy. This was sketched out for review, because it will be referred to again in this book. The need levels are generally described as physiological, security, belongingness or social, autonomy or self-esteem, and self-actualization. Before one becomes of major importance the preceding ones must be largely satisfied. Yet all are always present so that human motivation must of necessity be complex. Maslow's description of the self-actualizing person was also presented. The implication was that management must not concentrate on providing for lower level need satisfaction to the detriment of higher level needs. Management must take some responsibility for the personal growth of employees.

Next, we considered level of aspiration, for satisfactions and rewards depend on what the individual is trying to accomplish (or has set as his goal). Feelings of success and failure depend on past experiences and present group influences on the individual. Kurt Lewin with his field theory had a good deal to say about this; field theory emphasizes that motivation for behavior depends on the presently existing facts, including the feelings of the person and the pressures of the environment. In general, success raises level of aspiration and failure lowers it. This research finding runs counter to the incentive systems of some managers who feel that the constantly dangling carrot is the best incentive.

Competition and incentives were discussed. Although highly effective in games, competition is quite different in the work situation and the differences were pointed out. Only if work becomes a game can competition be a useful incentive. If competition is unfair because workers are poorly matched or feel they are being used, or if anyone suffers loss of esteem, the game ceases to be fun and is abandoned.

Money as an incentive is very important and the manager should never be blinded to this fact by his study of the human relations movement. But the actual influence of money remains an unknown variable because it symbolizes different things to different people. It cannot be considered on its own but takes on useful meaning only in the context of what it represents.

The motivation-hygiene theory provides some research support (although controversial) for Maslow's need hierarchy. Founded on a philosophy of the dual nature of man, it emphasizes that satisfiers and dissatisfiers must be kept separate and measured with a different yardstick. The major problem is that hygiene factors are easier to work with than motivators and the organization tends to concentrate its attention upon them thereby drugging its employees into becoming hygiene seekers. Although such employees are not sick, they are not healthy and become a constant source of difficulty to management.

Although not offering the often-asked-for ten easy steps to motivation, the conclusion urged managers to reexamine deep-seated ideas on motivation and to be prepared to experiment in order to discover what might be the best incentive system in their particular situation. More clues to such a discovery will be provided in a number of subsequent chapters; in the final analysis, this is what much of the book is all about.

2

HARMONY AMONG GROUPS

Because work is social, the manager finds himself in a position of responsibility for the social behavior of others. Only by ensuring that such behavior is effective can he do his job properly.

There are groups below the manager that he wants to run smoothly, but there are also groups all around him in other divisions of the organization which have no direct responsibility to him yet upon which he is dependent. There are other managers and groups of managers at his level with whom he must interact effectively. And there are those groups above him in the organizational hierarchy to which he must report and whose wishes he must put into effect by the proper use of his own group.

Part 2 looks first at different types of groups and organizations and how they "tick" as against how the social individual "ticks." It soon becomes obvious that the important links between groups and individuals are their communication processes. Problems develop because these processes are inefficient and so Part 2 looks at the communication net of which the manager is a part and how it works or does not work.

At this point we begin to see that because of subtle forms of communication the group will behave effectively only if there is an agreement or contract between the various parties (manager, group, organization). This contract is unwritten and is therefore referred to as a psychological contract rather than a legal one.

As psychological contracts involve attitudes of management toward worker and worker toward management, we next examine what social attitudes involve, how they are formed, and how they change.

The final chapter of Part 2 concerns changing people's minds—that is, their attitudes. Not that the manager is a manipulator, but he finds some members of his group more controllable and persuadable than others and he wants to know why.

6

WORK GROUPS AND ORGANIZATIONS

Now we want to look at the structure of the organization and the group the way it exists apart from the people who compose it. Why do we need organizations and groups; why it is we cannot simply work as individuals? What is a bureaucracy, and what are its advantages and disadvantages? Can the nonbureaucracy work in our technological age? Is there any truth in Parkinson's Law or the Peter Principle? Can organizations be typed any better than we type personalities? How can friction between subgroups of the organization be prevented? Is the size of the group related to the problems it experiences? What!—another committee!—what for this time? Can't we do without them?

Once, when I was being interviewed for a management position in a large organization, I asked my interviewers if they had a staff-line chart that I could look at to give me some picture of how the organization (over ten thousand employees) was set up. They looked at one another in dismay and one of them mumbled that he thought he had seen a chart around somewhere; one agreed and the other two disagreed that one had ever existed. Then they attempted to construct one—without success.

I was rather surprised by this experience (I withdrew my application for the position for a number of reasons) because at the time I had the rather naïve idea that any reasonable-sized company would have a clear self-picture to present to its employees and to strangers. After a few similar surprises—such as asking in-company management seminar groups simple questions about their organizational structure, and asking management trainees whom they report to in the organization and at what level—I have come to the conclusion that what I took for granted is not to be so taken.

All groups have structure, as we shall see in later chapters. The large organization particularly has a highly complex structure. Yet, reflecting on my personal experience, only in those organizations where I took the deliberate effort to piece together an organization chart, have I ever had an understanding of their structure. In most organizations the vast majority of members have little understanding of the organizational structure beyond their immediate supervisor and their immediate peer group membership. The naïveté of even senior and long-term employees in the organization is appalling.

This emphasis on group and organizational structures becomes understandable later when we find that communication patterns follow the lines of structure, power, and status. When the structure is not clear communications become misdirected and ineffectual. Often, I have tried to tell student reformers that their efforts to change the status quo of the university will continue to lack effectiveness if they persist in attempting to change or overthrow the system without any understanding of the structure of that system.

GROUPS AND ORGANIZATIONS

A group (sometimes called a *psychological group*) consists of two or more people interacting. This interaction requires that the behavior of each member influences the behavior of each other member and that the members share some common perceptions, beliefs, values, and objectives. We are all members of many such groups: family, work, friendship, educational and recreational, and so on.

Studying the behavior of groups, the psychologist sometimes restricts himself to examining the interaction of *dyads* (groups of two persons) or *triads* (groups of three persons) because the shared behaviors and influences within even the most simple group are extremely complicated.

When groups are related to one another in the sense that they have common objectives and ideologies (systems of thinking, policy, and ideas) they are referred to as *organizations*. In simple terms, an organization is a group of groups interacting to achieve some goal. Factories, hospitals, insurance companies, universities, and retail stores are organizations. Each has its unique structure, ideology, and other characteristics which influence its members in certain ways.

We refer also to both *formal* and *informal* groups and organizations. Formal ones are those set up with relatively clear and official roles for members, rules for interaction, and goals for achievement. They reflect the psychological and administrative assumptions of those who designed them but are rarely a true picture of what they are supposed to be. Informal groups or organizations refer to those unplanned sets of subgroups, friendship relations, and other informal relationships which inevitably develop when a number of people are placed in necessary contact with one another. These groups grow out of the personality characteristics and peculiar motivational needs of the unique set of individuals which comprise any group. No designer of a group can take all these factors into consideration and hence no one can predict all of the behaviors, attitudes, and feelings which are likely to be present in a formally designed group. It will become evident later that informal groups and organizational structures are at least as important for effective goal achievement as are the formal structures.

Officially, these informal groups and organizations do not exist and are not shown on even the most complete organizational charts. As they may vary considerably from the formal structure, there is potential conflict in objectives and communication lines between them.

THE PURPOSE OF THE GROUP

Any group or organization comes together or is put together for two reasons. First, because the group can do something which the individual cannot do or, at least, can do something better than an individual can do. Without a goal or objective there would be no group—whether that goal be to manufacture something, provide a service to someone, earn a profit, or whatever. Second, a group provides for the satisfaction of its members' wants. Unless the group meets members' needs or holds out some prospect of meeting their needs, it will not form, nor will it remain together if it ceases to satisfy these needs. It may provide its members with a monthly paycheck, give them an occupational role in the community, satisfy their social proclivities; or it may satisfy all these needs and more simultaneously.

We cannot say that one of these purposes is more important than the other; the fact is that we do not have a group without either. Yet there is always potential conflict between the group's major purposes for, often, the good of the individual must be held in check to reach the group's goal. If it is held too much in check and if it seems to the individual that the prospects of achieving his personal satisfaction no longer exists, he will then leave the group. When enough individuals leave the group, it ceases to achieve its objectives and goes out of existence. Yet, if the group concentrates solely on membership satisfaction and ceases to move toward its goal, its existence is again threatened and it can remain a group only by turning its efforts toward the goal again or by taking on new goals (in which case it may be considered a different group).

To steer the course between these two purposes is the main job of management. All experienced managers get the feeling from time to time that they are trying to serve two masters—their subordinates and the organization. The feeling is based on fact. They *have* two masters—the group goal and membership satisfaction. This always reminds me of the Irish priest's admonition to his parishioners that they "should always keep to that straight and narrow path that lies between good and evil."

For the manager there is no straight and narrow path, nor are there any means of always making clear distinctions between good and evil, nor can he separate the one group purpose from the other. Probably, he has to be as much a juggler as anything.

Diagrammatically, we can try to illustrate the problem in Figure 6-1. The more the group moves or is forced to move toward accomplishment of its goal *D*, the more is membership satisfaction going to decline from *A* to *B*. The more the group moves from *B* to *A* to meet membership satisfaction, the more is goal accomplishment going to decline from *D* to *C*.

FIGURE 6-1

RELATIONSHIP BETWEEN THE PRIMARY PURPOSES OF THE GROUP

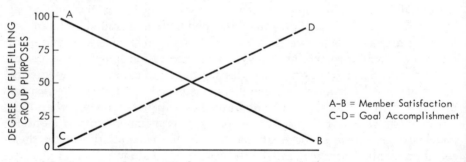

Moving too close to *D* threatens to destroy the group as moving too close to *A* causes it to deteriorate, be closed down, laid off, fired, or simply evaporate. The group may be held at a point close to *D* by means of tight controls and pressures but this causes tensions to accumulate because membership needs are not met and eventually trouble develops—strikes, sabotage, absenteeism, accidents, sickness, resignations, work to rule, lack of participation, or other such things. These are all attempts to rebalance the purposes of the group. On the other hand, when the group moves close to *A* and stays there for a prolonged time, they do not get the job done. This means falloff in profits and orders; underuse of time, space, and machinery; longer patient turnovers. The management tries to rebalance by tightening controls, threatening, firing slackers, enforcing regulations, closing down unprofitable units, introducing new incentives, and so on.

The whole of Part 4 of this book is devoted to the manager's role as leader of the group and the balancing of these forces. For the moment our main interest is in understanding how and why these groups and organizations are such complicated things.

Although I contend that the above holds true for all types of groups (recreational, social, educational, therapeutic, etc.), undoubtedly it is true of work groups. Everyone acknowledges that the work group has as its purpose the production of goods or the provision of services as effectively as possible. What so many neglect to see is that no group, work-oriented or not, can possibly achieve its goals effectively if it neglects too much and too long the other major function: the satisfaction of its workers. Even the most rigorously disciplined army and the most tightly controlled jail will suffer inefficiencies in some segment of functioning (morale, loss of equipment, higher operating costs, lack of creativity or flexibility). An escape-proof jail is more expensive than a prison farm and we have all heard stories of the rigidly disciplined army marching off the end of a dock or charging into vainglorious self-destruction.

High morale (membership satisfaction) costs money; lack of high morale costs even more money. Indeed, though it may not appear on the balance sheet as a direct cost, morale is probably the most expensive item on the budget of any organization.

THE BUREAUCRACY

Our Western civilization today consists of a vast interlocking network of complex organizations. Everyone in our society is influenced by them. It has been said that only the housewife and the preschool child are not a member of at least one. Whether or not they are members, they are certainly influenced by many organizations directly and indirectly—from the maternity hospital and the parish church to the supermarket and the municipality, not to speak of the local TV station, the political party in power, and an endless array of government services. Indeed, one of the greatest trends of our day appears to be to weave this interlocking network into a tight cloth so opaque that we cannot see through it. The municipality is tied to the hospital, the hospitals to one another, and they in turn are tied to the professional organizations, which are tied to the universities and colleges, which are tied to the lower educational institutions, which are tied to the school board, which is tied to the municipality, which is tied to the technical college, which is tied to the trades licensing board, which is tied to the trades unions, which are tied to the manufacturers, and so on. If one took the trouble to do it, he could probably demonstrate some sort of connection between any two organizations taken at random.

We contemporaries take these complex organizations for granted. Yet they are a product of the present day and represent the end point of social evolution. In our time we are all witnesses to the vast migration from rural to urban areas, to the closing down of the corner grocery and a host of other local shops, to the takeover by the international chain of the neighborhood gas station, to the merger of the factory down by the tracks with the national group, to the replacement of the family doctor by the private clinic. In our occasional reminiscences with our children about the good old days, we may mourn the passing of the butcher shop and the door-to-door visit of the vegetable truck but the truth is that, for all its depersonalization, the large organization is a more efficient vehicle for dispensing the goods and services produced by our civilization. (It has also multiplied the demand for persons with managerial skills.)

This has all become possible because of the development of what has come to be called "the bureaucracy." The popularization of the term comes from Max Weber[1] who used it to point out the growing importance of the large organization with fixed positions linked together in a hierarchical pyramid, with specialization, division of labor, and established rules for the interactions and behaviors of its members. Weber died in 1920 and his major work on organizations was not published until after his death. Although the term *bureaucracy* has taken on negative connotations as used by the layman, it is still a neutral technical term for students and researchers of the organization.

Weber pointed out that the bureaucracy has the following characteristics:

1. The principle of fixed and official areas of jurisdiction usually determined by rules, laws, or administrative regulations.
2. An office hierarchy and levels of graded authority leading to a firmly established system of super- and sub-ordination in which the higher offices supervise the lower ones.
3. The management of the office is based on a system of files and written documents.
4. Office management, and at least the specialized aspects of it, presupposes thorough and expert training of managers.
5. Official activity calls for the full working capacity of the official, even though the time he is obligated to be present at the office may be limited.
6. Management follows general rules which are more or less stable and more or less complete, and which can be learned by members of the organization.

Weber also wrote of the career of the bureaucrat as a vocation which keeps him in the bureaucracy and leads to normal advancement up the hierarchy, according to his experience and ability to meet the demands of his organization.

[1] Max Weber, *The Theory of Social and Economic Organization* (New York: Oxford University Press, 1947).

The bureaucracy is quite different from its predecessor organizations, held together by a series of personal relationships around a particular leader. The impersonality of the bureaucracy allows it to do things the personalized organization could not do. In one sense its members become replaceable parts. Because of filing systems and written rules, no man is indispensable in a job where he has the sole experience. At his resignation, promotion, or death another official trained in the company policy can be put into his place. This is to the advantage of both organization and individual for it maintains continuity of knowledge, procedures, and work behavior while freeing the manager to advance to new, higher, or more challenging positions according to his capacities. In fact, the bureaucracy does not operate as rigidly and impersonally as it is drawn up to do on paper, for informal organizations develop within it based on personal feelings and attitudes.

Without the evolution of such bureaucracies, we could not have achieved the level of industrialization and technological advance of today. Yet we all know that "bureaucracy gone mad" can ensnarl everyone in red tape. Recently, I collected a whole series of form letters including those from a pseudocollection agency when I tried to pay off a monthly account in one advance lump. As I intended to move, I wrote to the organization requesting the total amount due on my account so I could pay it off entirely. Computerized responses and form letters followed over several months, three addresses, and two countries until I finally received my answer and paid the account after seven desperate months that ended up with my writing threatening and insulting letters. When the bureaucracy works this way, it is fossilized and inefficient and cannot serve the purposes of the group.

Compulsory reading for all bureaucrats should be Franz Kafka's novel *The Castle*, especially Chapter 5. It describes in a manner which has come to be called Kafkaesque the ensnarlment of red tape which most of us have experienced.

But Weber described the bureaucracy as a thing of great efficiency and there is no need for it to become Kafkaesque under the guidance of intelligent and well-trained bureaucrats. Where there has been an unfortunate training emphasis on only the one major purpose of groups and an equally unfortunate training neglect on their other major purpose, the manager may well become the bureaucrat in the negative sense of this red-tapey inflexibility.

One further implication of bureaucracy which will become apparent later is that the mutual interdependence of parts means that what happens to one part happens to each part within the organization. Interdepartmental friction and rivalry can be very expensive to the total company; a decline in profits is a bad thing for the workers as well as for the shareholders;

and ineffective personnel at any level brings disadvantages to all members —to say nothing of patients, inmates, students, clients, and customers.

THE NONBUREAUCRACY

Because the bureaucracy *does* become a jungle of red tape and because it *can* choke itself into ineffectiveness, there have been recent attempts to design complex organizations which lack the ossifying elements of bureaucracy.

The objectives of some modern organizations are inimical, at least in part, to bureaucracy. The construction of TV programs, the allocation of welfare benefits, the new demands of university education, the reformation of delinquents and juvenile offenders, the constant demand for new products, and new treatment and teaching techniques put strains on a bureaucracy that may even bring about its destruction. The handwriting has been on the wall for some time. The phasing out of Ford's Model T in 1927 to meet newly developing customer preferences was a staggeringly costly operation made extremely difficult by the rigidity which had grown into the Ford system. No profit-geared operation can hope to compete in today's world unless it is prepared for maximum flexibility, and no public service or educational institution can live in a fantasyland of financing from a bottomless purse.

It is true that degrees of flexibility can be built into a bureaucracy and most viable bureaucracies readily incorporate new ideas, products, and procedures. Some even routinize change—the auto manufacturers do this as they automatically turn to the new year's models. Yet some of this flexibility is too superficial and too slow.

For us the question is what types of nonbureaucratic organizations should be able to achieve goals and satisfy members effectively. Perhaps the easiest changes to make in Weber's bureaucracy are the firmly ordered levels of graded authority (by the delegation of authority to subordinates) and the following of organizational rules (by allowing more freedom for individual initiative). The risk of delegation is often the loss of control over standards but when employees know more about materials, machinery, clients, and necessary procedures this risk must be weighed against advantages. Equally, allowing individual initiative (allowing line people to hire rather than having all hiring done through Personnel) must have its advantages and disadvantages weighed. Staff-line relations are one of the obvious areas for experimentation in debureaucratization. Giving staff functions (there are a number of possible ways to do it) to line authorities solves some problems but always raises the danger of reintroduction of problems the creation of staff was supposed to solve in the first place.

When it is necessary to have employees operate and make decisions away from central control (small foreign offices, forest rangers, branch libraries, certain types of salespeople), the bureaucracy may proliferate rules, requiring constant, time-consuming reports to headquarters, incurring the expense of "exotic" communications (telex, private long distance telephones or regular constant long distance telephone, closed circuit TV) to keep tabs on developments and problems. Or it may professionalize its employees through training or hiring processes or through developing new categories of technicians, as is now being done in hospital, medical, teaching, and computer work.

Experiments in the electronics industry, educational organizations, companies composed predominantly of professionals, and others have attempted to do away completely with the bureaucratic hierarchy substituting for it a series of councils and conferences and replacing managers with chairmen. Results have been mixed and controversial. One of the problems may not be so much the ideas that are attempted but the way they are introduced and followed up. Chapters 20 and 21 are devoted to guidelines for those who feel ready to experiment. Sometimes it is in overlooking a simple procedure or principle that the experiment goes wrong and incorrect measurements are taken.

Although most people probably prefer a nonbureaucracy as a place to work because it is antielitist, does not centralize power, has less rules, and allows the individual more say, the temptation is always there for the manager to bureaucratize those under him because it makes his life easier and more predictable. This is true even when the organization is innovative and expanding successfully.

In fact, there are probably very few "pure bureaucracies" and most large organizations contain a mixture of bureaucracy and nonbureacracy. In many organizations production or service is routinized, research and development is not, and marketing is in between. The optimal mix depends on the unique factors of each organization, including the degree of technology involved and the materials used. A typical picture usually displays a core of bureaucracy with a few nonbureaucratic units on the fringe; this is not necessarily the most effective setup. There are often places on the periphery of the organization which could be routinized and there are those in the center that could be debureaucratized.

PARKINSON'S LAW AND ALL THAT

Because it so often creaks, groans, and offends as it moves toward its goal, the ineffective organization and its rigidly bureaucratic members are frequently the butt of modern humor. Sometimes these witty jabs serve to pinpoint the weaknesses of the complex organization.

Among the best known such jabs is Parkinson's Law.[2] The law (also called "the rising pyramid") is stated as follows: "Work expands so as to fill the time available for its completion." Parkinson supports his law by arguing that work, especially paperwork, is elastic in its demands on time so that there is little or no need for any clear relationship between the amount of work to be done and the number of employees required to do it. There is a ratio, though, between the time it takes to accomplish something and its level of importance, for importance increases with time taken.

Parkinson points out that the increase of public officials in recent years is no reflection on the volume of work governments must do for, according to his law, there is no relationship between the two factors. The increase in public officials would remain the same whether the volume of work increased, decreased, or even ceased entirely.

What makes the law work, he says, are two *facts*. First, "an official wants to multiply subordinates, not rivals"; second, "officials make work for each other." Whether for good or for bad, the second of Parkinson's facts is true and we certainly do spend a good part of our administrative time reading the memos of our colleagues or writing our own for them to read. Unquestionably, it does become ludicrous at times as our filing cabinets become stuffed with messages from the person in the next door office which may continue to be unread, unanswered, unpondered, and unfindable if ever they are referred to again. And when colleagues are available there is the temptation to discuss intended decisions with them before reaching conclusions. In spite of Parkinson's humorous references, such actions have value while they also consume time.

Another tongue-in-cheek commentary is the Peter Principle, named after its proponent Professor Peter. The principle states that in the complex organization everyone eventually reaches his level of incompetence. This comes about because promotion to a higher level is based on demonstrated managerial competence at a lower level (regardless of ability to do the higher level job). Every individual who displays managerial competence will continue to be promoted until he no longer displays such competence. He has then reached his level of incompetence and will remain at that position for the remainder of his management career. In time this means that most organizational positions are filled with nonpromotable (displaying lack of competence in their present positions) managers. A further implication is that the organization promotes (and hence loses) its most competent people into positions of which they are not capable rather than leave them at the level where they do an excellent job.

We need our critics and we appreciate best those who can poke fun

[2] C. Northcote Parkinson, *Parkinson's Law: Or the Pursuit of Progress* (London: John Murray, 1958).

at our weaknesses at the same time as they make us think of ways of correcting them.

TYPING ORGANIZATIONS

As organizations differ not only in what they do but in how they are
set up to do it, there are always suggestions and theories that one type of
organization is likely to respond better to certain factors than to others.

One such typology is that based on the power or authority which the
organization uses. This classification has been proposed by Etzioni[3] who
describes four such types:

1. Predominantly *coercive* authority. These may be typified by concentration camps, prisons, custodial mental hospitals, and coercive
   unions.
2. Predominantly *utilitarian*, rational-legal authority, using economic rewards. Examples would be most businesses and industry, business
   unions, farm unions, peacetime military organizations.
3. Predominantly *normative* authority using membership as a desirable
   thing, status and intrinsic values as its rewards. Examples are religious organizations, political parties when they are ideologically
   based, hospitals, universities, social unions, voluntary and professional
   associations.
4. *Mixed* structures which combine the above three. Examples of *norma-
   tive-coercive* are combat units; of *utilitarian-normative* are most labor
   unions; of *utilitarian-coercive* are ships.

Etzioni goes further to distinguish three types of involvement that
the organization's members have in it. First, *alienative*, indicating lack of
psychological involvement; membership is maintained because of coercion.
Second, *calculative*, in which the person is involved in the sense that he
is willing to do a fair day's work for a fair day's pay. And, third, *moral*, in
which the individual is personally committed to the values and objectives
of the organization and he works because of his commitment.

If we now cast our organization types in graphic form with our types
of involvement we get a picture such as in Figure 6-2.

This shows us the nine possible types of relationship the member
could have with the organization. We notice at first that alienation goes
with coercion, calculation goes with utilitarianism, and moral involvement
goes with normative authority. We could say that the organization gets
what it bargains for. Coercive power gets members who would rather
not belong; utilitarian authority generates members who want economic
rewards for their performance but feel no necessity for personal involve-

[3] A. Etzioni, *A Comparative Analysis of Complex Organizations* (New
York: The Free Press, 1961).

FIGURE 6-2

ETZIONI'S AUTHORITY AND INVOLVEMENT TYPOLOGY

	Coercive	Utilitarian.	Normative
Alienative	Predominant		
Calculative		Predominant	
Moral			Predominant

ment; morally committed members value fulfillment of organizational norms because of their sense of rightness.

A historical shift in these relationships has been taking place and continues. Coercive organizations are a relic of the past. Coercive-utilitarian organizations are dying out because of pressures arising from the increasing complexity of many jobs and the increase in union power. Utilitarian organizations are still strongly evident because they are the most simple to conceptualize in our modern society (although not necessarily the most effective). Utilitarian-normative organizations are increasing because both management and worker (as well as work itself) are tending to become more sophisticated. Normative organizations have been around for thousands of years but are only now being seriously considered as possibilities for work organizations.

Where does your organization fit in this picture? (Or how does your university or college fit?)

In a study of classical management theory, Joan Woodward found that line-staff, specialization of functions, span of control, number of levels of hierarchy, and staff-worker ratios in 100 British firms had no particular significance as far as organizational success was concerned.[4] What she did find, though, was that her data made sense when all of the firms studied were classified into three categories, no matter what product was involved. The first type is unit and small batch production (custom clothing, prototype equipment, custom furniture, machine tools); the second type is large batch, assembly, and mass production (large bakeries, automobiles, mass-produced clothing); the third type is process production (oil, chemicals, and pharmaceuticals). These can be called *unit, mass,* and *process* systems and can be equated to increasing task complexity and the historical development of technology.

Firms within each of these three systems tended to have similar organizational structures regardless of their product. Going from unit to mass

[4] J. Woodward, *Industrial Organization* (London: Oxford University Press, 1965).

to process, increases were evident in the length of the line of command, the span of control of the chief executive, the proportion of wage costs to total costs, and some personnel ratios. The most successful organizations were closest to the average of their respective groups on these and a few other variables. Firms too far above or below this average did not do as well as those closer to the mean.

Woodward's conclusions support the theory of the dual purpose of the group we have already discussed—a technical function and a social function. The emphasis on either tends to vary with the type of organization. In process organizations the technical function is already designed into the plant itself leaving management free to devote more time to the social function. And, since the technical function is quite well ensured, more flexibility can be provided with the social function, or it may not even be fulfilled too well, and yet objectives are achieved. With unit firms it is necessary to tie together both technical and social functions because both are important. With mass systems the two functions tend to be in conflict and Woodward found the highest need for production control and rigorous sanctions in the mass systems. Staff and line did not fuse smoothly and production and social functions developed piecemeal. Unit firms tend to be dominated by engineering personnel, mass organizations are dominated by production people, and process systems are dominated by marketers.

In unit and process organizations the interaction of people is built into the system and so specific efforts to bring them together become less necessary. Internal group conflict was low in these organzations. However, in the mass production organizations Woodward found group relationships poorest when specific attempts had been made to put groups into inter-action where they had not traditionally interacted. This appears to support the ideas investigators have about the necessity of distinguishing between *coacting groups* and *cooperating groups*. The latter must work together to reach their goals while the former do not need direct contact.

Even long-accepted ideas about identification of workers with their company took a shaking up in Woodward's studies. Good staff relation-ships and identification seemed irrelevant to performance in process firms and could even be detrimental in mass production.

Woodward's typology should provoke further interesting research in the future.

THE GROUP VERSUS THE GROUP

As the complex organization is a group of groups interacting to achieve some goal, it is almost inevitable that there will be some conflict between groups. Indeed, some of this conflict is built into organizational structure—for example, staff-line conflict. Open hostility can develop between management and worker groups, as we know, but it also develops between other groups, as in the case of two university departments vying for control of an area of research which overlaps their respective disciplines. At other times the hostility is not so open (e.g., between junior and senior employees) or it may be that one group makes a mess of some job and then turns it over to another group as their responsibility. When one group can gain only at the expense of the other, it becomes a sum-zero game in which there must be a loser. Any win-lose proposition will generate conflict and any conflict is potentially destructive at many different levels and degrees of importance.

People usually develop a pride in the groups of which they are members and feel that their group is better in some respects than comparable groups. Sometimes it becomes a fierce pride developed by magnifying the faults and weaknesses of rival groups. Experimentally controlled research as well as studies based on observation of ongoing groups indicates that when they are put into occasional contact, at least through several of their members, a desire for more contact and for competitive contact develops. When competition does take place and is reasonably well matched, it is not difficult to fan it into conflict. Conflict generates perceptual error and biased judgment and once it reaches the boiling point it is difficult to cool it off. Far better it is to foresee it, head it off, and not require either group to lose face.

One way of overcoming conflict is by helping both groups to feel that, combined, they form one superordinate group. This is easier when the conflict is a non-zero game in which they have some important task to do together or face some common crisis requiring their combined efforts. It is not necessary that the groups merge into one formal group but simply that they act as a unified informal group. There are often pressures within each group to prevent a merger because a joint venture will represent a threat to the role and status of some members of both groups who may be happy to see the proposed merger fail.

When a win-lose conflict leaves no room for compromise or merger, a mediator, often the supervisor of both conflicting groups, may have to impose a solution. Depending on which side he favors, members of conflicting groups will see him as practical, fair, open-minded, impartial, and honest; or see him as biased, poorly informed, hasty in judgment, a bungler, and lacking in foresight and experience. If you are ever required to make such a decision, be prepared for a lot of follow-up fence mending. Later, we shall see that this is one of the requirements of a good leader—ability to withstand negative, even unjust reactions.

When bargaining or compromise is possible there is more hope for conflict resolution. Compromise and collaboration are hindered when both groups are confident, self-reliant, and able to get along without an agreement; when there is a lack of trust between groups or no visible guarantee that the agreement will be or can be kept; and when collaboration or compromise interferes with the independent operation of one group by the other.

Arbitration of conflict can be quite delicate. Trying to make differences disappear by rhetoric sometimes makes them more pronounced (see Chapter 10) and trying to gain personally from the conflict of subordinates is extremely dangerous. One suggested approach is to have each conflicting party or its representative express in the presence of one another what *they* think is the other's point of view. This may help to remove initial misperceptions. Conflict resolution at the level of the individual group member is something we will examine in Chapter 15.

In Chapter 11 we shall have much more to say about groups and how they form but one thing we can say in advance is that the more people have to do with one another in a social or mutual problem-solving way, the more they display a liking and a willingness to cooperate with one another. When conflict does arise between groups, it is often because no previous opportunities existed for members to interact with one another. Not that such interaction should be forced, but the professional manager who foresees conflict might arrange for some level of regular contact between the potentially conflicting units.

Most of us have had the chance of witnessing conflict between a group of which we were a member and another group. Think back on such a situation. Could it have been avoided? How? What would you do if you were supervisor of one of the groups today?

LIKERT'S LINKING PIN

Rensis Likert [5] has a good deal to say about the role of effective supervisors; we will discuss this in later chapters. He also has something important to say about how the group leader ties (or acts as linking pin for) his group to other groups and to the total organization.

The linking-pin concept is meaningful in the context of Likert's theory that the group leader must assist each group member to view his membership as supporting his sense of personal worth and importance, thereby satisfying his essential social needs. Only thus supported can each group member be part of an effectively functioning work team with a high sense of loyalty, effective membership interaction, and high performance goals.

The total organization will be effective only if it is composed of these

[5] R. Likert, *New Patterns of Management* (New York: McGraw-Hill Book Company, 1961).

highly effective groups which are coordinated by the fact that at least one member of each has a linking-pin function—membership in both a higher and lower (as leader) level group. Subordinate in one group and superior in another, he can provide both horizontal and vertical coordination at each successive hierarchical level. This is illustrated in Figure 6-3.

FIGURE 6-3

LIKERT'S LINKING-PIN CONCEPT OF ORGANIZATION

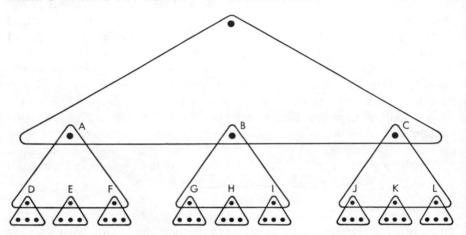

Persons A–L represent the linking pins for they have membership in both a subordinate and a superordinate group.

The total organization functions well when each linking-pin member is fulfilling his role well. When any member fails in his dual role, those groups under him will not be linked effectively to the organization and will not be able to perform as the organization requires. Any subordinate groupings of such a failing group will suffer corresponding ineffectiveness.

GROUP SIZE

A famous early study on group size was done by Wolfgang Kohler with tug-of-war teams. No one was surprised to find larger groups had more pulling power than smaller ones, but it was interesting that total pulling power does not increase in direct proportion to the number of men added to the team. As a matter of fact, as each new man (up to twelve) was added each team member pulled about 10 percent less hard than before. The reduction in per capita effectiveness can be attributed to increased communication demands and decreased group cohesiveness; both will be examined in other chapters.

A number of studies have found decreased satisfaction in larger groups compared to smaller ones, leading some people to postulate a direct relationship between group size and group motivation. It is easier to achieve consensus in small groups (five persons) than in larger ones (twelve persons). Also, it is easier to develop full member participation in smaller groups: one study showed that as group size increases the least active members of groups contribute less to the group's operation. Presumably, then, very large groups will have more deadwood.

One extensive survey of managers found that those in large organizations (more than five thousand employees) displayed no greater dissatisfaction than those in smaller firms. But those at higher levels of the large organizations showed less dissatisfaction than managers at the same level in smaller organizations; and those at lower level management in small companies were less dissatisfied than their equivalents in large organizations.[6] In general, managers in flat organizations (those with few echelons) seem to have more opportunity for self-development and self-actualization than managers in tall organizations (those with more steps in their hierarchy).

It has been reported that both plant size and departmental size affect absenteeism rates, tardiness, accidents, and strikes, with the smaller units having the better records. These findings have been confirmed in a number of surveys involving different types of organizations. This would indicate a tendency for higher morale in smaller than in larger groups.

Determining the optimal group size for any given task, one must consider several variables. Sometimes it presents the manager with a dilemma; he finds it necessary to increase size in order to provide the knowledge and resources needed to perform the task, yet performance is generally better in small groups. Also, smaller groups need less guidance from above and spend less time trying to clarify rules and standards. Yet technical, engineering, and architectural factors often call for larger units. One group of thirty workers may be set up with one supervisor; two groups of fifteen require two supervisors, or one supervisor and two assistants. Athough many theorists argue for breaking down large groups into smaller ones,[7] this still leaves the problem of holding in check the increasing number of supervisors and layers of supervision.

In any given organization it would be better to develop the flexibility required to determine the correct membership number, span of control, and number of levels of authority for each specific group and subsection by experimentation (see Chapters 20 and 21) than to rely on some mystical

---

[6] L. W. Porter and E. E. Lawler, "Properties of Organizational Structure in Relation to Job Attitude and Job Behavior," *Psychological Bulletin*, LXIV (1965), 23–51.

[7] E.g., Bernard M. Bass, *Organizational Psychology* (Boston: Allyn & Bacon, Inc., 1965).

number from classical organization theory which is supposed to apply to all groups, managers, and organizations regardless of what they are trying to accomplish. Some practical balance is needed between the approach of those who theorize "organizations without people" and those who theorize "people without organizations."

COMMITTEES

The camel, it is said, is a horse designed by a committee. And, truthfully, I have seen The Committee to Examine the Proliferation of Committees and The Committee to Establish Rules for Committees, and have been a member of The Committee to Examine and Recommend the Formation and Abolition of Committees.

Parkinson has a few words of advice on "the science of comitology." He says, "The first and most elementary principle of this science is that a committee is organic rather than mechanical in its nature: it is not a structure but a plant. It takes root and grows, it flowers, wilts, and dies, scattering the seed from which other committees will bloom in their turn." [8] I disagree with but one point in this statement. Only *some* committees die, others have to be killed or they will remain standing forever.

Bass [9] reports that 81.5 percent of executives state that their organization retains regular or standing committees and only 8 percent would abolish these if given a chance. Although they have the image of being inefficient, it is generally agreed that committees promote coordination, creativity, and informed decisions. The least support and the greatest criticism of committees and their work comes from the lower levels of management, the most support and least criticism from the highest management levels. It is difficult to think of organizations containing a high number of coacting groups (hospitals, universities, school districts) getting by without committees.

It is also to be noted that the higher the level of management, the more likely is the manager to be serving on committees. Also, the larger the organization the more likely is it to have a number of standing committees. Senior academic administrators often serve more than fifty committees simultaneously. This cuts greatly into their office time, private lives, and other essential duties. At the same time it facilitates many of their decisions and allows them to bring forward creative ideas leading to greater organizational effectiveness. There is probably no optimal maximum number of committees to which a person should be restricted (although the limita-

[8] C. Northcote Parkinson, *Parkinson's Law: Or the Pursuit of Progress* (London: John Murray, 1958).

[9] Bernard M. Bass, *Organizational Psychology* (Boston: Allyn & Bacon, Inc., 1965).

tions of the twenty-four-hour day and the seven-day week must be recognized) but when a ceiling is reached the executive usually starts to divest himself of the least important committees by resignation and delegation.

SUMMARY

Anticipating future chapters on communication and on group dynamics and leadership, some general statements about the organization and the group have been made in this chapter. The organization itself is a group composed of groups, and the principles of groups apply to organizations. Management theory of recent years has been characterized by a duel between those who emphasize the *structure* of the group (*classical* theorists) and those who emphasize the people who are *members* of the group (*behaviorists* or human relations theorists). (Both "classical" and "behaviorist" are, in fact, misnomers.) The practicing manager should be wary about such duels; usually, both sides have very valuable points and useful information which he can apply.

All groups have structure. The debate reflects the emphasis on whether the structure is imposed by the designers of the group or whether it is the result of the interaction of group members. In one sense this is something like the old nature-nurture controversy which psychologists abandoned some years ago. As the structure exists, regardless of how it got there, it is rather surprising how naïve most members of the organization are as to its shape. Often, the senior manager takes it for granted that those under him have as clear a picture of the organizational structure as he has, which is simply not true. Next time you corner the president or the general manager for a training session or seminar, it might be a good idea to ask for *his* picture of the structure and function of the organization.

Informal groups are another reality although they are elusive and are never displayed in the formal pictures of the organization.

The dual purpose of the group—to achieve a goal and to satisfy its members—was described. An overemphasis on one or the other is a threat to the achievement of the dual purpose. When either is frustrated the very existence of the group is threatened. The manager's greatest challenge is to ensure that both purposes are fulfilled; this is not an easy task for they are frequently in conflict.

The classical bureaucracy of Max Weber was outlined. The evolution of bureaucracies made the modern technological age possible but also brought with it the possibility of dehumanizing man. A justified reaction to this dehumanization is still taking place as man struggles for his right to personal existence in a highly complex world. Yet denial of the value of bureaucracy or attempts to destroy it take mankind backward rather than forward. Such destructive forces exist within our society and seem to be based more on fear of castration than realistic assessment of social evolution.

The nonbureaucracy can take a number of forms but mainly it is a softened bureaucracy which attempts to profit from the advantages of bureaucracy without dehumanizing the individual. The future organization will, hopefully, be of this nature. Otherwise, it will be a choice of Orwell's *1984* or "back to the farm" (and there will not be enough farms to go around in 1984). Some aspects of the contemporary organization can be debureaucratized better than others. Some should be and some should not be.

Parkinson's Law and the Peter Principle were mentioned as examples of the wit underlying the rejection of "pure" bureaucracy as incompatible with human frailty.

The typology of organizations was attempted by reference to Etzioni's coercive (alienative), utilitarian (calculative), and normative (moral) categories. Historical evolution points in the direction of a type of future organizational relationship which is more normative-moral. Joan Woodward's interesting findings were also outlined. Her types are unit, mass, and process. They follow technological evolution and the technical-social function of the organization parallels the dual purpose of the group. With different organizational types, one form of management and interaction of workers seemed more effective than others.

The conflict of group with group is inevitable within the complex organization. Some of these conflicts are built into organizational structure and others arise when the advantages to one group become losses to another. Optimal resolution of conflict comes by making both groups feel they have common interests and goals. The arbitration of full-blown conflict is difficult; it is a case where the ounce of prevention is truly worth a pound of cure.

Likert's linking-pin function of the group leader was outlined. It requires a member of each group to be simultaneously a member of both superior and subordinate groups. Without effective linking pins the effectiveness of the total organization is in danger.

Group size was considered. Although the evidence seems to favor the small group over the large group, reducing large groups present many technical problems. The optimal size for each group should not be set arbitrarily according to company rules but, rather, according to the specific circumstances of the people, task, and environment involved.

The usefulness and frustration of committees was the last point mentioned. Frustrating as they may be, they are invaluable to the large organization and look as though they are here to stay.

7

COMMUNICATION

Why are messages so often misinterpreted? What is more important than the words themselves? What are the major types of communication problems in the organization? Why do the standard solutions fail? Do you think people really listen to you? Does your organization have a special language? How come young people do not listen to their elders these days?

Once when I was a student I lived in a residence with forty or fifty other undergrads. Part of our housekeeping duty was to take a turn at helping the kitchen staff to dry and put away the dishes from the evening meal. It was difficult to keep good cooks from leaving for less demanding jobs in the restaurant industry in those times, but one day a new cook arrived. He was fresh off the boat from Italy, a short, mustachioed, volatile man with a ready grin and the ability to turn out cheap but tasty food. His only problem was that he could not speak a blessed word of English. A few days after Angelo's arrival I was on dish-drying duty with a friend. Angelo came into the dish room looking quite pleased with himself (he had produced an excellent meal), and we were introduced to him. I commented to him in English plus sign language how enjoyable his food was. He beamed and said, "You like?" My friend then turned to Angelo, smiling, patting his shoulder, and shaking his hand while saying in a congratulatory voice, "Angelo, you stupid little —— that was the most disgusting food I've ever tasted and if you ever serve spagetti again, I'll cut your mustache off." Angelo beamed with joy, shook my friend's hand vigorously, and repeated, "You like? You like?"

It was an unkind joke but no one was offended. I repeat the story here because it makes an important point about communication—namely, that the actual content of a message becomes so modified by the context and circumstances that it is often only these accompanying circumstances which are relevant parts of the communication.

In the jargon of social psychology we say that one person acts, either intentionally or unintentionally, so that he *expresses* himself and that the others will, in turn, be *impressed* by his actions. These expressions take the form of *signs* and there are two quite different types of signs involved in expressing ourselves. The first is called the expression that a person *gives* and involves the use of words, written or spoken, and other symbols which both parties agree to as the means of exchanging information. This is communication in the traditional and narrow sense. The second type of expression involves signs which a person *gives off*. These involve a very wide range of actions the person carries out both intentionally and unintentionally to convey information which cannot or must not be expressed by signs given, as well as those actions designed to misrepresent or hide true feelings. In the full sense, communication involves both signs given and signs given off and in practice it is difficult to separate them.

In the story about Angelo, my friend was *giving* a set of signs which were irrelevant because the receiver of the message could not interpret them; however, the signs *given off* were interpretable even though they contradicted the signs given, and it was these signs that brought the expected response. A similar thing happens when management tells employees it wants them to be members of one big happy family, that it respects them and wants them to develop in the firm, and that there is a great future for those willing to be devoted to the organization—and then displays by its actions that it is no more than superficially interested in them as individuals. The employees ignore the signs given and react to the signs given off.

COMMUNICATION AND INTERACTION

Communication for the social psychologist, then, involves far more than it does for the layman. We can communicate by the very way we dress or cough or eat at the table. Even the brand of whisky we order communicates something about us to our drinking companions—whether we do it deliberately or not. The way a man arranges his office and his desk can communicate warmth, aloofness, business, casualness, and so on. An organization's letterhead, quality of stationery, style of architecture or interior decoration all serve as signs to others about the image or message that it wants to give off (or gives off but does not want to). Thus the common platitude that all organizational problems are essentially communication problems might meet with agreement from the social psychologist—but then he would have to go on to say that communication involves perception, motivation, attitudes, group dynamics, leadership, organizational structure, and a few other subcategories. That is quite a wide range of behavior, of course, but these behaviors make sense only in the context of interaction and there is no such thing as interaction without communication.

Those who pursue the important question of how to get the group to accomplish its task effectively can get sidetracked into the examination of organizational structure, product engineering, marketing, and sales to the extent they lose sight of how critical is human interaction. Some of those who are reacting today against extreme emphasis on human relations in organizations are in danger of making an even worse error than those human relations proponents who ignore structure and engineering. For the value in studying organizational structure lies in the fact that it tries to make interaction and communication of members optimal, and the value in engineering is that it allows each member of the group to accomplish his task (as a group member, not as an individual) effectively.

Some researcher has estimated, I cannot recall whom or how, that more than 90 percent of human behavior is social behavior. If this excluded purely physiological behavior such as digestion or breathing (some of which *is* social), I would suggest that the estimate is low and that the figure should be closer to 100 percent. Even such biological acts as a sneeze or a burp or picking our teeth are social because the way we carry them out depends on the existing social circumstances, and whether we do them and how we do them conveys to people around us some expression in terms of signs given off or what kind of person we are.

Thus all social acts (or all acts) involve not merely *action* but *interaction* (or potential interaction) and so involve communication.

This is the important lesson of this chapter; from now on the book must become completely social psychological by assuming that all the human behaviors relevant to the manager are social behaviors, that they involve a form of interaction, and that they entail communication of some sort. As we progress, you may find that things you have tried to understand in the past will now make more sense in terms of interaction and communication.

COMMUNICATION AND ORGANIZATIONAL STRUCTURE (PROBLEMS)

The very nature of the organizational structure, designed as it is to facilitate interaction and move members toward goal accomplishment, provides barriers to effective communication. Or, at least, the very structure of the formal organization provides a climate in which attitudes inimical to effectiveness grow easily. It is not that the structure fails to accomplish its purpose (a fact often overlooked by the human relations theorist). It does what it is supposed to do. It establishes the correct and best channels for the majority of communications; it ensures that information is stored (files, reports, training, experience) at the key points in the organization for the application of that information; it clarifies the authority and priority of communications both within and outside of the organization; and more.

But across the same lines that facilitate communication, management complains that it is difficult to get people down the line to realize the importance of messages sent to them—and that things are not only to be done, but done in certain ways. Laterally and diagonally, we step on one another's toes, plan and work at cross purposes, and become involved in jurisdictional disputes in the large organization. Personally, on more than one occasion, I have seen thousands of high-priced man-hours invested by one committee completely discounted by another committee because the one claimed the other had exceeded its authority or its terms of reference or had not been properly constituted, to begin with. Finally, upward communication channels, complain the subordinates, do not exist. Communication in the organization, they say, is a one-way street—they get but cannot give.

Between these three structural communication problems, let us call

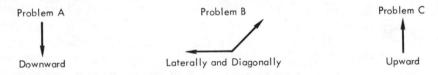

them, there is generated enough conflict, misunderstanding, hostility, ill will, lost time, wastage, duplication, and inefficiency to make even the structurally perfect organization ineffective. Overall solution of the problem will not be attempted in this chapter. No solution is possible without a fuller understanding of what takes place in the interaction of organizational members. There are no simple solutions, no ten easy steps. For now our focus is on:

$$A + B + C = \text{Ineffective Management}$$

Problem A

One industrial psychologist has pointed out,[1] "We all have problems in communication, though we are generally more aware of the failures of

[1] Henry Clay Smith, *Psychology of Industrial Behavior*, 2nd ed. (New York: McGraw-Hill Book Company, 1964).

others to understand us than of our failures to understand them." Then he goes on to refer to a study [2] to illustrate that graduate and undergraduate students in personnel courses (who, presumably, will soon be holding managerial positions in complex organizations) had very different ideas than workers did about job attitudes such as:

1. That they enjoy their work.
2. That they take pride in what they do.
3. What they think of seniority versus ability.
4. What they think of the company's customers.

The point is that if those who are about to become managers and supervisors *think* they understand what workers really want and perceive about their jobs while their thinking is opposed to what workers *actually want* or think, their communications to these workers will not be effective.

Further support comes from Kahn's [3] study in which there is a notable difference between the ranking of things the workers say are most important on the job and the things their foremen *think* the men will prefer:

TABLE 7-1

EXAMPLES OF RANKING OF JOB FACTORS
CONSIDERED MOST IMPORTANT

Factors	Men's Ranking	Foremen's Estimation of Men's Ranking	Foremen's Own Ranking	General Foremen's Estimation of Foremen's Ranking
Getting along well with people I work with	36%	17%	39%	22%
Getting along well with my supervisor	28%	14%	28%	15%
Good chance to do interesting work	22%	12%	38%	14%
Steady work and steady wages	61%	79%	62%	86%
High wages	28%	61%	17%	58%

number of workers = 2,499   number of foremen = 196   number of general foremen = 45
Adapted from R. L. Kahn.

[2] Ibid., p. 172.
[3] R. L. Kahn, "Human Relations on the Shop Floor," in *Human Relations and Modern Management*, ed. E. M. Hugh-Jones (Amsterdam: North Holland Publishing Company, 1958).

The obvious difference here is the overestimation by foremen of the importance of economic factors and the underestimation of social and interpersonal factors. (Actually, Kahn's study showed that the rating of factors for foremen, in which they ranked *their own* preferences, were quite close to their workers' rankings.) For our interest in communication the point is that the foreman communicating to his subordinates thinks that he understands what they want whereas the opposite is true. It would be as if my friend had assumed that Angelo could not understand English whereas acutally Angelo could understand English. Instead of being elated, Angelo would have been insulted. How often do foremen do things which they think will make workers happy whereas they actually make their workers unhappy?

The sad thing is that people in supervisory or managerial roles are in the same position they put their subordinates into, yet they do not realize this. A well-known study by Likert [4] showed that 90 percent of managers said their foremen felt free to discuss important aspects of the job with them—yet only 67 percent of foremen said they felt this way. Of the same foremen, 85 percent said their men felt free to discuss important aspects of the job with them—yet only 51 percent of their men said that they felt this way!

In the same study 70 percent of managers said that they got their foremen's ideas on work problems—only 52 percent of foremen agreed. Yet the same foremen said they sought their men's ideas on work problems —and only 16 percent of the men agreed!

Similar things were true about thinking that they tell their men in advance of changes in work procedures, times, and so on. Which reminds me of the time I was giving a midweek seminar to a group of supervisors from various companies. During coffee break I approached two men who appeared disgruntled and asked them why. They explained that they worked for the same company and just that morning had received a completely unexpected announcement via bulletin board that their hours of work were to be changed the following Monday morning from eight to four-thirty to nine to five. They explained what difficulties this would mean in leaving the car to the working wife, getting the children to school, arranging a new car pool, and so on. The striking thing to me was that two weeks before I had had lunch in the Chamber of Commerce with the very men who, in their organization, would be responsible for such a notice and we had been discussing the problem of upward-downward communication in the hierarchy with particular reference to Likert's study.

A number of studies confirm these findings of differences in understanding between manager-supervisor-worker and of disagreement on how

[4] R. Likert, *New Patterns of Management* (New York: McGraw-Hill Book Company, 1961).

each regards the other, the other's attitudes, and the other's job. The implications are that downward communications are distorted and misunderstood because of differences in attitude and feeling of those on higher and lower levels. The implications are also that upward communications are severely limited but more will be said about that under Problem C.

Problem B

Other than staff-line communication (which often has its built-in barriers), lateral or diagonal communication is largely coincidental or informal. It is an area of limited research by social psychologists although there is the beginning of some study on coacting groups. A great deal of informal communication of a lateral and a diagonal nature takes place when equal-level or approximately equal-level managers are called together for committee or other meetings. Indeed, sometimes chairmen have trouble calling their group to order, or bringing them back to order after a coffee break, because all around the committee room they have their heads together in little knots. These twosomes and threesomes break up only reluctantly after mutual exchanges of promises "to discuss it further over lunch later this week" and "I'll phone you and we can arrange a time."

The unmeasurable amount of information exchanged this way may well be what keeps the complex organization from grinding to a halt. A lot of such lateral and diagonal talk may be gossip, jockeying for position, and "politicking", but often it is talk of extreme importance in the function ing of subunits which do not have regular channels of communication and rarely need to come into contact. It is on that rare occasion when manager A says to manager B, "What is this I hear about your unit going into ——? You know, that has some implications for us," that such contact is important.

From personal experience as a veteran of uncountable committees of many levels and classifications, I testify that lateral and diagonal communications are often of great organizational value.

Other diagonal and lateral communications take place through other forms of personal contact, sometimes through mutual acquaintance emissaries and sometimes because one manager takes the initiative to contact another in a different line about what he perceives as a mutual interest. The emissary becomes important when lateral or diagonal contact is forbidden (e.g., when a senior manager tries to steal a key man from another group in the organization to be his new assistant). In these instances, as in many others, informality is emphasized by mutual tacit agreement not to exchange written correspondence, to work out "gentlemen's agreements" and otherwise to "bargain under the table."

There are even instances when informal communication may be underwritten by a senior person or senior body. For example, the president, chairman, or senior committee may find it necessary to carry out a discreet investigation of one of its units relative to a very "sensitive" area of the organization; it will then appoint a group to make such inquiries at diagonal, downward, upward, and lateral levels without keeping any formal notes or minutes and to bring back an informal report. Such a report may recommend a more formal discreet investigation.

Although some of these things may be contrary to bureaucratic structure and may even be forbidden in some organizations, there are probably few experienced and effective managers who would be willing to change such a system.

Problem C

One of the most common complaints of those at the bottom of the hierarchy is the difficulty they have in getting their ideas up the line. Their feelings are based on fact for a number of reasons. People at the bottom are often not as verbally fluent or as accustomed to presenting their ideas for consideration as are supervisors and managers; they may not be familiar with standardized procedures for presenting new proposals; they may get easily tongue-tied when presenting complex ideas; or they may be quickly discouraged by a criticism intended to be helpful and constructive. Further, those at the bottom do not have a breadth of understanding of the organizational structure. Thus they may overlook a detail needed to make their idea work or add a detail which will cause it to be discarded; or they may not know the best way to channel their communication upward.

No matter how willing the manager may be to listen, all these factors militate against his subordinates bringing their ideas forward. He must do far more than be passively receptive if he ever wishes to tap the great body of knowledge and experience stored in the summation of his subordinates. More will be said about this in another chapter.

The problem of upward communication is not merely a fact at the lowest level of the organization but also at intermediate levels. Read [5] has shown that the low-status to high-status communication barrier exists at higher levels and particularly is true of criticism and aggressively-toned comments which are screened out of upward-bound messages. This screening out is by no means accidental. The fact is that low-status members need the high-status members to help satisfy their needs for security and to reduce their anxiety. Consequently, the "lows" will always tend to act toward the "highs" in a manner which will maximize good relations and

[5] W. H. Read, "Upward Communication in Industrial Hierarchies," *Human Relations*, XV, No. 1 (1962), 3–15.

minimize feelings of unease or anxiety. This tendency will be the subject of more detailed examination in Part 3.

One of the results of such interaction between lows and highs is that pleasant matters are more likely to be communicated upward than unpleasant ones; achievements are likely to be recounted upward while information about errors, failures, and difficulties is screened out.

The screening will be at a maximum when the information could be construed as reflecting negatively on the low-status member. Information with possible negative connotations for the informer threatens his security or his progress upward on the line ladder. It has been demonstrated in several studies that most common to all managers is a desire for advancement (they also fear failure in achieving advancement). This leads them to screen cautiously anything which might impede advancement, and so the higher status manager hears very little about the current and unsolved problems of the lower level manager.

In Read's study it was predicted that the stronger the ambition of the manager to get ahead, the less accurately would he communicate upward those aspects of his work and performance which could be construed negatively. The higher his ambitions, the more likely is his tendency to communicate to superiors in a way that will maximize positive and minimize negative aspects of his work. He will tend to withhold, restrict, or distort information about current and unsolved problems in his daily work.

Two factors influence and modify this selective screening of information. The first is the *interpersonal trust* which the subordinate has in his superior. Distortions are more likely to occur if there is a lack of confidence between the two. They also take place in proportion to the subordinate's feelings that the superior might misuse or misunderstand the information to his own detriment. For example, he may fear communicating information about an unsolved problem to a supervisor if it may be used to hinder his progress and promotion. In other words, he may think the supervisor will perceive that he has difficulties solving problems on his level of command.

The second modifier is the subordinate's perception of the superior's *influence over his career*. The greater the influence the supervisor is perceived to have, the greater the tendency to withhold problem information, or to restrict and distort it. Here the supervisor is perceived as having the power to satisfy or prevent achievement of the subordinate's aspirations.

The important thing to notice, especially when we are studying leadership in later chapters, is that interpersonal trust influences upward communication and that attitudes of interpersonal trust should be fostered to ease the exchange of information. However, when the aspirations of the subordinate are high, even confidence between supervisor and subordinate does not eliminate the tendency to distort communication of problem information. One result is a potential strain between superior and subordinate.

Some implications of the study are as follows: First, unless the supervisor has other sources of information, his assessment of the subordinate's ability to cope with various types of problems is not likely to be accurate. Second, information about the type of work problems the subordinate's work unit experiences may not be known, to the detriment of the larger unit. Third, as the subordinate screens problem information from his supervisor, he is simultaneously cutting himself off from the experience and expert knowledge which the supervisor may have about solving the problem. This may mean that the organization is not functioning as effectively as it should.

Finally, it can also be concluded that distortion of upward communication at this level contributes to organizational effectiveness; it indicates that these problems are being handled at the level at which they should be handled and hence that the delegation of duties is effective. In other words, the upwardly mobile manager is learning to cut his teeth on problems and the senior manager is freed from lower level problem solving. Whether or not this last is a sound argument, there are probably grounds for considering that not every lower level problem should be communicated up the line. Sometimes when such problems are communicated upward, they are simply thrown back for lower level solution.

Now pause for a moment and think of your organization or one with which you are familiar. Which are its dominant communication problems —A, B, or C? Jot down some examples you have witnessed or experienced.

STANDARD SOLUTIONS

Having himself been the victim of distorted communications, every good manager resolves at the outset of his tenure in a new management position to be receptive to ideas, complaints, and even negative criticisms from downstairs in an attempt to overcome Problem A and Problem C barriers.

The most common attempt to achieve this is the so-called "open door policy." Using this technique, the manager advises his subordinates either individually or collectively, "My door is always open. If ever any problems arise, whether they concern the work or whether they be personal, just come on in. I'll always be pleased to try to help no matter what it may be."

The intent and attempt to fill the supervisory role properly are steps in the right direction. However, by themselves they are of little value. They may also sound so hollow as to raise eyebrows when uttered by a busy executive with thousands of employees spread over a vast area. (Yet I worked for one university president—fourteen thousand students—who kept an unscheduled free time each morning when he could almost invariably be contacted by any petitioner.) We have already considered the main reasons for failure of the open door policy: misunderstanding of what is important or relevant, fear the information could be misused, hostility toward the representative of the authority which is offending the person, lack of self-confidence in the ability to express one's ideas, and so on.

Most certainly, subordinates are not going to walk through the open door to tell their supervisor that they think he is unfair, unreasonable, inefficient, and stupid. And the worse the situation downstairs or the more unjust the supervisor is perceived to be, the more difficult it is to tell him so. An old story we are familiar with from childhood is called, "Who Is Going to Bell the Cat?" As a result, most subordinates who walk through the open door come to tell of something irrelevant or unimportant, to agree with supervisory decisions that appeared on the notice board, or to relate things stripped of potentially disturbing or potentially misinterpretable facts. Both the communication given and the communication given off will be geared toward keeping the supervisor happy and tranquil.

The good intent of the open door policy can be put to effective use, however, if it is accompanied by other appropriate signs given off. Apparently simple factors such as the type of secretary the manager has can make a difference. There are times when the hardheaded secretary who can put the fear of God into any petitioner and even cow a vice-president is truly appreciated. She saves us valuable hours in which we can get a bit of work done, but she may be an impassable obstacle course to a tongue-tied subordinate. Experienced secretaries are both boon and bane to the manager. Subordinates who do not have private secretaries of their own do not know how to cope with them. The ideal secretary is probably a creature who does not exist—a two-headed amanuensis-gatekeeper who must not frighten the timid yet is capable of cutting the legs from under the bold without lifting her eyes from the typewriter. Even Janus, the ancient god of gates, and Cerberus, the three-headed watch dog of Hades, did not meet this criterion.

Another factor militating against good intent is the very paraphernalia and trappings of management—the large office, the padded furniture, the forbidding mahogany desk behind which "himself" sits, the stack of files and row of telephones which give off signs of how busy he is and how little time he has for petty problems, and, of course, the heavy sacred door of the inner sanctum itself. A truly open door must really be open so that all passersby can actually see the occupant as available. Even the desk is a symbolic barrier and honest open door manager do not use it to frighten off petitioners. It is best to have an informal seating arrangement in front of or beside the desk or have it set so that it does not stand between the door and the manager; thus, with a swivel chair, he can attend openly to anyone who enters. The open, preferred hand is an ancient sign given off that no hostility is intended: the open office and unbarricaded manager give the same sign to his subordinates.

A second attempt to remove upward communication barriers is the famous (infamous?) suggestion box, the rightful target of many cartoonists. The simple suggestion box is a concession to fear. Once, when I made this statement, a manager approached me and irately explained, "But my employees want it!" I explained to him that was a terrible admission to make for it indicated what limited opportunities his employees had for expressing themselves openly.

The major problem with the suggestion box is that it is no receptacle for placing comments on complex organizational problems and complicated procedural difficulties. If used at all, it tends to become concerned with highly personal and trivial matters. And, even when the suggestion is put in that the heating be raised a few degrees, it is impossible to know how many people are quite content with the temperature as it presently stands. The suggested three extra hooks for the cloakroom or the request that the janitor put the right wastebins with the right desks are grounds for tearing the box off the wall for encouraging immaturity. These problems can be attended to in other ways. Yet a proposed design for a new organizational communication network is too big an issue to be simply popped anonymously into a box.

Successors to the suggestion box such as the company suggestion award program have as many critics as defenders. Some claim employees should bring forward their best ideas regardless of potential awards; or that the program inhibits suggestions because employees hold back on ideas they feel might not be acceptable yet which could be effectively modified in discussion with others; or that it allows a certain amount of plagiarization of ideas with consequent ill feelings; or that there are always envious comparisons between size of award and acceptance and nonacceptance of a suggestion—as well as charges of favoritism.

Nonetheless, many organizations are pleased with results. Effectiveness of award programs appears related to style of supervision and attitude of supervisors (as are many other factors in complex organizations related to supervisory attitudes).

Given the proper climate, both the open door policy and the suggestion box may have their place. But never should they be allowed to deceive management that upward communication exists.

Another formal technique designed to overcome communication barriers is the regular discussion period (e.g., the last working hour or half hour of the last Friday of each month). Some organizations employ such a mechanism; the total plant or large convenient sections of it hold a formal monthly meeting in the cafeteria or one of the shops. Foremen start the meeting by giving a report on company matters relevant to the workers— new contracts, vacation schedules, equipment replacement schedules, reorganization of the company, need for overtime, and so on. The meeting is then opened for discussion, questions, suggestions, and ideas. There may be requests that a department head or staff specialist attend a subsequent meeting to explain some proposal in more detail or to answer questions. The discussion may even take a rather rambling form in which nothing too relevant to work or policy is said. Yet anyone is free to speak, hoot, shout down his fellow's ideas, banter, or get things off his chest.

The side effects seem to be favorable even though some participants say it does not accomplish much. These feelings have been commonly expressed when this technique is employed: that foremen are helpful and explain things; that they themselves have a better idea what the company is trying to do; that they know better how they are getting on in the job; that they take more interest in the company, feel they are really part of it, and that it is one of the best to work for; and that it is easier to talk things over with foremen and get their ideas up the line.

More adequate solutions lie in the total climate and attitude of supervisors and of the organization itself. These will be outlined more fully when we discuss psychological contracts, attitudes and changing attitudes, group dynamics and leadership.

Finally, one study[6] which compared the recall or remembering effect of different types of downward communications found that a letter sent to the employees' home, combined with a presentation of the information by the supervisor, was superior to presentation by supervisor alone; and that either was far superior to sending a letter to the employees' home alone, to the bulletin board, and to the grapevine. Indeed, the bulletin board (there are over four hundred *known* bulletin boards at my university!) was no better than the grapevine!

SENDER VERSUS RECEIVER

Perhaps the most common source of communication barrier is that the receiver of the message *does not listen* to the message. This is a "kitchen variety" of barrier (it is very apparent in the kitchen arguments of husband and wife—"don't interrupt me!"; "will you just *listen* for a minute!"; "that's exactly what I'm trying to explain, but you won't let me!" etc.) but whereas the worker may even try to hold his hand over his wife's mouth in the kitchen to try to make her listen, in the boss' office he merely casts his eyes

[6] T. L. Dahle, "Transmitting Information to Employees: A Study of Five Methods," *Personnel*, XXXI (1954), 243–246.

to the floor and nods quietly, hoping the boss will shut up long enough to let him explain what he *really* came to tell him about.

How many times after the long-awaited critical interview with the boss has the conversation among peers gone like this: "What did he say about so-and-so?" "I didn't have a chance to ask him about that."

Daily in managerial offices all over the country there are one-way conversations. The subordinate has a list of things that he hopes to ask about or explain but after a few minutes in the office he sees that he "hasn't got a chance."

A good friend of mine, in charge of a regional office, developed a new and more effective work procedure. He wrote to the director at headquarters asking if he could come in and discuss the matter. The evening that he arrived he stayed at my house and we discussed the new procedure at length. We met for lunch the following day after his interview. He looked crestfallen. "He was so busy pointing to faults that I didn't get the chance to explain the whole thing. He shook my hand and told me not to be discouraged and to keep trying—but I honestly think that he didn't even understand what I was talking about. How could he? He didn't even let me finish!" A few months later my friend transferred to another division.

A number of studies point out the frustrations of receiving one-way messages without being able to send messages back. Studies also confirm that sending one-way messages to those who cannot answer back is quite comfortable, probably because negative feedback (criticism, being misunderstood, etc.) is blocked. However, studies show there is no question that two-way communication is more accurate for both and more satisfying for receivers than is one-way communication. Keep in mind, as implied earlier, that managers and supervisors often *think* that they have two-way communication when they do not.

The frustrations of being a receiver only are responsible for the feeling of workers that they are constantly subjected to unreasonable demands and pressures from management. This has no relationship to actual demands and pressures which are not felt as acutely when good two-way transmission is available.

COMMUNICATION PATTERNS

There has been much written about and much experimentation done with varieties of the famous wheel, circle, and line communication patterns. These studies have been carried out under laboratory conditions and it is difficult to know what contaminating factors of the organization might modify them. However, they do give us some guidelines about formal communication patterns. Their usual form is reproduced in Figure 7-2.

The more central a person is in the network, the less time it takes him

to solve problems requiring the receipt and transmission of inf
Unless demands from those on the periphery are too great or u

FIGURE 7-2

VARIOUS EXPERIMENTAL COMMUNICATION PATTERNS

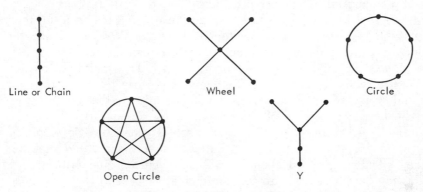

Five-member groups with lines indicating channels of communication available.

task to be solved with their information is too complex, the central person enjoys more work satisfaction than the others. Whether formally designated as such or not, he is also recognized as the actual leader of the group. Certainly, he does most *work* in terms of problem solving and transmitting answers.

These same feelings of satisfaction are available to those on the periphery if the communication net is changed from the wheel or chain to the open circle. But now the time to accomplish the simple task is increased and the number of messages to be sent is multiplied; thus there is *more* chance for errors to take place yet *less* chance for errors to go undetected.

Some reports are that the wheel is more effective in terms of productivity and time when the task is simple but less effective when the task is complex. Supposedly, the open circle is more effective for complex tasks but, when it has been operating for a while, the members of the open circle soon begin to treat one or more of their members as a leader; this means it is no longer truly an open circle net of communication for sending and receiving messages is not evenly distributed among all members. This makes it difficult to compare with other nets.

Regardless of the person in a central position (of a wheel), the job he does and his attitude toward that job will be strongly influenced by the communications the system imposes upon him. We might keep this in mind for later discussions of leadership.

SPECIAL LANGUAGES

We are all familiar with special and secret languages or codes from grade school gang or club. Family units have theirs that can bring peals of laughter from the family members at a wedding party but leave all outsiders with quizzical looks on their faces. Professions have ritualized theirs into complex jargons which bar outsiders from their discussions and reports. Some social psychologists are so jargon-heavy that they can lull their students and even their colleagues to sleep by the time they finish the introduction to their thesis or presentation. Although designed to clarify, jargon or special language can also be used to hide a multitude of sins.

We are reminded by Erving Goffman [7] that when theatre performers go behind stage they often talk of the audience in ways that the audience would be horrified to learn of. Backstage in the organizational sense is when one is in the presence of trusted peers at one's own level of the organization. Here customers, clients, patients, subordinates, and superiors may be ridiculed, gossiped about, caricatured, cursed, and criticized although they have just been treated with great respect in their presence. Plans may be hatched for "selling them," getting back at them, or pacifying them. Sometimes this involves referring to persons by their code name. In the *Caine Mutiny*, Captain Queeg was referred to as "Old Yellowstain" and equally, in the organization, a boss may be referred to by his initials, a nickname, or reference to some famous or infamous event.

In the presence of much lower or much higher status persons, or in the presence of customers, a colleague is often referred to as "Mr." or "Dr." or "Professor" instead of by his first name. When dealing with a nonmember of the group many forms of signs are given off in collusion with members. Thus, in the presence of a garage customer, the supervisor may ask the mechanic, "You checked Mr. Smith's tire pressure, didn't you, Bill?" implying that a positive answer is required whether it was checked or not. As an undergraduate weekend shoe salesman, I soon found out that retail salesmen have a vast private vocabulary which they use in the presence of customers to help close a sale. Often, the manager and his secretary work out a series of signals to terminate interviews: "I'm sorry to interrupt you, Mr. Jones, but don't forget you have a meeting coming up."

Through signs and private language, colleagues at all organizational levels can support, warn, and defend one another in the presence of noncolleagues. The quick side glance, emphasis of a key word in a sentence, or some unseen gesture is all that is needed to put the colleague on guard for correct interpretation of the innuendo, the veiled hint, or the purposeful kidding.

[7] Erving Goffman, *The Presentation of Self in Everyday Life* (Garden City, N. Y.: Anchor Books, 1959).

THE CHANGING RECEIVER

Although a well-known survey in 1950 showed that supervisors have an average reading ability equivalent to the tenth grade level, the implication being that downward communications were often written over the receivers' heads, a great deal has happened in the course of a generation. Two constantly changing factors in our ongoing social evolution must be kept in mind.

First, the average level of formal education of those young men and women joining the labor force each year is constantly edging upward. Some may still seem pretty thick between the ears, but they have been exposed to far more information and far more sophisticated learning techniques than their fathers before them. Even the informal education which children get daily from their TV sets equips them with a range of knowledge and a vocabulary superior to that of their fathers. In fact, we are dependent upon this increasing knowledge and sophistication to cope with our developing technology.

We also see many of the more senior workers and supervisors participating in mushrooming adult education programs through extension courses of various types. Many are studying advanced techniques and new theories and welcome the opportunity to apply them on the job.

Second, the young people joining our working force today have been exposed to a different environment than we have and one result is that they are better equipped to speak up and express their views. They are also more ready to decry "bull" from their supervisors than were the new workers of a generation ago. The generation of new workers today have been taught from kindergarten to be expressive, to speak up, and to say what they think. The students in the college classrooms today are positively "cheeky" compared with what we were in their place a generation ago. We would have recognized as readily that a professor was bungling something or had gone beyond his depth but we would merely smirk silently to ourselves. And, although today's university student is still quite conservative at heart, his training has led him to value speaking out against error and stupidity. Very few have not had experience in a few protest marches and other demonstrations against things they do not like.

This is what we have taught them and they have learned it well. Today even major civic projects often invite high school and college leaders to a seat on their planning committees and university students have voices on the senate and board of universities the length and breadth of the land. They are expected and encouraged to use that voice both by their peers and by their seniors. Unions and management alike have begun to notice the voices of youth in their midst, but far more is to come.

SUMMARY

The communication problem includes almost every form of human behavior when we consider communication in the broad sense of the social psychologist. When signs given off are added to signs given, perception, attitudes, group dynamics, organizational structure, and leadership become questions of communication. There can be no social interaction without the exchange of signs. Often, it is the indirect signs given off that have the real impact in the message whether we want them to or not.

Three types of communication problems were outlined—downward, lateral and diagonal, and upward. Cumulatively, they present enough potential threat to organizational effectiveness to undo the efforts of the best organizers.

Problem A is downward communication. Grounds for it are found in the research evidence that those at higher levels of the organization *think* they understand those below them and *think* they have good communication with those below them. The evidence is that this represents wishful thinking and the reverse is true. The potential for distortion and misunderstanding of communications to subordinates is a danger to good management.

Problem B is lateral and diagonal communication. Although formal lateral communication takes place between staff and line members, there is ample opportunity for it to be blocked or misdirected. A good deal of lateral communication takes place on an informal level and is often very useful for the organization. Unfortunately, it must depend on chance relationships and rumors.

Problem C is the greatest. The whole system militates against upward communication even when management wants to encourage it. At the lowest levels, the employee often lacks experience and ability in expressing himself and is given little chance by his supervisor and by the system. At middle levels, even the verbally fluent are inhibited from telling of things which they perceive might hinder their further advancement up the line. The stronger the ambition of the junior manager, the more he will hold back on potentially negative information. This can be modified somewhat by interpersonal trust and the degree of direct influence his supervisor has over his career but does not completely remove the distortion.

Inadequate solutions to the problems are mainly the open door policy of supervisors and the suggestion box. Reasons why both are inadequate were pointed out. Neither has to be abandoned, given the right climate, but they cannot be depended upon to do the job of removing communication barriers. The regular formal discussion seems to have some advantages as a technique to break communication barriers, even by itself, and in a healthy organizational climate should prove quite valuable.

We mentioned the duel between sender and receiver of messages. The problem is that managers are so accustomed to the sender role that they cannot seem to stop and listen and allow their subordinates to send messages to them. This is very frustrating to the person who really has a message and often leads to ineffectiveness when listening could have been effective.

Communication networks or patterns were mentioned. The wheel seems to have advantages over the circle for some tasks but the circle has advantages over the wheel for others. Probably, the best managers are able to convert their groups rapidly from one network to another to meet changing work demands.

A word was said about special languages. We all use them but are outsiders on some occasions and they could as well be used over our heads as we use them over the heads of others.

Finally, we noted two changing aspects of the message receiver. One is that he has more formal education than he had in the past. He is capable of more when properly trained and dislikes being spoken down to. The second is that he feels more freedom in expressing his true feelings today, even in the face of authority and opposition, than he did a generation ago.

8

PSYCHOLOGICAL CONTRACTS

On the basis of earlier chapters, we are now in a position to examine the fundamental relationship between management and its workers. In this chapter you should be able to see how pervasive the perceptual interaction model of social behavior is. What is a psychological contract? What are its major forms? What are their strengths and weaknesses? Which ones are you familiar with personally?

We have discussed some things people do without being aware that they are doing them as well as some things which influence a person's behavior although he may not know it. The present chapter deals with another of those things. What we will describe here is the most general and all-pervasive influence over a person's behavior while he carries out his work as a member of his organization. It is important for the manager to perceive and, when necessary, to alter this invisible influence on himself and his workers.

This discussion of psychological contracts flows from our discussion of communication in the last chapter and from earlier references to the principles of social perception.

One of the most fascinating stories in industrial psychology is that of the illumination experiments conducted in the Hawthorne studies.[1] The

[1] F. J. Roethlisberger and W. J. Dickson, *Management and the Worker* (Cambridge, Mass.: Harvard University Press, 1939).

story is as famous as it is fascinating so we present it here as a simple summary. One of the factors investigated at the Hawthorne works of the Western Electric Company in the 1920s was the relationship between illumination and productivity. It was expected that light intensity would be directly related to the amount of work a man was capable of doing. Yet the researchers were dismayed to find the relationship very erratic; in an attempt to pin it down, two small groups of girls (a control and an experimental group) were taken aside to be studied more intensively under rigidly controllable conditions. Even though lighting conditions in the control group were held constant while those in the experimental groups were varied, both groups continued to increase their productivity of small part assemblies. On one occasion an electrician came in to change the light bulbs but, in fact, replaced them with lights of the same wattage. Again the girls responded favorably! On another occasion some volunteer girls maintained a high level of productivity under conditions of simulated moonlight! They reported that they suffered no eyestrain and claimed they became less tired than when working under bright lights.

These and many other of the Hawthorne studies convinced the researchers that the social psychological factors were far more influential on worker productivity than engineering or environmental factors. The evolution of the human relations approach in industry is usually traced back to this point.

The engineer (the researcher whose main interest was in physical and environmental factors) had to give way to the social scientist in the Hawthorne studies. The evidence was overwhelming that the major influence on the worker's output was his own and the management's attitude and not the physical conditions under which he worked. During the experiments workers had come to feel that management was at last taking them seriously. After all, were they not consulted about their opinions on the lighting, given a more friendly atmosphere in which to work, allowed more freedom to talk and comment about the way the work should be done, even allowed some control over the actual work? Basically, for the first time in their experience, they were treated by management as human beings with personal lives, needs, and feelings. They responded accordingly.

Essentially, these workers were like the stuttering children referred to in Chapter 3. They perceived (correctly or incorrectly, it does not matter) that management had a high regard for them, had confidence in them, felt they were important to the organization—and they proved how important they were to management by "cooperating" and producing more.

THE NATURE OF THE PSYCHOLOGICAL CONTRACT

As we know from our study of perception, we all make assumptions and inferences about what people are like and how they are motivated. Consequently, we make assumptions about how to interact with them.

The assumptions of management will determine how the organization and its workers will be used in accomplishing its tasks. From these assumptions will flow the *management strategy*, the methods assumed to be optimal to deal with the demands of the task and the human and physical resources given to accomplish the task. The workers have their assumptions too. They make inferences about the organization and they expect the organization, through its management, to behave in certain ways toward them.

The interaction is one we have seen in Chapter 3 and it is diagrammed here in Figure 8-1:

FIGURE 8-1

MANAGEMENT-WORKER INTERACTION

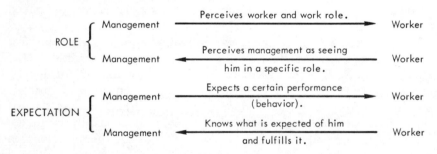

Here we see that the organziation perceives work and workers according to some general outlook or organizational philosophy. The result is a certain expectation of what work performance should be and how it should be treated (types of rewards given, etc.). But this perception-expectation also belongs to the worker. He perceives how the organization perceives him and he knows what is expected of him. He is like little Johnny who is perceived by the parents as their "problem child." He, perceiving their perception, rises to the challenge and meets their expectations. This is the self-fulfilling prophecy in operation again.

In every management-worker relationship, there must be some common basic understanding and a set of mutual expectations one of the other. Some parts of the mutual perception and expectation are spelled out openly and clearly (the worker agrees that he is to sign in at 9:00 A.M.

each morning and not leave till 5:00 P.M.; the organization states that it will pay him x number of dollars per month for his time). But the greater part of the mutual expectation remains unverbalized, unwritten, unmentioned (the worker expects management to treat him decently; management expects the worker to spend his time on the job working and not just fooling around; the organization expects the worker to respect its property; the worker expects the organization to respect his health and safety). These sets of unverbalized mutual expectations are what we refer to as the *psychological contract.*

I usually refer to the entire set of interactions by the symbol $M \longleftrightarrow W$. The M stands for management or the organization and its perceptions, understandings, assumptions, philosophy of work, and expectations relative to the worker; the W refers to those the worker has relative to the organization and the management, its representatives.

The organization does certain things *to* the worker and it does certain things *for* him. It also refrains from doing things to him. It pays him, gives him status, gives him job security, does not demand things of him which are not part of his specific job. He reciprocates by working hard and doing his job well; he does not criticize the organization in public or otherwise damage its image. The organization expects the worker to obey (submit to its authority through its legitimate representatives, the managers and supervisors); the worker expects fair treatment in return.

The organization enforces its expectations through the usual channels of authority and control systems, rewarding and punishing according to how closely the worker meets expectations. The worker enforces his expectations through his attempts to influence the organization by withholding participation or personal involvement and by the use of sanctions like strikes, apathy, go-slows, and so on. Each party to the psychological contract acts and reacts according to his perception of justice and fair play.

Hence we can consider the interaction between the management and the worker in terms of a psychological contract involving a process of reciprocal communication of perceptions, expectations, and behaviors. Their entire relationship and continuing interaction will be flavored by the kind of contract made between them.

The contract is a psychological one because it is based on an unverbalized exchange of assumptions rather than on a legal exchange of formalized documents. One may become conscious of a psychological contract but normally neither side is wholly aware of the extent to which it governs their interaction. Also remember that it is not a static thing but that the action and reaction of one side brings reaction from the other, and so forth in a cyclical manner. The influence of this informal organization is similar to the influences we shall discuss under the label of psychological contract.

Theorists over the past few years have come to identify four basic philosophies, based on four different sets of preconceptions and assumptions, which the organization's management holds as its part of the psychological contract.[2] As management is the dominant force in the $M \longleftrightarrow W$ interaction in our culture, its side of the contract has more influence on the outcomes of the relationship. From each of the basic philosophies there follows a different management strategy which, among other things, exerts pressure to make the philosophy true. We shall now examine each in turn.

RATIONAL-ECONOMIC MAN

The first psychological contract is based on one of the oldest philosophies known, that of hedonism, which we have discussed under motivation. Although it has taken many forms throughout the centuries, we know pleasure and pain defy objective definition yet hedonism persists as a theory. Adam Smith's ideas on economics are a good example of the philosophy as are some of the major theories of learning proposed by psychologists today.

Hedonism implies that man is motivated to behave in such a way as to maximize his own self-interest. The assumption is, as it were, that man (a *rational animal* distinct from the nonrational *brute* of the field) sits back, ponders his social situation, and arrives at a plan of behavior that is going to bring him the most satisfaction and the least trouble. Although this "obviously makes sense" on the superficial level, it is just as obvious that the earth is flat and not round. But, just as philosophers and scientists behave in their ordinary day-to-day activities as if the world really *were flat*, there is also the tendency in day-to-day behavior to work on the assumption that man really seeks pleasure and seeks to avoid pain.

Working on the basis of the rational-economic man theory, management tends to make the following assumptions:

1. Man is primarily motivated by economic incentives and tends to do whatever will give him the maximum economic reward.
2. As economic incentives are under the control of the organization, man becomes essentially a passive agent who can be controlled, motivated, even manipulated, by the organization.
3. Man is not only rational, he is also emotional. The emotions or feelings are really the irrational part of man and can interfere with good thinking. Man's irrational emotions must be prevented from "overcoming" him and preventing the rational calculation of his own self-interest.
4. Organizations must operate in such a way that they hold man's

[2] E.g., see Edgar H. Schien, *Organizational Psychology* (Englewood Cliffs, N. J.: Prentice-Hall, Inc., 1965).

emotions in check or, at least, neutralize the irrational side of his nature. This is for his own good as well as for the stability of the organization.

Proceeding naturally from these assumptions are the basic tenets of theory X management identified so well by McGregor,[3] which we have already mentioned in Chapter 6. Briefly, these add to the list:

5. Man is by nature lazy. He reacts to forces outside of himself and therefore must be motivated by outside incentives.
6. Man's natural goals run counter to organizational goals. To make sure that organizational goals are met, man must be moved by forces outside of himself. These forces are controlled by the organization.
7. Because of his emotional nature, man is really *irrational* and hence not capable of self-control and self-discipline.
8. On closer examination we must admit that there are *two* types of men. There are those who fit the above description and that minority who don't. Those who do not are more rational, more self-controlled, self-motivated, less dominated by emotion. These are the self-starters who do not let emotion interfere with rational calculation. Obviously, they are the ones who *should take the responsibility of management over the rest of the workers.*

At worst, the rational-economic man theory sees the individual as untrustworthy, money-motivated, and calculating, except for those self-starters who should be managing the former. At best, the theory makes man, the worker, a rather dull clod not knowing how to do things in his own interest without some direction and incentive.

These assumptions exaggerate and oversimplify man's nature. They may represent *some* men at *some* times but it is false to think they represent the majority. Yet the theory is not completely devoid of value. There are situations for which it and the strategy which comes from it have been proposed to work. The concept of the assembly line fits into the theory and the assembly line has proven efficient in innumerable instances. Certainly, money and economic incentives are an important part of the motivational exchange between organization and worker in most instances.

The pioneering work of Taylor [4] and the success of his system of Scientific Management also lent support to the rational-economic man philosophy. He and his followers seemed to demonstrate quite forcefully:

1. When each worker has one simple repetitive job to do, work proceeds

[3] D. McGregor, *The Human Side of Enterprise* (New York: McGraw-Hill Book Company, 1960).
[4] F. W. Taylor, *The Principles of Scientific Management* (New York: Harper & Bros., 1911).

most effectively. Therefore, complex tasks should be broken down to their basic elements.

2. There is one best way of doing a job. It can be scientifically determined.
3. Workers should be trained to do each job in the way it has been standardized by management.
4. Management determines the best way for each job to be done so any tendency of the worker to change the work routine must be controlled. Planning comes from above.
5. Because man responds to economic incentives, his pay should be based on the number of units he produces.

It is easy to be critical of Taylor today, even to take offense at his apparent attitude toward workingmen. To do so, however, might cloud the important contributions he made to industrial psychology.

A cumulation of hedonism, Adam Smith's doctrines, Taylorism, and theory X management leads to the following management strategy, still taught in the classrooms of schools of business and adhered to faithfully by so many senior managers. It is referred to as the four functions of management: *plan, organize, motivate,* and *control.*

The strategy is the fulfillment of a contract in which the time, service, and obedience of the worker is exchanged for economic rewards. Personal feelings, personal growth, and morale become matters of secondary importance to management. As the organization is paying for the service of the worker, it assumes the right of protecting both itself and the worker from the irrational side of man's nature through its control and authority systems. In turn, the worker must yield to the authority or power *position* regardless of the personality of the authority person or manager. This means that all members of the organization—workers and managers—are depersonalized and, as we have seen in discussing Weber's bureaucracy (Chapter 6), they become replaceable parts of the organization. If they were not depersonalized, it would be more difficult and hence less efficient to make them replaceable.

If something happens to lower productivity (or keep it from rising) or if worker morale declines, it is then the duty of management to redesign, redefine, and reassign jobs; or realign the organization structures; or change the incentive and control systems. Efficiency is sought through better use of human and material resources. As the workers do only what they are told according to how they are motivated, the responsibility belongs to management to plan, organize, motivate, and control better to bring about greater effectiveness. These responsibilities are usually fulfilled by clarifying staff-line functions, concentration on job description and job analysis, time-and-motion studies, and so on. Bonus schemes may be introduced and competition stimulated in an attempt to raise productivity. Control systems may be tightened, shirkers weeded out, pressures passed down the line. As everything is really dependent on management, the worker can be expected to perform only as well as good planning, efficient organization, stimulating incentives, and effective controls allow for or permit.

If one thinks of this rational-economic theory in view of our $M \longleftrightarrow W$ exchange or as similar to the perception-interaction examples of self-fulfilling prophecies which have been described, it can then be seen that even when people do not fit neatly into this theory there is little opportunity for them to express their difference. The psychological contract tends to make management's picture of the worker come true. As they are expected to be lazy, indifferent, hostile, and motivated only by economic rewards, that is what they tend to be. Argyris [5] claims this theory will produce and reward apathy, indifference, alienation, and noninvolvement.

Although the rational-economic theory has been presented here in its more extreme form, many of us probably are familiar with organizations that operate on these general broad principles. Indeed, some have been rather successful although most of those I know of personally have either been taken over or have suffered regularly from severe problems. Typically, such organizations have problems of ever increasing regularity and severity.

First, if pay is the only thing the worker can expect from the organization, he will continually want more as standards and costs of living rise in our industrial society. And, as he feels the purchasing power of his income decline, he will try to bank for the future with the highest possible pay increases now. Second, as technology develops and jobs increase in complexity, management has to rely more on the individual judgment, creativity, and loyalty of the worker. In other words, the organization of today has to expect more of the worker than merely time at work and obedience. Hence the contract begins to change for the worker, in turn, begins to expect more than economic rewards.

Over recent years researchers and theoreticians have increasingly pointed out that the myth of rational-economic man is an inadequate one for our society. It does not adequately describe the majority of workers and it tends to generate serious problems in the management-worker relationship.

SOCIAL MAN

Becoming gradually perceptible in the 1920s with the Hawthorne studies and not generally accepted perhaps until the 1950s, another myth of the nature of the workingman in industrial society began to replace

[5] Chris Argyris, "Individual Actualization in Complex Organizations," *Mental Hygiene*, XLIV (1960), 226–337.

the rational-economic theory. With it came a new series of assumptions about workers and organziations that became incorporated into a new 'psychological contract. We are going to refer to it as the *social man* psychological contract.

The Hawthorne studies pointed out dramatically that the need to be accepted and liked by one's fellow workers was at least as important and perhaps more important than economic incentives in determining how the individual performs on the job. The studies also showed how workers resist being put into competition with their fellows and tend, consciously or unconsciously, to band together to resist anything from management that might appear a threat to the individual.

The voices of social philosophers such as Rousseau and Karl Marx were being reexpressed in the writings of contemporary researchers and social philosophers. Modern industrial technology, they claimed, had taken the meaning out of work. The man-tool relationship had been reversed. The tool with which man created had now become a complex factory and, instead of the worker using the tool, it used him. The man, not the tool, had become replaceable. Indeed, he was just a replaceable part in a highly complex tool, depersonalized and *alienated* from the entire industrial process. He could spend his life in a factory and yet never see the end product it produced. Perhaps the best opportunity to see the product he makes is through TV commercials while his wife nags him about not being able to afford to buy it. Even in the 1936 movie *Modern Times* Charlie Chaplin turns an invisible wrench all the way home from the factory. He was a far cry from the craftsman of old who made shoes to fit the feet of his clients or the potter who put his creative spirit into his clay or the stoneworker who carved for the glory of God.

As he could no longer identify with the service or product which the organization turned out, the worker had lost the means of identifying himself in society. In the old days, names like Smith, Carpenter, Shepherd, Taylor, Fisher, and Cooper could tell of one's position in society but now he was just a man on the payroll, the same as thousands of others filing like ants into big buildings. The idea of an identity problem and of alienation has a certain romantic flavor, especially as the "Golden Ages" recalled were probably not as romantic as they sound in historical fiction. Yet, faced with the complexity of modern living, they make sense as do the ideas we saw underlying the philosophy of hedonism. Political movements, labor movements, social philosophers, psychologists, and others began stressing the social nature of man.

In this context the social man psychological contract evolved with a work philosophy based on the following assumptions:

1. Man is motivated primarily by social needs and gets his sense of identity through his relationship to other people.

2. Technological society has taken the meaning out of work and this meaning must be sought in the social relationships provided by the job.
3. Man is more responsive to the social forces of his peer group than he is to the incentives and controls of management.
4. The worker responds to management to the extent that the latter can meet his social needs.

This is a different myth than that of rational-economic man, and it requires a completely different management strategy. First, management cannot be attentive to task accomplishment only but must consider the social needs of the workers. Second, rather than be caught up with motivating and controlling, management must be sensitive to the worker's feelings of being accepted, his sense of belongingness, and his identity with the work group and the organization. Third, management must think in terms of group incentives rather than individual incentives. Finally, the supervisor is no longer responsible for planning, organizing, motivating, and controlling but, rather, he acts as an intermediary between workers and the impersonal organization, listening to their problems, trying to understand their needs and feelings, and being sympathetic. He is no longer the creator of work and the motivator but, rather, the facilitator and supporter of the worker.

I have presented a picture of the social man psychological contract in its full-blown human relations form. The important thing to recognize is that the contract has changed. There are other needs than mere economic ones. The organization specifies its goals for the group but allows considerable leeway for members to determine how best to achieve them.

The contract means that management and workers now expect more of each other. The worker has many of his needs satisfied through participation in the organization and he, in turn, becomes personally involved, giving greater commitment to his work, being more loyal to the company, and identifying with organizational goals.

If management frustrates, threatens, and alienates the worker, his perceptions cause him to develop norms running counter to the goals of the organization—that is, the social needs of the men are met at the expense of management. On the other hand, if management can harness these forces and get group goals in line with organizational ones, a reservoir of social energy and motivation then becomes available. If workers are alienated from the formal group and organization, they turn to satisfaction at the informal group level; but if management meets social needs, they will become involved with formal organizational goals.

As well as the Hawthorne studies and the conclusions drawn from them by Elton Mayo and others, a good deal of research evidence supports the social man theory. Some studies in manufacturing firms, for example, showed that productivity and job satisfaction had no relationship to pay and job status but were related to group membership. It was also demonstrated that most members of the group are happy and satisfied to conform to organizational norms if they are the same as the group norms, and it is the deviates in the work group who tend to be not satisfied with the way the group operates. Whyte's [6] famous studies of restaurant workers showed that absenteeism, job quitting, and customer service in the restaurant industry are related to social and group factors; if the group were well-knit, good relations and high-quality work were present. Assembly line studies pointed out that the major source of worker dissatisfaction is due to the breakdown of normal social relations—for example, the inability to talk to others at all or the inability to talk when the workers wish to do so. When assembly lines are redesigned to allow social interaction and teamwork, both productivity and morale go up. In another important study, Whyte [7] reached the following conclusions:

1. The percentage of production workers who are primarily motivated by money is very low, perhaps 10 percent of workers responding to individual incentive schemes and ignoring group pressures.
2. When incentive schemes do work, they often work for reasons other than that of making money; for example, the workers may perceive the incentive scheme as a type of game; or they work to keep on the good side of their supervisor; or they find that working quickly is less boring.
3. Rate busters have the type of personality in which social needs are minimized.

There have also been a number of studies which showed that the more highly productive groups in various types of organizations were employee-centered as against production-centered. Other studies pointed out the value of supervisors as social-emotional leaders as against task leaders.

Many other studies appear to lend support to the social man theory and advocate a different $M \longleftrightarrow W$ relationship than that discussed in the first theory. The evidence seems to point to man seeking to become personally involved in the organization for which he works. If this is true, it strikes at the very roots of the utilitarian psychological contract established on the basis of economic rewards and rational bargaining.

Carried to logical extremes, social man theory has resulted in birth-to-death fringe benefits for the worker, folksy company newsletters, and subsidized holidays at the firm's private lodge. These things are appreciated

[6] W. F. Whyte, *Human Relations in the Restaurant Industry* (New York: McGraw-Hill Book Company, 1968).

[7] W. F. Whyte, *Money and Motivation: An Analysis of Incentives in Industry* (New York: Harper & Row, Publishers, 1955).

by the workers—indeed, some of the fringe benefits have become social necessities—and it is not intended to discredit them here. However successful they have been in encouraging loyalty, high morale, and low turnover, it must be admitted that they are sometimes used as a thin veneer for exploitative ideas left over from rational-economic theory.

This very possibility leads us to examine the myth of social man with cautious objectivity; it leaves some questions unanswered and some problems unresolved. What do we do with the creative loner and the talented maverick? What about the rate buster who lives only for his wife and children? Or the worker so interested in financial reward that he would leave one firm to earn a few dollars a month more with its rival? It is difficult for the organization to have a workable social man psychological contract with these and others in spite of the obvious success it is with many. Some bright young graduates from today's universities would just as soon take their chances with the rational-economic theory, selling themselves for the highest price, as against being buried in brotherhood as an integrated part of a parochial-minded bubblegum factory.

The weakness of this psychological contract is that the worker is permanently bound to a parent-child relationship with the organization. The parent is benevolent, true, but the child never reaches maturity. Indeed, after some years of experience of a social man psychological contract the worker becomes incapable of standing on his own two feet. Unemployment becomes such a tragedy to him that he immediately falls back on the assistance of his godparent, the state, and only comes off the welfare or unemployment rolls when a new job has been found for him or the old company starts rehiring. Millions of today's young people demand brotherhood and equality but refuse it when it is offered conditionally by a parent-figure organization whose ultimate motives for existence they suspect.

On closer examination, the evidence for a social man theory demonstrates only the inadequacy and unacceptability of the rational-economic theory. The idea of the Industrial Revolution alienating man from his work and the need for social interaction can be used to support more than the social man theory. This leads us to a consideration of the third type of psychological contract possible in today's society.

SELF-ACTUALIZING MAN

With the same evidence used to reject rational-economic theory and support social man theory, we have data to support a third myth of the nature of man the worker. Although rooted in much earlier writers such as Goethe (1749–1832), the author of *Faust,* the idea of man possessing some inner need to develop his fullest capacities has received a great deal of support from students of personality in the first half of this century— for example, Carl Jung, C. R. Rogers, A. H. Maslow, Gardner Murphy, Gordon Allport, and others. As psychologists familiar with their writings turned their own attention to personnel, industrial, and organizational problems, they began to interpret the data supporting the social man theory to show how the contemporary organization was blocking the worker's search for self-fulfillment. Clinical psychologists and psychiatrists were especially aware of the price in mental health and personality growth exacted from organizational executives and speculated that the same might be true of all organizational members.

To discover whether or not there is the basis for establishing a psychological contract built on the concept of self-actualization, we must reexamine the idea that industrialization, technological development, specialization, and the assembly line have alienated man and taken the meaning out of work. It could be argued that the loss of meaning is related not so much to man's personal needs but rather to the fact that man as a complete human being has a natural, inborn demanding need to make use of his abilities and potentialities in a mature, constructive, and creative manner. Support for the argument comes from social philosophers, clinical and medical psychologists, industrial researchers, and even physiologists.

In industrial or organizational psychology the argument takes the following general form: the contemporary organization makes jobs so specialized and so fragmented that they neither provide the worker with the opportunity to make full use of his capacities nor permit him to feel any affinity with the end product or end service of the organization. Hence the worker is not permitted to use his potential to the fullest, or self-actualize, although by nature he needs to do so. In order to do a good job of anything and in order to achieve inner contentment, he must feel that he is doing something worthwhile, not merely wasting the only life he has doing trivial or nonimportant things like tightening nuts and mailing form letters.

The idea is called the *self-actualizing man* psychological contract and its basic assumptions are as follows:

1. The acceptance of Maslow's hierarchy of needs or some similar concept (this was outlined in Chapter 4).
2. Man seeks to be mature and independent in his work and, with adequate satisfaction of his lower needs, he can accomplish this. Management should help him to develop his special skills and abilities.
3. Man is primarily self-motivated and self-controlled. If nonself (external) incentives and controls are imposed by the organization, this will force man further back down the hierarchy of needs and motives.
4. There is no necessary conflict between self-actualization of the worker and the goals of the organization. Given the opportunity to self-

actualize through his job, the worker's own personal goals become integrated with organizational goals.

When the nature of man as a worker is perceived in this manner, the $M \longleftrightarrow W$ relationship and the management strategy will be similar to that of the social man theory—but with a few additional twists. First, management is less concerned with being considerate and babying the worker, as we saw in the extremes of the social man theory. Concern is about making the work challenging and meaningful. The overall objective will be to help employees find the type of meaning in their work which will provide them with a sense of pride and self-esteem. The manager is constantly seeking to find out what each worker finds challenging and rewarding and he is willing to delegate as much responsibilty as he feels each worker can handle.

In the psychological contract which forms we notice, first, that there is a shift in authority from extrinsic sources (economic, legal, and rational in the first type; social and group pressures in the second type) toward intrinsic motivation. It is accomplishing the task itself and taking pride in doing it well which the worker finds motivating. The organization mainly provides the opportunity or the climate for his intrinsic needs to be fulfilled and, consequently, they are fulfilled along the lines of the organizational goals. Blauner [8] has pointed out that if control in the work process is a critical determinant of a worker's subjective feelings of well-being on the job the question of whether industrial trends are increasing or decreasing man's control over the job becomes very relevant. Certainly, automation decreases his direct control. Yet studies of automated factories have shown that increased responsibility and control over the technical environment was a source of increased satisfaction and heightened status to the worker.

The contract proposed here involves the exchange of the opportunity for the worker to find intrinsic satisfaction and self-actualization for which the organization receives high-quality performance and creativity. The worker becomes personally involved in what he is doing and is allowed more say and more influence in his work. In return for this, management gives up certain of its traditional controls, most of which are external incentives.

In support of the theory, evidence from many different types of organizations shows that when the work is limiting or meaningless the workers create meaning and challenge by trying to outwit management or by banding together with others in work groups. (An excellent example

[8] Robert Blauner, "Work Satisfaction and Industrial Trends in Modern Society," in *Labour and Trade Unionism*, eds. W. Galenson and S. M. Lipset (New York: John Wiley & Sons, Inc., 1960).

of this is found in the ownership by the working group of an improved tool.[9] In this fascinating industrial case history the work group maintained control over their invention across four shifts, resisting all management's attempts to make them surrender it even for financial reward. A good part of the time saved by use of the improved tool was devoted to producing a higher quality work.) Manufacturing and technical workers often create fantastic gadgets to make their work easier or different. Workers also become involved in complicated moves designed to foil, fool, or frustrate their supervisor or the organization, often expending much more energy at such gadgetry or scheming than it would require to do the actual job for which they were hired. I once knew an ingenious fellow worker who almost religiously spent at least two hours outside of the office each day shopping, visiting art galleries, or merely sitting in the park and feeding the pigeons, all the time making management believe he was hard at work at his desk carrying out a rather dull and unpleasant job.

Henry Ford I stated in the early 1920s, "The average worker wants a job in which he does not have to put much physical effort. Above all, he wants a job in which he does not have to think." The young worker of today rejects this principle completely. He is of the same generation as the campus demonstrator. On some industrial shifts today the age of the average worker is in the low twenties. Recently, after winning what used to be considered a good contract in California, one senior union leader remarked, "The younger leadership is not satisfied, I don't know what they really want, what it would take to satisfy them." Increasingly, we old-timers in universities, business, industry, government, and union management are dealing with bright and vigorous young people who, although they do not always know exactly what they want, definitely know what they do not want.

The question does arise, though, whether any theorist seriously proposes that a self-actualizing man psychological contract could be worked out with all members of the organization. Is such a contract applicable to the lowest level employees? Could it be expected of those who work part time? What about those who are poorly educated? It is often readily admitted that such a contract becomes relevant when one considers the motivation of managers themselves, professionals, highly skilled technicians, and other specialized personnel. A number of researchers have shown that what makes such workers feel good about their jobs is related to the idea of self-actualization.

As far as lower level personnel are concerned, it must be remembered that what we are talking about here is the worker self-*actualizing*. The

[9] Paul Pigors and Charles A. Myers, *Personnel Administration: A Point of View and a Method* (New York: McGraw-Hill Book Company, 1956).

basic theory holds that no one is ever completely self-actualized because it is always possible for further personal growth to take place. Still, the theory holds that all people are *capable* of self-actualization at some level. Some workers, it is true, may do their self-actualization *off* the job by earning enough money *on* the job to provide for their self-fulfillment during leisure hours. But it can be argued that getting such people involved in self-actualization through their work as well as in their leisure hours would bring about an identity of personal and organizational goals and hence produce greater effectiveness. Members of cleaning staffs, janitors, and so forth often work out good contracts of this nature with their employers.

Remember that the concept of hierarchy of needs stipulates that self-actualization can take place only when the other more basic needs are satisfied. Presumably, then, self-actualization at one's work could never take place at any level of worker if such factors as inadequate salaries, poor working conditions, lack of job security, fear for the future, and the blocking of social needs were to force the worker to seek need satisfaction at a lower level in the hierarchy.

This psychological contract seems to offer a fair exchange. The highest human needs of the workers are satisfied and their personal development is encouraged; the profit for the organization is that it receives the creativity, involvement, and high-quality work of its members. It might also be added that this exchange tends to be profitable for society generally and some social philosophers and thinkers feel that the organization must accept the moral obligation of allowing optimal opportunity for its members to self-actualize. The fulfillment of this ideal in a universally progressive management would contribute toward positive social development and toward ending despoilment of the environment, plus adding dignity to the human race, while preparing society to enjoy the future fruits of technological advance. This is the type of maturity, insight, and responsibility that management must be prepared to underwrite in the remainder of this century. If the responsibility is rejected, the prophets of doom predict a very unhappy future for the human race.

COMPLEX MAN

The prospect of entering into a self-actualizing psychological contract with every man in the organization would make many experienced managerial people shake their heads in disbelief. It sounds great on paper but it is too good to be true, they would say. In practice, they know that almost everyone shows an unmanageable, greedy, cowardly, or selfish streak on occasion. And, with a large organization and enough "occasions" from most of its members, the entire management process could be reduced to chaos.

Admittedly, there are some good points to all three theories discussed, but all have their weaknesses too. Having examined the assumptions, psychological contracts, and strategies of each objectively, it must be admitted that none is wholly acceptable. The easiest way out of this difficulty is to try to build some agglomerate out of the best aspects of all three theories. In fact, this can be done in such a way that it looks like the simple and obvious truth that we have been overlooking all the while.

The error in the first three theories was identical in each case. The truth is that we *cannot generalize* about the nature of man, as each theory has tried to do. Each man is unique. There are many observable similarities across categories of people but even each of identical twins is unique. There is absolutely no guarantee that worker A will be the same as worker B or worker C. Given one set of circumstances, worker A may seem to fit perfectly into a rational-economic contract while B fits into a social man contract and C fits the self-actualizing model. Alter the circumstances and A no longer fits the rational-economic model while C does and B fits the self-actualizing theory.

This final theory of the nature of man the worker can be descriptively referred to as *complex* man and the assumptions that management brings with it to the $M \longleftrightarrow W$ interaction will be about as follows:

1. Man the worker is both complex and variable. He has many motives. These are arranged in some order of importance for each man but any hierarchy of needs is subject to change, depending on the given circumstances. In any event, the motive to work is not describable in any simple way but represents a complex package. Maslow himself has stated [10] that an act typically has *more* than one motivation and again that there are usually available various cultural paths to the same goal.

2. The psychological contract is a unique thing for each member of the organization and has come about as a result of his unique set of needs and his unique experience of interaction with the organization.

3. An individual worker's motivation may vary with different organizations, or with different groups within the same organization, with both formal and informal groups offering a combination of economic rewards, social need satisfaction, and the opportunity to self-actualize. Indeed, even different parts or aspects of the same job may offer him this range of need satisfactions.

4. Given the opportunity, the worker can become personally and productively involved with the organization on the basis of many different motives. The nature of his job, his own abilities and experience, and the people and the organization with which he interacts bring about a certain pattern of motive and feeling.

[10] A. H. Maslow, "A Theory of Human Motivation," *Psychological Review*, L (1943), 370–396.

5. The worker can respond to many different management strategies, depending on his complex motivation and the nature of his job. Thus it is impossible to set one correct management strategy as a guide for all workers, all circumstances, and all times.

The general form of management strategy which follows from these five assumptions calls for the best managers to be keen observers of people, able to understand those around them in the organization well. It is as if the manager were able to diagnose the motivation and ability of those he supervises.

Also, he will recognize the *value* of treating his workers as unique persons, rather than wishing they were all the same and as easy to manage as a group of robots. This, in turn, calls for a recognition of the value of being able to discriminate the qualities that make each worker different.

Finally, the manager must be flexible enough and possess a sufficient range of skills to treat each worker differently according to the demands of the circumstances. This takes rethinking, experimentation, and trial and error. We must be bold enough to discover what new things will pay dividends.

It can be seen that such a strategy does not contradict or conflict with those strategies already considered under the first three types of contract. Where the first three would be wrong is in oversimplifying, overgeneralizing, and lacking flexibility. In the complex man contract the manager may be directive in one instance and at another time permissive; he may use time-and-motion studies on one occasion and allow the group to design its own job at another time; he will support his workers in time of social needs, see that they get a raise when deserved, and ensure the climate in which they can grow mature in their work. In other words, he will be flexible, prepared to accept a variety of $M \longleftrightarrow W$ relationships, and will adjust to different types of authority and control systems.

To support the theory, we can refer to the research on alienation; we find that alienation from his work appears for a wide array of reasons and not merely as a problem of lack of identification. Studies of deviance from the work norm find that workers are underproducers and ratebusters for a variety of reasons. Other studies have demonstrated that different levels of management are concerned with different needs and are motivated at different levels of a need hierarchy. Even economic rewards represent quite different things to different people.

Do not make the mistake of thinking that a complex man psychological contract is the easiest of all to put into effect. It certainly does *not* imply a simple hodgepodge of ad hoc arrangements worked out according to the mood of the supervisor. It implies a steady and consistent policy of flexibility in meeting unique problems in unique circumstances with unique individuals in the best possible manner. This is nothing slipshod or haphazard. That is why it is the most difficult of all four contracts to effectively put into operation. But modern management calls for this. It is no longer good enough for the professional manager to hold his senior position in the organization simply because he has put in more time and has more "experience" (sometimes this amounts to years of experience in doing things badly). When I was an ambitious young man, a number of my colleagues and I left a potentially interesting civil service job because we felt that so many senior people in the organization had stayed the same over twenty-five years while the desks they sat behind grew bigger. Experience is one of the *worst* teachers if it does not teach people to explore, to experiment, to discover new and better ways to do the job better.

What the complex man contract calls for is the ability to recognize the value of individual uniqueness. This is not easy. Management would be so much simpler if men *were all alike*. One type of contract would be good enough for each for all time—one permanent management strategy could be taught to all interested and intelligent persons by means of a little pamphlet called *Ten Easy Steps to Being a Manager*. Well, if it were possible that is what I would be writing rather than a textbook full of ambiguities and half answers to questions. Yet these are the very reasons that a complex man psychological contract is the only workable one. They are the same reasons that a late twentieth-century manager must be an intelligent and knowledgeable professional. They are the same reasons you are studying a book like this.

Going a step further, many organizational theorists of today are of the opinion that enlightened management has much more of a responsibility to its workers than has been acknowledged throughout the Industrial Revolution and afterward. The psychological and spiritual growth of members of the organization must be regarded as a more intrinsically valuable thing than performance. (Not that performance should be ignored or neglected for the manager equally has the responsibility of optimal performance from those over whom he has supervision.) In fact, personal growth and performance are intimately connected. The personnel department through its batteries of tests and measurements can get some idea of an individual's *potential* for growth but has no sure way of measuring or ensuring *actual growth*. Within the entire complex organization only the manager can do this so the responsibility must be his. It is something like the responsibility of being a parent to a very young child. Yet the analogy of parent to child is a weak one for the worker is far from being an impotent child; what the manager must do is *not* treat the worker as a child. This is precisely where errors in management have been made in the past and it is precisely where errors must not be made in the future. As former chairman (representing the administration) of a university students' residence committee, I am very conscious of what the *now* generation think of anything which resembles authority *in loco parentis*. The people coming out of our high school and college systems today categorically refuse to accept one adult acting as a parent (in the parent-child sense) to any other adult (any other person beyond his mid-teens).

Yet, in spite of protests to the contrary, an easy trap for some workers and managers to fall into is to seek the line of least resistance. One of the most difficult challenges on the road to maturity is to accept change and to deal with complexity. To get away from the world of the child, people must learn (and be taught) to seek out complexity, not to fear ambiguity, to accept the challenge of responsibility in decision making. If the manager seeks to engineer all ambiguity out of work so the job can be done by a child or a retardate with minimal error and effort, he is not only "amputating" the human potential of his workers but following the line of least resistance, giving in to his own tendencies toward immaturity and failing to rise to the challenge of personal growth. As we shall see elsewhere, ambiguity, uncertainty, lack of predictability, and fear of the outcomes of our behavior give rise to our own sense of insecurity and childishness. We must overcome these things to achieve our own growth and self-actualization.

SUMMARY

Taking our earlier model of perception-interaction, our idea of the self-fulfilling prophecy, and what we know of communication, we have examined various possible relationships between management and the worker. Four possible philosophies of work or myths, such as were introduced in Chapter 2, were considered both in their historical context and in the strategies of management that followed from them. It is interesting to notice how the first three types of contract considered paralleled the various modes of authority (coercive, utilitarian, normative) discussed in Chapter 6. We see also how the major incentive systems (Chapter 5) fall into line with the type of $M \longleftrightarrow W$ involved.

The psychological contract itself consists of that set of mutually exchanged perceptions and behaviors we observe taking place between management and worker. Four possibilities along with supportive evidence and criticism of each were presented. The rational-economic man theory reduces all workers to the lowest possible denominator and leaves management with responsibility for its four functions—plan, organize, motivate, and control. True or not, there is no alternative but for this to become true when it is strictly adhered to. However, it is fraught with difficulties today and underlies many management-worker conflicts. Although still in operation in some segments of our economy, modern-day circumstances are forcing its abandonment by enlightened management.

Next, the social man theory was examined. It takes a higher view of the worker but at the same time tends to consider him rather like a child incapable of truly adult responsibilities. This is perhaps the most common psychological contract operative in North America today but we have seen that it has many weaknesses and must soon be replaced. The worker must be given the opportunity to grow up.

The self-actualizing man contract is the "in thing" in the organization of the late twentieth century. It is the symbol of enlightened and educated management and the best managers are trying to introduce it into their organizations, often against great opposition. It allows the individual to grow and to achieve his potential as a man in his work. It is criticized harshly but not well by the hardheaded managers for being impractically idealistic. They prefer a step backward. It is more wisely criticized by those who prefer a step forward.

The fourth theory, that of complex man, is more realistic than any of the first three. Its problem is the challenge of professionalization it calls for in the manager. Rather than accept such a challenge (i.e., of treating each worker as the complex and unique person that he is), even "enlightened" managers prefer the security blanket of one of the other three contracts. Yet the future will see it come over the heads of the incompetent and the fearful. The alternative is stagnancy and stagnancy is impossible in the human evolution. We must go forward or backward.

9

SOCIAL ATTITUDES

The objective of this chapter is to provide a basic understanding of the concept of attitude, for many of the following chapters will incorporate these ideas. What is meant by an attitude? What is implied by saying that attitude parts must be consistent? How does cognitive dissonance motivate behavior? What are the major functions of attitudes? Are some attitudes more changeable than others? What influences changeability? What is dogmatism and what effect does it have on attitudes?

One of the most thoroughly researched and written-about areas of social psychology is that of social attitudes. It will soon become apparent why the concept of attitude plays such a pivotal role in the study of people interacting. In fact, much of what has been considered in this book so far can be subsumed under the general heading of attitudes.

If only the attitudes of the people around us in the organization agreed with our own, or if they only held the attitudes we wished them to hold! How much easier the job of management would be! Sometimes it is just a minor discrepency in attitudes that causes the petty irritation—or, indeed, sometimes a minor discrepency sharpens our wits and proves stimulating. But the fact is that the attitudes held by others often have very serious implications for the work we are trying to accomplish and it disturbs us that people do not think and feel as we would have them do. How nice it would be to change their attitudes! Have you ever thought that they might have the same wishes about your attitudes?

This topic was as interesting to the ancient Greek philosophers as it is to modern writers such as Dale Carnegie with his *How to Win Friends and Influence People* (1937). Everyone seems to want a few tips on how to be persuasive. Very late one night, I received a telephone call from a stranger who displayed an emotion of near panic in his voice. He offered to pay me any price within his means if I could teach him the basic principles of how to be a "big closer" (a salesman who knows how to cinch a big deal). The popularity of books such as Vance Packard's *The Hidden Persuaders* (1957) show that the interest is not merely from the point of view of those who would influence but also of those of who might be influenced. Popular magazine or newspaper accounts of oriental brainwashing techniques always find ready readers.

We all seem to have a fairly good idea what an attitude is and do not hesitate to use the word. Among psychologists the word has many definitions but almost always indicates the idea that an attitude represents a person's readiness to respond toward a certain object or class of objects in a favorable or unfavorable manner. When we say that someone has a readiness to respond toward a certain object or the symbol of that object in a certain way, we are actually referring to a prediction we can make about that person's behavior. Ability to predict behavior is certainly what the manager needs. Sometimes it is quite simple. For example, when I know someone holds conservative social attitudes (he favors the social status quo or the "good old days" as against the upheaval in morality, religion, politics, etc.), I can then predict that he will not favor underground newspapers, that he will dislike drug users, and that he will be suspicious of bearded university students.

Therefore, we know a person's attitude when bits of information from his past behavior enable us to predict his future behavior in certain situations. However, we are going a step further by implying that the readiness to act is a "real thing" which the person carries around with him, which exists even when he is not thinking of it, even when he is asleep. In other words, the attitude is considered as an entity or a process which exists even though we are not able to observe it directly. This is what the psychologist calls a *hypothetical construct* and over the years psychologists have worked out many techniques for the indirect measurement of the constructs called attitudes. The measuring instruments involved range from straightforward responses to specially designed questionnaires through to the experimental use of hypnosis.

Our predictions of the likely behavior of persons, then, is generally based on what we perceive as their attitudes. Our accuracy of prediction depends on our observational ability. As we have seen earlier when discussing stereotyping (Chapter 3), this prediction could be made not merely of an individual but of a whole category of individuals—for example, the girls in the typing pool, the senior managers, the first-line supervisors. The value of being able to predict from knowing attitudes extends itself to whole categories of persons with whom the manager interacts. To a great extent the psychological contract we discussed in the last chapter is based on attitudes. There has been and continues to be a wide array of research on the attitudes of various types of workers. A quick glance through a bibliography reveals studies on attitudes toward pay, piecework, job satisfaction, leadership, working mothers, the handicapped, pay of subordinates and superiors, managerial performance, seniority, and so on.

NATURE OF ATTITUDES

Before going further, it would be best to examine more precisely what the psychologist means when he talks of this construct, attitude. *Attitude* differs from *belief* or *opinion* in that the latter do not carry the implication of feelings or *affect* about the object. I may have a belief and express as my opinion that the vast majority of men work for a living by use of their hands. To me this is as matter of fact as that my automobile runs on gasoline.

The belief or opinion consists solely of a *cognitive* component, the element of knowledge obtained from a perception of certain facts (either correctly or mistakenly). The attitude is regarded as having two further elements. First, an *affective* or feeling component: there is an emotional investment in the belief or cognition. Thus, beyond believing that the vast majority of men work for a living, an attitude holder might *feel* that it is good for people to work for a living and that if a man did not work at something it would sap his moral fiber. This attitude might carry a further feeling of resentment of men who try to get by without working by living on welfare receipts, unemployment insurance, or the good will of others. We also add to the cognitive and affective components of an attitude a *behavioral tendency* which refers to the predisposition to act toward the attitude object. Thus the attitude holder in our example may speak out against nonworking "freeloaders," may not wish to hire welfare recipients, may refuse to support organizations which offer food and shelter to those who do not work, and so on.

The attitude can be regarded as a *system* of these three components and we shall find that, once established, it tends to be a stable and enduring system. The object of the attitude may be anything which exists for the individual. Thus we have attitudes toward objects in the world around us (the weather, mountains, sports cars, stone buildings); many more toward objects in our social world (family, job, neighbors, street address, stylish clothing, men with sideburns, working in an office, working overtime); others toward political, economic, and social events (an election, the stock exchange, student anarchism, the assimilation of ethnic groups); as well as still others toward art, religion, philosophy, and ourselves. As long as the object exists in our psychological world we can have an attitude toward it. Incidentally, a *prejudice* is a negative attitude.

As well as considering attitudes as systems of three components, we notice that only rarely could an attitude be considered as standing on its own in a state of isolation from other attitudes. Most form *clusters* with other attitudes. These clusters are not always neat and orderly for we often find even incompatible elements tied together in one attitude package. We could think of an attitude cluster in which attitudes toward labor unions, strikes, wages of manual workers, blue-collar workers generally, and the relationship between education and income are all tied together in a neat package. But, equally, we may find inconsistencies such as positive attitudes toward equal work opportunities for all coupled with negative attitudes toward hiring Indians. But we shall have more to say about such inconsistencies later.

The concept of attitude is most useful to us if we keep it in context. In the context of understanding the individual we see it as a component of his personality. Attitudes and personality are interwoven and, in the broad sense, the structure of a person's personality can be considered as organized around a central system of values made up of related attitude clusters.

The personality types we considered in Chapter 4 could be explained this way. For example, the high-need-for-achievement person has certain attitudes toward risk taking, the use of his own skill, personal independence, responsibility in decision making, personal success, preparedness for the future, and so on.

Because attitudes are tied together in systems, we can expect that a change in one attitude will require adjustments in the entire system of which it is a part. Indeed, as the systems are tied together, it may require a change affecting the entire personality. This is not easy and in some cases is well nigh impossible.

AFFECTIVE-COGNITIVE CONSISTENCY

Perhaps the easiest way to understand the nature and function of attitudes as a prelude to understanding the problems of changing them is to examine some of the major theories of attitudes. We shall look at three of these theories. All are based on solid research and have generated both experimentation and discussion among psychologists in recent years. The first theory is called a theory of *affective-cognitive consistency* and is based largely on the research of Rosenberg.[1] The theory is called *structural be-*

[1] M. J. Rosenberg, "A Structural Theory of Attitude Dynamics," *Public Opinion Quarterly*, XXIV (1960), 319-340. M. J. Rosenberg, "An Analysis of Affective-Cognitive Consistency," in *Attitude Organization and Change*, eds. C. I. Hovland and M. J. Rosenberg (New Haven, Conn.: Yale University Press, 1960).

cause it is concerned mainly with what happens within the individual when an attitude changes. It proposes that the relationship between the affective and the cognitive components of the attitude change when an attitude is altered.

One aspect of the cognitive component of the attitude concerns what the person believes about the relationship between the attitude object and other objects which are affective to him (i.e., he has strong feelings about them) or which represent his important values. Rosenberg says that strong and stable positive feelings toward a given attitude object should be associated with believing that the object leads to attainment of a number of important values. Similarly, strong negative feelings (prejudices) will be associated with beliefs that the object tends to block the attainment of important values. Moderate positive or negative beliefs should be related to less important values, or at least be related with less confidence than important ones.

For example, a person may have strong attitudes toward socialism, setting a very high value on it as a means of achieving an economically just society (socialism and economic justice are related instrumentally for him). At the same time he favors the right to go on strike as a means (instrumental) to raise the wages of workers close to those of managers and owners; this would achieve a form of socialism which, in turn, is the means to economic justice (according to his thinking). A strong negative attitude—for example, prejudice against foreign workers—may be associated with fears for economic security ("they will take away my job").

Basically, what Rosenberg has demonstrated is that when a person has a strong positive affect toward an attitude object, he is likely to have a complex cognitive component in that attitude, believing it instrumental in achieving the things he values highly and preventing things he does not want. A person's attitudes, then, are anchored in his important values in a highly consistent manner.

Further, when the affective and cognitive components of the attitude are consistent with one another, that attitude is then stable (making it highly resistant to change). When the affective and cognitive components are inconsistent with one another beyond a level of tolerance for inconsistency, that attitude is unstable and will undergo a spontaneous reorganization until one of the following happens:

1. The force toward change (usually some communication or information from which the inconsistency originates) will be rejected. For example, if the attitude involves a positive feeling toward strikes and the belief that strikes lead to a higher standard of living, an editorial suggesting strikes lower standards of living for workers will be rejected.
2. There will be a fragmentation of the attitude in which the inconsistencies are separated. For example, the positive feeling toward

strikes is retained, not because they lead to a higher standard of living, but because they are the best means for the workingman to express the seriousness of his complaints. If his complaints are listened to, there is a possibility of his achieving a higher standard of living. In this instance the inconsistency ceases to exist for the attitude holder.

3. There will be an attitude change in which strikes are rejected as a means of achieving a higher standard of living.

The theory has been supported rather ingeniously by changing the affective component of attitudes of people while they are under hypnosis, then observing the changes in the cognitive components and related attitudes which take place following their removal from the hypnotic state. Changing one affective component results in a whole series of changes in basic attitudes.

COGNITIVE DISSONANCE

A second important theory of attitudes has been proposed by Festinger.[2] It is called the theory of *cognitive dissonance* and, at first sight, may appear similar to the affective-cognitive theory. The main difference is that it tends to tie in the third component of attitude (behavioral tendency) with cognitions about the attitude object.

Rather than deal with only one belief, this theory deals with the relationship a person's ideas have with one another. Briefly, it states that there are three types of relationships between all cognitions: dissonance, consonance, or irrelevance. Cognitions are *dissonant* whenever they are incompatible. They can be incompatible if they are logically contradictory, according to the person's own thinking (my job is fascinating; my job is boring); or if they are opposed to his experience about the relationship of events (the most junior and least qualified man in the shop will not be laid off during the cutback while the most senior and experienced men will be). Cognitions are *consonant* when one follows from the other on the basis of logic or experience (a well-qualified tradesman earns more than an unskilled laborer). Finally, cognitions can be totally *irrelevant* (construction workers wear hard hats and electric typewriters are faster than conventional typewriters).

According to the theory, the presence of dissonance gives rise to pressures to reduce or eliminate the dissonance and avoid the further increase of dissonance. Also, the more dissonance experienced, the more one is anxious to reduce it and to avoid further dissonance.

We can see here the implication of perceptual selection or selective

[2] L. Festinger, *A Theory of Cognitive Dissonance* (New York: Harper & Row, Publishers, 1957).

exposure, discussed in Chapter 3. It is when there is dissonance or the possibility of dissonance that a person exposes himself selectively to information. Also, the more dissonance, the more likely he is to seek out consistent information and avoid dissonant information. This is especially true when the cognitions involved are very important to the person and when a larger number of cognitions are involved. Let us say, for example, that a manager feels that his division of the organization has always been a happy and high-morale unit—that is, the cognitions of *his division* and *high morale* have always gone together. Let us say, further, that he takes great pride in what he regards as this fact; the cognitions involved are very important to him as he perceives them as part of his own responsibility. But morale in the group has been declining, the men have been grumbling and giving off signs of dissatisfaction, and it is obvious to the objective observer that things are not going well. Under these circumstances the theory would predict the manager would *not perceive* information that morale is bad (dissonance information) but would be more inclined to employ selective perception to see even the slightest indicators that morale is good (supportive cognitive information).

This example is based on personal experience interpreted in light of the theory. On one occasion I presented a three-day seminar to junior and intermediate supervisors of the regional division of a large organization. The major focus of the seminar, at their choice, dealt with communication problems in the large organization. The reason for the topic choice became apparent; I soon realized they were all perturbed by very poor communications within the organization, mainly due to the policies and practices of the divisional chief, a member of the old school of theory X management. The chief himself flew into town to attend the last session of the seminar and a formal dinner. After hearing me give the summing-up address, he came over to shake my hand and congratulate me. He said how interesting it had been, how the topic had always been among his favorites, how it was his carefully implemented policy to ensure optimal communication in his division, and he ended up telling me how high the morale was among his men mainly because every man who worked under him always felt so free to communicate with him directly. I knew, of course, that the opposite was true and my first reaction was that he was an obstinate old theory X hypocrite. However, his attitude and behavior make perfect sense in light of dissonance theory. It should have been predictable.

I have been present (and guilty) at policy-making meetings when the tip of the iceberg of some major problem bobbed up and everyone felt briefly uncomfortable about possible dissonant information and conclusions until it was decided to put off discussion of the problem "till the next meeting." Some organizations go month after month, even year after year, pushing a load of undiscussed but important matters of policy before themselves like a big bulldozer pushing an ever increasing mountain of rubble. We could speculate elsewhere on what will happen to the bulldozer. Right now our interest is in explaining why there are such feelings of satisfaction when a thorny problem is put off for later discussion. Festinger says simply that the existence of dissonance is psychologically uncomfortable and will motivate the person to reduce the dissonance and achieve consonance. What better way to reduce it than forget about it?

In fact, there are three techniques used for reducing dissonance:

1. Changing a *behavioral* cognitive element. Here, when knowledge of one's own behavior is dissonant with one's beliefs, the simplest thing would be to change the behavior. For example, if I think it is bad for my health to smoke and, in fact, I do smoke, then I can reduce dissonance by stopping smoking. Or if the manager thinks that it is a good idea to call policy discussion meetings frequently while, in fact, he rarely "wastes time" on these meetings, then all he has to do is arrange more meetings to reduce the dissonance.

2. Changing an *environmental* cognitive element. Here the person's behavior is dissonant with some element of the environment which can be changed—for example, he thinks that smoking causes cancer but, instead of quitting, he seeks out the companionship of other people who smoke and who tell him the statistical reports are inaccurate or he changes to filters. Or, if the manager thinks it is a good idea to call policy meetings, but cannot find the time, he can squeeze in a few minutes of policy discussion at regular business meetings; or he can ask members to submit their policy ideas to him in memo form.

3. Adding a *new* cognitive element. Here the person *cannot* change any cognitions involved in the dissonance; he can add new ones to outbalance the dissonant ones. For example, he thinks smoking causes cancer but he tells himself smoking helps him to relax his tense nerves and is thereby beneficial for his health. Or, if he feels policy meetings are good but never has time to call them, he can tell himself it is up to his superiors, not him, to call meetings for policy discussion.

One of the famous experiments used to demonstrate dissonance theory involved paying people to tell a lie and then finding out afterward how much they believed their own lie. (A lie causes dissonance because it juxtaposes a true cognitive element against a spoken false cognitive element.) The experimenter predicted that the less money the subjects were paid to tell the lie, the more dissonance they would experience and hence the greater pressure to reduce dissonance by starting to believe the lie; on the other hand, the more money they were paid to tell the lie, the less dissonance they would feel and hence the less pressure to reduce dissonance by believing the lie. The predictions were verified. High-paid subjects changed their opinion little after telling the lie; low-paid subjects did. This would certainly argue for a soft sell in trying to change someone's mind or get him to carry out some behavior contrary to his private attitude. The more pressure on him beyond the minimum required, the less his attitude will change.

The possibility is certainly arguable[3] that, because of this, a person working in one job for a long period of time without the possibility of changing it comes to think that his job is a good one even though he did not think so when he first took the job. This is what Festinger says when he states that the grass on the other side of the fence is *not* greener and then goes on to demonstrate his point in a number of different ways.

FUNCTIONAL THEORY

One of the older theories of attitudes is that a person holds them because they serve some functional purpose. One psychologist who has presented this theory well is Katz.[4] He feels that understanding the motivation for holding the attitude is the key to understanding attitude change and resistance to change. Four major functions of attitude are as follows:

1. *The instrumental, adjustive, or utilitarian function:* This is a hedonistic function whereby the person holds the attitude because it maximizes reward and minimizes penalties. The attitude would only be changed if it is no longer seen as a means of obtaining satisfaction. Thus, for example, an employment officer may hold positive attitudes toward certain categories of clients who reward him by being easily placed in employment, but negative attitudes toward those categories difficult to place because they make constant demands on him and provide him with little satisfaction.

2. *The ego-defensive function:* Here the attitude operates like a defense mechanism in one's personality, shielding one from unpleasant truths about himself or the harsh realities of his environment. Thus an insecure and inadequate supervisor may *project* (use the ego-defense mechanism of *projection*) his own feelings of inadequacy onto his subordinates, regarding them as inferior and incompetent; if they are inferior to him and less competent, then he must be superior to them and more competent.

3. *The value-expressive function:* In this case the person makes use of attitudes as a means of expressing his basic value systems or ideas about himself which he feels are important. For example, a person may take a strong public stand against a threatened labor strike to express his antiunion ideas which he feels, in turn, demonstrate his firmness of character to his fellow managers.

4. *The knowledge function:* Holding an attitude can serve the function

[3] D. J. Lawless, "Employee Attitudes Towards Self and Job According to Time at Work and Status Achievement" (Unpublished Ph.D. Thesis, University of London, 1969).

[4] D. Katz, "The Functional Approach to the Study of Attitude Change," *Public Opinion Quarterly,* No. 24 (1960) pp. 163–204.

of helping a person to structure and to make sense of his experience and his cognitive world. In this way those experiences which at first appear inconsistent with what he knows can be rearranged around his attitudes to help him understand the reality he observes. For example, the owner-manager who suddenly finds his men on strike and his plant being picketed by men who a few days previously had always greeted him with a smiling "good morning, sir" can reorganize this inconsistent information around a strong antiunion attitude and say, "Just look what the union does to decent men: it turns them into stupid animals."

It can be seen that there is some similarity in parts of this theory to cognitive dissonance discussed in the previous section. What Katz points out, though, is that when an attitude serves an adjustive function, one of two conditions must prevail before it can be changed: (1) the attitude and the activities related to it no longer provide the satisfactions they once did; or (2) the individual's level of aspiration has been raised. Let us say, for example, that a man held positive attitudes toward his compact car until he received a good promotion and now he wants a more expensive car commensurate with his new status. With a raised level of aspiration, the old car does not provide the same satisfactions and his attitudes toward it change.

Shifts in the satisfactions which come from our behaviors bring with them changes in attitudes. When new behaviors inconsistent with our attitudes bring us satisfaction, those attitudes then must be adjusted.

Ego-defensive attitudes develop readily in situations in which the individual feels threatened and also can be nourished by those in authority positions. Thus disgruntled and influential workers can promote negative attitudes toward supervision among their fellows quite easily if there is any fear or threat from management. Ego-defensive attitudes are strengthened by communications intended to reduce them. Katz says two conditions are necessary for change in ego-defensive attitudes. First, the reduction or absence of threat and the development of a relaxed atmosphere. Second, the opportunity to "let off steam" or ventilate feelings reduces the underlying support for the ego defense. Under these two conditions communications designed to help the person gain some insight into the ego-defensive function of his attitudes have the best chance to produce change—that is to say, those messages that help him understand the fears and insecurities that underlie his attitudes.

Now think of an attitude you observe or have observed in a group you are familiar with. What is its function? Does it or could it produce dissonance? If so, how could the dissonance be reduced? If not, how has dissonance been controlled? If the attitude were made unstable by the presentation of new data, what reorganization would make it consistent again?

RESISTANCE TO ATTITUDE CHANGE

Our definition of attitudes stated that they were enduring systems. In fact, we find degrees to their endurance and changeability. It has been suggested that we might categorize them on a dimension of depth, with the most superficial ones on the surface and the most profound ones at the core of our personality. On such a continuum we might describe four basic attitude depths and characteristics.

Superficially, at the first level, are those attitudes which are barely distinguishable from opinions or in which we display only a passing interest in the attitude object. I might, for instance, regarding myself as a rather amateurish fly fisherman, join in a cocktail discussion with fellow amateurs and during the evening express the attitude that I agree with my colleague's opinion that a Royal Coachman is a good choice when fishing mountain streams. However, someone else may readily change my long-standing attitude by a few forceful arguments plus the fact that I regard him as an authority on the matter.

At a second, still somewhat superficial level, are those attitudes we have developed through behavior repeated over a long period of time. Loyalty to brand names would fall into this category. Thus we have grown comfortably accustomed to ordering our "usual" brand of rye whisky, cigars, or tobacco. Under experimentally controlled conditions (see Chapter 20) we might not be able to distinguish "my rye" from Old Bushmill's Irish. When our brand ceases to be available, it is with only moderate discomfort that we shift to a new brand and soon build up an equally strong loyalty to it. These types of attitudes are the ones advertisers and propagandists are likely to have most success with for they do not appear to be tied in closely to attitude systems but are loose and disconnected.

At a third and deeper level are attitudes of true stability, closely interrelated with other attitudes into clusters and systems and giving rise to predictable behavior tendencies. These best fit the description of attitudes we have been discussing. They are quite resistant to change because they would involve change throughout the whole system. Only under certain circumstances will they break down and become altered.

On the deepest level, attitudes are locked into higher level constructs such as value systems, primary social attitudes, and personality traits. These factors go together to make up what we normally refer to as personality and could not be altered without change of the personality. They would contain the clusters of our basic attitudes toward religion, esthetics, political and economic philosophy, social philosophy, and so on in the very broadest sense.

These four depths should not be considered as distinct layers of attitudes but rather as observable points along a continuum stretching from our superficial behavior to the nuclear core of our personality.

The modification of attitudes is not as simple a thing as learning or developing them. Those attitudes developed by the child in the background of his home and reinforced by his family, neighbors, and playmates are those which become the foundation for the subsequently developed attitude networks. There appear to be four factors characteristic of those attitudes most resistant to change. First, they have been learned early in life. Second, they have been learned from direct experience, just as we would learn to fear and avoid objects and persons through unpleasant experiences or to like and approach them through pleasant experiences. Third, they satisfy our needs. Fourth, they have been integrated into our personality and style of behavior.

ATTITUDE CHANGE

The paradox of attitudes is that we need them to provide stability to our social world yet our social world is a changing one and we must change our attitudes to adapt to it. Just as we saw the value of perceptual and cognitive economics, we can say that our attitude systems enable us to react economically to a broad range of social facts. Without them we would be wishy-washy, uncertain of ourselves, bent by every current of opinion, unable to make clear decisions, and unable to stick to any we did make. Yet the rapidity of our social evolution requires a remolding of some of the basic values learned in our childhood. War is *not* glorious any longer, the only good Indian is *not* a dead Indian, the black-face minstrel show is insulting to a sizeable chunk of the world's population, Vatican II has produced previously unbelievable change in one of the most authoritarian institutions of history, walking on the moon is no longer science fiction, our attitudes toward environmental despoliation are hardening, and dozens of other changes, many concerning our work and our jobs, were barely conceived of as possibilities a few short years ago. Yet most of us were raised on attitudes toward these things that, if we continued to hold them, would put us sadly out of step with the late twentieth century.

Whether or not attitudes will change depends largely on the interaction of three things: the characteristics of the attitude, the personality of the attitude holder, and the group affiliations of the attitude holder.

We might notice that there are really two types of possible attitude change. The first we call *congruent* change and this involves an increase in the strength of an existing attitude, either to make a positive attitude even more favorable or to make a negative attitude more strongly negative. An *incongruent* change is one in which the direction of change is opposite to the originally held attitude. Thus a negative changing to a positive attitude or a less negative attitude, or a positive attitude changing to a negative attitude or a less positive attitude, are examples of incongruent change. Congruent change is easier to produce than incongruent change—especially when the attitude held is extreme, central in the attitude system, and interconnected with supporting attitudes.

The diagram below illustrates some possible changes. In Figure 9-1(a) we see that a change from A to B or from D to E should be easier to produce because they are congruent with the attitude already held. Changes from A to C or from D to F, although the same theoretical distance, are more difficult to produce because they are incongruent with the attitude held.

In Figure 9-1(b) changes from A to B or from C to D are easier to produce than changes from E to F or from G to H because A and C are more extreme attitudes than are E and G.

FIGURE 9-1

SOME POSSIBLE ATTITUDE CHANGES

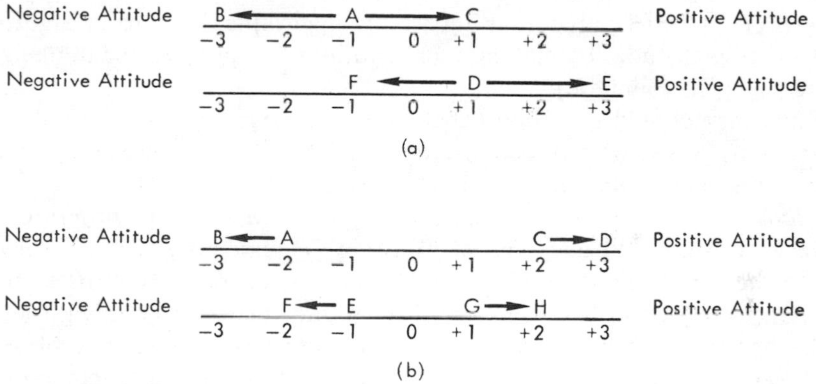

(a)

(b)

Another characteristic involved in changeability is the simplicity of the attitude. The number of facts involved in the cognition and the number of facts to which it is related make the attitude simple or complex. Although we shall see that the mere addition of facts has little effect on change, it is more likely to produce change in a simple than in a complex attitude. The degree of interconnectedness with supporting attitudes is also involved. With high-connectedness congruent change can take place more readily.

From a functional point of view, depending on how many social wants support it and the strength of these wants, the attitude may be more or less changeable. A congruent change of an attitude based on some social want or personality need could be relatively easy, provided the need could be magnified (calling for even more need satisfaction). For example, the worker anxious about the potential economic threat of immigrant workers could have his negative attitudes toward them made even stronger by being exposed to inflammatory speeches, articles, or other information which further magnified the economic threat.

In the next chapter we shall see in more detail some of the personal characteristics which make people persuasible or nonpersuasible. For now there are a few aspects of personality we might consider while discussing attitude change. Intelligence is one; it might be considered that more intelligent persons are more willing to accept new evidence that will produce change. Not so. At least, all attempts to prove or disprove the influence of intelligence by experimentation have been unsuccessful. One finds supposedly intelligent people swayed by quite primitive and illogical arguments as often as one finds highly intelligent people who remain adamantly stubborn even when the facts are shoved down their throats. Perhaps intelligence is not a good variable to consider on its own. In the context of other personality characteristics it might have some relationship to whether attitudes are changeable or not. From the point of view of attitudes being functional, it is conceivable that more intelligent persons are going to protect existing attitudes by making more subtle differentiations or thinking up more complex counterarguments.

Experimental evidence shows that there is a large body of the public which remains grossly uninformed on questions of politics, economics, social developments, cultural happenings, labor issues, and so forth. Many people, if they look at a newspaper, read only the sports and funnies; they rarely listen to a newscast and never listen to a news commentary. On TV they watch cowboys and Indians, sports, and comedies; on radio they listen to sports, noisy music, and badly informed open line shows; for reading they have the sports and skin magazines to look at and paperback adventure stories. News commentaries, editorials, business reviews, labor columns, and even the general news remains unheard and unread. Although such persons hold strong attitudes, and often prejudices, changing them by means of informed argument is almost out of the question.

What about the old folk myth that women are more easily persuaded than men? The next time someone mentions that one to you, ask him about the last argument he had with his wife and whether he won it.

Besides the nature of the attitude and the personality of the attitude holder, the third part of the interaction upon which attitude change depends is the group affiliation of the person. Those groups of which we are members ensure a good degree of "selective exposure" in a number of ways. For one thing specific topics are discussed only in the car pool and the cafeteria, or around the boardroom table and the water cooler. For another, group membership ensures exposure to the "correct" information through the company newsletter, the professional journal, the union bulletin, and so on.

More often, membership in the group prevents existing attitudes from being disturbed because information is "filtered" through the group. As we saw in Chapter 6, one of the powerful bonds which holds the group together is the fact that members think alike and those who do not think the same way are usually nonmembers. Information likely to cause dissonance or inconsistency is either omitted or perceived according to group norms with some modifications or is rejected or considered irrelevant. Also, as has been shown experimentally, attitudes which are temporarily unbalanced while outside the group can be rebalanced by interaction with group members, reading of group commentaries, and so on. Thus a member of group X holding attitude x might be taken aside by members of group Y who shake his attitude x and make him consider the possibility of attitude y. Upon returning to group X and discussing the matter with fellow members, there is a good chance he will be reconfirmed in an even stronger attitude x since members of one's own group are always more readily believed than are nonmembers, and persons from opposing groups are considered low-credibility sources.

We are not always exposed to information in the context of our groups, of course. Information which might change our attitudes impinges upon us from many sources. Even outside of the group, our membership still influences the way that new information is perceived. This is particularly true of primary groups such as family, friends, and fellow workers. The infamous systems of "brainwashing" were rarely effective without the captors first isolating the victim and breaking down his primary affiliations.

DOGMATISM

There is a style of thinking referred to as close-mindedness or dogmatism.[5] *Dogmatism* is a form of authoritarianism and we can consider it as a personality characteristic deserving of a brief discussion on its own apart from our previous discussion of personality.

To understand dogmatism, try to visualize all systems of cognitions being divided into two parts—a set of beliefs and a set of disbeliefs. Dogmatism is a relatively closed system in which the beliefs and disbeliefs are isolated from one another. It tends to be organized around some central authority theme which must be protected at all costs (e.g., a religious theme, a political theme, an economic theme). It provides an excellent framework for intolerance or qualified tolerance.

The greater the dogmatism, the more is the belief system differentiated

[5] M. Rokeach, *The Open and Closed Mind* (New York: Basic Books, Inc., Publishers, 1960).

from the disbelief system. If, for example, the highly dogmatic person sees something as bad, it is almost impossible for him to see anything good about it; a nondogmatic person might see it as bad but also allow for some possibility of good. The more dogmatism present, the more are ideological arguments considered irrelevant. Thus a highly dogmatic person opposed to draft dodgers might reject any argument in their defense and counter, "They are undermining democratic government, and besides they are all pinkos and homosexuals anyway." Finally, in dogmatism we find a denial of events which threaten the belief system. Here "the truth" becomes irrelevant and only "the cause" (the central authority theme) is important. I once witnessed a confrontation of two dogmatic and opposed historians, one of whom was anti-USSR and the other favorably disposed toward the USSR. The first said, "Before 1917 the Russian peasantry owned 80 percent of the arable land of Russia. Now they own 3.7 percent." The other countered, "That's not true. The czar and the nobility owned it all." As a non-historian, I did not know which statement was correct but, as a psychologist, I knew it was quite irrelevant to both as the only important thing was to make their point for "the cause."

Rokeach has developed scales for measuring dogmatism. Two samples from the scale follow:

1. It is only natural that a person would have a much better acquaintance with ideas he believes in than with ideas he opposes.
2. When it comes to differences of opinion in religion, we must be careful not to compromise with those who believe differently from the way we do.

Agreement with items like this are scored as close-mindedness.

In dogmatism one finds a high rate of rejection of opposing beliefs, a relatively low level of interconnection among belief systems, and complex cognitions about positively valued objects as against cognitions about negatively valued objects.

Although close-mindedness is not always immediately apparent, one is sometimes able to observe a cluster of atttudes over a period of time which, taken together, indicate dogmatism. I have an acquaintance who, over time, has expressed the following beliefs and attitudes which, taken together, indicate dogmatic thinking: (1) Trade union members, as a group, have the highest standard of living of any group in the country. (2) Tradesmen cannot expect to be as well off as people with a higher formal education. (3) A lower standard of living motivates the manual worker to try to better his lot through hard work. Rokeach gives an example of close-mindedness in the response of a person who, when requested to return a borrowed book, says, "I didn't borrow your book in the first place. Besides it was torn when you lent it to me. Furthermore,

I have already returned it to you." The statements are illogical but systematic and designed to protect some central authority theme (in the second example they protect the self).

Some further observations can be made about dogmatism:

1. The *time perspective*
   a. The present is regarded as unimportant in its own right but important as a stepping stone to the future.
   b. Drastic revision of the present can often be brought about only by force.
   c. The future is predicted in confident detail although there is no confidence in the predictions of those in disagreement with the belief system.
2. *Authoritarianism*
   a. There is admiration of those in authority and hatred for those opposed to authority.
   b. There is a strong belief in "the cause" and a decreasing tendency to admit that other causes might be valid. There is a constant guard against subversiveness and no compromise with ideological enemies.
   c. There is a strong belief in an elite (political, religious, intellectual, hereditary, activist, etc.).
3. *Intolerance*
   a. There is a clear-cut polarization between the faithful and the unfaithful, the friendlies and the enemies, the good guys and the bad guys.
   b. Disbelievers are rejected as enemies of, for example, God, the country, the working class, the fine arts, science, progress, youth, the revolution. Those who are accepted are accepted on the condition that they are believers. Intolerance for the renegade is most severe.

The type of close-minded dogmatism we are describing is not restricted to political and religious systems. We find this form of authoritarianism among all walks of people: the liberals, the radicals, the conservatives, and the middle-of-the-roaders. Student activists, philosophers, nurses, scientists, managers, labor unionists, educationalists, government functionaries, psychiatrists, anarchists, literary critics, and corner grocers are all represented among the close-minded.

SUMMARY

For some social psychologists, the beginning and end of their discipline can be found in the study of attitudes. Certainly, we can all see the wide range of implications the understanding of attitudes has for good management. Once the system of cognitions, feelings, and behavior tendencies with respect to the job forms and hardens, it remains highly change-resistant.

We have had a brief look at some major theories of attitude. The affective-cognitive consistency theory ties together the person's beliefs about the attitude object and his feelings about it. The holder of strong attitudes feels his ideas are related instrumentally to the achievement of his important values. The importance of the theory of cognitive dissonance is the link it provides between the cognition and the behavior tendency. It allows us to make certain predictions about behavior; this is one of the important reasons we study attitudes in the first place. Also, we saw the importance of understanding attitudes as functional and outlined some of the reasons people hold attitudes in the face of apparently contradictory evidence.

Once formed, the attitude endures. As part of our personality it is almost completely change-resistant. At a more superficial level are attitudes and beliefs which are somewhat more susceptible to change. Whether or not they will change seems to depend on a combination and interaction of factors relating to their nature, the personality of the attitude holder, and his group affiliations. When change does take place it is more likely to be of a congruent than an incongruent nature.

A certain type of close-mindedness called dogmatism is representative of authoritarian and intolerant persons; it is highly resistant to any type of change because of the way its cognitive systems are structured.

Ultimately, the concept of attitude remains most useful for us if we see it as part of a person's personality, if we understand that he has a purpose in holding it, and if we can use it to describe categories or groups of persons.

In the following chapter we are going to examine further some aspects of changeability in which we shall see further implications of the personality, the communication process, and the influence of the group.

10

CHANGING
PEOPLE'S MINDS

Changing people's minds involves changing their attitudes. What do we know about the receivers of messages in regard to change? What about the sender of the message; what makes a person a persuasive communicator? How should a message be constructed to make it convincing? What are some of the unexpected responses to communications we should be aware of? How can group membership be used to effect attitude and behavioral change?

Social philosophers, from the days of the great Athenian thinkers, have written, preached, and speculated on how the human race might become a utopian "empire of reason" if people could only be brought to understand and accept the reasonableness of logic, justice, and virtue. Among the least naïve were writers like William Godwin (eighteenth century) who thought that vice and injustice could be banished from England through the education of the population in "the dictates of justice." Today's social movements seek to redesign the human race through a whole gamut of techniques from the harsher forms of communism to psychedelic drugs. The basic principle underlying them all, whether acknowledged or not, is that when a human being is given a clear choice between truth and untruth he will as a rational creature choose truth. Social psychologists have shown time and time again that such an approach is naïve and simplistic.

However factual, the presentation of information alone is rarely a determinant of attitude change. New information is incorporated into pre-existing attitude systems to keep attitudes consonant. We know that attitudes do not always correctly reflect "the facts" although "the facts" are "valid" in the sense that the cognitive components of the attitude correspond with or are based on fact. Reality cannot be ignored. Distorted cognitions would soon lead to distorted behavior; but recall from our chapter on perception how the cognition takes on quite different attributes once it is placed in an appropriate cognitive system.

Some years ago a study [1] on attitudes toward fluoridation revealed that among "the facts" underlying opposition to fluoridation were the following: it is rat poison, Nazi; ruins batteries, radiators, and lawns; causes hardening of the arteries and veins, premature aging, loss of memory, nymphomania; and that it weakens the will.

Managers are frequently confronted with opposing facts in which the values of the organization, its individual members, and the community come into apparent conflict.

Experts on almost any issue are always offering advice through magazine, newspaper, TV, and radio commentaries. One can easily quote contradictory authorities on economics, politics, financial trends, how to raise children, the effects of drugs, and so forth. Little wonder the manager seeking the facts begins to doubt anything which he cannot see, hear, or touch for himself.

We can easily spend our entire waking life reading persuasive advertising, publicity releases, and editorials as well as hearing and seeing them on radio and TV. But, in order to get any work done and preserve our health and sanity, a large part of these messages must be perceptually excluded.

Some of the things we saw about attitudes in the last chapter might lead us to wonder whether it is ever possible to change people's minds. Given that any attitude change usually disrupts a host of other attitudes, would it not be easier to cling to attitudes for life once they have formed? Not so. Our cognitions do change throughout life. In order to cope with our world, to get our satisfactions, and avoid punishment, we must keep our cognitions in line with reality. If my stomach gets in the way when I try to cut my toenails, I may be forced to admit as facts what my wife has been telling me about putting on weight.

Stephenson [2] has pointed out that any attitude change has to involve a *tripartite* interaction between a person (X), a medium or social mechan-

---

[1] M. Davis, "Community Attitudes Toward Fluoridation," *Public Opinion Quarterly*, XXIII (1959), 474–482.

[2] William Stephenson, *The Play Theory of Mass Communication* (Chicago: University of Chicago Press, 1967).

ism (Y), and a message (Z). There tends to be a common error among message senders and would-be persuaders to omit the intervening vehicle (Y). For example,

one can promote soap (Z)
to housewifes (X)
because supermarkets (Y)
make it easy for X to purchase Z
but,
it is difficult to sell civic responsibility in voting (Z)
to citizens (X)
because there is no facilitating social mechanism. (Y)

In this latter case, one might make voting mandatory by revalidating the rationbook, driver's license, and so on, at the polling station.

Ultimately, we are more interested in changing people's behaviors, although we are talking about changing their minds or attitudes. This requires us to look closely at the recipient of the persuasive communication, the sender or vehicle of the persuasion attempt, and the message itself.

THE RECEIVER

Persuasibility is the tendency of a person to accept a persuasive communication. It commonly refers to a response to a direct influence attempt. *Suggestibility* is a broader term implying response, not merely to persuasive attempts, but to any action or communication of another person whether or not it was intended to change behavior.

Do people differ in terms of persuasibility? The following sample quotations from an early study [3] on the effect college life has on a student's general attitudes illustrates the range of individual differences in persuasibility:

> I came to college to get away from my family, who never had any respect for my mind. Becoming radical meant thinking for myself and figuratively, thumbing my nose at my family. It also meant intellectual identification with the faculty and students that I most wanted to be like.

> I wanted to disagree with all the noisy Liberals, but I was afraid and I couldn't. So I built up a wall inside me against what they said. I found I couldn't compete, so I decided to stick to my father's ideas. For at least two years I've been insulated against all college influences.

[3] T. M. Newcomb, *Personality and Social Change: Attitude Formation in a Student Community* (New York: Dryden Press, 1943).

A good deal of research on persuasibility has been done in this area by Hovland and Janis.[4] They conclude that a person might be highly persuasible on certain topics but not at all on others. Susceptibility to persuasion might vary depending on the form of appeal, different communicators, different media, or some other aspect of the situation. One person could be quite persuasible to communications coming from authority figures but quite resisting to threatening communications and so forth.

People are generally persuasible to a similar degree on different topics and about the same to subsequent communications designed to change their attitudes back in the opposite direction (countercommunication). Yet the research shows that persuasibility is inconsistent. To explain this, the terms topic-free and topic-bound persausibility are used. By *topic-free* is meant the general tendency to be persuasible to more or less the same degree on different topics. By *topic-bound* is meant the difference in persuasibility on each distinct topic. Figure 1 illustrates how the same person can be both topic-free persuasible and topic-bound persuasible.

The conclusion is that persuasibility is somewhat consistent in people across different topics and types of communications, including those that

FIGURE 10-1

PERSUASIBILITY IS BOTH TOPIC-FREE AND TOPIC-BOUND

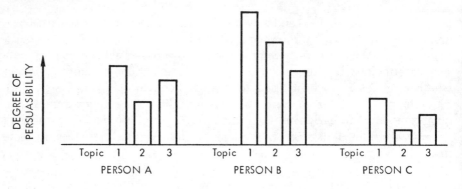

run counter to his attitudes and those of which he has much or little knowledge. At the same time there is a wide range of responsiveness according to a combination of circumstances.

We might notice a few other things about the personality of the recipient of the persuasive communication. First is his level of self-esteem.

[4] C. I. Hovland and I. L. Janis, eds., *Personality and Persuasibility* (New Haven, Conn.: Yale University Press, 1959).

The more inadequate a person feels and the more social inhibitions he has, the more likely is he to be persuasible. People with a great deal of confidence in their own intellectual abilities are not only more resistant to change but more willing to expose themselves to discrepant information. Experimental evidence indicates that when a person has confidence in his ability to refute discrepant arguments or in the correctness of his opinion, he is quite willing to confront opposing arguments and information. Also, it is easier to learn and remember arguments supporting one's own position and to learn implausible arguments opposing one's own position. A ludicrously poor argument by one's opponent is something one enjoys remembering but a stupid argument from a well-intentioned supporter is better forgotten. It is satisfying to think that all the wise men are on our side and all the idiots are with the opposition.

The personality of the receiver of the message should not be overemphasized. Persuasibility makes much more sense in the context of the total communication situation. This becomes clearer in a theory of attitude change we have not yet examined.[5] It describes three forms of influence a communication can have on the person.

First, *compliance* takes place when a person accepts influence from another person or group because he hopes thereby to achieve a favorable reaction (or avoid an unfavorable one). The compliant person may disagree privately with what he expresses but expressing it helps him to avoid some punishment or gain some satisfaction. For example, one company used to require its representatives always to wear a hat when making their business or sales calls. Some removed their hats when they thought they would not be seen by their superiors for they disagreed with the policy and disliked wearing a hat. Compliance, then, refers to those opinions expressed publicly to the influencing agent but disagreed with privately.

Second, *identification* occurs when a person adopts the behavior of another person or group because this behavior is associated with a satisfying self-defining relationship with that group or person. The identification is a means of defining oneself as having a certain type of relationship with the person or group although the behavior or attitude itself is not intrinsically satisfying to the individual. We see, for instance, junior supervisors or managers adopting the habits of dress, of speech, of working hours; displaying the same attitudes toward the board of governors, clients, and nonsupervisory staff; frequenting the same restaurants, choosing the same drinks, and so on of the senior managers whom they admire—or adopting the habits of the general managerial group.

[5] H. C. Kelman, "Processes of Opinion Change," *Public Opinion Quarterly,* XXV (1961), 57–78.

Finally, *internalization* takes place when the person accepts an influence because the behavior induced is congruent with his value system. This type of behavior or attitude is intrinsically satisfying to him. Thus the manager may support a new company policy on adult education for members of the organization because it is congruent with his value and attitude system concerning the responsibility of management.

Which form of influence takes place depends partly on the source of power of the influencing agent. When the agent has strong control over rewards and punishments which will follow from the behavior or attitude, compliance is then likely to occur. In the organization where rules and procedures are enforced severely this commonly occurs. Also, when the influencing agent is able to closely observe the action or statement of opinion, there is more chance of compliance. When the severe boss, for example, tells his subordinates he has been thinking something over for a long time and has finally come up with an excellent idea, the likelihood is high that the subordinates will tell him that they agree it is an excellent idea.

When the relationship to the influencing agent is a satisfying one there is more likelihood of identification. In a pleasant organizational climate the newly appointed young supervisor is more likely to imitate his manager's behaviors and job attitudes. This is particularly true when he can carry out behavior which the manager himself carries out as part of his work role—for example, correcting rather than reprimanding a subordinate.

Finally, we are most likely to observe internalization when the influencing agent is highly credible or believable and when relevant values are activated.

A particular situation may not yield a pure example of compliance, identification, or internalization. Frequently, two or all three take place simultaneously. Thus the school principal who is a strict disciplinarian but is liked and respected by the teachers may persuade them of things congruent to their exising attitudes thereby evoking compliance, identification, and internalization.

CHARACTERISTICS OF A PERSUASIVE COMMUNICATOR

Aristotle wrote over two thousand years ago that people are more likely to be persuaded by a speaker's character when he presents his message in such a way that people think him credible. He felt people are more likely to believe those they thought were "good men." Up until recent times it was widely held, even by psychologists, that when a message came from a prestigious person it was likely to be persuasive whether or not it was logical. A few years ago a social psychologist named Asch (we shall see more of his ideas in Chapter 14) pointed out that the prestige of a communicator was not as important as the fact that the recipient of the message perceives its *content* differently depending on how he sees the communicator.

Hovland and his associates at Yale University have also done research into the characteristics of communicators. They feel there are two primary characteristics which affect whether a communication is accepted by its recipients. These are the *expertness* of the communicator, or the extent to which his audience believes he is capable of giving the correct or best information; and the *trustworthiness* of the communicator, or the degree of confidence his listeners have in his intent to give them the best information. Taken together, these are referred to as *credibility*. Expertness can usually be determined by the communicator's specialized training or education, his background of experience, and, to some extent, by general characteristics such as age, position, and social status. Trustworthiness is more difficult to identify but position and status, as well as certain personality characteristics, mannerism, physical appearance, and modes of speech, are often associated with trust. The important thing is the audience's *perception* of the communicator's *intent* in giving the message. When the communicator is perceived as having a definite intention to persuade, it is more likely he will also be perceived as having something to gain and thus as less trustworthy. This is why, regardless of the message, people tend to suspect the communications of salesmen, radio and TV commericals, and politicians. It also accounts for the skepticism workers often have about statements which come from management.

When a message is presented by a high-credibility person, his message is judged more favorably than an identical one from a low-credibility person. However, experimentation with *actual attitude and behavioral change* is not so consistent, for low-credibility messages also tend to affect people. This is something we shall examine in more detail soon.

The more favorably disposed the recipients are to the communicator (the more *attractive* he is), the more will his influence be accepted. This conclusion about *attractiveness* of the communicator should not surprise anyone; it is mentioned here because a good deal of research and experimental evidence supports the principle. Groups or individuals who are liked by the persons receiving the message can persuade them more easily than those who are less attractive.

Another communicator characteristic found to affect the degree of influence is the *similarity* between communicator and message recipient. Similarity causes the communicator to be perceived as more attractive, among other things, but similarity alone can account for persuasiveness. This being the case, it is possible that a persuasive message received by workers from a credible fellow worker or from their representatives (union officials, political representatives, sympathetic spokesmen) has more impact than an equivalent message from management or its spokesmen because the latter may be perceived as dissimilar to the workers. Equally, messages from representatives of the workers may be discounted by management while statements from the board of directors should have more chance of inducing changed attitudes and behavior among company officers, stockholders, and associates.

In summary, those characteristics of the communicator which would make it more likely that his persuasive messages have effect are his expertness and trustworthiness (which, together, we call his credibility), his perceived intent to induce change, his attractiveness to the recipients of the message, and their perception of his similarity to themselves.

What would happen if a credible and attractive person were sent by the governing body of an organization to try to persuade a dissident group and he started out by saying, "I have been asked by the board of directors to talk to you about this problem. . . . ."? Why?

CHARACTERISTICS OF A CONVINCING COMMUNICATION

Having seen some of the traits of a persuasible person and some of the attributes of a persuasive communicator, we now turn to the characteristics of the persuasive message itself.

For centuries, debaters have wondered about the rhetoric of even mentioning the arguments of the opposition or, indeed, of acknowledging the opposition's existence. The idea was that one could make the opponent's argument and then discount it or defeat it to give one's own argument more strength. Not until World War II was there any experimental attempt to answer the question of whether the best persuasive message is *one-sided* or *two-sided*. When the war in Europe ended, many American soldiers felt the Pacific war would be short and they could get ready to go home. Fearing this might be wishful thinking, the government investigated the best way to convince them the Pacific war could be a long one. Two types of persuasive messages were used. The one-sided communication merely argued that Japan was a strong nation and that the war would be a long one. The two-sided communication gave the same information plus a few arguments that might have been made by those who disagreed with the point. When possible, these arguments were refuted. With both types of communication the conclusion was the same: the Pacific war would take at least two years to win. Contrary to expectations, the experimenters (Hovland and his associates) found both types of communication to have the same effect. However, closer examination revealed that when the men were initially opposed to the message (they expected a short war), the two-sided message was more effective than the one-sided. The one-sided message was more effective for those who initially agreed with the communication, merely bolstering their opinion. The two-sided message was less effective for those who initially agreed with the opinion, probably because it planted a few seeds of doubt where none existed previously. Also, the one-sided message was more effective for the poorly educated soldiers while the two-sided was more effective for the better educated.

The conclusion is that one should present a two-sided argument to an intelligent audience that is initially opposed to one's opinion; but one should not mention the opposition's arguments when talking to an uneducated group which agrees with him from the start. However, before adopting this generalization too widely, there is another point to keep in mind. When the recipients of the persuasive communication are subsequently exposed to countercommunication (arguments from the opposition), those who received an initial two-sided message are much better able to resist the countermessage than those who initially received only a one-sided message.

Two-sided persuasive communications are said to have an *inoculating* effect. That is to say, having heard some weak counterarguments or the presentation of counterarguments along with rebuttals for them, the recipient is immunized against counterargument at a later date, or at least the effect of future counterarguments is weakened. Also, one might expect that the inclusion of some negative material in an overall favorable context could produce higher credibility. This is a point advertisers used to overlook but now they take advantage of it.

A number of studies on the inoculating effect were a result of the concern about the lack of resistance American prisoners of war seemed to have against Chinese propaganda during the Korean War. A congressional committee had suggested the problem would be overcome if soldiers received more instruction in "Americanism." Social psychologists argued and demonstrated the opposite. What the soldiers needed was the immunizing effect of exposure to the Communist position along with arguments against such a position. Because of a number of social forces operating in the United States at that period of time, many soldiers had never received any exposure to Communist thinking and arguments against it. Just as medical inoculation is carried out by the injection of a weak virus, so inoculation to persuasive communication is carried out by injection of a weak countermessage.

A question people have wondered about for many years is whether, in arguing a case in a court of law or during a formal debate, the advantage goes to the first speaker or the last speaker. Some have argued the case for first impressions (which we saw are important in Chapter 3). Others have argued that the person who gets in the last word has the advantage because his points are more likely to be remembered and cannot be rebutted by the opposition. This controversy is known as the *primacy-recency* question. Current research points out that some factors give advantage to the first communication, some factors give advantage to the last. Exactly what these factors are is yet to be determined. Remembering and forgetting the content of the messages is likely one and the period of time between receiving messages may be another. For the present the advantage in practical settings probably lies in getting your strongest argument in before the opposition does. As a final caution, it appears better to put pleasant information forward before unpleasant information if both must be presented.

The *fear-arousing communication* is one which has been popular in some management messages. How effective is it? We can think of those subtle and not so subtle threats—for example, that one more wage demand is going to force the company out of business, or kill its export market causing a subsequent personnel cutback, and so on. Does such a threat really cause the workers to vote against strikes or be willing to settle for a smaller demand? What about the supervisor who issues a direct threat to his subordinates designed to make them change job attitudes?

There is quite a bit of experimental evidence on fear-arousing appeals. One of the most famous is a study by Janis and Feshbach [6] in which they tested the effects of fear appeals on attitudes and behaviors related to tooth-brushing. Some recipients were given a *strong fear* message about tooth decay, pain, and disease with vivid films on mouth infections, and so on. A less dramatic *moderate fear* message was given others on the consequences of neglecting oral hygiene. A third group received *minimal fear* messages in which infection and decay were scarcely mentioned. As predicted, the minimal fear message was most effective. It produced a net desired change of 36 percent compared to a net change of 8 percent in the strong appeal. Also, the group which received the minimal fear message proved most resistant to a countercommunication by a dental authority one week later.

Follow-up and similar studies show that those who listen to frightening messages make many more statements rejecting the messages, think that the communication lacks objectivity or is alarmist, and are less likely to repeat the argument. The conclusion is that a high level of fear motivates people to develop psychological resistances to the communicators' arguments, conclusions, and recommendations. This could be interpreted in

[6] I. L. Janis and S. Feshbach, "Effects of Fear Arousing Communications," *Journal of Abnormal and Social Psychology*, XLVIII (1953), 78–92.

light of the theory of cognitive dissonance discussed in the last chapter. The fear-arousing message contains many elements of dissonance which would be most easily avoided or reduced by rejecting the message.

Health campaigns, drivers' safety appeals, and others are now taking these findings seriously, as much of their former fear-arousing propaganda proved quite ineffective. Management would be wise to move in the same direction to have its messages more readily received.

There is still no unanimity on the question, though. A number of recent researchers feel that fear appeals are effective up to a certain point, only after which the strong fear reduces the effectiveness of the communication. Others feel that persons with a characteristically high level of anxiety may be sensitive to fear appeals. Still others propose that it all depends on the complexity of the issue. As with so many issues in psychology we shall have to wait for more evidence before being able to provide a refined answer to our question.

THE TOTAL SITUATION

While examining piecemeal some characteristics of the recipient of the message, the sender of the message, and the message itself, it would be well to keep the *Gestalt* or total situation in mind. Even when one designs a message guaranteed to catch anyone's attention, has it endorsed by the most credible authority, and constructs it with utmost cunning— it may still be rejected. Nothing makes a person change his attitude against his will. Especially when the information is controversial, the message recipient can always refuse to accept the communicator's facts.

The entire *Gestalt*, the total situation, in which the persuasive attempt is successful must include a climate which will facilitate the message and a communicatee who is willing to accept the information. For example, those who have recently endured personal frustrations are more likely to accept aggressive communications and less likely to accept pleas for patience and consideration. One might expect, then, that in a climate of work frustration workers will be readily aroused to aggressive and hostile action and less likely to accept even the most sound arguments from the most credible communicators urging them to be patient. Even the momentary mood of the recipient—depending on what happened to him that day, that morning, or that week—may affect his receptivity to various types of recommendations.

In most nonexperimental settings the communicatees have the opportunity to discuss their objections to the message soon after receiving it. The support one receives from peer groups must not be overlooked. "Brainwashing" techniques have always made the breaking up of the primary peer group the first step in their procedure as support from even one other person is a tremendous asset in helping us stick to our opinion.

There have also been experiments to test the hypothesis that when food is eaten during the presentation of a persuasive communication it will increase acceptance of the message. The prediction has been verified. Even when the communicator is not the donor of the food and when the donor of the food did not endorse the communication, the pleasantness of the situation appears to help get the message across. When the food donor also endorses the message of the communicator there is an extremely high opinion change. It is possible that the consumption of a desirable food induces a momentary mood of compliance toward the donor that is strongest at the time the food is being eaten. There is some evidence that willingness to change decreases in strength rapidly after the food has been eaten. As far as your author knows, there is no research on the effects of *drink* during the presentation of a persuasive communication. However, the evidence seems to support the value of taking a client to lunch or introducing news of policy changes at company-sponsored dinners.

SOME SPECIAL EFFECTS IN ATTITUDE CHANGE

A couple of situations are worth noting in which the effect of the persuasive communication is the opposite of its intent. This is commonly referred to as the *boomerang effect*. Thus a communication designed to change an attitude or behavior in one direction can produce a change in the other direction.

For example, the response of authoritarian persons (determined by a personality measurement to hold, among other things, power and status as central values) to nonauthoritarian attempts to change their prejudices usually boomerangs.

The importance of the *perceived position* of the communicator must be taken into account if one wants to predict the effectiveness of a communication. There is only a certain range within which the communicator's position will be judged by the recipient as fair and unbiased. The closer one's own stand to the attitude statement, the more favorably does one evaluate it. (Known as the *assimilation effect*.) In those situations where the issue at stake is of great personal concern to the receiver of the message and where the credibility of the communicator is not great, the message of the persuasive attempt must not deviate very far at all from the position of the communicatee or it will surely boomerang (*contrast effect*). In the latter circumstances it would be wiser to employ a series of communications spaced over time gradually moving the recipient of the message away from his position.

On the other hand, when the issue at stake is of little concern to the communicatee and the communicator is highly credible, effective change can take place even though the communicator's position is quite far from that of the communicatee.

The last of the unexpected results of persuasive communication we shall examine is the *sleeper effect*. In one of Hovland's experiments on credibility, messages were delivered by a high-credibility communicator and a low-credibility communicator. As expected, the high-credibility person produced much more attitude change when this change was measured immediately after the message was delivered. However, in a follow-up study conducted four weeks later, a startling finding emerged for the difference in effect of the high- and low-credibility communicators had disappeared. Two things had happened. First, the passage of time had produced a decrease of effectiveness in the high-credibility communication. Second, in the same period there was an increased acceptance of the position advocated by the low-credibility communicator.

The sleeper effect refers to the fact that after the passage of four weeks there is no significant difference between the effectiveness of high- and low-credibility communicators. The suggested reason for this is that the low-credibility message may have been discounted at first hearing. However, with the passage of time it may be easier to remember *what* was communicated but not *who* communicated it, allowing for the acceptance of the low-credibility position.

The amount of material remembered from credible and noncredible sources remains about the same after a passage of time, communicator credibility having its maximum effect immediately after the communication. The influence of trustworthiness and expertness depends, then, on whether the recipient of the message remembers its source.

An incidental finding from studies of the sleeper effect is that prediction of attitude change can be far more accurate if the credibility of the communicator is known relative to the specific topic involved rather than just as a general abstract credibility. Thus a prestigious professor from the School of Engineering and the minister of transportation combined may not produce as much attitude change on driver safety as a relatively little known local racing car driver.

GROUP EFFECT ON CHANGING PEOPLE'S MINDS

We now turn our full attention to group effects on changing a person's mind for the group has the greatest force in determining whether or not change will take place. There are a number of ways in which such forces work.

First, the so-called *two-step flow of communication* indicates that when issues call for opinion change or for the reception of new information which will change behavior patterns, communications normally pass through several levels or steps (it usually involves more than two steps). Major issues are popularized by national and international opinion leaders (usually public figures of various sorts) through mass media via newspaper columns, TV interviews, magazine and journal articles, and so on. Before the "rank and file" take these new facts and suggestions into their cognitive and attitude systems, they first discover the reaction of their *local opinion leaders*. Normally, these leaders pass on their reaction to the issue to less active persons by word of mouth or they may be quoted by third persons in conversations with other members of the rank and file. Local opinion leaders vary with the issue. On new work techniques, it is one person; on TV program selection, a second; on marketing shifts, a third; on labor issues, another. Once the leader has reacted by changing his behavior, expressing his opinion, or deciding not to change his behavior, the rank-and-file members of the group or of the local community will then decide whether or not to follow suit.

Most organizations and work groups will have their local opinion leaders, and it should not be too difficult to discover who they are on many types of issues by observation over a period of time. Studies on opinion leaders have shown that they have a specialized area of information or behavior and also that they have some consistent characteristics. First, they represent or personify the values and attitudes of their group more closely than others. Second, they are more competent in the sense that they have more expert knowledge and are more in touch with the latest information (often they read more, subscribe to more technical publications, attend conferences). Third, they are "centrally located in the social structure"—that is, they have a wider range of friends and acquaintances and belong to more organizations making them a focal point of informal communication. In other words, they are far more active than other group members in relation to the particular issue.

One could certainly enhance the possibility of his persuasive message getting across if he could insure that local opinion leaders of the groups he wished to persuade would react favorably. On the other hand, if local opinion leaders would tend to oppose new ideas and behaviors, the chances of general adoption would be considerably reduced for they are imitated by others even when they make no direct attempt to influence.

Before leaving the local opinion leaders, we must not be so naïve as to believe that every bit of information from the mass media or other major sources must be screened by them. Their role varies considerably, depending on the topic of influence. Certainly, important news reaches each member of the public directly through radio, TV, and newspaper.

Could you identify a local opinion leader in your office, classroom, factory, department, etc.? How do you know?

The more closely knit is the group, the more influence it has both in resisting unwanted persuasion and in strengthening acceptable persuasive attempts. Even on those issues which are not of particular relevance the group exerts some pressure on members who deviate. Removed from the support of his major groups, a person becomes much easier prey to various types of persuaders.

Attitudes which had originally been perceived differently, which were ambiguous, which involved a misperception, or the implications of which remained unknown are clarified through interaction with fellow group members. These forces can be used directly for persuasion.

A famous pioneer of group dynamics, Kurt Lewin, was the first to demonstrate how the group could be used as an agent of change.[7] His technique usually involved a series of steps. First, the *issue is presented* in the form of a lecture or statement suggesting a course of action compatible with the existing motivation of the audience. Second, those present are asked to discuss their *feelings about cooperating* in the proposal of the communicator and are also encouraged to voice their objections. The third step involves the communicator recognizing and *accepting objections* without disapproval and, in fact, acknowledging the right of group members to raise objections. In step number four the discussion leader tries to answer any *requests for information* or clarification raised by group members. Fifth, he encourages the group to discuss the issues in a way that will *meet the objections* raised at least to some extent. Next, the group members are asked to *make a decision* as to whether or not they will carry out the desired behavior. Finally, there is the opportunity to see how many others agree (*perceived group consensus*) by show of hand or other public statement.

Many of these seven steps involve practices familiar to us from other procedures such as swearing on the Bible, signing a pledge card, making a public commitment (e.g., in Alcoholics Anonymous), and so on. When compared to other techniques, the group decision process was more than ten times as effective in producing changed behavior. (32 percent as against 3 percent). Lewin saw the procedure as a three-step process: unfreezing group attitudes which might ordinarily produce resistance to change; establishing new attitudes; and refreezing the new attitudes.

Group decision process involves things which normal persuasive attempts do not. First, it gets participants actively and personally involved. Second, they perceive that others are willing to abandon their old attitudes. Third, as the leader is permissive they feel nothing is being forced on them. Fourth, and important, they are required to commit themselves to

[7] K. Lewin, "Group Decision and Social Change," in *Readings in Social Psychology*, 3rd ed., eds. E. E. Maccoby, T. M. Newcomb, and E. L. Hartley (New York: Holt, Rinehart & Winston, Inc., 1958), pp. 197–211.

change. Finally, also very important, they have the opportunity to see others commit themselves.

Choice and commitment are important factors involved in the process. Deliberately choosing to carry out a nonpreferred behavior could be said to increase cognitive dissonance which must then be reduced by attitude change. In fact, the more unpleasant the behavior a person commits himself to, the greater will be the pressure to reduce dissonance through attitude change. When simultaneously the person witnesses others around him committing themselves to change, group pressures then act further on him to carry out the behavior to which he is newly committed. Because commitment is voluntary, a greater amount of attitude change is likely to take place.

CONCLUSION

Aldous Huxley wrote in an appendix to his book, *The Devils of Loudon* (which deals with religion and persuasibility) that even highly civilized people would lose their sense of judgment and their critical objectivity if exposed long enough to ritual drumming, chanting, and hymn singing. He felt even the most educated people could be reduced to savages, given the appropriately controlled circumstances. Equally, other writers have felt that, given the deployment of the correct psychological-physiological-perceptual techniques, whole cities and societies could be brainwashed or hypnotized. It is great stuff for popular magazine articles, science fiction movies, and antiutopian writers. Fortunately for us all, the best evidence is that this is fanciful thinking on the same level as trips to other galaxies. The long-term effects of the most sophisticated forms of brainwashing are on a par with good old-fashioned torture. Probably the simplest way to make a person change his behavior is to point a gun at his head and keep it there. This is not only unhuman, it is also extremely wasteful of resources, for it requires one supervisor for one worker. It has been used, of course, to raise some impressive monuments, but civilized men reject it.

That being the case, there are only four ways left to change people's minds and behavior:

1. *Providing them with more information.* This is ideal but often impractical for reasons we have seen in the last two chapters. When it can be used effectively, we can heave a sigh of relief, let a brief feeling of pride pass through our breast since we are working for a good organization, and quickly get back to work to keep it that way.

2. *Change can be enforced.* The law or the heavily sanctioned rule is sometimes the only way we have of forcing the facts of life down reluctant throats. Although we may espouse the cause of the perfectibility of man,

we might shudder to think what would happen if there were no traffic or parking regulations. The parking chaos of some European cities today and the subsequent traffic chaos would be enough to convince the objective observer that, failing all else, the law should be enforced to the utmost severity. At times the manager is thankful that he can quote chapter and verse on safety rules, equipment maintenance, hours of work, and many other regulations. Yet I recall the case of a friend of mine in his first management assignment, a public service office of about twenty-five people, who tried to convince his men that when greeting visiting clients they must display the utmost courtesy. After several discussions of this point, in a fit of frustration he *ordered* that every man dealing with the public must greet each new male client by shaking his hand. The men complied. One clique, however, as soon as they shook the client's hand and sat him down excused themselves, went to the washroom, and washed their hands, insisting to the dismayed manager that it was within their rights for the protection of their health. Predictably, the manager did not last long in this position.

3. *Changing people's personality.* Normally, this is a drastic and costly procedure with no guarantee of effectiveness. It would be advocated only in the extreme case of the unbalanced. But, on another level, if we consider personality change in the broad sense of helping people to grow and mature rather than in the restrictive sense of emergency psychiatric treatment, the manager can do a great deal to encourage personal growth through in-training, sponsoring, and supporting off-job education, and generally taking the stance of teacher. More will be said of this in Chapter 18.

4. *Changing group affiliation.* At first glance this may appear to be something controllable only by the individual, with the odds being that he will improve or get worse depending on the change of group affiliation. In fact, the manager has a lot of control here. The next chapter will provide some hints on how a person can be put into the right group to achieve the right behavior. As managers it is often within our power to switch a person from one group to another to help him achieve his potential as a person as well as to achieve the goals of the organization.

SUMMARY

This chapter is most valuable when taken in conjunction with Chapter 7 (Communication), Chapter 9 (Social Attitudes), and Chapter 14 (Normative Behavior and Conformity). Indeed, it ties in closely with much of the rest of the book. It is important in management to get our message across in such a way that it results in behavior change both for overall effectiveness and for the good of the worker (also for our own peace of mind).

Stubborn and old-fashioned thinking of both workers and management are deterrents to organizational effectiveness. Sometimes the attitudes are deep-seated and long-lived, based on old prejudices and fears for security of the self. This makes them all the more difficult to change.

Our main consideration has been how to get our facts accepted as facts by others—our peers, our superiors, our subordinates, or the general public. First, we looked at the recipient of the message to see whether there were any peculiarities or differences to take into consideration. There are. Some people are more persuasible than others. Having said this, we had to go on to qualify that some people are more persuasible on certain types of topics. The concluding saw-off is that persuasibility is both topic-free and topic-bound. One of the most readily observable characteristics of the persuasible person is his level of self-esteem or confidence. Confidence in his ability to refute a persuasive attempt makes it more difficult to change a person's mind. Kelman's theory of attitude change was examined in the context of personality. The three stages of compliance, identification, and internalization were considered with their implications. The three stages may overlap. In concluding the overview of personality and persuasibility, we must point out that it would be erroneous to consider personality outside the context of the entire communication situation.

The next major consideration was the communicator. A number of characteristics make him an effective persuader. His expertness and trustworthiness combine to make him a credible or noncredible communicator. Expertness can usually be determined readily. Trustworthiness is more difficult but hinges on the audience's perception of the communicator's intent. His attractiveness and similarity to those receiving his message also influence his persuasiveness.

The message itself should be one-sided or two-sided depending on who the recipients are (one-sided for the less bright and for those already on one's side). But that is not the only consideration. Longer term inoculating effects of a two-sided message must be taken into consideration. The person who has never been exposed even to weak arguments from the opposition is easier prey to countercommunication. The question of primacy-recency is still debatable with good points for both sides. In practical application, it seems better to get the best punches in first. The fear-arousing communication must be held in suspicion, according to the most extensive research. It tends to raise cognitive dissonance which can be reduced most easily by rejecting the message.

The total situation in which communicator, communicatee, and communication interact must always be kept uppermost in mind. When this total situation is a pleasant one (e.g., while eating good food) the persuasive impact is greater. Momentary moods and situations of general frustration complicate the persuasive attempt. This is particularly true because, as we have seen in Chapter 7, managers often do not get a good picture of the feelings of their subordinates.

Rather than risk a boomerang effect, many situations should be dealt with in several short steps. The sleeper effect has been well documented and is rather discouraging to deal with if one wishes long-term attitude change to take place against even low-credibility opposition. Perhaps the best way of dealing with it is to provide more frequent persuasive messages until the point has become well established, for research with the sleeper effect has been restricted to one-shot communications.

Finally, we considered the all-important influence of the group in changing people's minds. The local opinion leaders are the keys in the two-step flow of communication and in many types of attitude and behavior change they make the major communicators' job easy or near impossible. Lewin's group decision process involving unfreezing-establishing-refreezing has proven one of the most potent techniques in producing attitude and behavior change. It must be remembered that the technique depends on message recipients who are not motivationally opposed to commitment toward the new cause of action. The deliberate choice and commitment appear to make the technique really work.

3

GROUP DYNAMICS

The first two parts of the book have shown us how complex social behavior is and have given us some idea of the importance of membership in the group. Part 3 leads us into the very heart of group behavior; here we stop to take a self-conscious look at what happens to us as group members. Questions such as "Do we really have any control over what happens in the group?" will nag us constantly. But before we finish it will be seen that the people in groups are not at all the same as the molecules in a chemical reaction.

First, in Chapter 11, we examine why groups form and what makes them maintain their existence in spite of destructive forces. How to form an effective team will be our major concern. In this context we are introduced to the important theory of exchange. The next chapter deals with the mystery of power and its different forms, where it comes from, who has it, and how it works.

Chapter 13 deals with status, how it is achieved, and what it does to the group and its members. Norms and conformity come next in Chapter 14, and by now the student begins to realize the dynamic forces operative in the group to make it work effectively and noneffectively. Finally, the concept of role is examined and we find that group dynamics begin to make more sense for the individual is seen as an individual again and not merely a puppet controlled by group forces.

11

THE GROUP AS
A TEAM

Why are some groups capable of functioning as a unit whereas in others it is every man for himself? What is sociometry and how can it be used to analyze groups? What underlies our preferences in choice of other people? How does exchange theory account for smooth interaction? How does a basic group form? What changes are likely to take place in the ongoing group? What can interaction process analysis tell us about an established group? How can we recognize morale? What effect does it have on productivity?

Sitting watching excerpts from a soccer (football) match on TV, I notice how a small group of men devote every possible ounce of energy to achieve the group goal. When it is achieved their satisfaction is exuberance—jumping, dancing, singing, lifting one another from the ground. In the last minutes of play they call on hidden sources of energy, exhausting the last muscle, the last drop of sweat, the last bit of oxygen in the blood—in a superhuman effort to accomplish what they are there for. But they are not individuals, they are a team. A chance for glory comes—but the odds favor a chance for a fellow player by a slim margin. There is no hesitation. The pass goes to the fellow and personal glory is forfeited. Have you ever watched a National Hockey League game in which the players deliberately "fed" a fellow player who was close to the top scorer in the league?

From the handful of professional players I have known, it seems that their jobs are in many respects similar to ours. They get paid for their work and they get into disputes about income and fringe benefits. There are threats to their security, thoughts about playing with the other team, petty jealousies after they have left the locker room, a wife and kids who are already asleep when they get home, and concern about whether they should look for another job which demands less sacrifice or provides higher pay.

I have never coached as much as the kindergarten league but I have wondered how it feels to be the manager of a professional team, standing on the side, munching a cigar, and knowing full well that, win or lose, your men have given every blessed ounce of knowledge, experience, and physical energy in their power to achieve the goals for which the organization was set up. I have also wondered whether managers in other business, industrial, government, educational, and other organizations ever experience the satisfaction the coach must feel about the effort his team puts into their job.

This question is raised here because, although we have seen something of the nature of the group in Chapter 6, to date we have concentrated on the group as a structure while now we want to know something of its internal dynamics. It was Kurt Lewin who first emphasized the concept of group dynamics. We know what a group is now but by *dynamics* we refer to the adjustive changes that take place in the group structure as a result of change in any part of the group. A part, of course, may be simply an individual. According to Lewin's philosophy of science, a change in a part brought change throughout the entire group analogous to the change witnessed in physics when observing the electrical or magnetic field. This also implies a tendency for any action to be balanced by a counteraction.

Our consideration is not so much *why* groups form (as it was in Chapter 6) as *how* groups form. Some groups have no choice, such as family groups. Other groups, such as most working groups, have little choice. They also vary in degree of cooperation. At the other extreme from the athletic team, I can think of the days I spent working on the docks as a longshoreman. We showed up at 7:00 A.M. for the first shift. The boss read off the names of those he wanted and the rest of us waited until 8:00 A.M. for the next shift. At 9:00 A.M. there was another reading. We never knew whom we would be working with or, indeed, if we would work that day. At that time the pay was about the highest per hour in North America for manual workers, but we never knew from day to day whether or not we would work and how many hours we would get. Cooperation was so low and competition so high, in contrast with the athletic teams, that I can remember watching with two friends the stub of a cigarette burning off half the lower trouser leg of a foreman who had thrown it unknowingly into his own pants cuff; none of us were gentlemanly enough to point it out to him although we all enjoyed watching it work slowly and cruelly.

How many work groups secretly or overtly relish the agony and frustration of their supervisor or manager as we did as against those who, like the hockey or football team, suffer the depth of each agony with him?

People sit in the classroom together or ride the elevator together and even share the same office, but what is it that makes them feel they are part of the same group? We can be physically close to other people yet feel no affiliation to them. I can recall another day in the shipyards when we were carrying out minor repairs on a naval ship. Her full crew was still aboard. It was a big day because Prince Philip, Duke of Edinburgh, was visiting the port. As his ship came cruising into the harbor every naval ship afloat was decked out in its finery. Every bridge was loaded with brass and ribbons. Each crew was lined up smartly like wooden toys. Bos'n pipes whistled, bands played. We civilians sat down out of the way and opened our lunchboxes to enjoy the show during our coffee break. At a given signal, a young seaman started running along the deck from midships aft pulling the end of the line that would string the bunting the entire length of the ship and spell out the appropriate nautical greeting to the prince. On every ship in the bay the bunting went up smoothly and smartly. Not on ours. As the young seaman raced past us a few yards his foot tangled in the ropes and he went head over heels in a snarl. The bunting hung loose and ludicrously like a broken spider web. The air on the bridge turned blue as it became obvious that there was a direct ratio between the amount of brass one wore and the loudness of voice and the most practiced obscenities. Down on the deck the junior officers took up the scream in their younger voices, one young looie being less than fifteen feet from the seaman who, now in a complete state of panic, looked like a ball of twine gone crazy. We sat only a few feet away and calmly slurped our coffee out of the thermos tops. The young fellow's mates stood not too far off still looking like wooden toys. The officers increased the pitch and speed of their obscenities. The bunting flapped foolishly in the breeze fouling itself even more grotesquely to spell out some undecipherable message. No one moved. The only movements were the twitches on the skipper's face, the screaming jaws of the officers, the barely discernible side glances of the seamen, the calm deck-to-mouth movements of our thermos cups, the derisive swinging of the bunting, and the poor ball of twine flapping like a dying fish on the deck. What a contrast to the athletic team! One man tumbles on the ice during the hockey game and reflexively another is doing two jobs doubling for him. Just as we had sat calmly watching the foreman's trouser leg burn, here we sat watching the seaman's agony, sympathizing with him but rather enjoying the consternation of the brass.

Why is it that people prefer to help, work with, enjoy the company of, be in the same group as—or reject, refuse to help, sabotage—others?

Some years ago Jacob Moreno[7] developed the sociometric test as a means of obtaining quantitative data on the preference of group members for associating with other group members. The technique has since been employed in many theoretical and practical researches.

SOCIOMETRY

What we observe regularly in any group is that each individual tends to choose certain persons and ignore others. These choices are based, in part, on liking or *positive affect* toward the other person. This liking for persons and their reciprocal feelings toward us are among the most important aspects of social life. They influence all the dynamics of the group and form the basis for the group's very existence. Feelings of positive affect lead to increased association and thus contribute to shaping all forms of group and social behavior. The very formation of groups is based on the attraction people have to one another for whatever reason. Even in the large and highly formalized organization a pattern of positive and negative affect influences who associates with whom, what the communication pattern will be, who has status and power, how conflict will be resolved, and whether the formal leaders will get the cooperation or noncooperation of their subordinates.

The patterns of attraction which we observe during the group's interaction are called the *affect structure*. It is these we wish to examine in terms of a *sociometric structure*. Basically, any sociometric test is a means of getting information on the liking preferences of group members. When administered as a formal test, care is normally taken to ensure the privacy of the individual's choices. Typically, the test asks a few specific questions such as "Who do you prefer to work with in this group?", "Who do you prefer not to work with in this group?", "Who do you like in this group?", "Who do you not like in this group?" Depending on the nature of the specific sociometric structure being examined, the questions may be, "Who would you prefer as your leader out of this group's members?", "Who would you prefer as a partner on job x?", "Who would you prefer to study with (travel with, share an office with, etc.)?" Since Moreno's first proposals, many different procedures have been developed for determining sociometric choices and rejections. Sometimes an unlimited number may be chosen; at other times the number is specified (it may be only one). Variations ask the chooser to guess who will choose him in return. It may not be obvious at first glance but, depending on what the person is choos-

---

[1] J. L. Moreno, *Who Shall Survive?*, 2nd ed. (Beacon, N.Y.: Beacon House Inc., 1953).

ing for, his choices often differ. Also remember that the sociometric test measures the *desired* association rather than the *actual* association.

The results of a sociometric test can be described in a number of ways. Perhaps the best known is the *sociogram*. The sociogram in Figure 11-1 might be typical of a small work group with the solid arrows representing choices and the broken arrows representing rejections.

FIGURE 11-1

SOCIOGRAM OF A SMALL OFFICE GROUP

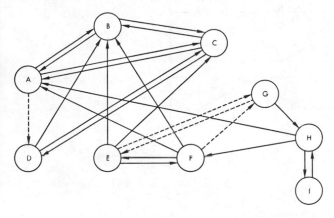

Here we can see that persons A, B, and C are the focus of many solid lines. The highly chosen or "overchosen" (in the sense that more than the average number of choices go to them) members of the group are called the sociometric *stars*. Other persons such as G are relative *isolates*, chosen by no one and possibly disliked or distinctly not chosen by some group members. Isolates usually choose few people themselves. In this particular sociogram there is a mutual dislike between E and G. A, B, and C form a distinct subgroup or *clique* in this sociogram with D, E, and F aspiring to clique membership.* Cleavages between subgroups are usually represented by the distance of lines between them. Here, within the total group of nine, the readily identifiable subgroups are (A, B, C), (A, B, C, D, E, F), (E, F), (G, H, I), and (H, I).

One can see that a sociogram of a much larger group would be a cumbersome thing and difficult to interpret at first glance. This would be

* The terms clique and cabal are sometimes used in another sense with *clique* having the implication of older malcontents who turn inward toward themselves as they foresee little hope of further advance within the organization; *cabal* implies an upwardly mobile group attempting to expand the interests of its members and to "capture" influential organizational members to its membership.

particularly true if group members were allowed a large number of choices. The information in figure 11-1 could also be cast in a *sociometric matrix* as in Figure 11-2.

FIGURE 11-2

SOCIOMETRIC MATRIX OF A SMALL OFFICE GROUP

	A	B	C	D	E	F	G	H	I
A		1	1	-1					
B	1		1						
C	1	1		1					
D		1	1						
E		1	1			1	-1		
F	1	1			1		-1		
G				-1				1	
H	1					1			1
I								1	

The rows across indicate who each person chooses (or rejects with a -1) and the columns down indicate who chose or rejected each person. The stars and isolates are easily discernible in such a matrix even for larger groups.

Another technique useful for some purposes is *index analysis*. For example, the choice status (*CS*) for each group member can be worked out in index form by indicating the number of persons choosing him divided by the total number (*N*) of possible choices for him. The formula would be:

$$CS = \frac{\text{number of persons choosing}}{N - 1}$$

The index for each person could be worked out with a range from a maximum of one to a minimum of zero. Thus in Figures 11-1 and 11-2 the index for A would be $CS = .50$; for B it would be $CS = .625$; for I it would be $CS = .125$; for G it would be $CS = 0$ (or $-.25$).

If the major interest is in the structure of the group rather than in the individual members, another type of index can then be employed such as the *cohesiveness index*. This is determined by dividing the number of possible mutual pairs in the group into the number of actual mutual pairs.

$$\text{Cohesiveness} = \frac{\text{number of mutual pairs}}{\text{number of possible mutual pairs}}$$

Again, in Figure 11-1 and 11-2 we find the index is .167.

Our sociogram represents a fairly normal office group with a clique of high status members, its side group of low status members, and one person who is an isolate. Unless G is a rather extraordinary person the prediction would be that he will not last in this office. As the sociogram represents a true group, you may know that G started off well in this group but his unrealistic ambitions put him into direct rivalry with E; after about six months he transferred to another section with the blessing of almost everyone in the office.

The value of sociometric techniques is that they give some specific measurement of group cohesiveness, enable one to discover natural leaders (such as local opinion leaders), pinpoint problem members of the group (often isolates turn up to be inadequate persons in need of psychological help), and determine natural communication nets.

A number of studies have made use of sociometric techniques in designing work, training, and military groups. A study of construction workers by Van Zelst [2] is an example. Here carpenters and bricklayers were given the opportunity to indicate their first, second, and third choices for preferred teammates rather than the somewhat arbitrary assignment by foremen. Noticeable improvement in turnover, material costs, and labor costs for housing units resulted.

Sociometric techniques can be used for a number of purposes. Obviously, the privacy of the individuals who are asked to make choices must be ensured and the information obtained must be used judiciously; otherwise, one may encounter lack of cooperation and other problems.

THE REASONS FOR CHOICE

A number of psychologists have concerned themselves with why some persons are overchosen sociometric stars while others are underchosen isolates. Some have tried to identify the personal characteristics of those with high choice status and those with low choice status. A number of tendencies affect the pattern of sociometric choice in the group.

First, persons tend to choose those with whom they have the most chance to interact. Sheer physical distance is a factor here. It is easier to interact with someone at *this* end of the office than with someone at *that* end of the office and hence easier to choose him (or it is easier to choose him and hence easier to interact with him?). This may not be the sole factor but it is influential. In one case with which I was familiar—I made recommendations which were not heeded—poor communication patterns and relationships existed through a succession of office incumbents in the

[2] R. H. Van Zelst, "An Interpersonal Relations Technique for Industry," *Personnel*, American Management Association, 7 (1952), pp. 68–77.

relevant offices, while in an identical branch there was a succession of good relationships. These are diagrammed in Figure 11-3.

In Figure 11-3A the working relationship between first-in-charge and second-in-charge were always good (so was the relationship between their secretaries). In Figure 11-3B the relationship of first-in-charge and second-in-charge was always one of complaining about "not keeping me informed." This was true over a succession of two incumbents in both offices. In

FIGURE 11-3

PHYSICAL DISTANCE EFFECTS INTERACTION

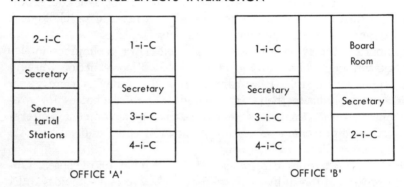

OFFICE 'A'   OFFICE 'B'

office *B* for both incumbents there were always snide remarks about the relationship between the number one manager and his secretary and the secretary herself was always considered by the rest of the office staff as overbearing. These remarks were probably not justified on objective grounds. Although other factors could certainly have been involved, sociometric choice favors interaction and choice between the two senior managers in office *A* but does not favor it in office *B* unless other factors are stronger.

There is a string of studies demonstrating that physical nearness favors mate selection, alphabetical order of surnames favors choice among students, common domicile favors friendship selection, and people who live near doorways and elevators in apartment blocks are sociometric stars while those at the ends of corridors are sociometric isolates among inhabitants of those apartment blocks.

A second trend is to choose those considered as having characteristics which are desirable according to the norms and values of the group. Thus brighter people choose others who are bright, religious people choose those who are religious, pretty girls are overchosen by both boys and girls because prettiness is valued, and so on. Those who adhere to the norms and standards of behavior which best typify the group's behavior are overchosen among student groups and working groups. Even those who reflect the dominant trends in political and economic issues are most chosen.

A third general trend is that we choose others who are similar to ourselves. Many studies have demonstrated a strong preference for those with similar personality characteristics, attitudes, value systems, and social background characteristics. This is true even for children. Religious belief, ethnic group membership, racial membership, socioeconomic status, and background experience all seem to influence choice.

Finally, on analyzing sociometric choices, we notice a strong tendency to select those who mutually choose oneself. A causal sequence involves the perception that one is liked by another person which results in choosing that person. This indicates that choice cannot be considered on its own but must be seen as a two-way effect in which the liking of another influences that person's liking. This is related to the fact that we choose those whom we believe perceive us in a favorable manner or whom we believe see us somewhat as we see ourselves—in short, persons in whose company we achieve some basic satisfaction of our needs.

This book stresses the fact that behavior can be better understood as interaction rather than in terms of acts of an individual person. To make the point in this context of choosing and attractiveness, let me tell what happened among a group of graduate students some years ago. Having studied the basic principles of choice, attractiveness, and perception, they decided to try an informal experiment. Unknown to the "victim," five male graduate students decided to use a rather average-looking and shy female student as their subject. Systematically, they approached her for dates. When one had dated her, another would call up the next day and ask for a date on the same night. They tried to get her to break her dates with the other students. When one took her to a dance, others would cut in on the dance floor. When one took her to a party, others would try to talk her into abandoning her date and going home with them. This "game" continued for several months. Finally, the students had to abandon their project; this mousy little girl had become such a popular student on campus that it was virtually impossible to get a date with her because of outside competition!

We are left with the old philosophical conundrum: Which came first —the chicken or the egg? Or, Which comes first—one is chosen because he is attractive or one is attractive because he is chosen? The question is too complex for an either-or answer.

EXCHANGE THEORY

The empirical evidence that "birds of a feather flock together" is quite substantial. Similarity in attitudes acts like a magnet to draw people together. Once together for some time, they begin to become dependent upon one another (or they are dependent upon one another so they interact—it does not matter, only that the dependence begins to increase) for information about the world around themselves. What we all need from other people is information about how fitting or proper or just or correct or right any thought, action, feeling, thing, person is in terms of our pre-existing cognitive and attitude systems. When we interact with someone whose attitudes are at variance with ours, there is a constant potential strain about which one of us sees the world correctly (it is rarely the other fellow). On the other hand, when we interact with someone of similar attitudes, not only is the danger of contradiction and strain reduced but there is a constant feedback from him to indicate that the way we see the world is the correct and best way. This is called *consensual validation* and this consensus of opinion we receive from others is perhaps the most powerful of social motives. Without it we would not likely be able to retain our sanity and our grasp on reality; the world would become an anxiety-producing, completely unpredictable, chaotic, and terrifying place.

The greater the importance of the common attitude and the more relevant, all-pervasive, and directly related to the consequences of their behavior it is to the persons involved, the stronger will be their attraction to one another.

In discussing exchange theory, our emphasis is on the interaction rather than the personal characteristics of those who interact. We shall use the most simple group, the *dyad*, or group of two persons, as our example to explain the theory. This dyad or two-person group forms the basis for all groupings. The theory will involve the rewards exchanged and the costs incurred when the two persons interact.

There are four basic terms employed in the exchange theory:

First, *reward*. This is an elementary psychological term implying the satisfaction or payment or reinforcement that a person or animal receives for carrying out some behavior. The implication is that the more rewarded the behavior is, the more the person likes to do it (this is the Law of Effect which we shall have more to say about in Chapter 18). We have already seen that such things as consensual validation are rewarding. In this sense the reward can be considered the incentive that makes a person persist in his behavior. In exchange theory, reward can refer to any thing or activity of one person which contributes to the gratification of another person. Thus a raise in pay, a promotion in status, a letter of recommendation, the opportunity to work in peace and happiness, help in overcoming anxiety, the chance for self-improvement, a word on one's behalf to the right person, willingness to help out or listen to a person's problems, even a smile and a friendly handshake can be considered rewards.

The second term is *costs*. This has broad reference to anything which is the opposite of rewarding. It would include all those things which could

be considered punishing as well as the carrying out of behaviors less rewarding than possible alternative behaviors. Reprimand and demotion
are obvious costs. Less obvious are crabby supervisors and fellow workers,
lack of freedom to discuss one's feelings, noisy or otherwise undesirable
working conditions, providing service to an angry customer, being asked
to do work beneath one's accepted organizational status, and having to
work while the rest of the group is having coffee break.

Outcome is the third term. It refers to rewards less costs. If the outcome of an interaction is positive, it is called a *profit;* if it is negative, a
loss. Many interactions involve both a profit and a loss simultaneously.
For example, I may be enjoying a delightful conversation with someone
I like but at the same time realize that I am getting behind in important
work which must be done in the very near future. For attraction to take
place the interaction must either yield a profit or:

Fourth, the outcome of the interaction must be above some level of
minimal expectation or *comparison level.* A comparison level is influenced
by past experience with this type of interaction and its outcome, the experiences of similar interactions, the estimate of what others receive as
outcomes in similar interactions, and the outcomes available if one were to
engage in alternative relationships with other persons.

Using these concepts of exchange, we can then observe what makes a
member of the group overchosen. The sociometric star is a person who
facilitates rewarding interaction for a number of others. Studies demonstrate that he helps others, protects others, prevents them from receiving
costs or reduces their costs, and increases the value of rewards of those
who interact with him. The star is a type of leader and he contributes to a
positive group atmosphere through various means. Each overchosen person
broadens the opportunity for others (and indirectly for himself) to participate in potential group interaction by pulling others into group activities, introducing new ideas and behaviors, helping members to be tolerant
of one another. Often, such stars feel uncomfortable when other members
are unhappy or left out of activities.

Another characteristic of the overchosen is his personal stability and
ability to control moodiness, depression, or anxiety. Those interacting with
him do not incur his costs. He rarely confides his personal problems and
worries to others, except to a select friend. Others have no fear of costly
interaction by picking up his troubles. He appears able to establish quick
and effective understanding with a wide range of different types of personalities, being able to identify with them and comprehend their feelings. They
put confidence in him and he can speak for them or act on their behalf.

Several studies confirm this picture of the overchosen as a person with
the traits required to increase rewards and decrease costs to others. Consistent with the idea of exchange, the sociometric isolate and the rejected

person tend to be domineering, belligerent, and inconsiderate, raising the cost to other people in interacting with them.

These characteristics of the overchosen and the rejected person tend to be carried with them from group to group. This accounts for the relative consistency in choosing them throughout groups. Nonetheless, we must keep in mind that some modification of choice may result from the special characteristics of other group members, the general characteristics of the group as a whole, and the special situation in which the group interaction is taking place.

In his readings and use of sociometry, the manager should keep in mind a distinction made by Jennings [3] between psychegroup and sociogroup. The *psychegroup* uses some criterion of leisure time as the basis for its choice. It is composed of those people with whom the person would like to go to a party or picnic, to a movie, to play cards with, and so on. Generally, persons chosen for such groups satisfy the chooser's social-emotional needs, provide consensual validation about the world, and reciprocate the choice. Psychegroups have a sociometric structure indicating fewer but mutually reciprocated choices. The *sociogroup* is a working-to-gether or living-together group. Choice is more on the basis of the person's role in the group, conformity to group standards, and contribution to smooth interaction. Mutual choices in this type of group are much less noticeable as choice tends to concentrate on those sociometric stars whose role is important in fulfilling the group purpose.

FORMATION OF THE DYAD

To profit from this book from now on, I would like to see each student and reader begin to become more self-conscious of his interaction with other people in terms of exchange. Not that he should be cynical about attractiveness and rejection, nor become so cold and analytical that he loses his human spontaneity, but, rather, that he become a practicing student of the objective observation of interacting people. This can become for him a valuable tool in effective management. Before starting to "analyze" too finely the behavior of immediate associates, it might be better to practice by watching people in subways, at cocktail parties (an excellent location for observing social interaction), in bars, and so on.

Two cautions are necessary. (1) Do not play God. The very best social psychologist would be very reluctant to make firm judgments on people during "field observation." Field observation is the type of study involving natural observation as against experimental observation wherein

---

[3] Helen H. Jennings, *Leadership and Isolation,* 2nd ed. (New York: Longmans, Green & Co. Ltd., 1950).

it is possible to control the personal background and environmental variables of the observed subject. In field observation there are too many un-
controlled, unknown, and uncontrollable variables. (2) For the sake of your
own personality development, let me tell you a little story from my own
experience: When I was a graduate student, I observed at first hand one
of my friends go through a rather interesting stage of development. He was
involved in the study of personality and of clinical psychology. He started
to read the works of Sigmund Freud, the founder of psychoanalysis. A
bright student, he soon mastered the concepts and jargon of Freud. He
grew a goatee and mustache as Freud had worn, changed his glasses for
some with frames like Freud wore, and ceased to speak the Queen's
English, substituting for it "pure psychoanalytic Freudian." Nothing that we
did, said, gestured, wrote, or did *not* do missed his gaze and his psychoanalytic interpretation. In a short time he was universally considered a
"screwball" and became a sociometric isolate ignored by all and taken
seriously by no one. Fortunately, a series of traumatic incidents helped
him pass through this rather childish stage and he later rejoined the ranks
of the normal. I would imagine that the same type of compulsion could
seize someone who saw social interaction solely in terms of exchange theory
—with similar unfortunate consequences.

A number of factors contribute to the initiation and subsequent
strengthening of the dyad. First, there is the necessary physical propinquity
which provides the initial opportunity to meet and the frequency to meet.
If you ride in the elevator with the same person every morning over a
long enough period of time, this physical fact increases your opportunity
to speak to him, get to know his name, and even become good friends,
even if the final friendship relation takes several years to form. As George
Homans, a famous proponent of exchange theory, once stated, "You can get
to like some pretty queer customers if you go around with them long
enough." Every adolescent lover aspiring for a happy relationship with the
beautiful young thing on the next block knows that if he walks past her
house enough times, the opportunity to see her, be seen by her, meet her,
learn her name, date her, be loved by her, and marry her will be increased.
Unfortunately for him, the physical propinquity involved is not as advan-
tageous as working in the same office, sitting in the same classroom, or riding the same elevator.

Second, we notice that people who are physically close often have
more similarities than those who are physically distant. Living in the same
neighborhood often indicates the same socioeconomic background, as does
attending university (even the specific faculty of attendance is indicative
of socioeconomic status and major interests), or doing the same or similar
type of work in the same type of organization. Sometimes ethnic and religious affiliations are also tied in with neighborhood of residence and occupa-

tion. Eating in the same restaurant or cafeteria or carrying lunch to work and eating it in the same park also increases likelihood of similar background while increasing the possibility of meeting.

A third obvious way of increasing attraction through interaction is the result of the communication following this interaction. This involves the direct and indirect exchange about one another which, in turn, increases the degree to which persons might be known to be similar and hence become attractive to one another. The very fact that the personnel office has put groups together often influences the formation of very strong friendship and other sociometric ties.

Fourth, as two people continue to interact with one another, they become better able to predict one another's behavior. This results in increased rewards and decreased costs throughout their interaction with the greater likelihood of a profit outcome for both. When the other person's behavior can be predicted, it is easier to prevent him from receiving costs and it becomes less costly to provide him with rewards. The same is true vice versa. The possibility of a mutual profit outcome above some expected minimum increases attractiveness.

Finally, interacting with people who are physically closer in terms of time and effort, rather than with those who are physically distant, increases the likelihood of further interaction. The barbershop, dental clinic, coffeeshop, and corner bar which are closest stand a better chance of getting our business than those farther away. When there is an architectural firm in the same building, it is easier to use it than another one on the far side of town.

THE SEQUENCE OF DYAD FORMATION

If we were to examine the sequence of events leading from nonchoice to fullest choice, we might see something like this: Suppose there was a national convention of paper clip producers and John Jones from the West Coast was there for his firm while Bill Brown from the East was there representing his company. After a few speeches and discussions of mutual interest, there is an adjournment for coffee break. John knows few people at the convention on other than a casual basis. When he picks up his coffee and turns around, he notices that everyone is breaking up into little informal conversational knots, shaking hands, laughing, renewing acquaintancs. The person to his left is shaking hands with an old friend, the person to his right has his head turned to converse with someone else. John steps away from the coffee table and quickly observes that almost everyone is engaged in conversational groups.

He steps into one small group, introduces himself, and *samples* their discussion. It is not particularly interesting to him; they are talking about football and he prefers to talk business. He is soon on the periphery of the conversation but keeps his eye open to make *estimations* of what other groups he might join which could yield a higher profit than this one. He sees one person standing alone at the far end of the room; he looks like an attractive person but, if he were to leave his present group and walk all the way to the other end of the room, that person might go somewhere else or be joined in conversation with an intimate friend by the time he got there. Thus physical distance rules him out for sociometric choice. Also, the potential cost of having to break into a new conversational circle rules against this choice.

Now he notices another single person just leaving the coffee table, apparently also looking for conversation. He is close. John breaks away and introduces himself to this stranger who turns out to be Bill Brown. His face is familiar and John recalls that he spoke from the floor during the morning's discussion. "That was a good point you made this morning," he says (in fact, he cannot recall the point but he is trying to facilitate interaction by giving Bill a reward). According to the etiquette of social interaction, Bill should acknowledge receipt of this unsolicited profit by refraining from giving John costs and endeavoring to give him a reward in exchange. He should not ask, "What point was that?", for instance, for this might be embarrassing for John (a cost exchanged for a reward). "Ah, you mean my reference to competition from staplers?" Now John remembers and they engage in discussion, providing each other with rewards when possible and avoiding costly disagreement. After the first polite exchanges, both parties attempt to discover what they have in common through direct signs given and signs given off: where do they come from, what organization, their organizational rank, whether they know so-and-so, what is each organization's approach to the latest developments. Depending on the strength of the need for interaction each will disclose more or less information. Weighing the costs and rewards, making estimates about future interaction relative to future alternatives, both John and Bill enter an interaction phase referred to as *bargaining* (although both probably remain quite unaware of the actual process). Each is behaving in such a way as to motivate the other to produce rewarding behavior. Such bargaining usually involves types of strategies which make the other person perceive that he is receiving much and can expect much more for having offered very little. John may be more interested in one aspect of the business than Bill and while he talks about it Bill exaggerates slightly his interest in that specific aspect. This involves little cost on Bill's part yet may result in the receipt of later rewards from John. The strategy also involves giving progressively greater rewards to the other which prompts progressively greater returns, accompanied by mutual attempts to reduce costs.

If Bill and John receive a satisfactory exchange, they will cease sampling and estimating the possible interactions they might have with others and make a *commitment* like "Let's have lunch together and discuss this matter further." A possible long-range result of their interaction may result in the public *institutionalization* of their relationship by means of a business agreement between John's west coast firm and Bill's eastern firm about data, markets, and products.

I have oversimplified the exchange between John and Bill to illustrate the sampling-estimation-bargaining-commitment-institutionalization process. Many exchanges never reach the final stage of institutionalization although all partnerships, legal agreements, trading agreements, and employment of consultants are as much institutionalization as is the exchange of marriage vows. Obviously, the entire process tends to take a much longer time than implied in our example. Also, it must be kept in mind that the entire process is usually below the threshold of the participants' awareness. People who enter the bargaining phase coldly and calculatingly will probably not be found too attractive for friendship relation and, unless the expectation of a good business profit is perceived, the other party may continue the sampling and estimation elsewhere. One highly rejected aspect of interaction is the perception and thought that one is being used by another or being taken for a ride. Only those with strange psychological twists to their personality allow themselves to be used by others.

CHANGES IN THE DYADIC RELATIONSHIP

We can never consider the relationship between two people as static. Consequently, the group and the organization are never static. This is why we are interested in group dynamics with its implication of constant change. I often think of the group or the organization as I would a piece of my mother's bread dough: while it is working the superficial changes are gradual and slight but one is ever aware of the microscopic chains of restless activity beneath the surface.

These changes in the basic dyads of the organization come from a number of sources. First, they may simply be a function of the exchange. In some European countries it is customary for business partners, friends, and colleagues in the same office to greet each other with a handshake on arrival at work in the morning and again after lunch. After a few years the exchange, which may have had an original high reward, has become a perfunctory ritual, yet to omit it without good reason would risk giving the colleague an undeserved cost and so it continues ad infinitum. Although the North American and British ritual is not so elaborate it is comparable. Any type of reward produced for another person may become increasingly costly because of the loss of alternative rewards, embarrassment, or simple fatigue; at the same time the value of rewards recieved may diminish because the needs of the person receiving them become satiated. Also, as a result of long-term interaction, a more effective and less costly reward may be produced. The good assistant or secretary can anticipate the needs of the one he assists thus providing rewards at reduced costs to both.

Second, we may see shifts in characteristics of members of the dyad. As a result of experience, new attitudes, new ambitions, and promotions, new needs emerge and new goals are acquired. An anticipated or confirmed promotion changes the relationship with colleagues and former supervisors. In a growing organization the frequency of such changes brings a constant reshuffling of dyadic relationships within the total membership.

A third change can result from sources outside of the dyad. A new colleague joining the organization, who has more in common with some people than older interactors, may upset a series of regular dyads.

Fourth, neutral behaviors associated with rewarding behaviors may take on new cost-reward values. Take a case of two friendly colleagues A and B. Because they met and worked in the same office together they eventually ended up being good friends. One day A introduced B to another friend, C. B was not particularly drawn to C but because C was A's friend, B interacted with him and was pleasant to him (if B had not been friendly to C, this would have been costly to B's friend A). But over the months C has become a very good friend of B. Indeed, because of the profitable interaction B and C have enjoyed, B would now choose C over A.

Another thing to remember is that, although cost and reward may remain relatively the same, the affect choice may change because of changes taking place over time in the comparison level. A rise in comparison level sometimes takes place as the initial glow of the early stages of a relationship settle onto an even keel. One often witnesses the exuberant glow of affect exchange between the manager and his new assistant, the boss and his new secretary, the foreman and his new tradesman. After a few days the affect subsides to a normal friendly relationship.

Although it may appear that affect choice always involves positive attraction one to another, this is not necessarily the case. The loveless marriage is an example of this. The married couple may receive very low satisfaction from their continued interaction, so low that it would not result in a positive attraction. Yet they maintain the relationship because they know that the alternatives available would result in even less rewards or even greater costs. Guilt, stigma of divorce or separation, fear of loneliness, financial costs, and so on may raise the *comparison level for alternatives* so high that neither partner wishes to terminate the relationship. The same thing certainly happens in employer-employee, teacher-student, doctor-patient, customer-supplier relationships; the potential consequences of terminating the relationship are too risky.

In one sense the final structure of a group always involves a series of compromises. Group structure moves toward an equilibrium in which each person's position in the affect structure is the best he can obtain in terms of cost-reward outcomes. This means a tendency toward mutuality in choice and the choice of those who are of equal status with oneself. To perceive that the person one likes does not reciprocate the liking produces some strain on both parties which can be reduced by decreasing one's affect toward the person chosen. When choice is based on personality likeness, each partner will have similar ways of expressing and receiving affect which will facilitate mutual satisfaction.

The final form of group cohesiveness depends on the extent to which members find a reward-cost outcome exceeding their comparison level. The rewards can come from three major sources: the interaction of the group (cooperative and friendly); rewarding activities (exciting research team); membership achieves further desired goals (status among nongroup members).

If such outcomes or their possibility exceed a comparison level of what might have been available in alternative relations outside the group, the group will remain cohesive. Because of this, even those low-status and underprivileged groups characterized by low pay, poor working conditions, and little opportunity for personal improvement can remain highly cohesive. Such a comparison level for alternatives outside the group can be the result of low-level outcomes previously experienced, perception of what other persons like oneself receive as outcomes, as well as the perception of even lower quality outcomes in alternative relations. Certainly, one witnesses low-status work groups of great camaraderie, loyalty, and cohesiveness (e.g., garbage workers).

INTERACTION PROCESS ANALYSIS

Another technique used to analyze interaction of group members is interaction process analysis, developed by Robert Bales.[4] It requires an observer to watch the group in action and classify their individual activities into separate categories. It differs from sociometry in that people do not have to be asked anything because their actual behaviors are observed and recorded. Bales developed his system so that it could be used to study *any* group, regardless of its purpose, background, and membership. The categories he devised are meant to be mutually exclusive and logically exhaustive systems—that is, the observed behavior of a group member can be put into only one category, and all his behaviors can be put into one of the twelve categories provided. Table 11-1 summarizes these categories.

[4] R. F. Bales, "Some Uniformities of Behavior in Small Social Systems," in *Readings in Social Psychology*, eds. S. E. Swanson, T. M. Newcomb, and E. L. Hartley (New York: Henry Holt, 1952).

The System of Twelve Categories covers all the group's possible behaviors. The observer records each unit of behavior in one category.

TABLE 11-1

Human-Relations Positive	1. *Shows solidarity,* helps, rewards, raises other's status 2. *Shows tension release,* jokes, laughs, shows satisfaction 3. *Agrees,* shows passive acceptance, understands, concurs, complies
Task Area Positive	4. *Gives suggestion,* direction, implying autonomy for others 5. *Gives opinion,* evaluation, analysis, expresses feeling, wish 6. *Gives orientation,* information, repeats, clarifies, confirms
Task Area Negative	7. *Asks for orientation,* information, repetition, confirmation 8. *Asks for opinion,* evaluation, analysis, expression of feeling 9. *Asks for suggestion,* direction, possible ways of action
Human-Relations Negative	10. *Disagrees,* shows passive rejection, formality, withholds help 11. *Shows tension,* asks for help, withdraws out of field 12. *Shows antagonism,* deflates other's status, defends or asserts self

Using this technique, an observer puts every segment of verbal or nonverbal behavior into one category. For example, a simple sentence would be a unit, but a complex sentence may represent more than one unit. Nonverbal behaviors are usually scored at one-minute intervals.

Bales provides us with an example of his technique used while observing a budget meeting. The chairman is coded 1, the members in order around the table are 2, 3, 4, and 5 while the group as a whole is coded 0. The chairman says, "Well we have ———; what do you think we should do about this piece of equipment?" This is scored by the observer as 1-0 in category 9 (the chairman addresses a problem-solving question asking the entire group for suggestion). Member 2 says, "I think we should get it." This is scored 2-0 in category 4 (member 2 answers a problem-solving question by making a suggestion to the entire group). While member 2 is giving his supporting reasons, member 3 breaks in with a counterargument and soon the discussion gets heated. Meanwhile, member 5 who has said very little appears quite bored and the observer gives him a score under category 11 (withdraws out of the field). While this is happening member 3, in the heat of the argument, directs a humorous but antagonistic remark at member 2 and the others laugh. The observer scores this under category 12 (antagonism) and category 2 (jokes, tension release).

As the meeting goes on and the various interactions are recorded, it soon becomes apparent what kind of a group is operating. The total number of acts of the group can be computed and plotted on a graph showing the relative frequency of the twelve types of group interaction. Reducing these to a percentage of the total number of acts, any group can be compared directly on a graph or a group can be compared with itself over a series of meetings. Figure 11-4 illustrates such a comparison between two groups, a "satisfied" group and a "dissatisfied" group. We see that the satisfied group produced a higher rate of suggestions with a corresponding higher rate of agreement as against the dissatisfied group's negative responses and questions.

Average groups appear to spend about one quarter of their time on positive human relations activities (Bales categories 1, 2, 3) and about 10 percent on negative human relations activities (categories 10, 11, 12). Negative task behavior takes about 5 percent (categories 7, 8, 9) and about 50 percent of time is given to positive task behavior (categories 4, 5, 6).

Using the Bales technique, it is also possible to draw up a matrix of who-to-whom giving a picture of who speaks, for how long, and to whom.

FIGURE 11-4

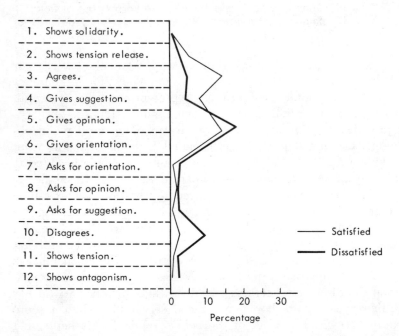

1. Shows solidarity.
2. Shows tension release.
3. Agrees.
4. Gives suggestion.
5. Gives opinion.
6. Gives orientation.
7. Asks for orientation.
8. Asks for opinion.
9. Asks for suggestion.
10. Disagrees.
11. Shows tension.
12. Shows antagonism.

——— Satisfied

——— Dissatisfied

0   10   20   30

Percentage

Profiles of a "satisfied" and a "dissatisfied" group on Bales's 12 Categories showing their major differences and similarities.

Patterns vary from group to group, depending on how formal or informal their structure and how task-oriented or human relations–oriented their purposes. Generally, each member receives back approximately one half of what he puts out, low-status persons (who usually speak least) tend to direct their words to specific individuals, while high-status persons tend to speak to the group as a whole. A *basic initiating rank* can be computed from analysis of the matrix and is found to relate both to productivity and ability to guide the group. The larger the group gets, the more tendency is there for the high-status member to do most of the talking, speaking to the group as a whole rather than to individuals, while the ordinary members do the listening and provide a climate of positive feedback.

The Bales technique has been used to study many different types of discussion groups and has been found extremely reliable and useful. Although it is relatively simple to use, an observer should have a chance to practice it and compare his findings with those of others observing the same situation. Until he has developed some degree of sophistication, too much weight should not be put on his findings.

GROUP MORALE

Membership in a group serves a function for the individual. His various wants and needs are satisfied—physiological, social, and personal. Yet different persons satisfy different needs through participating in the same group activity. One person is a member primarily because of the status it provides, another because of the money it pays, another because he finds it more interesting than other jobs available. Also, the apparent or professed reasons for being a member of the group are not always the true ones; hence the stated functions of the group are not always its true functions. We all know that membership in the Squash Club, the Canoe Club, or the Golf Club is not always intended as an outlet for one's athletic needs. Again, the purposes and needs satisfied by the group now may not be those it satisfied in the past. In Canada many veterans' organizations continue to prosper in spite of a shortage of wars and a military service which is cut almost every time the budget goes to Parliament Hill.

A number of things may mislead us in judging a group's morale.[5] The orderliness of a highly structured group such as the military platoon may be deceptive. The same may be true of the teacher's classroom and the high productivity work group or office. These may reflect high discipline rather than high morale. An orchestra can produce beautiful music under a tyrannical conductor. High productivity can be a misleading indicator of high morale for the two are not necessarily related. Finally, a lack of

[5] Joe Kelly, *Organizational Behavior* (Homewood, Ill.: Richard D. Irwin, Inc. and The Dorsey Press, Inc., 1969).

conflict in the group does not necessarily indicate high morale. Indeed, it is difficult to picture a truly effective group which does not experience some degree of conflict. Effective groups deal with conflict positively, ineffective groups are disrupted by it.

The high-morale group is held together by internal cohesiveness rather than by external pressures. Friction or disagreement is not divisive but is marked by attitudes of "We can sort this out among ourselves." Good will, cohesiveness, and adaptability to its internal changes are marks of morale. Consensus on goals and positive attitudes toward them are also common. The group is valued as a thing with its own existence; all members wish to maintain it for its own sake.

Low morale is characterized by disintegration and factioning of the group under pressure, by mutual distrust and carping criticism by members of other members. When tensions arise the group cannot resolve its problems. It lacks adaptability and cannot improvise and create when unique problems arise. Consensus about group objectives is lacking and individual aims sometimes differ from group goals. Negative attitudes toward objectives and a deficient sense of identity are also apparent. As can be expected, such groups are not long-lived.

Membership in a high-morale group offers the individual a wide range of support. If he is frustrated or threatened, the group provides him with some sense of consolation, protection, and strength to face his particular adversity. Thus, in the face of failure of a prize project or a reprimand from above, the individual can seek solace and reinvigoration from his fellow members giving him the strength and courage to continue and to try again. A supervisor of a high-morale group would find it difficult to browbeat an individual member, as contrasted with the "bossy" stand he can get away with against a worker isolated from the group.

Related to the concept of general supportiveness is the influence the group has on the psychological health of its members. A famous study of changed production techniques in British coal mines demonstrated this point well. The predicted rise in productivity resulting from the introduction of sound new engineering techniques did not take place. Instead, there was an outbreak of psychosomatic disorders on an epidemic scale. Morale dropped to a very low ebb and absenteeism, personal conflicts, and tensions increased sharply. Eventually, the major cause of the trouble was traced to the disruption of the old groups by the new technology, which prevented the socialization and collaboration formerly enjoyed by the wokers and provided them with no new substitute social arrangements to guard mental health and morale. It has also been shown in other studies that group cohesiveness lessens work-related anxieties. The more cohesive the group, the less likely are members to feel nervous or jumpy.

Studies on desertion from infantry combat groups as well as the replacement of soldiers in veteran combat groups have also demonstrated the value of a feeling of pride in one's group as a means of support when danger and anxiety are high.

Turnover and absenteeism, very costly items in running any large organization, have also been shown to relate to group cohesiveness. In themselves they are often taken as an index of morale. Research supports the hypothesis that membership in a cohesive group increases job satisfaction while reducing absenteeism and turnover. Even in the face of strong feelings of antagonism to the organization, the sense of group solidarity and belongingness prevents turnover and minimizes absenteeism.

MORALE AND PRODUCTIVITY

It used to be a fairly common error in the earlier days of the human relations movement to assume a cause-effect relationship between morale and productivity. The mistaken conclusion some drew from the Hawthorne studies was that the formation of a tightly knit group in the relay assembly test room was responsible for the steadily increasing productivity. It takes only a little reflection, though, to realize that a highly cohesive group could be fanatically dedicated to the very destruction of the organization. Industrial and commercial organizations in North America and Europe are relatively free from this type of cohesive group at the present time. University administrators, law enforcement agencies, and some other public organizations have had some recent experience of it, though. A tiny group of radicals bent on disruption can bring the whole organization to a standstill.

The Hawthorne studies drew attention to the restriction of output by group pressure to control productivity. This subject will receive the full attention it deserves in Chapter 14 but for now it is well to remember that the highly cohesive group should be considered neutral relative to actual productivity. At the same time its potential for either high produc tivity, low productivity, or disruptive activity must be recognized by the manager.

On the average, cohesive groups produce the same as groups which are not cohesive. Those which represent the extremes of high and low productivity, however, tend to be highly cohesive. But individual members of the cohesive group all tend to produce at the same level—high or low! Actual production level is influenced by other factors. Deviation from average productivity is related to the way cohesive groups perceive the larger organization as supportive which, in turn, is often interpreted from the attitudes of the supervisor. Cohesiveness is associated with higher productivity when confidence in management is high and with low productivity when this confidence is lacking.

Group pressure (to be examined later) is also implicated in morale and productivity. Coch and French [6] give us an excellent example of a worker who exceeded group productivity and was subsequently scapegoated by the other members until her output level dropped even below the group norm. When the group was broken up and the scapegoated girl remained on the same job, her productivity doubled within a few days and stabilized at that level.

The higher the cohesiveness, the more likely are members to report their job as ranking "better than most" in the organization. Cohesiveness also relates positively to number of years of service; and it generally decreases as group size increases. It is *not* related to similarity in age and educational level.

Effective cohesive groups have been described as one of three possible types of "team." First, the *natural group*, limited in number to a maximum of six or seven and resulting from the spontaneous attraction of members whose work is clearly related. Many types of such natural groups are in the complex organization because of the nature of the division of labor. Second, the *family group* which can be somewhat larger in size. It is based on the existence of a core of old hands whose long years of service and knowledge of the organization have been acquired through experience. Because of their seniority, these people can set the example (as the norm or standard) for new workers who respect their experience. Some minimal time is required for such teams to form. Third, the *organized group*, skillfully cemented together by the capable supervisor whose understanding of group dynamics enables him to integrate his unit into a cooperative team.

It is to help achieve this third type, the organized group, that this chapter has been presented. Today's manager cannot gamble on being lucky enough to stumble into a situation where the first two types of effective cohesive group exist by accident.

SUMMARY

We began and ended this chapter with a consideration of teamwork. It is possible that circumstances of the group make it behave as an effective group like the professional athletic team but the intelligent manager is not going to rely on circumstances to do his job for him. The patterns of attraction one to another which underlie the formation of the group were referred to as the group's affect structure. Within this structure we can isolate the stars or overchosen persons and the isolates or underchosen persons by means of sociometry. Sociometric tests provide us with both graphic

[6] L. Coch and J. R. P. French, "Overcoming Resistance to Change," *Human Relations*, I, (1948), 512–532.

and statistical pictures of stars, isolates, mutuality of choice, and whether or not the group is a cohesive one. Ultimately, cohesion depends on the degree of mutuality of choice among members.

We examined the basic dyadic attraction in terms of exchange theory, a concept which will underlie a good deal of what we have yet to say about group dynamics. Reward, cost, outcome (in profit or loss) and comparison level are the bases for exchange. The overchosen person is one who provides a consistent profit outcome for many people while the isolate is one who provides a minimal profit outcome for few or none.

In spite of eventual equilibrium and mutuality of choice in the stable and long-standing group, we must never forget the dynamics of change taking place during interaction. Much depends on the group itself—whether it is a psychegroup (leisure group) or a sociogroup (work group)—as to who are to be the sociometric stars.

The basic steps in the process of dyad formation were seen to be sampling-estimation-bargaining-commitment-institutionalization. Not all dyads go through all stages and those which do require the passage of considerable time. Even once institutionalized, there are possibilties for change because of changes in the cost-reward outcome or in the comparison level for alternatives. Although affect choice nearly always involves positive attraction in the first instance, it does not have to be positive to remain in existence for the alternatives of greater loss may keep the dyad or the entire group together. Inevitably, the final form of any dyad or group will involve compromise of those interacting, each obtaining the best of what he can reasonably expect from the interaction.

Interaction process analysis, the Bales system, was explained and some of its uses in comparing groups and determining who does what in the group were pointed out. It is quite simple to use, given a bit of practice, and yields a very simple profile of what is going on during the interaction.

Group morale, what it is and what it is not, was next. It is internal cohesiveness rather than external pressure which holds the group together. The high-morale group is a force for the general and mental health of its members and can usually be noticed for its low absenteeism and turnover which, in turn, are indicators of its members' health. The supportive atmosphere of the cohesive group can hold it together even when it no longer retains its primary purposes.

Our final consideration was the relationship between morale and productivity. There is no necessary causal relationship between high morale and high productivity. On the other hand, the highest producing and lowest producing groups in the organization will be among the most highly cohesive. Given the correct supportive environment and the proper supervisory attitudes, the highly cohesive group has the potential to be among the most effective in the complex organization.

12

POWER

Managers want power. Perhaps some have it but do not know how to use it. How does seeing power as a function help us understand it? What is the underlying basis of power? Are there different kinds of power? Why does it cost a powerful person to use power? What is meant by power imbalance? How can imbalance be balanced? Can power be maintained in imbalance? Does delegation of power mean loss of control?

The meaning and implication of power has been both a fascinating and mysterious topic of discussion for thousands of years. Mysterious, very largely because people have never truly understood what power is, where it comes from, and how it works. Anything on which our understanding is so ambiguous has about it the air of mystery. For example, we talk of the power of God, will power, nuclear power, the power of the sea, the power of a witch doctor, and so on. These are all difficult for us to understand on more than a superficial level. True, we all know that nuclear power involves the interaction of atomic particles but even the theoretical physicist has confronted mystery when he tries to understand nuclear power in depth.

One problem of understanding what power is and how it operates is the common tendency to regard it as a quality residing in an individual person rather than as the result of an interaction, or an exchange, between people in which the power consists of elements of their interaction. What

I shall argue here is that power is *not* a quality of a person; that it does *not* reflect the *characteristics* of a person; that it is *not* something which we perceive as belonging to a powerful person or a person with some mysterious gift of persuasion. Rather, power grows out of the interaction of people and belongs, not to the people themselves, but to the interaction.

Until recent years almost the only basic writing on power and its operation was done by Aristotle more than two thousand years ago, by Machiavelli four hundred and fifty years ago, and by Hobbes about three hundred years ago. Their concept was that a person *possessed* power and was able to force others to do his will. Machiavelli put some emphasis on the circumstances in which the power was used, but it still required possession. This idea of power has been carried forward from the days of Aristotle, Machiavelli, and Hobbes into today's thinking.

WHAT POWER IS

Every time people interact to influence the behavior of one another, then power, as understood by the psychologist, is involved in their interaction. As we all interact with others in various formal and informal groups, we can witness the *existence* of power, our attempts to exert power, and the influence attempts of others to change our behavior. The very operation of the group involves exchanges of power.

Smooth operation of any organization (and of society itself) takes place through the complex power or control processes built into that organization (or that society). At times group members are to exert power; and sometimes they are to resist it. The coordination of the whole organization toward the accomplishment of its goals requires the existence of a *power structure*. This means some formalized structure in which it is considered legitimate for one person to exercise power over other persons by sending influence attempts to them and, further, that they allow themselves to be influenced by such exercises of power. These built-in controls also allow for, even call for, the resistance of some people to influence attempts. Without a power structure the organization would become anarchistic; it would lack rules for the exertion, resistance to, and compliance with influence attempts.

Often, the controls or the power within the organization are in the hands of a relatively small number of persons. (Incidentally, this is one of the complaints of the student activists on today's campuses—that the control or the power within the university structure is concentrated in the hands of a relatively small number of persons whom they feel are not qualified to exercise it. These same students are becoming members of the professions, the working force, and the labor unions, and will be numbered among the leaders of society at the turn of the twenty-first century. We may feel the impact of their doubts about concentration of control or power in the hands of a few senior members of the organization.)

The concentration of authority or control in the hands of the relatively few can deprive the thousands of opportunity to exercise their individual initiative. This may result in labor and student unrest, apathy, disloyalty to company policies, and nine-to-fiveism; this makes it important for the manager to understand the complex operations of power.

For more than ten years, writers such as McGregor have advocated theory Y management as against theory X managemnt. In spite of the call for a more truly participative management and a more truly democratic leadership style in the contemporary organization, writers and theoreticians still express concern that power in the organization is increasingly falling into the hands of relatively few persons.

The prophets of doom fear it is only a matter of a few steps between Whyte's Organization Man and Orwell's Big Brother and from there, with the knowledge of genetics and programmed learning we have acquired in recent years, who knows what society could become by the year 2000?

POWER AS A FUNCTION

Let us try to analyze the operation of this mysterious power. Hopefully, removing some of the mystery will allow for the proper use of power to make the group or organization effective and will also allow for the resistance of power when it is misused.

We can begin by examining power in terms of the *intent* of one person to influence the behavior of, or the events controlled by, another person. This process is shown diagrammatically in Figure 12-1.

FIGURE 12-1

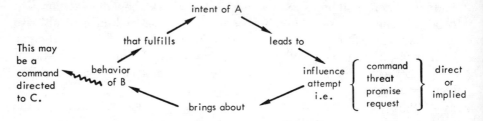

BASES OF POWER

Power as a function of people interacting involves three important variables: resources, dependencies, and alternatives.

First, *resources*. A resource is a property of an individual. It is something he owns Perhaps it is just himself or the way he behaves or the way he looks. Good looks, for instance, could be considered a resource; or brains or brawn or experience or knowledge; or being in a position to recommend someone else's promotion or to contact other people who are considered to have resources. Whatever its form, it enables the person with the resource to, in some way, determine the rewards or costs of other people interacting with him. I could determine your rewards, for instance, by allowing you to share in my knowledge or experience; I could determine your costs by making you feel uncomfortable. In these cases I use my resources to provide you either with a rewarding or a costly interaction with me.

Now the value of the resource is not determined solely by its possession, but also by how much another person has *dependency* on it. For example, a girl's relative beauty might be a resource to her in some circumstances. Under other circumstances it might not be considered a resource at all. If she were visiting an army camp, perhaps her beauty would take on great value. Among a bevy of Miss Universe contestants it would be of very little value to her. There is an old Spanish proverb which states, "In the kingdom of the blind, the man with one eye is king." We may have knowledge or experience, or good contacts, but they may not enable us to exercise power over others.

Third, power is also a function of the availability of *alternatives*. Dependent on someone's resources, we may turn to alternative persons' resources thereby reducing the power of the one on whom we were dependent. An employer, for instance, may have resources in terms of being able to offer employment but he may lack power because the employee can seek alternative employment. The threat or possibility of going over someone's head reduces his power. Of course, if there are no alternatives, the person with the resource has then increased his power over the other. If it is impossible for the employee to get alternative employment, he may have to put up with the working conditions of his present employer.

TYPES OF POWER [1]

Examining the operation of power in light of these three variables, we can see that there are a number of different types of power.

1. *Reward power*. A person has power over the other because the other perceives that the person can mediate rewards for him. That is, a person has control over things which another considers worth having. This would include any things, situations, or personal characteristics which the

[1] Adapted from J. R. P. French, Jr. and B. H. Raven, "The Bases of Social Power," in *Studies in Social Power*, ed. D. Cartwright (Ann Arbor, Mich.: The University of Michigan Press, 1959), pp. 118–149.

other might find satisfying—for example, promotions, answers to questions, recommendations, a good word with the right person, and so on.

2. *Coercive power.* With coercive power the other perceives that the person can mediate punishments for him—fire him, reprimand him, embarrass him, make him carry out unpleasant tasks, and so on. The cutting off of satisfaction to the other as controlled by the person would also be considered a punishment.

Reward power and coercive power are similar. First, they are limited. The power of a person over another does not extend beyond the limits of the reward or punishment which he can mediate for the other.

Second, it depends on what the other perceives are the probabilities the person can or will reward or punish him. The person may be very strong physically, for instance, but if the other thinks he will not strike him or exert physical strength against him, his physical strength will not generate power.

Third, the degree of power will be determined by how the other has observed the person to use his power of mediation in the past. True, the person may be able to either reward or punish, but if the other has never observed the person exercising his power in the past when it might have been expected that he would exercise it, that power is diminished. For example, the boss may say either directly or indirectly that he will fire employees who consistently come late for work. However, if other employees consistently come late to work but never get fired, the resources of the boss to influence tardiness are diminished.

3. *Referent power.* Referent power is based on identification with the person who has the resources, or the desire to be like that person. Originally, it may have been reward or coercive power but the other becomes attracted to the person and wants to identify with him. The most common example of this would be the child who, as he grows older, begins to identify with his parents, wanting to be like them. We also see examples of referent power in the organization; originally, the manager holds reward or coercive power over the employee but, with the passage of time, the employee comes to see that maybe it would be a nice thing to be a manager. He then begins to act like the manager, to wear the same clothes, to work the same hours, and so on. If the manager works after five o'clock, the employee will work after five o'clock; if the manager takes long lunch hours, the employee will take long lunch hours.

Referent power is perhaps the most extensive form of power; the person with resources may exercise power even when he is not present and even when he has no intention of influencing.

4. *Expert power.* Expert power is based on the other perceiving that the person has expert knowledge in a given situation—for example, he sees his boss is expert at solving a particular type of problem and so when that

type of problem arises he takes it to the boss and asks for assistance in solving it. When told to solve it in a certain way, he then agrees to try that solution.

5. *Legitimate power.* Legitimate power is based on agreement and commonly held values allowing one person to have power over another person. For example, one person is older than the other or has more seniority on the job or has been formally appointed or designated as group leader; hence he has the agreed right to exercise power. Here the power lies in the acceptance by the other of the underlying norms or agreements or values.

All five types of power can be understood on the basis of the relationship of resources, dependencies, and alternatives. The types of power become clearer to us if we think in terms of the exchange theory discussed in the last chapter.

POWER AND EXCHANGE

So, for instance, having reward power or coercive power allows the holder of the resource to determine the profit-or-loss outcome of the other depending on the other's alternatives.

As for referent power, the closer the other can match the behavior of the referent who is his model, the more satisfying it is. If he carries out behavior which he thinks his referent would not carry out or would not like him to carry out, he feels guilty and anxious and dissatisfied with himself, incurring a loss. With expert power, the other allows the person to influence him because the alternative of not accepting expert advice may be an error and the other may feel guilty or anxious about the possibility of making a mistake. A profit outcome is more likely to result from accepting expert advice.

Legitimate power is similar. Here the person incurs a profit from adhering to accepted standards whereas rejection of the group or organizational or social norms could mean his costly rejection by fellow members.

COST OF USING POWER

One thing to keep in mind is that it always *costs* something to use resources to influence another. True, the boss can fire the employee, but if he does so he has to hire another, which may be difficult (hence inconvenient and costly). Also, he may risk the chance of being perceived by other employees as unfair or unjust or harsh; or he may have to do a lot of explaining to his own superiors about why he found it necessary to fire an employee; or he may have to do a lot of explaining to himself about how he allowed a situation to develop in which the only way to solve the problem was to fire the employee; and so forth. The more costly it is to use a resource, the less power it holds over another person. As an extreme example, think of the jilted lover who says, "If you don't marry me, I'll commit suicide." He has a resource by which he would like to influence the loved one but to use it would be extremely costly.

The cost of using resources could be put in some order of importance. For example, it is less costly to reprimand than to fire someone; it is less costly to release someone at the end of a probation period than to release him before the end of a probation period.

If a threat is involved in an exercise of power, the power of the threat depends on whether the other thinks the person will really use the resource. Each time you allow someone "to get away with something" your power is proportionately reduced.

Even the use of expert power is costly. As the expert uses his resources to solve the problems of others, they learn better how to solve the problems and become less dependent upon him. (This is not a bad thing, as we shall see elsewhere.) Unless his expert power becomes referent power, it may decrease.

THE POWER PROCESS

Power cannot be considered as a static thing. It is part of group dynamics—an ongoing thing. Whenever it is exercised, the relationship between the user and the person influenced changes at least a little bit, and often considerably. This is what is meant by saying that power is not something which belongs to a person but, rather, is a function of interaction. As it is a function of people interacting, each person has some power over the other. And, because a person has power *relative* to another, he becomes dependent upon the other for the exercise of his power. In a sense this makes him not powerful, but dependent.

POWER BALANCE

Considering power as a process rather than as a static relationship, we can say that the power of a person over another depends on the amount of resistance the other can put up against the influence attempts by the person.[2]

If we call one person A and the other B and then examine the power relationship between A and B in terms of A's resources, B's dependencies, and B's alternatives, we can say that the power (P) of A over B is equal to the dependency (D) of B upon A, and the power of B over A is equal to the dependency of A upon B. Or:

[2] R. M. Emerson, "Power-dependence Relations," *American Sociological Review*, XXVII (1962), 31–41.

$$PAB = DBA$$
$$PBA = DAB$$

These power relationships can be considered *balanced* when A and B have equal power over and dependency upon each other. Or:

$$PAB = DBA$$
$$= \quad =$$
$$PBA = DAB$$

The relationship would be considered *unbalanced* when either A or B has more power or dependency than the other.

First, consider a balanced power relationship. In balanced power (e.g., a partnership, a friendship), each person has power over the other and each has a dependency on the other and their relationship is harmonious. There are various ways in which they can maintain the relationship balanced, keeping it stable and effective. They can, for instance, assign different values to each other's activities. In a partnership, one partner may have creative and design resources whereas the other, lacking in design resources, is a good salesman of the product designed by the first. Or, again, they may alternate the exercise of power so that each makes decisions on certain types of issues, and so on.

BALANCING IMBALANCE

But what about power in imbalance? An unbalanced power situation is unstable because it encourages the use of power by A over B. When power is used, it automatically brings about behavior designed to reduce the cost to one member thereby bringing power back into balance. We know from the last chapter that when one member constantly incurs cost in interaction there is a tendency for the relationship to be terminated at the first alternative. So if, for example, A tries to use his power to the disadvantage of B, B will then try to reduce the cost of being dependent. This he can do in a number of ways. Here are a few.

1. *Withdrawal.* If B sees his outcomes are simply not worth it, the alternative of terminating the relationship may be less costly than submitting to A's power. Of course, the very fact that he can withdraw (or threaten to) places a limit on A's use of power so that A cannot take advantage of B.

2. Forming *alternative* relationships. Here B tries to build up A's dependency on B by, for instance, forming a relationship with C. The very fact that he can interact with someone of equal or greater resources allows an employee to inhibit an employer from putting him at a disadvantage.

3. A third balancing operation involves what we call *status evaluation.*

The more powerful member of the interaction achieves status by having less powerful individuals dependent on him, and this status is a source of satisfaction.

The more he wishes to retain his status, then, the more dependency he feels upon the persons who are dependent upon him, bringing his power into balance. The manager who values his status is reluctant to use power over subordinates in such a way that his competence will be questioned because of the number of complaints, resignations, or requests for transfer from his division.

4. The formation of *coalitions* brings about balance. Forming coalitions involves the tendency on the part of the weaker members of the power interaction to form closer relationships so they can resist the power attempts of the person on whom they are dependent. Employee cliques are a common example of this, and one major aspect of the labor union reflects an attempt to reduce the power of large organizations.

5. Finally *continuous interaction* between two people produces a tendency in the direction of equality of power. Take the simple example of the boss and his secretary. The longer they interact with one another (that is to say, the longer she is his secretary) the better she gets to know him and gets to know his work and his job. This enables her either to facilitate his work or to make it difficult for him. She can distinguish people he wishes to see from those he does not wish to see; she knows the type of correspondence she can handle without reference to him; she learns where the appropriate files and information are; she becomes a buffer for him in his interaction with other people; she reminds him of appointments. Eventually, he becomes dependent on her, which leads to a harmonious power balance.

MAINTAINING IMBALANCE

Now, of course, there are situations in which we do not want balanced power. The foreman does not want to be dependent on his charge-hands, the Governor-General does not want to be dependent on his aide-de-camp, the boss does not want to be completely dependent on his secretary. Rather, they want to maintain a formal relationship that might be called having a degree of *psychological distance* between them.

What can they do to maintain this psychological distance? In fact, we find it is relatively simple to set up psychological barriers to maintain distance. An obvious barrier is pay differential. The fact that one person, having a higher salary than another person, can afford to live in a different way, eat in different restaurants, and wear different clothes, prevents them from interacting frequently off the job. Other barriers are the separate office, different washrooms, perhaps separate eating facilities, location on different floors of the building, and so on. Distinct titles also carry the implication of a different psychological status. For example, the boss can come into the office in the morning and say, "Good morning, George." But George has to say, "Good morning, *Mr.* Jones." Mr. Jones can say to George, "How are the wife and family these days, George?" But George cannot say to his boss, "How are your wife and family, Mr. Jones?"

Through these means the power structure is maintained in such a way that one person can, when he wishes, exercise authority over another. This formalization of the power structure is important for such factors as objective decision making and policy making within the organization, as when dealing with release of personnel, promotions, and assessments.

REACTING TO POWER

Because of experience in power relationships from childhood (parent-child relationships), most adults have become quite sensitive to power balance or imbalance in daily situations. People understand quite readily what the various power relationships are within their groups and they behave accordingly. There is experimental evidence to support this common observation.[3]

As people perceive power relationships readily, we might expect them to employ balancing and imbalancing operations just as readily. Common observation confirms this.

Take, for instance, the car salesman who approaches his potential customer with a beaming smile and a firm handshake. The customer has a certain amount of power over him because the salesman has a dependency upon the customer's money resources, and the customer has many alternatives in terms of where he will buy his new car. The salesman must reduce the imbalance and one way will be to try to change the salesman-buyer relationship to the appearance of a friend-friend relationship. A good car salesman tries to make his customer react to him like a lifelong friend.

On the other hand, the customer may fear that, because the salesman is a smooth and experienced talker, unless he is on guard he will pay more than necessary for a car. So he will want to maintain his power position. He may set out to play "hard to get" by feigning an air of indifference.

The salesman may try to close psychological distance toward friendship by introducing himself by his first name. The customer may attempt

[3] J. P. R. French, Jr. and R. Snyder, "Leadership and Interpersonal Power," in *Studies in Social Power,* ed. D. Cartwright (Ann Arbor, Mich.: The University of Michigan Press, 1959), pp. 150–165. G. Levinger, "The Development of Perceptions and Behavior in Newly Formed Social Power Relationships," in *Studies in Social Power,* ed. D. Cartwright (Ann Arbor, Mich.: The University of Michigan Press, 1959).

to retain psychological distance (and hence power) by disclosing only his surname, thereby forcing the salesman to address him as "Mr." or "sir" while he addresses the salesman as "Bill."

The salesman may employ a bit of subtle flattery, raising the customer's status and making him dependent on the salesman for maintaining the status. Having given the customer status, the salesman may communicate subtle hints of threatening to reduce the status or make the customer feel silly.

At the same time the customer may make frequent references to his alternatives,—the other cars he has seen advertised and their advantages over the ones he is being shown—to remind the salesman of his dependency on the customer's resources.

If power is maintained in balance, a good deal may be made and both parties will feel satisfied.

POWER AND CONTROL

Before the development of the modern organization with all its complexity and technology and means of instantaneous communication to members and nonmembers, it was often felt necessary by the organization's leaders to centralize power and control for the firm, even heavy-handed, use of a few key leaders. The technique appeared effective to them and perhaps there was some necessity for it, given other conditions within the old-fashioned organization. Concentrated control might have served the function of holding the organization together by assuring adherence to norms (see Chapter 14) and preventing role conflict (see Chapter 15) among members.

Modern developments, however, have made heavy-handed centralized control both unnecessary and ineffective. Internal communication systems, coupled with the increasing technical and general knowledge of its members, allow everyone to participate in organization affairs. Interaction among members moves in a series of unbroken circles of information output, input, and feedback; only relative concentrations of power and control are required to keep the information cycle well oiled.

Decentralization of power and control seems inevitable, given the conditions developing within the modern organization. Undoubtedly, this will be a stumbling block to those accustomed to a traditional heavy concentration in the leaders. Decentralization is even contrary to the Protestant ethic which called for firm individual effort and striving. It calls, rather, for closer, warmer, more human interaction and cooperation.

The philosopher Thomas Hobbes, writing in the seventeenth century, thought men constantly pursued power, which could be gained only at the expense of the power of others. The modern organization has no place for

Hobbesian power, "a perpetuall and restless desire of Power after power, that ceaseth onley in Death." Yet Hobbes realized power could lead to brutish and chaotic conditions and he advocated surrender to a centralized authority. Today we have moved a few steps forward and should be looking not to philosophers of the past like Hobbes but to philosophers of the future like Teilhard de Chardin who foresees the inevitable drawing together of human beings into ever closer forms of communication without loss of individual personality. The recently popular fantasy writings of Tolkien warn in *The Lord of the Rings* how the ordinary person would not be able to cope with the possession of absolute power.

With a greater understanding of power we can avoid its misuse. Hardly any issue has only two sides. To reduce problem solving to a win-lose debate between adversaries, in which the more powerful member can always force his choice, does not make for a smooth interaction and can interfere with effectiveness within the organization. Indeed, even resolution of issues by majority versus minority vote, with the combined power of one group forcing the issue against a less powerful group, can be employed only with great caution in restricted circumstances. Misuse of power can lead to the loser's reaction of "Wait till next time" or "Don't come asking me for cooperation to implement this decision."

POWER STRUCTURE

Because we can conceive of an organization as having a structure, it is easy to conceptualize a power structure following somewhat the lines of a personnel chart. Just as we can make a sociogram of affect, so we can make a diagram of the power relationships among members.

As power can be either direct or indirect, the power of A in Figure 12-2 can be considered equal in both instances.

FIGURE 12-2

INDIRECT POWER CAN BE EQUAL TO DIRECT POWER

Through connections of indirect power, it is easy to see how a "power elite" can develop within a large organization or among certain members of different organizations which have dealings with one another. Figure 12-3 represents an example of such a power elite in which we see that A, B, and C, although working for different organizations, have balanced power relationships with each other which could be based on friendship, club membership, or other common interests. The indirect power of *A, B,* and *C* could be considerable in such an instance.

FIGURE 12-3

A HYPOTHETICAL POWER ELITE

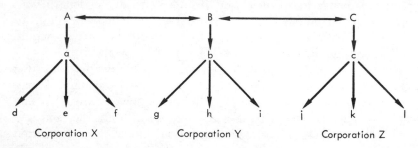

Corporation X   Corporation Y   Corporation Z

POWER BLOCS

These days it is popular to refer to certain types of social movements as power blocs. For example, there are Black Power, Red Power, student power, and many other catchy titles to indicate that large groups of persons with limited individual power have banded together into coalitions in attempts to reduce the power of those upon whom they have dependency.

Predictably, according to the model used in this chapter, it can be seen that when power is used it brings about a lack of stability in social interaction. This tends to happen in these power movements. For example, student power blocs tend to bring about a reaction on the part of education officials designed to reduce student power and retain stability.

We have seen that power cannot be considered a static relationship but a dynamic and ever changing one. Those involved in power bloc friction such as union-management strife should be seeking optimal ways to bring power into harmonious balance rather than playing the "one-upsmanship" game of trying to maintain imbalance. According to our model, if one side wins and maintains power to the disadvantage of the other side, further balancing operations are inevitable in time. The modern organization cannot afford temporary or pyrrhic victories.

SUMMARY

This brief outline of power and its operation should provide some idea of what the psychologist means by power and how he attempts to explain it. We started off by emphasizing that power is not something which exists in an individual but, rather, something which comes out of the interaction of one individual with others. It is an attempt of one individual to influence the behavior of another individual. Whether or not his attempt is successful depends on the three variables referred to as resources, dependencies, and alternatives.

Five different types of power were outlined: reward power, coercive power (these types are rather similar and both have rather severe limitations), referent power (in which the person imitated has the ability to influence the behavior of the one who imitates him), expert power, and legitimate power. It may be nice to have power, but the use of resources is always costly. Power is effective when held in balance. As soon as power is *used,* it gets out of balance and the person *against whom* the power is used automatically resorts to some activities designed to correct the power imbalance. In conclusion, there are some situations in which it is necessary for us to maintain power in a state of imbalance for the sake of organizational effectiveness.

Arguments for decentralization, based on the changing nature of the organization, were presented.

Power structures are a type of sociogram and should include indirect relationships.

Power blocs are coalitions and are governed by the same rules as the exercise of individual power.

Understanding what power is and how it operates in the organization is a resource which today's manager cannot do without if he wants to remain an expert.

13

STATUS

The objective of this chapter is to understand status as more than simply "snobbishness." What does status really involve? How do we get it? What effect does it have on our relationship to others? Why is a status structure an integral part of the organization? Is there a pecking order in the human organization? Does occupational prestige affect work? What is the typical background of various levels of occupations? Does labor suffer because it lacks status relevant to management? What is the relationship between status and communication?

The organizational world has many jokes about status and status symbols. They are excellent subjects for the magazine cartoonist's wit because each of us wants to give off signs to the world that he is a certain type of person. As we cannot go around broadcasting our personal opinion of what we think we are, we do the next best thing and set up a public symbol.

To the social psychologist, however, status means more than this. It provides the manager with another opportunity, like affect choice and power, for understanding the dynamics of the groups with which he must work.

Status is the rank we confer on a person according to our perception of him. Sometimes it is a formal rank such as "world champion," "the richest man in the world," "Nobel Prize scientist." More often, it is not formalized but is recognized by those who know as falling at some approximate point between the highest and the lowest rating for members of a specific class or category of people.

Setting ourselves the task of ranking all members of our organization in terms of their organizational status, we might be fairly clear about the top and the bottom, still relatively clear about those in senior positions, and make reasonable guesses for the middle and the rest. As a manager you might take it for granted that all members of the organization could make some sort of ranking like this. In fact, this is not the case. Few university students could adequately rank university administrators or even those of the department in which they are taking their major. I remember when working as a tradesman in the shipyards that ranks were always distinguishable by the width of the white stripe on people's hard hats. As few of us knew who the foremen or the senior brass were, other than our own foreman and a couple of the charge-hands, the general rule was, "Stop fooling around and look like you're busy if you see anyone with a wide band or a white hat."

The psychologist defines *status* as the worth of an individual as estimated by a group or class of persons. The estimation of a person's worth depends on his characteristics, qualities, possessions, position, activities, and so forth which others perceive as contributing to those values and needs shared by members of the group or category of persons. What these specific things are will depend on those making the status evaluation. They may be related only to the values of a small group (ability to read Syro-Aramaic) or to widely regarded means of satisfying needs (possession of wealth). Sometimes these attributes are broad (knowledge of management, of psychology, of history, of investment markets, etc.).

SOURCES OF STATUS

Status, then, is given by the group. As with power, it is not a thing a person possesses on his own. A Kwakiutl Indian chief in early British Columbia could achieve status by burning all his tribe's blankets and possessions and flinging every bit of wealth and money into the watching crowds. The more he destroyed, the higher his status. But we, as non-members of his group, would grant him no status for his acts, probably regarding him as a great fool. I recall one day after the introduction of minicabs in London when I was being driven down Threadneedle Street by one of the partners in a new independent minitaxi company. He was describing to me the difficulties they were having in getting established in opposition to the old traditions of London taxis. As we passed the Bank of England a number of tall-walking, straight-backed individuals in bowler hats, top hats, striped trousers, and tails, carrying umbrellas (brollies) were noticeable. "There go the tea-and-bun boys," said my loquacious driver. "The what?" I said, not understanding. "The tea-and-bun boys. I call them that because they strut around like peacocks in their bowlers and tails but they only make enough money to afford to eat tea and buns." Here was an excellent example of a nongroup member not being impressed by the status symbols of a group. Not being a member of the group, it is easy to scoff at those status symbols others consider all important. Can you think of a few examples for groups within your own organization?

That attribute which provides the greatest reward to the greatest number is going to be associated with maximum approval and will bring its possessor maximum status. Unfortunately, it is also necessary for such an attribute to be relatively rare. A problem faced by the Canadian Forces recently was the result of a new policy; a private would almost automatically be promoted to the rank of corporal after a minimum of time as a private along with maximum training and skill level. The increased pay and prestige of the higher rank was supposed to enhance morale, increase productivity, and reduce the rate of resignations from the Canadian Forces. It did not appear that the policy would cause a loss of experienced personnel, but the prestige of the rank of corporal was seriously eroded. Senior corporals were disturbed at the loss of prestige which they had acquired with much more difficulty, and the disproportionate resignations produced a serious decline of needed personnel.

Being perceived by the group as receiving rewards or incurring costs also brings the individual status. The very fact that one is seen to receive things valued by the group or society brings one status—for example, high income, citation by a professional society (whether or not the reason is known); being a guest panelist on TV (whether or not one contributes anything useful). This is also true with costs. Receipt of the Victoria Cross (whether or not posthumously) indicates the degree of sacrifice willingly incurred on behalf of the group. But costs must also be seen as valuable to the group. Occupational drudgery and occupational responsibility are both costly but only the latter contributes to high status.

Another way to acquire status is through investment. Seniority is perhaps the best example of this. It has no intrinsic value of its own but it is accorded a certain value by group consensus. Along with it go certain privileges—longer vacations, higher pay, job security, less road trips, choice of offices or working hours. This all results from the investment of time alone.

COMPARING STATUS

Underlying the concept of status is that interaction is based on the comparison a person makes between his own status and that of others. This comparison can be made in terms of rewards, costs, and investments.

Depending on the comparison, the person is either satisfied or dissatisfied.

Two principles help us to understand the reaction to these comparisons: distributive justice and status congruence.

Distributive justice refers to the perception that a person's outcomes are directly proportional to the rewards and costs he has invested. In practice, we do not measure this proportion with cold calculation but merely compare our standing relative to others on the same outcome, considering oneself higher, lower, or equal to them. If our outcomes are the same as those of other group members, according to the amount we have each invested, distributive justice is achieved. If somebody has seniority over me, has invested more time and money in the preparation of his professional career than I have, knows the job better than I do, and is promoted over me, this is distributive justice. On the other hand, if I have seniority and better experience and knowledge of the job but he is promoted over me because he is the president's fair-haired boy, I then feel an acute sense of the injustice of this situation.

A number of reports in the research literature tell how the lack of distributive justice brings disharmony to the organization. Most managers have some experience of their people coming to ask for a raise or a promotion "because X gets more than I do but doesn't have the same responsibilities (cost), doesn't have the same background and experiences (investment)." One study reported that when workers knew others had higher education and more seniority, only a relatively small percentage complained about the others getting high salary; but when they regarded themselves as equals, a great majority were dissatisfied that the others received more than they did.

The second principle is *status congruence*. This ties in directly with distributive justice and merely implies that all the characteristics and attributes of a person are greater than, equal to, or lower than the corresponding attributes of a person to whom he can be compared. Thus the director as compared with the assistant director must have higher income, larger office, more experience, and better stationery. In other words, the things he has and receives should be congruent with his status.

Status congruence also implies that the higher status person works harder (incurs more costs) than the lower status person. Salaried workers in the front office often work late for nothing extra while those in the shop get time and a half for overtime. And there really are some management people who carry home more than an empty lunch bag and scratch pads for the kids in their attaché cases. Often, the workers with seniority and high pay feel or say that they like to work harder, faster, and produce higher quality than the young men or the new men to show they are "better."

Status congruence is tied in with status symbols, as we have implied. The symbol itself may have no intrinsic value (colored telephones as against black ones) but it comes to symbolize status through regular association with high-status persons. Every organization has its own peculiarities with regard to status symbols—office size, curtains, number of telephones, cost of office furniture, size of carpet, fresh or plastic flowers on the desk, washroom keys, and so on. Each of us has his favorite anecdote about the humorous situation which evolved when the accepted practice for symbols was offended. My own deals with the assistant director who brought his own wall-to-wall carpet into the office one weekend.

Incidentally, that is where our expression "being on the carpet" comes from; only senior people had the status of a piece of carpet in front of their desk. The underling would stand on it while being reprimanded.

Both distributive justice and status congruence serve important functions in the complex organization. First, we feel cheated when our profits are out of line with our investments because high investments should bring high profits. As for status congruence, our experience teaches us that when we present certain signs to others they will treat us accordingly. If the signs we present are the same as those given off by lower status persons, their treatment of us will then be inappropriate and ineffective. For example, if the boss wore the same clothing and had the same type of office as the clerks, he would constantly be receiving communications from others intended for action at a lower level; while, simultaneously, persons would be uncertain to whom they should address high-level communications. Lack of status congruence makes interaction unpredictable and studies have demonstrated that where it is lacking there is interpersonal conflict; where it exists, the group is more congenial and reaches decisions more readily.

In comparing ourselves to others to clarify our status, the incomes, skills, and job demands of only certain people are of direct interest to us. We use only relevant others to judge the degree of distributive justice involved in our outcomes and theirs. Depending on the comparison, we may feel angry, embarrassed, content, satisfied, or extremely pleased with ourselves.

So status and its symbols, although easy to joke about, are very serious matters in the complex organization. Each person must be able to observe the costs, investments, and rewards of those fellow members similarly positioned to himself so that he can make an accurate comparison with his own outcomes. If too many people come to the conclusion that the organization is lacking in distributive justice and status congruence, rivalry and friction will then result, with people and factions jockeying for their "rights" and a danger of reclining effectiveness.

THE STATUS STRUCTURE

As a stable structure is desirable, a number of group processes ensure distributive justice and status congruence. First, any changes that disrupt them will be resisted. An example would be bribery. I once spent a couple of months in an organization where bribery was rampant. I was astounded on the third day after I reported in when a client slyly inquired whether or not my wife had a fur coat. After a few weeks of witnessing those around me tucking bottles of whisky and cartons of cigarettes into their desk drawers or carrying them carelessly sandwiched between file folders, I began to comprehend the reason for chaos in the office. There was a genuine spirit of competition among employees to give quick and clandestine service to those with the biggest bribes to offer. The top brass appeared to keep a blind eye to all this, and I wondered privately whether they were getting kickbacks themselves. A few days before I left, a large truck came into the parking lot and backed into the shipping portal. Prior to leaving for the day we were all invited to visit the storeroom. There we found cases of liquor, cigarettes, and cigars piled mountain high awaiting us. Needless to say, the competition, rivalry, friction, and factions in this office made it the most unpleasant of several branches of the organization I worked in and I found that, throughout the larger organization, decisions coming from this office were always suspect.

We can see the problems in terms of status. Here was an opportunity for a person to increase his rewards without increasing his costs or investments. When it became obvious that a low-status person was getting undeservedly high outcomes, the pressure was on the higher status person either to "put him in his place" or try to better his own outcomes by taking a bigger slice of the pie or by slicing bigger pies. Status congruence and distributive justice did not exist and chaos resulted.

We also see an advantage of status structure stability is that it leads to group consensus. When status congruence is appropriate and distributive justice is visible, all members can be in agreement about the values of the group. Since the traits and attributes of members are evaluated according to how they contribute to the furtherance of the group's values and according to how rare they are among group members, then the greater the consensus on values the greater the status stability.

Another important thing about status structure stability is that it calls for (allows, encourages, and demands) a person to act in a manner appropriate to his status. It is "beneath" the high-status person to not take the lead in time of crisis, or not to set the pace and the example, or not to defend the actions of the organization in public when they are challenged, or not to stand up for low-status persons when they are threatened. In other words, the high-status person must behave in such a way as to "validate" his status in the group.

Related to this is a process called *status conversion*. This involves the manipulation of events, circumstances, or words in such a way that a person uses his status as a resource to bring himself rewards on a different level. Thus a judge accosted by a police officer for a minor traffic infraction may emit signs of his status with the intent of avoiding a ticket; a teacher may use his authority to silence a student asking a question that he cannot answer; and a senior man may use his status in the typing pool to get priority for his work over the work of a junior man. A number of studies report how this operates in a factory setting when a lower status person can borrow tools or ask advice from a higher status person, but high-status tradesmen rarely borrow or ask advice from low-status tradesmen without disguising their intent by pretending they want to compare notes or to discuss a technical problem of mutual interest. We also see the same thing among managers and supervisors on the same level.

A further tendency supporting stability is to perceive people who are frequently seen together or who belong together as having equal status. By this simple mechanism one person is able to participate in the prestige of another. We all know, for instance, that the wife and children of a high-status person are accorded the privileges of high status. Often, the wife is expected to bear the costs and investments of her high-status husband. Other than these obvious situations of status by association, there are many other instances in which we see that status "rubs off." The director's secretary, executive assistant, and other functionaries pick up a certain amount of status just because they are close to him and are frequently seen interacting with him.

Even among those at the bottom of the structure stability is desirable. When there is some prospect of those of low status achieving the group values, they respect them. Also, regardless of what a person may say, everyone knows in practice that money, skill, and knowledge are useful things to have for day-to-day living and so their possession automatically confers status. Finally, the low-status person can get direct gains from the high-status person he supports. Low-status persons can pass off responsibilities to those of higher status; can demand extra compensation for overtime while the high-status persons cannot; can require help of higher status persons without fear. I recall a low-status civil servant once telling me slyly, "I have never signed anything in my five years here. That way, if anything ever goes wrong, they can't pin it on me."

We might notice that persons can distort their perception of their own status by means of rationalization. This way they can think of themselves as higher status than they actually are without disrupting the true status structure. This is done by emphasizing some dimensions of status while denigrating other dimensions. The senior worker can emphasize the value of his seniority and experience and downgrade the value of a formal education. Thus the remark to the new recruit, "You may have a college degree, but I am a graduate of the school of hard knocks."

THE PECKING ORDER

Some years ago researchers confirmed an old barnyard truth that there is a social order with a status hierarchy among chickens. This is probably the origin of our term "henpecked." Subsequent observations confirmed this among monkeys, other animals, and humans.

Among chickens the strongest and most powerful hen or rooster displays his or her status by pecking all other chickens into obedience. The one who is second in order pecks all others below him or her; the third, all those below him or her; and so forth down to the lowest order chicken. The poor hen at the bottom is pecked by all and has no one below herself to peck. She is the weakest and least attractive—and little wonder.

High status in the pecking order brings certain privileges. Those at the top get the choice food, water, roosts, and so on (hence maintaining their strength and condition). In some animal groups it also brings responsibilities—such as among baboons, who march in packs, with the high-status baboons occupying dangerous positions.

The instinctive value of this situation is apparent among animals. A hen, for example, will not mate with a rooster below her in pecking order; hence the roosters on top of the hierarchy sire most chicks and keep the strain strong. Even the rooster who is not particularly sexually aggressive keeps the lesser roosters from mating. Regrettably, hens high in the pecking order mate less than hens below them. If the hen is the leader of the flock, she may never mate.

It is relatively easy to observe this same pecking hierarchy in human children. Thus the leader of children, the second in charge, and so on are given their status by the tacit consent of those at the bottom of the hierarchy. As with the pecking chickens and the aggressive baboons and monkeys, one child will act aggressively toward another for no apparent reason than to confirm his status relationship. This type of aggression is not necessarily the result of frustration but merely the symbol of status order.

A classic study reported by Whyte [1] noted that the bowling scores of his famous street corner gang corresponded to their self-confidence and group status. When a low-status person's bowling score rose out of line with his status, he was heckled mercilessly until his confidence was shaken and his score dropped. The same thing has been found by a number of re-

[1] W. F. Whyte, *Streetcorner Society* (Chicago: University of Chicago Press, 1943).

searchers in the relationship between group status, self-confidence, and predicted future performance in a dart-throwing game. It is also reported that students' performance in several areas of study are related to their self-concept of their own ability.

The point for the manager is that, although the worker is far more complex than the chicken or the monkey, his status and performance are related.

OCCUPATIONAL PRESTIGE

It has long been noted that workers in different occupations and industries tend to display different job attitudes. One of the factors accounting for this is occupational prestige. It has been argued that prestige provides the best explanation for these differences and that if all occupations were ranked in terms of their job satisfaction and also ranked in terms of public esteem, the correlation would be higher than for any other factor related to job satisfaction across all occupations. The prestige of an occupation depends on the amount of skill the job calls for, the degree of specialized education and training it requires, the level of responsibility and autonomy involved in work performance, and the income which it brings. All these factors have a direct relationship to satisfaction and at the same time are linked to status.

High-prestige jobs are valued for their status rewards even though many aspects are quite unpleasant; low-prestige jobs are equally undervalued and disliked even though the work involved might be quite pleasant. Blauner [2] points out that "the lowliness or nastiness of a job are subjective estimates. A doctor or a nurse, for example, or a sanitary inspector have to do some things which would disgust the most unskilled casual laborer." Nonetheless, these jobs carry high occupational status and prestige. Above all, it is the prestige of the working group and his position within this group which influences a worker's job attitudes.

Professionals and business executives have the highest occupational prestige in our society. That they also have the highest level of work satisfaction has been borne out by many studies. White-collar workers tend to be more satisfied with their jobs than manual workers even though the income and skill level of office workers is outranked by blue-collar workers. The manual workers have a lesser social prestige. Outside of North America this prestige difference appears to be even more pronounced.

Among blue-collar workers as a category, there are also occupational ranks just as there are among professionals. Higher positive work attitudes

[2] R. Blauner, "Work Satisfaction and Industrial Trends in Modern Society," in *Labor and Trade Unionism*, W. Galenson and S. N. Lipset, eds. (New York: John Wiley & Sons, Inc., 1960), pp. 340–354.

are consistently found among skilled workers than among the semiskilled and nonskilled.

One does find occupations with a relatively high prestige where job satisfaction is not as high as it should be. This should warn us that it is not occupational status alone which must be considered when predicting satisfaction. There are other factors; some have been considered and others we shall treat in further chapters.

The responsibility, respect, and recognition that go along with the material rewards of high status contribute not only to a sense of satisfaction but also to a sense of self-esteem. The higher the managerial status, the less deficiency in self-esteem. This would indicate high level satisfaction, according to Maslow's need hierarchy. Self-esteem which goes along with high status also appears related to mental and physical health. It has been shown that the higher the self-esteem, the less frequently are employees likely to visit the company dispensary. Increase in job status brings a decrease of such visits while moving down in job status is accompanied by an increase in dispensary visits.

STATUS AND PERCEPTION

Recalling our chapter on perception, we know that putting people into categories helps us economize when dealing with our social world. Status is such a category, and the activities of a person at one status level are perceived by us differently than the activities of a person at another level. For this reason we may react differently if the file clerk is late with a promised delivery than if the president is late with a promised delivery. This links status to communication in a very important way, as we shall soon see.

Even though two persons behave in an identical manner, the difference in their status causes a person perceiving them to assign different motivations for their behavior. When a person of lower status than oneself complies with a request, we perceive him as *having* to cooperate. When a person of higher status than us complies with a request, we perceive him as *wanting* to cooperate. One result of this is that we tend to express more liking (affect choice) for the high-status person than for the low-status person even though their behavior is identical. Presumably, we give the director more credit when he says "Good morning" to us than when the janitor says it.

Persons may tend to interpret events differently, depending on their position in the organizational hierarchy. In one of her studies, Morse [3] asked a group of clerical workers and their supervisors, "How does a person get ahead here in the company?" Supervisors tended to explain it in terms

[3] Nancy Morse, *Satisfactions of the White-Collar-Job* (Ann Arbor, Mich.: Survey Research Center, The University of Michigan, 1953).

of "merit" while workers were more likely to make cynical references to knowing the right people or "just plain luck."

It has also been shown that high-level managers and their immediate managerial subordinates differ substantially in their descriptions of what the subordinates' jobs involve, even though written job descriptions are available. Less than half agreed on more than 50 percent of the topics concerning the job duties of the subordinates. An even greater discrepancy exists in perception of the obstacles these persons see as hindering the subordinate from performing well on the job. Obviously, there is an area of potential conflict here between the managers and their managerial subordinates along the lines we have discussed in our chapter on communication.

SOCIAL BACKGROUND

It was stated earlier that the class background of workers sometimes accounts for typical behaviors. Thus those from working class city backgrounds tend to have greater respect for working class values and adhere closely to norms established by their work groups. Rate busters and isolates within work groups tend to come from rural farm backgrounds. McClelland claims that American Catholics and Jews born around 1920 tend to be high achievers.

Contrary to the popular myth about the origins of American business leaders in working class and farm-based families, studies of business leaders born between 1785 and 1920 show that the clear majority of American business leaders always have and presently do come from relatively well-to-do families. The proportion coming from working class families has tended to be small.

A study by Lipset and Bendix [4] gives comparative data on social mobility in a number of industrialized countries. It was found that from one generation to another all countries showed a high rate of mobility, with from one quarter to one third of the population moving upward from working class to middle class or downward from middle class to working class. The total mobility in all countries compared tended to be much the same. Thus in the United States 33 percent of sons of manual workers moved up into nonmanual occupations while 26 percent of nonmanual workers moved down into manual occupations. The total mobility of men moving across the manual-nonmanual line in either direction was 30 percent. In Germany the figures were 29 percent, 32 percent, and 31 percent; in France 39 percent, 20 percent, and 27 percent; in Japan 36 percent, 22 percent, and 27 percent. It was also found that the rate of interclass marriages was similarly high in all western countries for which data was available. In the

[4] S. N. Lipset and R. Bendix, *Social Mobility in Industrial Society* (Berkeley: University of California Press, 1959).

broad sense this would indicate that the persistence of class position is an illusion, due mainly to the fact that the change tends to take place slowly and to the fact that the class character tends to persist beyond the actual class change.

It seems that modern industrial societies could not function effectively without this social mobility. An expanding industrial society calls for increasingly more managers and professionals. As the upper class cannot meet the demand, the recruits come from the lower social levels. Those born into the upper strata who lack the motivation and ability to succeed in professional, technical, and managerial positions gradually gravitate downward.

A number of sociologists have found that upward mobility is greater among middle-class persons than among the lower classes. This is related to the difference in achievement motives and achievement values between the social classes. One study of adolescent boys showed a clear difference between the upward-aspiring and the downward-aspiring. The former were lively and energetic; the latter inactive and apathetic. The upward-oriented showed a long-term time perspective, internalized personal controls, greater family independence, more self-acceptance, and higher social confidence than the downward-oriented adolescents.

Even sexual behavior appears related to occupational status, according to Kinsey's famous report. Three occupational classes (based on the parental job) of 16- to 20-year-old males revealed a relatively low frequency of masturbation and a relatively high level of premarital intercourse in the semiskilled labor class compared to the professional class. The lower white-collar class appeared to be in transition between the other two classes. The really surprising thing about the data, though, is that a boy from the skilled labor class who ultimately moves into the professional class displays a sexual pattern in his youth that is in line with the professional class pattern. Similarly, the downward mobile skilled labor class youth has a sexual pattern resembling that of the unskilled labor class.

LABOR, MANAGEMENT, AND THE COMMUNITY ELITE

Although power in the social and group dynamic sense was discussed in the last chapter, it may be well to have a quick look at the influence in the community held by various categories of persons depending on their status rank in organized labor or in business and industry. There has been a general agreement that the community elite of businessmen in North America not only control the community but know that they do. In spite of this, they occasionally decry the unrestricted influence of organized labor. Labor leaders, in turn, often consider the local community as the tool of business although on appropriate occasions these leaders claim to represent an important power bloc.

C. Wright Mills [5] has suggested that labor sees itself as a pressure group which wants a bigger share of the social structural power. They want to join high-status owners and managers in running the corporate system, rather than being a cowering minority at the mercy of the business class.

A study done in Michigan in 1960 [6] reported about one fifth of "persons who, singly or collectively, have enough influence and power to put across a major project or settle a major issue in the community" as union officials. These labor influentials showed "remarkably little stereotypical imagery either of itself or management." However, they did think that there was a small and active clique of decision makers who mediate most community projects and issues and that labor's representation in this clique was small and inadequate.

Organizations can be considered as having status in the sense that the public tends to rank them in a similar manner to individuals holding social status in the total community. Retail stores are obvious examples of this; they are judged on the quality of merchandise and type of clientele as well as on service. When seeking jobs, high school and university graduates also rank organizations in status, just as professors and top graduate students rank universities.

Educational level and deportment of employees is a gauge we use in ranking organizations. Even the *type* of education and where it was obtained is counted. In countries like England the school tie is still very important while more subtle signs are used in North America. The American myth is that "Where are you going?" is more important than "Where do you come from?" As a native North American who has lived, worked, and studied in North America, England, Ireland, and continental Europe, I notice the different *style* of acceptance of class background on the east and west side of the Atlantic but an element of snobbery seems to exist on both sides. The North American style is more disguised, possibly to uphold the myth. Once, when I was giving an address at Oxford, a student group invited me to dine with them. Part of the evening's good-natured banter centered around British class snobbery and one very pleasant young man was being joshed because, they claimed, regardless of what he did in life he would be a success for his schooling background was Cheam, Eton, and Oxford.

The things which provide status symbols to the organization are the quality of architecture and interior decoration, use of office equipment

[5] C. Wright Mills, "Labour Leaders and the Power Elite," in *Industrial Conflict*, A. Kornhauser, R. Dubin, and A. M. Ross, eds. (New York: McGraw-Hill Book Company, 1954).

[6] R. William, H. Form, and W. L. Sauer, "Organized Labour's Image of Community Power Structure," *Social Forces* (1960), pp. 332–341.

(style and color of typewriter and telephones), degree of computerization, and so on. Banks, trust companies, and insurance companies are easy to compare on status rank even to the casual observer in terms of architecture, depth of frontage, existence of patios, sculptures, quality of paintings or mosaics or tapestries, amount of nonutilitarian space, and so on.

Individual members of the organization often have distinguishable insignia depending on rank. The military is the obvious example of this but others like hospitals, ecclesiastical institutions, police, and universities have their appropriate dress and badges. What the waiter wears tells you more about what a meal will cost you than will the menu.

STATUS AND COMMUNICATION

Although we have already devoted some time to the consideration of communication, many of the problems raised earlier can now be seen more clearly in the context of status. The first thing we would observe is that the consistency of who communicates (or does not communicate) to whom and how often is directly related to the status of the individuals concerned.

Communication tends to move upward in the status and power hierarchies, being more frequently directed to high-status persons. In terms of exchange theory, upward communication is risky because of possible rebuff which confirms low status but the chance for public reward from a high-status person makes the estimates of outcomes a worthwhile risk under appropriate circumstances.

Studies also show that persons equal in status are more likely to communicate *with each other* than persons of unequal status. In terms of exchange theory, this is a safer form of communication for equality of costs and rewards is ensured.

Finally, we notice that when the equality of status of two persons is in doubt they are likely to avoid communicating with each other. When such uncertainty exists, it makes prediction of outcomes difficult and may confirm low status instead of equality. Thus when doubtful of each other's status persons avoid interacting. Take note of this the next time you see two people introduced ambiguously. When status is clearly either equal or unequal, they will tend to communicate something to one another. When their status is ambiguous, most of their initial communications are designed to discover directly or indirectly what their status relationship really is.

SUMMARY

In spite of our humorous jabs at status and prestige, we are now in a position to see the value of status and status symbols for keeping the complex organization running smoothly. Status is worth according to the estimate of a category or class. The individual member of the work force can have a different status according to which group is ranking him on his worth—the general community, the total organization, or his specific work group. The specific traits or attributes ranked depend on the group doing the ranking and its values.

The sources of highest status, then, are possession of those characteristics which can provide the highest rewards to the greatest number of members of the category. These attributes must at the same time be relatively rare among those doing the rating. Costs, rewards, and investments are the bases for attaining status.

One great value of status is the feedback it provides on our standing and progress. We get this by ranking others on status and comparing ourselves to them in terms of distributive justice (outcomes versus costs and investments); and by observing status congruence to see whether people have the appropriate things that go along with their status. Status symbols are signs of congruence. When distributive justice and status congruence do not exist in the organization, its members can be expected to be dissatisfied, noncooperative, and competitive with one another.

A stable organization status structure is a desirable thing, not because it preserves a privileged position for the few, but because it enables members at all levels to work smoothly. In fact, the privileges of the high-status individuals are accorded them willingly by the low status because they are expected to shoulder responsibilities and burdens which the low status do not want. If it is apparent to all that promotion, pay, and privilege come only from bearing costs and investments, and possession of those things valued by the organization (in other words, on the basis of merit), then, no matter where he is positioned, each member knows he will be dealt with fairly when the goodies are handed out.

Mechanisms such as rationalization are used as means of distorting one's own perception of status position without disrupting the actual status structure. Indeed, the way we perceive the relationship in status between ourselves and others with whom we interact will determine how we perceive their actions and communications and how we interact with them. Thus we talk differently to our boss than to our secretary.

Although it is necessary to be cautious when bringing animal social behavior into comparison with human social behavior, we looked briefly at the pecking order in animals and noted something similar in human children. The physiological factors involved in the pecking hierarchy would never be sufficient in themselves to account for the complexity of social status ranking.

We concluded with a brief look at some of the sociological data on occupational prestige (which is not truly objective in any society) and at the social background and social mobility of the so-called managerial class

There are more similarities than differences across all industrialized nations which have been studied. Occupational status appears to have a closer relationship to job attitudes and satisfactions than any other factor. The prestige of management and labor was also mentioned with some speculation about their influence in the community.

Finally, the very important link between status and communication was made. Communications tend to go upward to high-status persons and across to equal-status persons, and tend to be very scant to persons of ambiguous status relationship.

"I knew he was a miner, for he stirred his coffee with his thumb," says the old folk song. It is funny, yes, this status symbol, but only because of it was the waitress able to judge that the customer was of the same status as she and hence a suitable partner in love. So status and its symbols make a good joke but they also make a complex social life far easier to manage.

14

NORMATIVE BEHAVIOR AND CONFORMITY

The rules for interaction among members of a group are largely unwritten. In this chapter we want to find out how these rules come into existence and why people adhere to them even when they would prefer not to. How are these norms communicated within the group? Do people stick to the rules when no one is watching them? What social factor allows people to defy the rules? Is defiance costly? Is there a conforming personality? How are deviants brought into line? What is the best way for a manager to change the unwritten rules?

Once the group comes into existence, it can remain in existence only by all group members agreeing to some formation of norms or rules for their interaction.

The highly formalized group, of course, establishes written laws and books of rules. But even then there remain many unwritten rules for behavior which anyone who claims membership must conform to: even the most detailed company manual will not tell you that you should say "Good morning" to your colleagues.

A norm is a standard or behavioral expectation shared by all members of the group; it is against this norm that the group member can gauge the appropriateness of his feelings and by which his behavior and the behaviors of others can be evaluated.

In order to achieve stability and to minimize any tension we may experience in dealing with our social environment, one thing we all need and for which we all depend on other people is a means of validating our way of interpreting our social world. It is the group which provides us with this validation. Members validate each other's interpretations through exchanging signs given and signs given off. Both the extent of and the conformity to norms will be due, in part, to how much the individual depends on the group for the satisfaction of his needs.

Let us take a look at an example of normative behavior as demonstrated by Sherif's [1] famous studies of autokinesis which have been replicated in many variations.

In the autokinetic experiment, subjects are exposed to a tiny pinpoint of light in a completely darkened room. The light is turned off for a few seconds and then turned back on again. The subject is then asked by the experimenter, "How far do you think the light has moved?" or some similar question.

Now the thing about the autokinetic effect is that the pinpoint of light *does not move*. Indeed, the light is usually fixed to some permanent stand. Nonetheless, the subject gets a distinct feeling that the light *has* moved.

This sensation of apparent movement is something like an optical illusion; even when you are aware it is an illusion you still experience it. When coupled with this sensation he hears the experimenter's question "How far has it moved?" the subject's perception of motion is supported and he makes a guess of the distance.

Now the experimenter can introduce other variables to complicate the experiment slightly. He can bring in a number of subjects and expose them all simultaneously to the same autokinetic effect.

Let us say, for instance, that the experimenter brings in five naïve subjects and exposes them simultaneously to the autokinetic effect. Starting at one end of the row of subjects, the experimenter asks how far the light has moved. Let us say that the first subject, uncertain about the distance of apparent motion, makes a guess of two inches. Then the experimenter asks the second person in the row how far the light has moved. This person has all the information of the first subject plus the added information that one person sitting beside him has just said that *he* has experienced the light moving a distance of two inches. Now, depending on whether he thought that two inches was a generous guess or an underestimate, let us suppose he says the light has moved one and one-half inches. Then person number three is asked. He has all the information the first person had but he also

[1] M. Sherif, "A Study of Some Social Factors in Perception," *Archives of Psychology,* No. 187 (1935).

has two additional "bits" of information—that one other person has esti-mated a distance of two inches and a second person has estimated an inch and a half. Suppose he guesses one and three-quarter inches.

For the fourth person it is a simple thing to make a guess between the extremes of the range, or to extend it a half inch or so at either end. This will demonstrate that he sees the world around him in approximately the same way that everyone else does. If he chooses to extend the range slightly, the final subject will then have the option of a somewhat wider range.

TABLE 14-1

A GUESS IN THE DARK

Three hypothetical groups of five persons each exposed to the autokinetic effect and asked to guess the distance of movement of the pinpoint of light.

	Subject 1	Subject 2	Subject 3	Subject 4	Subject 5
Group 1	2 inches	2 ½ inches	1 ½ inches	2 ¼ inches	1 ¾ inches
Group 2	6 inches	4 inches	5 ½ inches	4 ½ inches	5 inches
Group 3	¼ inch	½ inch	¾ inch	½ inch	¾ inch

Keep in mind that all subjects have been exposed to exactly the same light stimulus. The only factor that differs is the "guess" of Subject 1 in each of the three groups. This demonstrates that the "goodness" of a guess is influenced by what other people have been seen to guess.

If you refer to Table 14-1, you will see the results of three hypo-thetical groups of five naïve subjects exposed to the autokinetic effect. It is apparent that the first guess is used as a gauge for what is right or fitting. However, if Subject 1 makes a bizarre guess, the rest of the group will try to get him to modify his estimate to a more suitable distance. If they succeed, all will be satisfied they are perceiving their world correctly. A hypothetical demonstration of this is provided in Table 14-2.

What we witness in these illustrations is the gradual formation of a norm or standard which each member can use to determine whether his way of thinking or guessing or seeing is appropriate. Before he witnesses the guesses of his companions he has no way of knowing this. They are all in an equally ambiguous position at the start and so they are all equally dependent upon each other.

As we have seen in Chapter 10, some people are more persuasible

TABLE 14-2

A hypothetical group of five persons exposed to the autokinetic effect on three occasions. Subject 1 makes a bizarre guess the first time he is asked but the group eventually modifies his estimate.

	Subject 1	Subject 2	Subject 3	Subject 4	Subject 5
First Guess	3 feet	8 inches	6 inches	7 inches	5 inches
Second Guess	12 inches	6 inches	5 inches	6 inches	4 inches
Third Guess	7 inches	5 inches	5 inches	5 inches	4 inches

(Remember the light is stationary and has not moved at all.)

than others. Indeed, Sherif reported one subject being influenced to the extent of making guesses about the distances of motion which were greater than the length of the experimental room!

This raises another interesting aspect of the experimental design. It is quite simple to plant one or more confederates in with a naïve subject and by means of prearranged signals alter the guesses of the naïve subject. This is illustrated in Table 14-3.

TABLE 14-3

A hypothetical group of three persons exposed to the autokinetic effect in which one person is naïve and the other two are confederates of the experimenter.

	Subject 1 (confederate)	Subject 2 (confederate)	Subject 3 (naïve)
First Guess	½ inch (prearranged guess)	¼ inch (prearranged guess)	½ inch
Second Guess	18 inches (prearranged guess)	24 inches (prearranged guess)	15 inches
Third Guess	¼ inch (prearranged guess)	⅛ inch (prearranged guess)	½ inch

(Remember the light is stationary and has not moved at all.)

At first glance, autokinesis might seem remote from day-to-day managerial problems. Before carrying the discussion further, we shall look at another similar type of experiment modeled after those carried out by Asch.[2]

I drew up a series of eight by twelve inch cards, each with one heavily drawn vertical line in the center. The lines varied from one inch to ten inches in length. Seven students were chosen from the classroom and given instructions as follows:

> Tomorrow morning you will go to the cafeteria and sit at two different tables for coffee at the beginning of the class hour. I want one group of you to sit with a lone student, preferably a first year student who has never taken a psychology course. Talk with him and treat him as one of the group. After a few minutes I shall send another student from our class to the cafeteria to collect eight "volunteers" for a classroom demonstration. You will all volunteer and, if the naïve student does not volunteer along with you, coax him to join you in the classroom demonstration.
>
> When you come to the classroom I shall ask you to sit in an arc at the front of the room with the naïve student second from one end. Then I shall show you these cards one at a time and explain that you are to guess the length of the line on each of them. Make normal guesses on the first five cards which will vary from long to short. The sixth card will be a short one—about an inch long. However, you are each in turn to report this sixth card to be within a length range of eight to twelve inches. I shall start asking from the student furthest away from the naïve student.

Figure 14-1 illustrates the classroom setting. The original experiments were done by Solomon Asch. In the demonstration referred to, the confederates are seated in a classroom with one naïve subject, all facing the card stand where the lines are exposed by the experimenter one at a time.

During such demonstrations the naïve student has the opportunity to notice that everyone else in his group sees the world more or less the same way as he does: they all guess the approximate length of lines the same as he does within tolerable limits. But then, suddenly, he sees that something has gone wrong! These people who think and perceive the same way that he does have suddenly started seeing things in a manner opposite to the way he sees them. Who is right? They? Or himself? They outnumber him. It is now his turn to make a public guess. A whole classroom is watching him. Six people have already reported seeing the opposite of which is right in front of his eyes. What should he do? Conform to meet the norm? Or risk the chance of being considered an oddball?

In classroom demonstrations the author has had more students conforming than saying what they actually saw. Those who went against the

---

[2] S. E. Asch, "Studies of Independence and Conformity: A Minority of One Against a Unanimous Majority," *Psychological Monographs*, LXX, No. 9 (1956).

norm and reported what they really saw said afterward that they felt very uneasy and hesitant at stating the true length of the line to be opposite to that reported by other group members.

FIGURE 14-1

PRESSURE TO SEE THE SAME THINGS

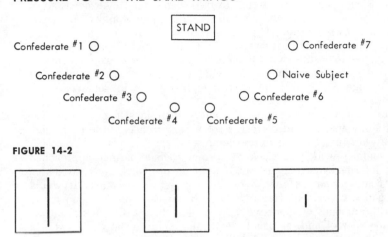

Confederate #1 ○

STAND

○ Confederate #7

Confederate #2 ○

○ Naive Subject

Confederate #3 ○

○ Confederate #6

○ ○
Confederate #4   Confederate #5

FIGURE 14-2

Typical line cards with straight vertical lines varying from twelve inches in length to one inch.

In his experiments Asch reports a considerable conformity in about one third of his subjects, and a partial conformity in most of the rest. He also reports that those who resist conformity do so with great discomfort.

Now let us take a step closer to the everyday work situation. Bear with me while I tell a little anecdote about my youth.

Because my family was in the construction business I used to earn my pocket money and school fees as a roofer, mainly applying asphalt shingles. There were eleven roofers in the company, and we used to work in crews of from two to six depending on the particular job. In those days we considered it a good day's work to apply about 6½ "squares" (i.e., 650 square feet) of shingles in an eight-hour day. This meant about 1 "square" an hour with time for extras like chimneys, valleys, ridges. The boss (my cousin) always felt we worked too slowly and insisted that we could average 8 squares a day. Presumably, he was of this opinion because occasionally we would apply 8 or even 9 squares a day but usually this would be followed by a day or two of 4½ to 5 squares each.

The work routine called for each man to carry his own shingles up onto the roof. Usually, we each made a pile of a few squares and worked from it till more were required. If a roofer were feeling energetic some day, he would apply more than the average or norm. Indeed, occasionally we used to have contests to break the monotony on larger roofs. In such contests men often applied a square in twenty minutes.

Nonetheless, if a man consistently applied 8 to 10 squares per day over several days, or if he persisted in applying several squares more in a day than his fellow workers, strange things tended to happen. For example, he would come to get more shingles from his pile and find a fellow worker sitting on the pile having a cigarette and offering him one. This would slow him down by ten to fifteen minutes. If he persisted in breaking the norm, he might go down to get more shingles and come back to find his roofing hatchet missing, or in severe cases his nail bag nailed to the roof. In fact, there were dozens of tricks the roofing gang could employ to insure that all members of the crew would come to realize that the optimal way of perceiving a day's work was of consisting of five to eight squares of shingles in eight hours with an average of about 6½.

Because older and experienced roofers than myself perceived 6½ squares a day as good and correct, I soon came to accept the norm and, over the years, passed it on to newcomers.

One summer work was slack. A former roofing partner approached me and informed me that he had bought an old truck and was taking roofing contracts on his own. Would I join him? Of course. It would be fun and we would be free agents with our earnings being in direct ratio to the amount of work we were willing to do. Our first contract was a normal roof and, as usual, we were on the job at 8:00 A.M.. At 4:30 P.M the roof was almost finished—it just needed a bit of trim and we had applied 31 squares—an average of 15½ squares each! We didn't feel that we had worked extraordinarily hard and, on the way back home, we talked in wonderment about our 31 squares and the old days when we averaged 6½ squares a day.

By now you see a great similarity between the pinpoint of light in the autokinetic effect and the determination of how many squares a day a roofer should apply. It is very difficult to say what is a day's work. We are all aware of offices, hospitals, or work crews which are considered "hard working" or highly productive and also of those which are low producers. Within the same building or factory are some units in which people expend far more energy than in other units and yet they all consider it quite natural to work according to the group norm.

Norm formation comes about, as we can see, through the general acceptance by group members that the way relevant behavior is carried out (reporting the movement of a light, guessing the length of a line, applying asphalt shingles, attending to classroom lecture, carrying out any day's work) is the appropriate or fitting way to carry out such behavior. It may not be the fastest or the neatest or the best way, but it is the *fitting* way. It fits the perception of members of the group and hence is considered "the way things are done around here." Behaviors contrary to the norm are "*not* the way things are done around here."

INFLUENCE AND NORMS

Once norms have been formed, both under experimental conditions and in the natural laboratory of the factory and office, they no longer need the group to keep them in effect. When the individual has formed norms in the group, he maintains them even when the group is no longer present. If autokinetic norms are formed in a group, they are maintained even when the individual is tested alone. The roofer who has learned the norm of 6½ squares a day in the working crew will maintain it even while working alone for a few days.

If norms are learned outside of group situations, however, they will tend to change gradually to meet group expectations if the individual is subsequently put into an established group. Autokinetic experiments demonstrate this just as readily as our observation of the new roofer with an individual norm of nine squares a day gradually coming down to an average closer to that of the roofing crew. Of course, the individual who alters his norms remains completely unaware of the change and may deny that he has been influenced by what other people think or do. It is important to keep this point in mind for norms are formed through group processes of which the individual remains quite unaware. This leaves the average person open to a certain amount of manipulation. The manager should not forget that norms can change upward just as easily.

One of my brighter students once reported several years after he had graduated that he thought the most important thing he had studied at university was norm formation and Sherif's experiments because it made him aware of the various attempts at manipulation to which he had been subjected since graduating. So, although we are not generally aware of norm formation in process, we make ourselves aware of the processes to some extent when we have some understanding of them.

While still considering influence, it might be noted that persons with high status influence norm formation more than other group members. We shall see the implications of this later when we look at leadership for the leader has high status in the group.

NORM-SENDING

Much of what has been discussed about norm formation involves norm-sending. Norms can form in the group only as long as information is communicated from member to member about what each considers to be fitting perception, fitting behavior, fitting reaction, and so on. But norms are communicated largely by signs given off, indirectly.

Norm-sending refers to the communication involved in norm formation. In its full sense it involves three components:

1. The definition of correct attitudes and fitting behavior (defining and agreeing upon perceptions and action in the particular situation).
2. Monitoring the degree of conformity to the norm (observation by others of whether norms are being broken or adhered to, possibly with a formal monitor, for example, the group leader).
3. Application of sanctions (either positive or negative reward or punishment applied for conformity or nonconformity).

Let us take an example of how norm-sending operates in a practical setting:

A new man is hired to work as one of six punch press operators on the machine-shop floor. The punch presses carry out a number of relatively simple operations to service the needs of the machinists, boiler makers and other technicians in the shop. The personnel office does the formal hiring and explains company policy to the new man. Among other things, he is advised by personnel that the company has a strict policy about quitting time. There is a "five minute" whistle at 4:25 P.M. and only when it blows can the worker stop working and start cleaning up his machine and himself for the day. Also, he is not to leave the shop premises until the final 4:30 quitting time whistle blows. This is an example of direct and explicit norm-sending by the personnel officer through signs given.

The man is next directed to his shop where he meets his foreman and assistant foreman. They tell him more about the shop routine and turn him over to his supervisor. The supervisor takes him to his machine, introduces him to the other five operators and tells him that one in particular, the senior man, will "teach him the ropes." In the process of breaking him in to the details of the job, the senior man tells him that the punch press operators start putting away their jobs and cleaning up their machines around 4:15 P.M. This is so they will be ready to leave their machines immediately when the 4:25 whistle blows, pick up their lunch pails and jackets, and be ready to leave the shop premises at first sound of the 4:30 whistle. As this is contrary to the direct information given by the personnel office and as he is concerned that he might be found to be unacceptable to the company if caught defying their policy, he listens to this new norm information intently.

At 4:15 he notices his five fellow workers gradually cease actual job work and start straightening up around their machines. By 4:20 all of the machines have been closed up for the night. A couple of operators call to him to "knock it off" for the day and, reluctantly, he begins to follow their example. One of them comes over with some comradely advice that he has to start cleaning up sooner or else he won't get out of the shop "on time" (exactly at 4:30). With the example of his five co-workers and their direct advice, he now knows the group norm both in terms of signs given and signs given off.

So far the first part of norm-sending has been accomplished. The job attitudes and the correct job behavior have been explicitly and implicitly defined for the new man by his fellow group members. He now knows what correct and fitting behavior is in this group with regard to quitting time.

On the second day he is again the last one to turn off his machine and a couple other operators call him to "pack it up." Again he receives brotherly advice about quitting time. On the third day he is the last to quit again but no one tells him to stop. He notices that everyone is giving him "dirty looks." In these situations the norms are being monitored by all group members. Which is the second aspect of norm-sending.

On the fourth day all punch presses have stopped by 4:15. The new man is still finishing up one piece. The biggest, toughest operator of the other five comes over to the new man's machine. Without saying a word, he takes the strip of metal which the new man is finishing out of his machine, bends it double over the corner of the workbench, throws it casually into the metal scrap bin, and walks silently away. The new man sees that all other operators are smiling their approval. On the fifth day he goes to join the other operators at coffee break and they all turn their backs to him. These are examples of the third aspect of norm-sending—sanction. The new man is being punished for not adhering to a clearly defined norm.

If he does not adhere to the norm now, he will experience great difficulty on the new job and will either be forced to quit or take a job outside of the shop.

PUBLIC AND PRIVATE CONFORMITY

There is a distinction between conforming in public—when working in a group where the normative behavior is visible to others—and conforming in private—the fire watcher off in his forest tower. When norms are formed in a group there is a strong tendency for them to be adhered to even when the person is in private. But norms formed in private tend to change when the person becomes a member of a group.

Very few jobs are completely private. Even our fire watcher has to make his reports and account for his district. (Your author once knew a prospector working for a geological exploration company whom his fellow prospectors suspected of not doing much work—but no one could really prove it.) But parts of many jobs are carried out privately.

One thing which influences conformity, public or private, is whether the work itself is intrinsically satisfying. Skilled crafts and professional and technical work activities are often interesting in themselves and hence the worker maintains a high work rate regardless of whether he is under public surveillance. On the other hand, when the work is monotonous, repetitious, and apparently purposeless a high degree of public surveillance seems required. If it were left up to the individual to carry out such work in private a much lower norm would be in effect. Military groups in peacetime are often quoted as examples of this. Much of the ordinary peacetime soldier's routine becomes monotonous so the military must maintain organized systems of surveillance and sanctions.

The wise manager, keeping this in mind, should do what he can to prevent work activity from becoming boring and repetitious and try to make tasks interesting for his subordinates. If all workers were highly skilled or professional and all tasks were interesting, there would be much less need for surveillance, threats, and sanctions while productivity, excellence, and creativity would be high. This is an ideal, but worth striving for.

Conformity to group norms is high both publicly and privately when the person feels reasonably well accepted by his fellow group members and feels he has the chance to be even more accepted by them. On the other hand, when he thinks he is not well accepted by the group and is not likely to be accepted, he tends to conform publicly but not privately. Generally, then, insecurity brings a tendency toward public but not private conformity.

Experimental evidence also seems to indicate [3] that under conditions of coercive power and nonlegitimate power, public conformity is observed along with strong resistance to any conformity at all. We have seen some of the limitations of coercive power but this is another caution to be considered when it is available for use.

SUPPORT FOR NON-NORMATIVE BEHAVIOR

In the demonstrations of autokinetic movement and guessing the length of lines, we have seen that the pressure to conformity comes about from a sense of anxiety that others are doing things correctly while one is not. The more ambiguous the task and the more complicated it is to define correct behavior (how does one find out how many squares of shingles should be applied in a day?), the greater is the tendency to relieve the anxiety by stepping into line with the other members of the group.

Remember that, when referring to anxiety, we are not necessarily thinking of the hand-wringing and breath-stopping type but simply that "sneaky hunch in the back of the mind which makes us hesitate before committing ourselves."

Some of Asch's further experiments showed that, even though other members of the group reported seeing the lines differently than the naïve subject, he did not feel the same pressure to conform as long as there was one other person who supported his opinion. Our own personal experience bears this out. If a person is arguing with a group and they all insist that he is in complete error, it is difficult for him to adhere to his point of view without feeling uneasy, especially if the point is an ambiguous one. However, let *one* other person in the group support his view and he can con-

[3] J. R. P. French, Jr., H. W. Morrison, and G. Levinger, "Coercive Power and Forces Affecting Conformity," *Journal of Abnormal and Social Psychology,* LXI (1960), 93–101.

tinue to press his point confidently in the face of all arguments and evidence to the contrary.

The same is true in work groups. The pressure on a deviant from the norm to "step into line" is greatly reduced by the presence of another deviant or a group member who is willing to tolerate his deviance.

WORK UNITS AND NORMS

Each job is unique and even a simple repetitive job like working on an assembly line can be considered to be divided into many work units. Copy typing can be considered relatively simple, yet even typing a form letter involves selecting the proper form, typing the address correctly, adding the relevant information, inserting into its own (not another) envelope, filing the copy, and directing both letter and file to the correct baskets. One could talk, then, of "mailing a form letter correctly" as a unit of behavior subject to normative control in an office typing pool. But one could also talk of a subunit of this behavior, such as "typing the correct address correctly" or "tagging the file," as behaviors subject to normative control.

So the typing pool could have norms about mailing form letters which insured that each girl did her share or that a minimum and maximum number of letters were done each day or that certain types of letters received priority treatment. But, equally, one could talk of norms for the subunits of behavior. Such norms could require that letters be addressed neatly as against casually, or that addresses rarely be erroneous as against frequently erroneous, or that letters be directed in such a manner that postage costs are saved because of the address groupings.

As well as these units and subunits of behavior, we can also think of different aspects of the behavior the worker carries out. For example, the work may be done cheerfully, or quickly, or quietly, or with a minimum of wastage, with inventiveness, and so on, as against gloomily, slowly, noisily, wastefully, without improving methods. All these aspects of the work behavior are also subject to normative controls in the group. If all the other girls in the pool show their disapproval at the wastefulness of one group member, there will be pressure on her to work more carefully.

The group itself is not a simple thing to define. Norms are formed in the group, yes, but most of us hold membership in a number of groups simultaneously and each influences norm formation and conformity. Our copy typist belongs to the group in the copy typing pool. Probably, she also belongs to the general group of female typists, stenos, and clerks in the total office. If more than one organization occupies the same office building, she is part of the larger unit of girls in the whole building and of more intimate friendship groups who regularly eat lunch together. She may be considered a member of other groups on the basis of her age, seniority, and marital status. She will be considered a member of the larger organizational group as well as of her own smaller units. Each will influence certain aspects of her norms. Some will put more pressure on her than others.

Keeping in mind the complexity of even the ordinary job, we see that a whole series of norms are operative simultaneously in any work group. Depending on the degree to which he feels pressure to conform to different parts or aspects of the job, a worker may conform strictly to one aspect, less strictly to another, and not at all to a third. For one part of the job he may conform publicly but not privately and for another aspect he may conform both publicly and privately.

Our copy typist may maintain the norm of working quickly both publicly and privately; she may defy the office norm of low wastage "because Mr. Jones himself wastes more paper in a day than the whole typing pool does in a week"; she may maintain the norm of neatly typed envelopes (public behavior) but deviate from the norm of adding the relevant information to the form letter properly (private behavior, because no one else in the office can monitor it or sanction it).

CONFLICT

The whole discussion of different groupings having influence on different work norms raises problems of conflict between norms. We have seen in our example of the new punch press operator how he was given one rule by the personnel office and another by his work group. Ultimately, his problem might be resolved, depending on which group he feels is putting more pressure on him to conform. So very often in the course of our working day when we get that uneasy, twisted-stomach feeling, it is because we are caught in such a conflict. We know one group expects one thing of us while another group expects something different.

A fuller discussion of the problem will have to wait till the next chapter when we examine the problem of role strain and its resolution. For the time being, it is sufficient for the manager to be aware that in the vast majority of instances the employee who defies the rules and company policies (its norms) is not doing so out of sheer perversity and maliciousness but because some other group norms are more important to him. Perhaps the resolution of his conflict will be in leaving the group which is of secondary importance (the company) but the organization may lose a lot of good employees if it tries to compete with the norms of such important groups as the family, the ball team, or friendship groups.

THE COST OF DEVIATION

A discussion of conflict leads us, in turn, to a discussion of what it costs the individual to be a deviant or a conformer. In our introduction to the study of groups in Chapter 6, we saw that one of the major reasons for the existence of the group is the satisfaction of its members. The operation of norms in the group ensures such satisfaction. The more the individual requires or values his membership in the group to satisfy his needs, the more willing he is to conform to group norms and the more pressure he will put on other members to conform. Particularly, we have seen that behaviors which contribute to the accomplishment of the group task are subject to normative controls because they lead to goal achievement, member satisfaction, and avoidance of failure. The norms will ensure member cooperation in accomplishing the task and similarity in attitudes toward things relevant to the group; also, they will put sanctions on behaviors which would lead to group failure.

Norms among roofers are often developed to ensure cooperation in work which can be dangerous if the men fail to work as a team. Cooperation on high or steep roofs is essential and on other roofs it makes the work more pleasant. Norms determine when it is acceptable to use the shingles or material which another man has carried up onto the roof and when it is not. Ladder use, turns for driving the truck, having to ride in the back of the truck, doing the hot side of the roof, or doing the dirty and dangerous jobs come under normative control to ensure work is done under the safest and most pleasant conditions. If the job is not done well, the boss may get grumpy, the building contractor may complain of the workmanship, or competitor roofing crews may scoff at the shoddy job. (When a roof leaks and a roofer is called to repair it he usually asks in a scornful tone, "Who put this roof on?")

The degree of conformity in groups varies but, in tightly knit or highly cohesive groups such as roofing crews, deviants are not tolerated; although idiosyncrasies and personal work styles may flourish, heavy sanctions are applied to nonacceptable behaviors. Such cohesive work groups usually overlap to some degree with leisure hour friendship groups so that workmates golf, fish, curl, and drink together. Often these friendships extend to the worker's family so that wives, brothers, or neighbors are tied to the work group through overlapping friendship groups. This makes the price of deviation extremely costly.

Adherence to norms, then, is related to cohesiveness. First, there are the face-to-face work groups, then the larger sections containing more personnel, then the divisions in which only a small percentage of total members know one another, and finally the total unit where almost the only thing members have in common with the majority is that they work for the same organization. Depending on the nature and size of the total organization, company-wide norms which put more pressure on the individual than his more intimate work groups are likely to be rare. This is why, in the example of the new punch press operator, company policy will lose out to the norms of the small group unless the supervisor has influence over work behaviors.

Those interested in management have probably deduced that norms are not greatly influenced by *fiat* or company policy. As norms serve a purpose at the grass roots level, it is here that the changes must be truly accepted.

This is not to say that changes in company policy or fiats do not change work behavior. First, if the required change does not interfere with established norms, there is no reason to defy it. Second, even though it may require normative change, it may not prevent group satisfaction and new norms may thus be acceptable. Third, the fiat may change behaviors not subject to normative control—for example, changing the workday from eight to four thirty to eight thirty to five.

CONFORMITY, DEVIATION, AND PERSONALITY

Some people obtain a certain satisfaction from behaving according to group norms, not only because it helps to achieve goals, to ensure fitting behavior, and to reduce anxiety, but also because normative behavior satisfies certain of their personality needs. Personalities with a high need for affiliation, for instance, enjoy normative behavior in friendly, cooperative groups. On the other hand, personalities with marked hostility feelings find that deviation is a means of expressing this hostility. High achievement needs in the personality tend to make the person task-oriented, as we have seen (Chapter 4). If high achievers are skilled at the group task, they enjoy normative behaviors which lead to its accomplishment.

Persons with low self-esteem, made to feel comfortable and accepted in a group, feel strongly attracted to the group and are great conformers. On the other hand, self-confident persons are less dependent on the judgment of others, and studies show that they conform to a lesser extent.

"Rate busters" who deviate from the norm by exceeding work output of the group tend to differ from those who hold to normative work output both in their background and in their personality. They tend to be individualistic and to have family backgrounds where economic independence is valued (a farm family background would be an example). They do not have as strong social needs as the average worker.

Those with low affiliation needs probably get their major satisfactions in life from other things than being accepted by group members. Indeed, it is possible that some types of personality may even get satisfaction from not being accepted by others.

"Rate holders" who conform to the working group norms tend to come from city working class families and have stronger social needs (they tend more to be "joiners" of various social groups).

When Asch interviewed the subjects in one of his major experiments, he found that only a very few stated they had perceived the false majority estimates as actually correct. Most yielders said they saw the lines as being one way but believed they must be perceiving them incorrectly. A third form of conforming was based on a fear of appearing different from the others. These persons disregarded what was right or wrong and paid attention only to what they should say to agree with the majority.

In similar types of experiments, Crutchfield [4] studied fifty professional men and found that from 30 to 70 percent conformed to the incorrect group consensus on certain types of items, including items reflecting false group attitudes. In another experiment he asked subjects to agree or disagree with an item such as "free speech being a privilege rather than a right, it is proper for a society to suspend free speech whenever it feels itself threatened." When faced with an affirmative group's consensus, 58 percent of the subjects conformed and agreed with this statement!

Crutchfield found that some persons submitted many times over a series of trials whereas others yielded only once. He found that the independent person is more effective intellectually, more mature, more confident, and less rigid. The independent and conforming persons also have different attitudes toward parents and children. Conformists tend to idealize their parents whereas the independents are more objective and realistic. Conformers are more restrictive in their attitudes toward child training while independents are more permissive. The personality traits that characterize persons most likely to conform in these settings are similar to those which would describe the authoritarian personality. We have seen in Chapter 10 that some types of persons are more persuasible than others and we can now see that these personality differences are responsible for different attitudes toward normative behavior.

PRESSURE TO CONFORM AND THE DEVIANT

Norm-sending with its monitoring and sanctions is designed to reduce the number of deviations in the group. However, there are times when even the most persistent deviant is not pressured to conformity by the group. Our earlier example of the new punch press operator could have been carried to this extreme. If the new man had persisted in being a nonconforming, rate-busting deviant, direct norm-sending would have ceased in another day or so. He would still have been subjected to sanctions but with the difference that the sanctions would have been designed to punish him and not to correct him. The persistent deviant from group norms is not sanctioned to conform but just for being "bad." He is considered an irredeemable sinner. One does not have to look far for examples of such behavior. When children play, often the child who does not conform to the

---

[4] R. S. Crutchfield, "Conformity and Character," *American Psychologist*, X (1955), 191–198.

rules of the game is advised by norm-sending only once or twice that he is "out of step." If his deviant behavior persists, he is pitilessly treated by his fellows as incorrigible and is no longer permitted to play. He is sent packing by the largest members of the group, often enough with a physical reminder of his perversity and sinfulness. In children's games there are few "errors" and many "sins."

One classroom demonstration of this I employ is to give the class a case history of an adolescent with an extremely unfortunate childhood background full of slums, drunken parents, criminal elder brothers, overly harsh police treatment, and so on, who is on probation for a delinquency and gets into petty trouble again. After the lengthy case history, the class is asked to decide what should be done with the boy. They are given five possible suggestions ranging from doing nothing or being extremely lenient to the opposite extreme of very harsh and lengthy punishment. Most young students in the classroom tend to judge the delinquent leniently but I always "plant" a vociferous student who argues in the class discussion for the most severe punishment regardless of what other members of the class say.

At first, other members of the class try to argue gently with him and change his mind. Gradually, their arguments display a loss of patience. After a few minutes of his "persisting in his perversity" they cease arguing with him, ignore his questions, pay no attention, ignore his vote, and generally "freeze" him out of the discussion.

The same things happens to our perverse norm-defier in the work group.

Try to think of a persistent rate buster that you have come across either as a student or in a work setting. How was he regarded by his fellows?

CHANGING THE NORM

Having read the chapter on norms this far, the hard-pressed manager may feel discouraged about the possibility of changing his work group's behaviors now that they are ongoing.

Not every deviation from the norm is sanctioned. Indeed, one could have creative groups in which certain types of deviations are fostered to enable the group to better accomplish its task. But of major interest here is the way that power, status, and leadership influence norm formation and produce changed normative behavior.

First, with reference to power, researchers [5] have noted that norms are an excellent substitute for the use of power. (We have noted the prob-

[5] J. W. Thibaut and H. H. Kelley, *The Social Psychology of Groups* (New York: John Wiley & Sons, Inc., 1959).

lems which can stem from power use.) The use of power as an influence attempt may produce undesired behavior as a reaction. For example, the boss of the roofing crew may use his coercive power to get the roofers to apply more squares a day. However, if they resent this coercion, they may form a coalition and may put the shingles on carelessly or be uncooperative in other ways. The resulting situation is not satisfactory to either party. On the other hand, both parties can reduce the cost to themsleves by establishing a norm which both find satisfactory, or at least less costly than what results from an actual use of power.

A number of studies have shown that high-status members of the group conform more closely to norms than average group members. As we shall see more clearly later, the group member with the highest power and status is usually the group leader. The group leader, then, has the greatest pressure on him to conform. Yet at the same time the leader must deviate from the norm by introducing changes in work procedures and goals. So the high-status leader has two strong contrary demands put upon him by the group—first, to be a conformist and, second, to be a deviant.

As groups are ongoing processes of interaction change must take place for them to be effective. It is the leader's role to introduce these changes in the norms.

Hollander [6] has shown that such *deviation* from group norms on the part of the leader in fact is *conformity* to what the group expects of him. He finds that in the early stages of interaction leaders are strong conformists, thereby building up their status and power. In the process of doing so, the leader acquires "idiosyncrasy credits" which he can "bank," as it were, against the "discredits" of deviation.

If the leader's power is based on expert power or legitimate power, he is also freer to deviate from group norms.

When the high-status person "takes a chance" on introducing a change, the outcome is in his favor. If his choice of deviation is *not* favored by the group, he can draw on the balance of his idiosyncrasy credits. If his choice of deviation *is* favored by the group, he confirms his high-status position. This situation allows the leader to be both conformist and deviate.

Some interesting observations were made of nursery school children a few years ago.[7] Groups of children were selected by their teachers as "followers" and were put together over a number of days so that they could form their own rules and traditions (norms) respecting play, toys, special language, use of objects, and so on. After each group had developed its own clear norms, a new child was introduced to it. These new children

[6] E. P. Hollander, "Conformity, Status, and Idiosyncrasy Credit," *Psychological Review*, LXV (1958), 117–127.

[7] F. Merei, "Group Leadership and Institutionalization," *Human Relations*, II (1949), 23–39.

had been picked by the teachers as having more initiative and directing power, giving orders more often than following, and being a bit older than the members of the groups. With twenty-six such leaders it was found that all but one were forced to accept the rules and traditions of the group. At the same time each was able to maintain his leadership position.

The researcher pointed out that leadership was maintained by the leader tending to follow one of three strategies:

1. *The order giver.* The leader gives orders, makes suggestions, and bosses the children in the group. He tends to be avoided and ignored while the group carries on according to its own norms. Suddenly, the leader changes behavior. He joins the group, learns the rules, and *then* orders them to do what they would have done anyway. In this way he maintains his status, power, and leadership but does not alter the group norms.

   We can probably all think of the "boss" who just "bosses" but who contributes little to the group's development. He retains his legitimate power position and monitors group norms strictly. He appears to be more concerned with maintaining the status quo and his own power position than seeing the group do anything constructive.

2. *The proprietor.* The child takes leadership by taking possession or control of group property. The toys and objects of the group become "his" and can be used according to the usual group norms as long as their "ownership" is acknowledged. In this way he maintains his authority position but does nothing to alter the group norms.

   Once again, we can probably all think of this supervisor or manager who keeps all the necessary information for group operation to himself. All the "toys" are his. Only he knows about the group's progress, problems, and requirements. Access to information about the group's relationship with the rest of the organization can be obtained from him only one piece at a time with acknowledgment of his authority and key position. Thus he remains leader but does little to change the group's normative behavior.

3. *The diplomat.* This child leader accepted the rules and traditions of the group and joined in the ongoing activities. He introduced very gradual changes and became the leader of the new games and behaviors. Later, he was able to introduce more drastic changes without being rebuffed by the group.

   The diplomat is a better model for the leader who is willing to understand and respect what the group values, yet he is a true leader introducing normative changes which are acceptable because they meet the requirements of the members' need satisfactions.

Here, then, is the key to changing normative behavior. First, keep in mind that the norms are established consciously or unconsciously to control those behaviors necessary for the group to satisfy its major purposes and accomplish its major tasks (as perceived by the group members). Second, deviations are rejected and sanctioned because they threaten to interfere with this need satisfaction and goal achievement. Third, a normative change perceived as providing the same or better need satisfaction and goal achievement will be accepted if properly introduced to the group—especially when introduced by a high-status, high-power, or high-leadership member.

SUMMARY

A norm is a standard shared by all members of the group. It provides the means of validating the appropriateness of behavior. Sherif's autokinetic effect studies and Asch's line studies were described to illustrate how norms form and remain in effect. The same thing applies to work groups as seen in the roofing crew.

Norm-sending involves the communication to members of which behaviors are appropriate or inappropriate, either directly or indirectly. An example of norm-sending by punch press operators was given.

Whether or not behaviors are private influences how closely a worker adheres to norms. If formed in the group, they are influential even when private, as they are when the work itself is interesting.

Norms apply to all relevant behaviors and may extend from general activity to subunits of the job. This means a whole series of norms are operative for the average worker. It also means there may be conflict between what is appropriate behavior in one sphere as against another sphere of behavior.

Deviation is costly, the more so when a group is highly cohesive or is related to other cohesive groups.

Personality factors influence willingness or desire to conform. This raises the question of persuasibility again, as considered in an earlier chapter. There is a difference between the average rate holder and the average rate buster.

The group puts pressure on the deviant to conform but when they consider him "perverse" they apply sanctions only for the sake of punishment.

This chapter on norms is relevant mainly because the manager is in a position to influence their development and change. If he does so correctly, normative behavior and conformity provide a key to group effectiveness. When he has no control over norms, he can be randomly their victim or their beneficiary.

15

ROLES

The behavior we expect from a person depends largely on the role we perceive him to have. How does the role we perceive ourselves to have affect our job attitude? How does a person get into role conflict? How does understanding role help us to understand why people in the same organization clash with one another? What are some unavoidable role strains? How can their effects be reduced? What steps can a manager take to prevent role conflict? How do we make decisions when faced with conflicting obligations? Are managers moral? Must managers be manly?

As norms form and individuals are assigned a status rank, the organization's social system acquires a structure in which persons take on specified roles to which are attached behavioral expectations. These roles help clarify and guide the form of interaction which will take place in the group. Later, we shall see that a pivotal role in this interaction is that of leader. As the organization evolves or undergoes marked change, new roles with their accompanying expectations emerge and old ones are abandoned. Because the role exists apart from the person (it is that place in the modern organization into which the individual is fitted as a replaceable part), he sometimes fits into it rather uncomfortably. When the round person is fitted into the square role he will either fail or something will have to give. It is these roles, the accompanying role strain, and its resolution which will now occupy our attention.

Perhaps we all can recall experiences similar to mine in one of my first supervisory positions:

I had known X for several years, and we had been good friends with similar interests and educational backgrounds. He had a couple of years' seniority in the organization, but we were at approximately the same level of responsibility and income. One day I was delighted to learn he was being transferred to my division. We had some good social evenings when he arrived, and our wives got along well together. We cooperated closely in the office and spent many lunch hours and coffee breaks together. I began to notice that the quality of his work was inferior and that he did not accept work norms easily. However, our role of mutual friends was well established, and I tended to turn a blind eye to his weaknesses and quietly corrected some of his work which came across my desk. Two or three months later I was promoted and found myself his supervisor. He was genuinely pleased for me in spite of his seniority. However, I now found my dual role as his good friend and supervisor an uncomfortable one. Complaints about his work reached me, and some sections were willing to cooperate with his section only when I urged them to be patient, and even then with reservations. Before many weeks passed a serious case of his negligence was brought to my attention. I called him in to discuss it. "Come on, old friend," he said in his jovial way, "don't take these things too seriously. That can be fixed up easily enough. I'll do it over again more carefully." I was in a bind and I knew it. Every attempt on my part to play the role of supervisor was met by his reacting in the role of friend.

It is situations like these—and their actual form is multiple—which start many managers on their way to the ulcer or the coronary. This is one of the important reasons we need to understand social roles and their implications clearly.

THE NATURE OF SOCIAL ROLES

Perceptual interaction gradually leads members of the organization to develop shared perceptions about what behaviors belong with which positions in the group structure. Norms provide the background against which the validity of these behavioral expectations and the appropriateness of the attitudes accompanying them can be evaluated.

The role behavior of a person can be anticipated and predictability of others makes it possible for us to shape our behaviors accordingly. We can do this not only for the person-in-a-position but also, because of our experience of persons-in-a-position reacting to us, we can do it for a person-in-a-position-in-a-situation. In other words, we can predict not only how the director is going to react when we tell him things are not going well in our district but also how he will react when we tell him so in the context of things not going well in similar districts across the country. Our experiences with role incumbents called "director," then, enables us to make predictions of his attitudes in new encounters simply by placing him and situation into an appropriate category. His experience enables him to do this for us as well.

By role we mean categories of persons occupying a place in a social relation. The terms president, director, divisional manager, chief clerk, personnel officer, typist, file clerk, and janitor all refer to role categories. But so also do terms like old man, young woman, friend, taxi driver, wife, customer, patient, and student.

Role expectations and *role behaviors* must be distinguished. The expectation represents how the person (the actor) who fills the role category is supposed to act (the manager is supposed to view "goofing off" on company time as a misdemeanor). The role behavior refers to how a specific person in a role category actually behaves (Mr. Jones, the manager of B division, is very casual in his treatment of workers who are low producers). Some individuals fit into roles very well; others do not. All the training and experience the company can give him may not make Mr. Jones an effective personnel manager, even though he is a nice person, fairly intelligent, and has a good formal education.

The expectations which go with a role specify particular behaviors relative to the occupants of other positions. Just as barber specifies behavior relative to barber shop client, so vice-president of planning specifies behavior relative to president; assistant manager specifies behavior relative to manager. These other positions are often referred to as the *counterpositions* and there can be no such thing as a role or a role incumbent without persons to occupy counterpositions—no generals without armies, no sons without mothers, and no managers without people to manage.

Along with the role and its counterpositions go a series of obligations, rights, and privileges. The manager may have the *obligation* of not endangering his subordinate's health by ensuring adequate working conditions, the *right* to expect job cooperation from him, and the *privilege* of being addressed by him as "Mr. Jones." The subordinate may have the obligation to report to the manager on his section, the right to expect fair treatment from him, and the privilege of being groomed by the manager for a more responsible position.

ROLES AND THE ONGOING INTERACTION

At any given moment a person may occupy a number of positions simultaneously. Thus the manager may be the supervisor of section B, the close friend of the manager of section A, and the person who told his subordinate, Bill Blokes, to do the job in a certain way. Now Bill Blokes comes to him and says that the manager of section A has reprimanded him for doing the job in that certain way. The manager's expected behavior is different according to the three simultaneous roles. As manager he has obligations to the company to achieve maximum effectiveness, his friend expects him to be friendly, his subordinate expects his support.

However, at any one moment a person never fills all his possible role categories. Some remain or become latent, while others are active. From his awakening in the morning a succession of roles emerges to activity then become inappropriate to the social setting—husband, father, carpool friend, manager of section A, advisor to a subordinate, respondent to a senior manager's request, representative of the company at a downtown meeting. The expected and appropriate behavior for each, in turn, is completely unexpected and inappropriate for the next.

ROLE EXPECTATION AND JOB ATTITUDES

Role expectations are *anticipatory*, (there is a regularity to the expected behavior of both role partners) and *obligatory* (we feel a person is obligated to fulfill our expectation). If I approach a fellow worker in a friendly and cooperative manner on what I perceive as a mutual problem, I *anticipate* that he will be cooperative in return, and I feel that he is *obligated* to be cooperative. This means the expectations are shared between us (and others) and that they are, in fact, *normative*. If the role partner does not fill his counterposition as expected I shall feel upset about it. When we deal with someone correctly or even go out of our way to do our duty politely and he is impolite or spiteful to us, we feel disturbed by the nonconformity of his behavior.

Thus the role is normatively controlled, shaping behavior in the direction of shared values; it is enforced by the behavior of other people; it may be specific to the group or generalized to all of society; there is a limit on the range of behaviors considered appropriate or permissible. When things are slack in the office or shop and the employer or manager orders a worker to do something nonappropriate to his role (e.g., wash the manager's car—I have seen it happen) he is acting contrary to role expectation and will surprise, anger, disgust, or confuse the person in the counterposition.

The term *values* has been used a number of times in the past few chapters. Values refer to the ideas that group members share about desirable things. For example, they may feel that the group should be friendly; that high-quality work is better than high-quantity work; that members should help one another; and that the group should be respected by other groups. These values can be ranked in terms of importance. They are related to role behaviors that are expected to fulfill or support group needs, and acts contrary to such values will be sanctioned.

Enforcement of such normative behavior is ensured both by formal sanction (the late employee has his pay docked according to how many minutes he is late) or by informal sanction (the noncooperative worker is shunned by his fellows). Sanctions can also be internal and private, as feelings of pride or guilt for having done a good or a shoddy job.

In an interesting study, Lieberman [1] demonstrated how closely work attitudes are tied to role in a cause-effect relationship. (It also bears out the validity of common expressions such as "You would never recognize him since he became a foreman.")

The company which was studied employed about two thousand five hundred in its factory and about one hundred fifty first-line supervisors. The shop was unionized and had about one hundred fifty stewards. A questionnaire dealing with attitudes toward the company, the union, and the job was completed by all factory workers including foremen. Fourteen or fifteen months later the same questionnaire was completed again but in the meantime some workers had been promoted to foremen and others had become shop stewards.

Lieberman was then in a position to ask the question, "What impact does being placed in the role of foreman and the role of steward have on the role occupants?" Compared with those workers who had not become foremen or stewards, he found, first, new foremen had changed their attitudes toward seeing the company as a better place to work, had a more positive perception of top management officers, and felt more favorably about the incentive system. Compared with those who had not become stewards, the new stewards had come to look more favorably upon labor unions generally, had a more positive perception of top *union* officers, and tended to prefer seniority rather than ability as the basis for moving workers into better jobs. The major general finding, then, was that workers put into the role of foremen changed their attitudes in the directon of pro-management while workers put into the role of shop steward changed their attitudes in the direction of pro-union.

Second, it was found that this attitude change was more pronounced for those who became foremen than for those who became shop stewards.

Third, it was found that new foremen became more antiunion, whereas new stewards did *not* become more antimanagement.

Having had the opportunity to complete this research, Lieberman had a stroke of good luck (unlucky for others, as we shall see). A short time after his second survey the company found itself trapped in an economic recession and had to cut its work force. Many workers were laid off and a number of foremen returned to nonsupervisory positions. Simultaneously, a number of shop stewards had not run for reelection or were not

---

[1] S. Lieberman, "The Effects of Changes in Roles on the Attitudes of the Occupants," *Human Relations*, IX (1956), 385–402.

elected. This unusual set of circumstances enabled the researcher to attempt to answer the question of whether the change of attitudes which had come with the new foreman and steward roles was a permanent one.

A third set of measurements of the same persons revealed that workers who became foremen and remained foremen retained their promanagement attitudes or became even more favorably promanagement. The demoted foremen showed fairly consistent readoption of attitudes toward management which they held before promotion.

The study as a whole demonstrates the importance of the neglected function of role. Once again we are back to the philosophical conundrum "Which comes first, the chicken or the egg?" As social interaction is an ongoing process and as group dynamics is a thing with seemingly no beginning and no end, it is difficult to know where to break into the cycle of change-producing-change. The question of role and interaction will crop up again when we consider leadership: Who should be promoted, the man who displays promanagement attitudes or the man who, in spite of current attitudes, has talent to get the job done? Indeed, how do we know he has the required talent until we put him into the position?

ROLE STRAIN AND ROLE CONFLICT

The term *role conflict* refers to that situation in which a person confronts competing or conflicting expectations. *Role strain* is a broader term which includes not only role conflict but other situations as well in which the person has difficulty meeting role expectations. This section will deal mainly with the broader concept of role strain.

When group members do not hold expectations in common, or behave contrary to them, interaction may then become difficult or impossible. This type of strain brings about conflicting tendencies to act; feelings of inadequacy, embarrassment, or guilt; and frustration of needs. Let us say, for example, that a subordinate approaches a manager with a difficult work problem. He expects the manager will take the problem seriously and offer advice for a solution. If, contrary to expectations, the manager treats the matter with levity and makes some pseudohumorous suggestions for solutions, the subordinate will not know whether to laugh or maintain his seriousness (conflicting tendencies); may feel embarrassed or inadequate; and will not have his needs satisfied.

The more clarity and consensus about roles, the easier it is to conform and hence the smoother the interaction. Strain comes from uncertainty of what roles involve and which behaviors are appropriate. Lack of clarity often appears when newly created positions are filled even though the job was explicitly defined before it was occupied. It also appears when a new role incumbent takes on an old established position and changes its character. The higher his position in the hierarchy, the more likely it is that he has some elbow-room and hence the more possibility of strain in the early stages. This is equally observable when the organization attempts to introduce new policies calling for adjustments in roles down the line.

Whenever role expectations are not clear for any reason, role strain will result and we witness periodic attempts by persons to clarify their roles. The large organization commonly develops a company manual. In some organizations a brief handbook is sufficient; in others we find it runs to several volumes (in a perpetual state of being amended). Sometimes role incumbents have to prepare elaborate job descriptions which are then adjusted so that all counterpositions are in harmony. Some of these techniques are useful but others become cumbersome because they are too elaborate. No matter how elaborate they are, it is impossible to foresee all the possibilities of strain and sometimes the good old-fashioned "lover's quarrel" is the only possible solution for redefinition and clarification of roles.

ROLE CLASH

Lack of consensus on role expectations can come from a number of sources. One or more role occupants in the organization may disagree with what is expected, resulting in a lack of concerted action and some degree of friction and anxiety. I have often heard interpersonal conflict in different types of organizations referred to as "personality clash." True personality clash is probably rare. The problem is far more likely one of role conflict. Labeling a conflict as personality clash is usually taken to mean that it is "unfortunate but unreconcilable" and hence it is impossible to do anything about it. Such ostrich-like attitudes should be replaced by an understanding of role strain.

Disagreement on expectations takes a number of forms. Here are some of the major ones:

1. Disagreement on the situation in which the role applies—for example, does one have to treat the role partner with the same respect outside the office as during the workday?
2. Disagreement on whether the expectation is mandatory or preferred—for example, is it necessary or does one have some option on whether to show the boss a sensitive piece of correspondence?
3. Disagreement on what expectations are actually included in a given role—for example can one communicate directly with another sector of the organization or must the communication go through the manager?
4. Disagreement on the range of permitted or prohibited behavior—for example, with reference to expense accounts or disbursement of petty cash.
5. Disagreement on which expectations should be honored first when there is conflict—for example, the typist is told to put aside whatever

she is working on and complete *this* piece immediately by two persons of approximately the same organizational rank.

Several or all of these disagreements may be present simultaneously.

When the role partners define roles and expectations differently from each other and the resulting conflict cannot be avoided or resolved, we can expect to witness sanctions like withdrawal of cooperation or even self-sanctions in the form of ruminations of guilt. Sanctions may also be imposed by others related to the role partner: for example, manager A is in conflict with vice-president Mr. X; he confides the conflict from his own point of view to manager B and together they impose sanctions of non-cooperation on vice-president Mr. X.

The greater the formal training and preparation leading to role occupancy, the more agreement there will be on expectancies for role positions—for example, medical doctors interacting with nurses. Also, there is some evidence of greater consensus when certain roles are very clearly defined, as the role of security guard or watchman. Finally, those with a great degree of contact agree more on their respective roles (boss and secretary).

According to a well-known study on school board members and superintendents,[2] members of groups with high consensus on their positions receive more gratification from their jobs and higher evaluation from their superintendents. It also suggested that in organizations which involve both professional and nonprofessional workers, the satisfactions received by the professionals are based partly on how well the nonprofessionals facilitate the achievement of professional goals. Other studies support this suggestion in industrial settings. When foremen and union stewards tend to define each other's roles in the same way as their role partner's (foremen to stewards and stewards to foremen) they reported easy relations with one another.

BUILT-IN CONFLICT

Some positions come with ready-made conflict or competition within the same role. The senior professor in the university, the senior doctor in the hospital, the senior administrator of many organizations finds increasing demands on his time as he is put on more committees, asked to take over supervision of a new section, elected an officer of another professional society, and so on. He soon finds the twenty-four-hour day and the seven-day week are far too short to meet all the role expectations required of him. Some of these expectancies will have to be sacrificed and those in counter-

[2] N. Gross, W. S. Mason, and A. W. McEachern, *Explorations in Role Analysis* (New York: John Wiley & Sons, Inc., 1958).

positions will feel the strain, as will the role incumbent himself who may soon begin to feel harried and pestered with petty details.

Technical or highly trained personnel brought in as staff specialists and traditionally lacking the authority to enforce their ideas and recommendations have a lot of potential strain. They also impose potential strain on the regular *line* workers who often regard staff men as inexperienced newcomers with different backgrounds of education, experience, and values.

Another type of built-in conflict belongs to the nature of the role. Private ambulance drivers are expected to help the injured at the scene of an accident but also want assurance that the ambulance bill will be paid; dentists are guardians of our oral health but aggressive bill collectors as well. Persons in managerial roles have these types of built-in conflict; leadership requires them simultaneously to keep group members focused on the task and to be sympathetic to personal needs.

Some role conflicts we are faced with as managers, professionals, university teachers, or just plain people come from expectancies in the community outside of our work organization. The community project, the church study group, the PTA, various groups devoted to helping our fellow man in need, the local political organization when election fever is in the air, and others (including our own family) have legitimate demands on our time. Sometimes they demand some of our experience and expertise as well. On occasion they try to pressure us into using office time, facilities, stores, and influence. Perhaps you have all felt that twinge in the stomach when you know a report is due to the school of nursing advisory board tonight and an important memo must suddenly be prepared for the company president for tomorrow morning while the wife is sullen because you will not be able to join her at the Smiths' cocktail party till at least ten o'clock.

Of increasing relevance these days is the conflict of the working mother. She often finds herself torn deeply between job, children, husband, and her personal development.

It comes as a surprise to some to learn that one of the major precipitating causes of the severe behavior disorder is a promotion. The literature on clinical personality disorders is full of case histories of men who have struggled to achieve top positions and a few weeks or months later have suffered severe personality disorganization or "nervous breakdown." Part of the reason appears to be the role strain which results from the discontinuity between the old role and the new one: the demands on and expectations of the new president are quite different from those he experienced as general manager; the demands on the foreman are quite different from those he was used to do as a nonsupervisory worker.

Finally, it might be noted that Western society, particularly in North America, provides a basic role strain for anyone in a supervisory position. This is because of our cultural stress on egalitarianism (the idea that all men are equals) which is taught us from childhood onward. Those younger persons, especially, who find themselves in their first supervisory position may feel quite uncomfortable on finding themselves treated as the "superior" in a superior-subordinate relationship. Even the words "superior" and "subordinate" tend to be avoided in textbooks and seminars, because the implication of the terms runs contrary to the cultural myth of equality. The young supervisor may feel uncomfortable when a pretty stenographer addresses him as "sir" and the older manager may feel role strain when his elders address him with deference even while outside of the work environment.

REDUCTION OF STRAIN

From the foregoing examples of role strain it might seem that every managerial role carries with it enough potential conflict for each incumbent to develop a new ulcer a day. If enough potential role strain were actualized it would soon lead to the breakdown of the organization. Such ineffectiveness could not take place if the purposes of the group were ever to be achieved. Part of dynamics is devoted to reducing strain in such a way that all role incumbents can perform their jobs appropriately.

When a crisis results from conflict, the obvious need is to seek a consensus of what are the rights and obligations of each. This may take the form of one marching into the other's office demanding, "It's time we got things straight around here," which, hopefully, will be turned by calmer minds into a valuable heart-to-heart talk leading to agreement on future behavior. Many organizations have negotiating committees, grievance committees, shop stewards, and so on to whom formal complaints can be brought when someone feels his rights have been offended. Those who have been on such committees know that the vast majority of cases can be resolved through discussion even when the initial appearance is one of impossible complexity and conflicting expectations.

Even better is the committee set up to prevent conflict. The coordinating committee or the liaison committee is such a group, although it may take many different forms and operate at many different levels. They are extremely useful when different groups share the same facilities, equipment, or environmental area; or when new facilities or environmental space is being planned and prepared for use by more than one group.

Role obligations in any social system are arranged in some sort of value hierarchy even though the members of that society may not be fully conscious of it. We are all familiar with the phrase "Well, I'd like to, but I can't because—" followed by the appropriate insertion of the obligation to fill some senior role. The morning off to attend a funeral; the extended lunch hour to visit the dentist (role of protector of one's health); leaving an hour early to prepare for the company banquet; excused from other evening obligations to prepare for an examination the following morning;

all these "excuses" resolve a role conflict because all parties involved accept a given priority of social roles.

BUILT-IN STRAIN REDUCTION

Protection from role strain is often built into organizational structure. Not allowing a person to hold more than one position simultaneously if there is the likelihood of clash is a good example of this. The law prevents lawyers from taking both sides in the same case and often we do the same thing in the organization. We get an independent consultant to check our books, to recommend on hiring or promotion of key personnel, to advise on locations for new plants, as well as on many other important decisions. This not only ensures that we have the advice of experts but that the information will be objective and that temptations to the decision makers to fill another of their roles at the possible expense of the organization will be reduced.

Spatial and temporal separation of the situations involving conflicting role expectations is another technique. The most obvious is the separation of the role of husband-father from the role of workingman. The man who works out of his own home is often faced by expectations from wife and children which conflict with requirements of doing his work well. In times of disaster or community danger this role strain becomes apparent. At the time of the great Winnipeg Flood (1950), many persons found they were simultaneously trying to meet the demands of protective parents and homeowners at the same time as they were defending the community and their places of work. Firemen, policemen, municipal engineering workers, and utilities workers felt the strain especially severely.

Protection from sanctions for persons holding pivotal positions also helps to reduce strain. Just as lawyers and priests have the privilege of withholding sensitive information, personnel officers, school principals, faculty deans, and many others in managerial positions also have to keep certain information in confidence, excusing them from normal expectations. The union steward is normally protected from sanction by guarantees of job security even though his role sometimes requires action contrary to management's expectations. Within the cohesive group one often finds reluctance to attack fellow position holders even when they err. Usually, managers are quite understanding of fellow managers who have fallen victim to role strain and made the wrong decision for they know how easily such a thing could happen.

Another technique we notice over a period of time when two roles are in conflict with one incumbent is division of the group. Although separate divisional chiefs may report to the same manager, the strain on the latter is not the same.

Finally, we have the famous *rites of passage* as a technique. This anthropological term originally referred to the ceremonies which accompanied changes of role in primitive societies, such as in puberty rites (change of role from childhood to manhood). In fact, we use similar things in industrialized societies to indicate that a person has passed from one role to another. We go so far as to change a person's name when he is promoted; thus, for example, the name plaque on his desk as a junior man was "Bill" but now the name on his door is "William C. Smith" and the clerks no longer call him "Bill" but "Mr. Smith." We also have our promotion parties at the office, the announcement with photograph on the business page of the newspapers, and so forth. We even have the "honeymoon" for new role incumbents; during this initial period of occupancy we overlook his foibles to give him a chance to "get the feel of the new job." Passage to higher positions or the hiring of new recruits can also be eased by orientation programs, special training programs, probationary periods, and so on.

CHOOSING THE ALTERNATIVES IN CONFLICT

Just as role strain must be reduced to prevent group ineffectiveness, so it must also be reduced in the individual to prevent his anxiety level from rising above a limit of tolerance. The easiest way of doing this is by restructuring his perception of the situation either to rule out conflict completely or to make the choice between alternatives more simple. A typical bind for the manager is one in which expectations of his superiors are contrary to those of his subordinates. By a simple *rationalization* ("They don't realize it, but it's better for them this way"), he can usually reduce any anxiety produced by his choice.

Because we tend to be somewhat consistent in resolving role strain, even in dissimilar situations, a rough dichotomy of personality can be drawn describing the way persons resolve conflict. One category of choice is *particularistic*, favoring a friend or an individual; the other category of choice is *universalistic*, favoring the group or society generally. Thus a person who tells a lie to protect a colleague whose expense account is being questioned, is resolving role conflict (friend role vs. employee role) particularistically. Recommending not to hire the nephew of a friend in favor of a more suitable candidate is universalistic. These two personality types can be measured by psychological tests.

A theory of conflict resolution has been developed by Gross and his colleagues.[3] They explain that a person faced with conflicting expectations A and B may:

[3] Gross, Mason, and McEachern, *Explorations in Role Analysis*.

1. choose to conform to A or conform to B
2. choose to compromise by meeting both expectations in part
3. try to avoid conforming to either expectation.

Diagrammatically, this can be illustrated as in Figure 15-1.

FIGURE 15-1

THREE POSSIBLE RESOLUTIONS OF ROLE CONFLICT

a) Conflict

b) Resolution I: either–or

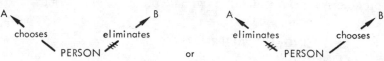

c) Resolution II: compromise

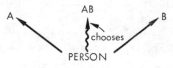

d) Resolution III: avoid

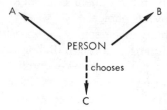

The actual choice is a function of three variables:

1. How legitimate the expectations are perceived to be.
2. How strong the sanctions for nonconformity are perceived to be.
3. The personality orientation of the person relative to legitimacy and sanctions.

First, legitimacy or illegitimacy depends on what the person perceives others have a right to expect. People tend to conform to legitimate expectations and avoid illegitimate ones. In terms of the diagram in Figure 15-1, if one expectation is legitimate and the other illegitimate, the former will be honored; if both are legitimate, a compromise will be attempted; if both are illegitimate, a response to either will be avoided.

Second, persons choose expectations which enable them to avoid strong negative sanctions. Again, in terms of Figure 15-1, if one expectation carried strong negative sanctions and the other carried weak sanctions, the former would be chosen; if both carried strong negative sanctions, compromise would be attempted; if both carried weak negative sanctions, the choice would be determined by legitimacy and personality orientation and not by sanction alone.

But legitimacy and sanctions can work at cross-purposes. For example, a worker may decide to carry out a personal errand during lunch time which will cause him to return late. He tells a colleague to cover for him if the supervisor comes. In fact, the supervisor does come looking for him and, finding him absent, asks the colleague directly, "Is he goofing off again?" Now the colleague has a friend-employee role conflict. It is illegitimate to cover for the friend but it also carries a strong negative sanction to betray him. The friend had no right to ask him to carry out an illegitimate act and the supervisor has a right to sanction him for not cooperating should he not tell the truth. To predict in a case like this, we use the third variable.

This is the personality difference between a primary orientation to legitimacy or a primary orientation to sanctions. Three such personality types are outlined. One gives primacy to legitimacy (a *moral orientation*). This type of person rejects illegitimacy and chooses legitimacy; if both are legitimate, he will compromise; if neither are legitimate, he will avoid choosing. The next type of person gives primacy to sanctions (an *expedient orientation*) and will choose the expectation with the strongest negative sanction for nonconformity; will compromise when strong sanctions are equal; and only when sanctions are weak in both choices can we predict his behavior on the basis of legitimacy. A third personality tends to take both variables into account simultaneously (a *moral-expedient orientation*). In his behavior he always tries to balance legitimacy or sanction, depending on the stronger factor in each case. When they are equal he compromises but otherwise he chooses on the basis of net balance.

On the basis of the theory, Gross and his colleagues were able to make correct predictions when school superintendents were faced with role conflict expectations concerning hiring and promotion of teachers; salary increases for teachers; budget priorities for financial or educational needs; allocation of their own after-office hours. Accurate predictions were made in 264 out of 291 cases of role conflict.

Using the same basic model, other studies have made predictions on conflict resolution among business executives, company training directors, and labor leaders [4] as well as among police officers and trainees.[5] Their predictions have not been as good as Gross's but have still been reasonably accurate.

For a final word on the resolution of role strain by the individual, we might keep in mind that there are always a few persons who do not accept even the central values of a society, or who have commitments to contradictory values. To explain what ultimately happens, we can view the role relationship as a *bargain* [6] in which a *role price* is set through interaction. An individual could perform his expectations well ("pay high") if he wants to carry out a particular role obligation as against other ones. This means, for example, that a man will devote much more time and energy to his job if he really enjoys the work or is deeply committed to its aims while devoting less energy to his marriage because he feels that it has not worked out well. In such a situation he would settle for the best bargain for each role keeping the total outcome in mind.

MANAGERS AND MORALS

The issue of morality is not often raised in a textbook written by a psychologist. Perhaps this is because it is perceived as related to the taboo topic of religion. However, if morality has a place in a book for managers, it is probably right here while we are discussing how the individual decides to resolve situations entailing role strain.

A study of business ethics was carried out a few years ago and reported in the *Harvard Business Review*.[7] About one thousand seven hundred executive readers of HBR responded to a lengthy questionnaire on attitudes to business practices. The results showed how executives are aware of their social responsibilities, profess lofty ethical aspirations, but feel that many other businessmen carry out unethical practices.

Almost all respondents agreed that they regarded untempered profit maximization as immoral. Only one in a hundred disagreed with the idea that sound ethics is good business in the long run. They view the corporation as more than a moneymaker and are conscious of its responsibilities

[4] F. A. Shull, Jr., and D. C. Miller, "Role-Conflict Behavior in Administration," a paper read at the American Sociological Association, New York, 1960; quoted in *Social Psychology* by T. F. Secord and C. W. Backman (New York: McGraw-Hill Book Company, 1964).

[5] J. Ehrlich, J. W. Rinehart, and C. Howell, "The Study of Role Conflict: Explorations in Methodology," *Sociometry*, XXV (1962), 85–97.

[6] W. J. Goode, "A Theory of Role Strain," *American Sociological Review*, XXV (1960), 403–496.

[7] R. C. Baumhart, S. J., "How Ethical are Businessmen?" *Harvard Business Review*, XXXIX, No. 4 (July-August 1961), 6–31.

to the people and the society to which it owes its existence. On some matters nearly all agree that practices are always unethical; for example, padding expense accounts, providing call girls.

The influences on whether a man makes ethical decisions were given in order as personal code, actions of superiors, company policy. Influences for unethical decisions were given in order as actions of superiors, ethical climate of the industry, actions of equals, lack of company policy, personal financial needs. These findings can be interpreted variously but, regardless of the interpretation, they point out the responsibility of managers: I am my brother's keeper. If you want to have an ethical group working for you, set the pace for them by personal example. Further, as Edmund Burke said, "All that is necessary for the forces of evil to win in the world is for enough good men to do nothing."

The great majority of respondents felt there were unethical practices in their industry. The ones they most wanted to eliminate were, in order: gifts, gratuities, bribes, and call girls; price discrimination and unfair pricing; dishonest advertising; unfair competitive practices; cheating customers, unfair credit practices, and overselling; price collusion; contract dishonesty; unfairness to employees and prejudice in hiring.

The major role conflicts reported by the executive respondents concerned firing and layoffs (getting rid of senior but less productive workers); honest communications (best advice means a lost sale or a lost customer); collusion and gifts (price differentials); pressure from superiors (to edit or "doctor" reports for clients, for higher production).

THE MANAGER IN THE ROLE OF MAN

Although the feminists may chip away at our hegemony, it looks like men will dominate management positions for a long time. Because of their role in our society and the expectations that go with such a role men have very strong advantages over women as managers. This is to be expected, for men have given the cultural definition to management (although women and children have concurred in the definition). Indeed, successful women managers often display some characteristics which are generally described as masculine.

Nonetheless, the role of manliness called for in the manager sometimes works to his disadvantage. Certainly, one can speculate about the relationship between the masculine role requirement of being tough, objective, unsentimental, emotionally unexpressive, and achieving and the fact that men die younger than women in our society.[8] The man who displays tender-

[8] S. M. Jourard, *The Transparent Self* (Princeton, N.J.: D. Van Nostrand Co., Inc., 1964).

ness, who shows emotion by weeping, or who exhibits his sentimentality is likely to be scrutinized carefully when promotions are considered. Although we males seem biologically and historically capable of expressing as broad a range of emotion as women and of having an unfathomable depth to our feelings, wishes, and fantasies, our maleness (particularly when it is magnified by a managerial role) requires us to hide much of our true selves.

There is evidence that men conceal more about themselves from others (as well as from themselves) than do women. It is as if we wore a protective suit of personality armor. When we venture into strange or dangerous territory (such as the world of management) it is necessary to buckle this armor tightly and hold our shield close for naked truth exposes our vulnerability. "Manliness," especially that called for from the manager, burdens us with chronic stress which could contribute to our shorter life span.

Our advantage, however, is our ability (which women often lack) to relate to other people impersonally. In the next section we shall see that effective managers retain an optimal psychological distance from their subordinates preventing personal matters from contaminating objective judgment.

A disadvantage is that, trained from youth to "grin and bear it" rather than to sob soft feminine tears, we often do not notice or even ignore the signals of strain which precede our ulcers, coronary, or nervous breakdown. We may also have become experts at concealing our needs for love and affection even from our wives and children and much more so from our employees and subordinates. Indeed, for a subordinate to witness a display of deep emotion other than anger in a manager might give him cause to suspect his boss is "cracking up."

No wonder, then, that managers so often feel alone and isolated. Frequently, it is they alone who understand the full implication of what is going on in the organization around them. Most of the others do not really seem to care. Even the good wife at home offers her sympathy but fails to understand the import of managerial problems, doubts, and strains. This heavy burden can be a danger to the physical, mental, and spiritual life of even the broadest-shouldered, most masculine manager. Even after their retirement, men—more frequently than women—suffer disintegration of personality, age rapidly, and die sooner.

We have been trained from youth to put up a good fight, not to be quitters, and to enjoy the game and its competition. As well as this we must learn, for our own personal development, that the player is more important than the game; that survival beyond the game is valuable; that existence in itself holds meaning and excitement. Without these attitudes we may never live long enough to get our gold watches.

SUMMARY

The question of social role fulfillment seems, at first sight, a rather secondary interest to managers. On closer examination, it involves us in an understanding of some of our greatest problems and headaches. The value of clearly established roles lies in the predictability they bring to an otherwise ambiguous social interaction. When occupants of each role and counterposition agree on rights and obligations, cooperation and coordination follow even in complex interaction.

That the role one fills in the organization influences his attitudes toward the job and toward the organization is clearly demonstrated by Lieberman's study of foremen and shop stewards.

However, multiple role occupancy, disagreement on normative demands, the emergence of new roles, passage to higher status, and many types of disagreement on role expectations can lead to role conflict and role strain. What often passes as the clash of incompatible personalities is more usually explainable in terms of role conflict.

The higher the consensus on what one's organizational role involves, the more likely we are to find job satisfaction. Many organizational roles come with an unavoidable, built-in conflict—for example, the conflict potential between staff and line workers.

Different mechanisms can be used to counter these, varying from the heart-to-heart talk to the formal coordinating committee. Protection from sanctions, restrictions on multiple-role occupancy, physical and spatial separation, and role mergers are other ways of protecting individuals from the consequences of strain.

A person's solution to a role conflict can be predicted if it is known whether he has a particularistic or a universalistic tendency in his personality. Gross and his associates set up a theory of resolution based on the three possible alternatives (choice of one alternative; compromise; avoidance) by which quite accurate predictions of solution could be made in terms of the three variables: legitimacy-illegitimacy; strength of sanctions; and personality orientation in terms of moralistic, expedient, and moral-expedient tendencies.

Brief reference was made to business ethics and it was pointed out that the typical executive is very aware of his social repsonsibility and that of his organization. It is easiest to be an ethical manager if one has ethical superiors.

Finally, the role of the male in general was examined. The masculinity of managers serves both to their advantage and disadvantage. The greatest disadvantage is that masculinity imposes role strains that femininity does not; the consequences for mental and physical health as well as the early death rate of the male have been well documented. The most healthy approach to management lies in the realization that our personal development must not be neglected because of our commitment to our managerial duties. In fact, the two should not be incompatible.

4

LEADERSHIP

There is a vast amount of research literature on leadership, both in the business and industrial setting and in other social settings. Some of the research is "pure" and some of it "applied." The main focus in Chapter 16 is to clarify the concept of leadership in light of the research psychologists and sociologists have given us. The question of who the leader of the group really is and how he gets this role and the problem of how he can be described are brought out in this chapter. In Chapter 17 some of the major research findings are brought into the management setting so they can be directly applied to day-to-day problems.

Chapter 18 points out some of the neglected responsibilities of today's leader. It shows how fulfillment of the role of leader-teacher allows both individual and organization to realize their potential by applying the principle of learning to management. A few basic learning concepts are described and their practical application to work problems is discussed.

16

THE ROLE OF LEADER

Although it is a common assumption that good leaders have a number of common characteristics, the present chapter attacks this popular belief. Can leadership be understood better in the context of group dynamics? In what ways do the concepts of group leader and individual leader conflict? What are the true qualifications of leadership? How does leadership role tie in with group purpose? Are there different styles of leadership? What are the functions of leadership? Authoritarian or democratic—which is better? Can we assume it is the latter?

For centuries people have asked what it is that makes a good or a powerful or an effective leader. Many perhaps thought that if they knew the secrets of leadership they could enjoy the fruits and advantages that great men received (perhaps forgetting the problems of exile, imprisonment, and violent death that great leaders also received).

Until relatively modern times leaders were generally *born* and not made (see Chapter 5 for reference to the social background of business leaders). A man's socio-economic status depended upon an accident of birth. The son of a nobleman or landowner was likely to receive an education of sorts and learn to read and write; he was also likely to have servants, money, and better food to eat (hence be larger in size and in better physical condition). Consequently, he would stand out among men by his very speech, dress, and bearing and have a greater chance of exercising acts of leadership.

However, there were always those few not so blessed at birth who rose up from slavery or poverty to become leaders. Were they also born with some qualities of leadership or was this something they acquired in the process of growing up and experiencing life?

Questions like these were relevant because until quite recently the only way answers were attempted was through studying the lives of great men. The ambitious and the concerned studied and imitated the lives of Alexander, Caesar, Napoleon, and others. The sayings and advice of famous men were seen as keys to success. Much of today's population has not moved beyond this stage; they read the biographies of politicians, businessmen, and military leaders for some clue to effective leadership.

Starting less than one hundred years ago, a few writers began searching through the lives of famous leaders for factors which they might have in common. Some of these studies showed that leaders were taller than followers (bishops were taller than clergymen, university presidents were taller than college presidents, sales managers were taller than salesmen, etc.). This was alright when referring to an outstanding tall leader like Charles de Gaulle but it was not much help in explaining a short leader like Napoleon Bonaparte. Height may correlate with leadership but it is certainly not the sole—nor an important—factor. In fact, nine studies have reported leaders were taller than followers—but two have reported they were shorter! And two found no difference.[1]

Other physical factors such as body size, health, physical energy, and physical appearance have been studied with somewhat similar results as the studies of height. Not all effective leaders have been healthy and, indeed, some, like Franklin Delano Roosevelt and John F. Kennedy, have had physical defects.

It soon became apparent to writers on leadership that a search for physical correlates would take them nowhere; when techniques for measuring psychological characteristics became available, the search turned to such things as intelligence. Were leaders the most intelligent members of groups? (They tend to be more intelligent than average but are certainly not the most intelligent members of groups.) Personality factors were also examined; aggressiveness versus submissiveness, extroversion versus introversion, and so forth. But the results were similar to the studies on intelligence (five studies found leaders more extroverted; two studies found them more introverted; four studies found no difference) and researchers

[1] R. M. Stogdill, "Personal Factors Associated with Leadership: A Survey of the Literature," *Journal of Psychology*, XXV (1948), 35–71.

gradually began to believe that the personality characteristics of leadership were too complex to measure with standard psychological tests.

The problem with all these early studies on leadership was that they used a *trait* approach to the question. In other words, they tried to discover what trait or combination of traits was required to make a good leader. After his extensive research of the literature, Stogdill states, "The findings suggest that leadership is not a matter of passive status [i.e., is not merely something which the leader may possess such as being the son of a king or duke] or of the mere possession of some combination of traits." [2] (The comment in brackets is mine.)

This implies that the opposite to "leader" is *not* "follower" for the characteristics of a leader are not opposed to the characteristics of a follower. If there is an opposite to leader it is "the indifferent," for the apathetic or indifferent are those who are incapable or unwilling either to lead or to follow. The further implication is that a person who is a leader in one situation may be the follower in another. And this is certainly what we witness each day. The good supervisor or manager who leads his unit effectively becomes a good follower in a superordinate group.

Although many books have been written and many conclusions drawn about what it takes to be a good leader, Stogdill's findings, supported by a number of others, puts most books on leadership written prior to 1950 on a list headed "For Research or Historical Interest Only." Unfortunately, our public (and private) libraries are still well stocked with such books which are not so marked.

LEADERSHIP AND GROUP DYNAMICS

The failure of the trait approach underlines the importance of understanding leadership in the context of the group. Leadership is a role stemming from the interaction of the group members. It cannot be understood apart from choice, power, status, norms, and the very nature of group purpose. This is why so many studies (Stogdill reported nineteen) confirmed that the pattern of leadership traits differed with the situation.

The group, in order to survive as a group, must differentiate one of its members to fill the leadership role. Otherwise, its very existence is threatened by lack of achievment of its purpose or lack of membership satisfaction (see Chapter 6). Leadership belongs to the group and not to the individual; therefore, to seek leadership traits is to look in the wrong direction, and to understand leadership we must look at what the group is trying to achieve. Then we may find that leadership falls to one, or to several, or to many members of the group.

[2] *Ibid.*, p. 66.

It is a common misperception to seek the locus of cause for leadership within the person rather than within the situation; historically and culturally, we have always tended to emphasize the names of individual heroes of battles, successful politicians, great statesmen, explorers of the unknown, inventors, and outstanding executives. But the heroic general would be nothing without his foot soldiers, the politicians could not succeed without supporters, inventors stand on the shoulders of earlier inventors, and executives do not become outstanding without a pyramid of subordinates.

We have a mythology about leadership which often stands as a direct stumbling block to effective management and the effective organization. Centering attention on the concept of one-man leaders who supposedly have some personal trait or talent to get the job done leads to impractical and inefficient use of the potential residing in the members of many small groups. Although most groups within the organization have a formal leader whose status is ratified by the organization, concentrating on what *he* does prevents us from even looking at what is actually going on as the group proceeds to fulfill its purposes. Without realizing it, our tendency to concentrate on the one-man leader, his traits and actions, requires an implicit assumption that he is some type of magician in complete control of his social environment. Yet our movies, TV plays, novels, even textbooks and university courses—to say nothing of our day-to-day organizational behavior—support this folklore.[3]

To make sense at all, leadership must be understood as those behaviors of group members which are

1. functionally related to the achievement of the group's goals
and/or
2. functionally related to the very maintenance and strengthening of the group's existence.

The first category of leadership acts is instrumental in achieving goals and would include such things as making suggestions for action, evaluating movement toward goals, preventing activities irrelevant to the group goal, helping to set norms, providing solutions to goal barriers, and so forth. The second category of leadership acts is existence maintaining and includes such things as encouraging other group members, helping release tension which may build up within the group, allowing everyone to express himself, and rewarding useful behavior of other members.

[3] The thinking of many contemporary social psychologists, supported by research literature, is exemplified in the work of George A. Borden et al., *Speech Behavior and Human Interaction* (Englewood Cliffs, N.J.: Prentice-Hall, 1969), p. 134 ff.

Given some reflection, it can be seen that these are acts which almost every group member perfoms from time to time—or *can* perform. Does that mean that every member of the group carries out leadership acts? Yes it does.

GROUP VERSUS INDIVIDUAL LEADERSHIP

The concept of group leadership will not go unchallenged by experienced managers in spite of the forewarnings in the first chapter that one intent of our book was to upset some thoroughly ingrained management myths. Therefore, I shall sketch out the reasons such an approach is superior to the traditional concept of one-man leadership and how it can add to organizational effectivenss.

The group approach means that the leadership act originating in the newest, low-status, introverted member of the group may be as important to fulfill group purposes as an act of the assertive, high-status, experienced, formally appointed chairman or manager. It is the context of the act which is important—the group and the larger organization. Understanding this, all group members, including the formal leader, are in a position to encourage leadership acts which will lead to the group goal and to inhibit acts likely to interfere with its achievement.

The group approach also means that all members are employed in the verification process; the critical thinking of all can check the faulty reasoning and incorrect information of other members. When we have one or even several formal leaders, the false can be mixed with the true, the mediocre with the brilliant, and the stultifying with the creative, and the best will be accepted while the worst goes unchallenged. From our study of status we know that a middle-status member is not likely to challenge a high-status member who is a recognized producer of good ideas (even when he also produces poor ideas).

This is not to say that the formally designated leader is a hindrance to the group's progress. He need not be and, indeed, hopefully, he will help rather than hinder it. In the complex organization groups could not function effectively without formal leaders. In practice, such leaders tend both to help and to hinder the group's effectiveness. Ideally, they should only help, but in practice what we should strive for is increasing the ratio of help over hindrance so that the latter becomes negligible.

Some tasks and some aspects of tasks in any complex organization call for, even demand, a highly directive leader. Crises demand a decisive leader who can act quickly and alone, confident that his group supports him to the fullest. Indeed, research has shown and many of us have personal experiences of the fact that the formal leader who fails to act this way in a crisis will, figuratively, be stripped of his mantle of authority while group members turn to an informally designated leader for decisive action. (With the crisis past they generally turn back to the formal leader.) But other day-to-day tasks call for directive leadership. In these it is sufficient for the leader and all members to be alert to the potential of leadership acts emanating from any group member. This bring us back to so many points made earlier on communication and group dynamics—in which context the whole concept of leadership must be viewed.

When one man, formally designated as leader, by his presence or position in the group produces an atmosphere wherein others surrender their initiative and are inhibited from producing any kind of leadership act, that group is immeasurably debilitated en route to fulfillment of its dual purposes—task accomplishment and member satisfaction. Such a stance makes peripheral members passive, exonerates them from responsibility in accomplishment, and leaves the central leader open to blame if the task fails or the group deteriorates.

Contemporary social psychologists are divided between those who favor a *total group leadership* approach and those who favor a *modified group leadership* approach leaving some emphasis on the formal leader. These latter (I include myself among them) feel that one person plays a guiding role, putting pressure on the group by suggesting directions and enforcing procedures (making an agenda, terminating debate, calling for formal motions, interfering in conflict, requesting experts to voice opinions). In the task-oriented group in which the work to be done is quite straightforward, the amount of direction called for is even greater; once the group is "locked on" to goal achievement, the leader must interfere when suggestions arise which will retard progress or deflect the group from its course. The ideal leader is flexible enough to lead the group through a series of variations from completely open, leaderless behavior (brainstorming) to ruthless insistence on fulfillment of duties calling for personal sacrifice. Now the group-leader theorists argue that it is impossible for one man to preempt all the procedural insight in a group unless he is so much more experienced, trained, or gifted than other group members that the group becomes superfluous: the leader is capable of doing the job alone. This argument is invalid, I submit. First, because a modified group-leader approach does not assume that the leader is in some sense capable of doing the job alone. Second, because the group itself calls for directive leadership when one member begins to behave foolishly and disruptively or persists in repeating boring personal arguments. Third, because the formal leader is often in the position of having more facts, more experience, and a broader range of understanding of overall goals than is the group.

Having presented the arguments, we are now in a position to examine the pros and cons of the two basic concepts of group leader as against individual leader. They are in the following table:

One Leader	Group Leader
Personal motives dominate group objectives whether or not they are identical with group or organizational motives.	*Depersonalizes motives to concentrate on task.*
Unique personality both helps and hinders group function.	*Unique personalities of all are used but not allowed to interfere with task and purpose.*
Unique experience is used as guide for group behavior.	*Formal leader's experience is used and is buttressed by experiences of others.*
One man helps others and contributes to task.	*All help and contribute.*
Leader holds major responsibility for success or failure.	*All are responsible for success or failure.*
Group depends on leader for effective action.	*Whether leader is present or absent, the group is able to function effectively.*

QUALIFICATIONS FOR LEADERSHIP

Whether or not the act of leadership comes from a formally designated leader, the actor must possess recognized skill and knowledge. A designated leader must possess considerable skill and insight for he has to prevent his formal designation from interfering with leadership acts from other members. Such a leader needs insight into group dynamics and membership behavior, developed by his successful participation in many groups and by his lengthy and systematic observation of the group communication process. Depending on his degree of skill, he will either be able to actualize the potential of his group or he will dominate, ignore the contributions of others, and alienate its members.

The group requires that various of its roles and functions be specialized. Borrowing from a division from Haiman,[4] we could say that style of leadership (formal or informal) follows from three things: *individual differences, need for personal stability,* and *division of labor.*

First, the unique differences among individuals would include their talents, personality, experience, knowledge, and specialized training which would equip them to perform some group roles more readily than others. One will be better able to carry out certain group functions (chairing a committee, directing a work group, supervising task performance); another will like to do certain things better than others (carry out the mathematical calculations, prepare a background report, contact a nongroup member on

[4] F. S. Haiman, "The Specialization of Roles and Functions in a Group," *Quarterly Journal of Speech*, XLIII (1957), 165–167.

behalf of the group). Because of these individual differences, some members may be capable of carrying out many of the group's functions, some capable of carrying out a few, and some capable of carrying out rather limited functions.

Second, we know that everyone is dependent on his group for feedback and consensus about the appropriateness of his perception and his behavior. In other words, each member must be able to depend on aspects of his relationship to others and their relationship to the rest of the group members. This shared consensus underlies personal stability in one's world. Because ambiguous situations and unclear role expectancies are frustrating, anxiety-producing, and inefficient to at least some of the group, members are readily labeled either consciously or unconsciously as leader, follower, high-status, low-status, and so on. The expectations of their behavior and situations of interaction are also readily labeled and stereotyped. One is labeled "the fact man," another "the spokesman" for certain interests, a third as one who can get things done, a fourth as the joker, and so on.

This labeling often has the effect of encouraging the person to carry out those behaviors expected of him even more than does his possession of certain characteristics. We know from our study of perception and self-fulfilling prophecy (Chapter 3) that when everyone expects a person to be the witty joker of the group and reacts to him as though this were one of his major group functions, he behaves accordingly, perhaps even abandoning any attempt to fill other roles such as that of "serious contributor."

The third factor from which leadership acts follow is the division of labor among group members. Ineffectiveness would result if all were supervisors or assistants, or if all were architects and none were draftsmen, or if all produced and none sold. This means that roles, responsibilities, and tasks will be divided among members on a fairly regular basis so that each can provide service to the group by moving it toward task accomplishment and freeing other members to do things they are better at or enjoy more. Of course, a specialization of functions complicates relationships among members because the implication it carries for communication, power, and status may interfere with cohesiveness and solidarity.

In one sense it may seem we have come full circle. We started by pointing out that the one-leader concept was invalid. We are now back to the point of admitting that specialized ability, the expectations of others, and the specialization of functions requires one group member to carry out specialized leadership acts more than other members. We call this person the "leader."

The difference is in our understanding of what leadership acts involve, why they are carried out, and the threats that a trait approach or a one-leader concept entails by suppressing and the leadership acts which all members are capable of performing, and thereby of decreasing the group's effectiveness.

As Gibb [5] explains:

Thus, the particular role an individual member achieves within the group is determined both by the functional or role needs of the group-in-situation, and by the particular attributes of personality, ability, and skill, which differentiates him perceptually from other members of the group. Leadership is a function of personality. It is also a function of the social system. But more basically it is a function of these two in interaction. (pp. 215–216).

LEADERSHIP AND GROUP PURPOSE

A group does not exist without a leader and a leader can certainly not exist without a group. Our theoretical lone man on a hypothetical desert island who has never had any contact with other human beings could certainly not have leadership characteristics. Leadership acts can be carried out only because of the dual purpose of the group: task accomplishment (instrumental) and member satisfaction (existence maintaining). In an informal group, such as at a bus stop, leadership may shift rapidly from one member to another in succession—as the first person in line steps into the bus, the others take a step forward to follow him, but now he is gone and another replaces him. The large public reception is another example, as we see people swirl about and we see groups form and dissolve, with new leaders ever arising to start new conversations on new topics or to make suggestions for action like going to the bar for refills.

In informal groups leadership may fall to one member rather than another because he is taller (hence can look directly at all other members over the heads of shorter people), because he has a louder voice and can be heard above others, because he is older and hence is accorded more respect when he makes suggestions, or because he is the biggest coward and runs at the first sign of danger, followed by the others who become confused.

The unruly crowd or mob often follows the leadership act of a sociopath or a psychotic; these persons may have less inhibition about urging people to carry out illegal acts, or may set the pace by throwing stones, attacking police, or breaking windows and stealing. Sick people or highly prejudiced persons can become crowd demagogues when tensions are high and group purposes are ambiguous.

The type of leader who emerges and the type of leading that is done depends on the group's purpose. If it is primarily to accomplish a task (getting prompt medical attention to the injured at the scene of an accident; scoring against an opposing team; finishing a customer's job by

[5] C. A. Gibb, "An Interactional View of the Emergence of Leadership," *Leadership,* ed. C. A. Gibb. Penguin Books, Inc., 1969.

four-thirty), the person who is most directive, displays greatest knowledge, or has most formal authority is given leadership by the group. If the major purpose is member satisfaction (a house party, a group therapy session, or a PTA discussion group), the leader is the one who produces most laughs, reduces most anxieties, or provides the most interesting information.

As most of the groups we are interested in fall between these extremes, who gets the leadership role? First, remember that it does not have to be one person. It could be two—one to urge the group to the task, the other to relieve tension when work is monotonous or demanding. It could be more than two members, as we have seen, and it might involve all members performing various leadership acts as demanded by the situation.

LEADERSHIP STYLES

The formal or generally recognized leader, depending on the purpose of the group and upon his personal characteristics, may spend a greater part of his effort initiating and directing group actions toward problem solution or in helping and satisfying members. The first is known as a *task leader* or *job-centered* leader; the second is known as a *social-emotional* leader or a *member-oriented* leader. The two possible emphases are often referred to as the two dimensions of leadership: the *initiating and directing* dimension and the *consideration* dimension.

In a famous study done some years ago, Robert Bales [6] set up a series of five-man discussion groups that had to arrive at a single solution to a human relations problem within a specified time. The groups were composed of relative strangers and met a total of four times. At the end of each session they had to answer a series of simple questions: Who contributed most ideas? Who did most to guide the discussion? Whom do you like? Whom do you dislike?

At the end of the first session the best-liked member tended to be judged as having contributed most ideas and guidance. But by the end of the fourth session the person best liked was more often *not* the one judged to contribute most ideas and guidance—and the one who did contribute most was often the most disliked man! The most liked usually stood second or third in terms of his contributions. (A corollary of this is that if you are going to be a leader, be prepared to be disliked.)

Bale's study raised a number of interesting questions but our main interest is in noticing that there are two major leadership roles in his groups. It was the task leader who kept the people at the job and insisted it be accomplished according to the specifications. For this he was liked

---

[6] Robert Bales, "The Equilibrium Problem in Small Groups," in *Working Papers in the Theory of Action,* eds. T. Parsons et al. (New York: The Free Press, 1953).

and respected. But, as he continued to force people to focus on the job, certain personal satisfactions (the enjoyment of new friendships, interesting gossip, telling of jokes) were frustrated. These personal need satisfactions were interfering with the task and that is why the leader inhibited them. But as group frustrations built up the members began to direct their hostilities toward the task and toward the task specialist who was pushing them to accomplishment. As these frustrations represent disruptive forces capable of preventing both the job from being done and the members from achieving satisfaction, it is necessary for a new leadership role to be differentiated. This was the social-emotional leader; it was his role to reduce tensions and prevent accumulated frustrations from destroying the group's dual purpose. His leadership acts help boost morale and defend the values, attitudes, and norms of the group which have been deemphasized, denied, or threatened by the required focus on the task.

The two dimensions or emphases are not opposites. The quality of being production-centered or task-oriented as a leader should be considered as independent of being employee-centered or member-oriented. The good supervisor or manager combines both dimensions in his leadership style, working out his own creative synthesis of the two. Yet an inflexible emphasis on either one can get the manager into trouble. If he emphasizes only the job-centered dimension, he is then regarded as a taskmaster and risks lack of cooperation from the group. If he emphasizes only the consideration dimension, he tends to be regarded as a superficial popularity man and can be used by his subordinates to their personal advantage and to the disadvantage of task accomplishment.

Whether two obviously different leaders arise in any work group, as they did in Bales's study, depends on how much the achievement of group goals frustrates individual satisfaction. When the two are mutually compatible, both dimensions of leadership can then be fulfilled in one formal leader. When task and member satisfaction collide, the degree of differentiation between roles depends on how much frustration and hostility is generated and on the leader's skill at preventing such frustration.

We also find this differentiation or bifurcation of leadership roles when there is a different level of involvement in the task among group members. In the work group the supervisor and highly skilled members are often more involved in the task than are other members; thus the formal supervisor becomes the task leader while some other member carries out many leadership acts of an informal social-emotional nature (e.g., imitating the boss in his actions, making jokes about the job, and being able to "stand up to the boss" in a mock-serious way that relieves tension). Such informal leadership acts may even come from low-status members of the group.

When we find two quite distinct roles within the group or when we find a formal leader tending to emphasize the one dimension or the other, we see that the personalities of the two are likely to be different. The effective task specialist tends to be an emotionally detached person (he cannot be emotionally involved for this reduces his ability to exercise power by increasing his dependency on others). He differentiates between followers to a higher degree, seeing their personalities as quite distinct and liking some more than others. He is capable of withstanding negative attitudes and reactions from others. The social-emotional expert likes people and they like him. He likes other group members strongly and equally. The disadvantage of this is that he depends on others and is upset by their negative reactions to him.

The more a person is perceived as the legitimate leader (established in his position by a higher authority); deserving of his position; personally involved in accomplishing a legitimate task and not merely satisfying his own needs (making a reputation for himself or being ambitious beyond his capabilities); the more the perceived costs of carrying out his orders are not considered great by group members and do not arouse much conflict with the satisfaction of their personal needs. When the leader is perceived by the group as illegitimate, as holding power by boot-licking his own supervisor, and so on, the costs of carrying out his instructions and demands are perceived by group members as much greater. Frustration results and secondary leaders are needed to fulfill the social-emotional dimension of leadership.

FUNCTIONS OF LEADERS

In their book on social psychology, Krech and his colleagues [7] provide a list of functions which all leaders may serve to some degree.

The *executive* is top coordinator of group activities with the responsibility for execution of group policies and objectives. Normally, the work is not carried out by himself but delegated to other members. Lack of delegation cuts down involvement of other members as well as their responsibility for work outcomes.

The *planner* role results from a broader knowledge of long-range as well as short-range goals and closer contacts with key nongroup people. However, this function can be overplayed by keeping others in the dark thereby cutting off their talents and experience as well as reducing their involvement and responsibility.

The *policy maker* has three sources for his function. Superordinates may dictate what he must get his group to do. Subordinates establish work

[7] D. Krech, R. S. Crutchfield, and E. L. Ballachey, *Individual in Society* (New York: McGraw-Hill Book Company, 1962).

norms from below. The formal leader himself may be given autonomy both from above and below to make policy decisions.

As *expert*, the leader is a source of information and experience and often possesses highly needed special skills. This talent may be the ability to draw on the specialization of his technical subordinates and his assistants and coordinate their efforts toward goal achievement.

The *representative to nongroup members* is an important function in a large organization for the formal leader is the point of official contact with other segments of the organization and with the organization as a whole. Both outgoing and incoming messages are channeled through him.

The leader is *controller of internal relations*. He influences the structure of the group more than any other member. In some types of groups he is the hub of a major part of the communication and group dynamics.

He is the *purveyor of rewards and punishments*. It is the leader who must ultimately apply the formal sanctions—both positive and negative. Even when he does not administer them, he recommends or approves of them—for example, promotion, handing out the "pink slips."

As *arbitrator and mediator*, he acts as judge and conciliator when conflict arises within his group. Whether conscious of it or not, he may play an important part in the formation or reduction of in-group factionalism and bickering.

The leader must be *exemplar*. He is the model for the behavior of members and must set the pace through contagious enthusiasm for the task. We discussed this point in our chapter on norms where we found the leader adheres to group norms more closely than other members to gain idiosyncrasy credits.

The leader is the *symbol* of the group. In some types of groups this is most important. The head of the family, the head of state, the chairman of the board, the director of an institute, and many others symbolize or stand for the group.

Every experienced manager knows that the leader is *substitute for individual responsibility*. How often are we begged through signs given off, or even deceived for this purpose, to give our formal stamp of approval, to countersign for the timid or the terrified subordinate. (We must admit that, although this is often a bothersome stupidity, sometimes our act of "magnanimity" gives us a feeling of vain but satisfying pride.)

For some groups the leader is *ideologist*—when he is the primary force behind the formation of the norms, beliefs, and group values. The high school football coach, the father of the family, and some types of political leaders (e.g., Lenin) are examples of this. It is less important in work groups but could exist in some segments of the organization. Military and ecclesiastic groups provide another possibility.

The leader is sometimes the *father figure*. In this sense he is the focus of individual identification and private emotional feelings. Sometimes he is even referred to both seriously and in jest as "the old man," or "the great white father."

Experienced managers are also aware of another important leadership function, that of *scapegoat*. The leader becomes the target for aggression when things go wrong as easily as he is the father figure when all is rosy. In time of frustration or disillusionment, it is he who must bear "the slings and arrows." Every time I think of this, I think of Mussolini. How they loved him when he was on top and how they dragged his naked body through the streets when his empire and his dream tumbled!

Some of these functions are far more important than others. Some we have already discussed in detail. Some will be fulfilled much more often by the manager in his routine work. Some he may never really fulfill. But potentially he can fulfill all of them.

A few minutes of reflection should enable you to ascertain which functions are most relevant in your group.

AUTHORITARIAN AND DEMOCRATIC LEADERS

A distinction sometimes drawn between leadership styles is that of authoritarian leader, democratic leader, and laissez-faire leader. These can best be distinguished in terms of the communication and information nets operative in their groups.

The *authoritarian* exercises more authority over members. He controls all progress to the goal and interrelation of members. He resists attempts to change his leadership functions. His most effective technique in maintaining this position is by withholding knowledge of goals, not sharing information required for the task, and not providing feedback to members on their progress. As he is the only group member with complete knowledge of all functions and accomplishments, the members are dependent upon him for goal achievement. This means that the communication net is of a wheel form with the authoritarian leader at the center.

Now we know that the most common structural feature of the organization involves a basic wheel form—for example, as in Figure 16-1. Structural forces tend to push the manager in the direction of authoritarian leadership. Obviously, the larger the group over which he has supervision, the less direct contact the manager is likely to have with peripheral second- and third-line subordinates.

A common result of this form of leadership is that the group grinds to a halt in the absence of its chief and, pending instructions from him, no decisions are made and no new activities are initiated. When an authoritarian leader clings to the reins even during a prolonged hospitalization the organization may suffer irreparable damage.

FIGURE 16-1

EXAMPLES OF LEADERS IN WHEEL STRUCTURES

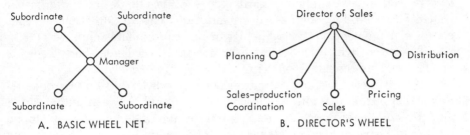

A. BASIC WHEEL NET   B. DIRECTOR'S WHEEL

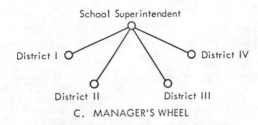

C. MANAGER'S WHEEL

The *democratic* leader uses a different approach. He may have as much power as the authoritarian leader but he uses it by distributing responsibility rather than by concentrating it. He tries to keep as many members as possible personally involved in problem solution and in awareness of goal progress. The sociogram describing the communication net for this type of leader is more like an open circle; members are encouraged to communicate with one another and with the leader. During his prolonged absence for sickness, accident, or vacation, the group is able to function effectively.

The *laissez-faire* leader is really no leader at all. He holds the formal leadership position and acts as the group's figurehead. He may have achieved his position by fighting hard for it or by nepotism. The actual leader may be his assistant, a general manager, or some other senior person. Laissez-faire leaders are occasionally found in military, government, ambassadorial, and philanthropic organizations but also crop up in the profit-making company. I knew a shipyard foreman who did nothing but play cards from eight in the morning till four-thirty at night day after day. A senior charge-hand effectively ran his group. Often, when such a laissez-faire leader decides to "do the rounds" or "show the flag" on a monthly visit, the workers hold their breath hoping that he will not feel moved to issue any instructions, for his knowledge of what is going on is so out of date and irrelevant that it will simply upset work procedures.

Although the democratic group is more effective, some situations may call for authoritarian or laissez-faire leadership. Equally, some groups prefer nondemocratic leadership. There seems to be a preference among insecure minority groups (e.g., immigrant groups) to prefer authoritarian leaders, and also scientific-technical groups often choose an authoritarian leader. Some production-oriented organizations choose authoritarian leaders for management positions whether or not subordinates approve of this. Also, the group which has successfully adapted to a laissez-faire leader is not likely to prefer either of the others as his replacement.

An early classic study on the various types of leadership was done by Lewin, Lippitt, and White.[8] Differences they found between authoritarian and democratic groups were that the authoritarian-led tend more to be either aggressive or apathetic (aggression directed inward, apathy replacing aggression when the leader is absent); members make more submissive approaches to the leader; there is less group cohesiveness; constructive work decreases when the leader is absent; in the presence of frustration the group deteriorates and blames individual members for problems. In the last situation the democratic group attacks the source of the frustration.

There is a parallel between the task-centered and the authoritarian leader and between the social-emotional and the democratic leader. However, each involves a distinct aspect of leadership behavior and cannot be fully equated. The task leader is not always authoritarian nor is the social-emotional leader always democratic.

SUMMARY

There are many things still to be said about leadership but this chapter has attended only to those things which the leader normally does or is expected to do. The assumption throughout the chapter has been that the leader is the person formally designated to lead the group. In spite of this, a strong argument was made against the adequacy of the one-leader concept. Any member can, does, and should be encouraged to perform leadership acts.

Leadership is a function of the group. Only if we rid ourselves of the idea that it is the function of an individual can leadership make any sense. The argument was made that the group-leader concept was superior to the one-leader concept in terms of effectiveness for a number of reasons. As a function of the group, leadership must be understood in the context of the dual purpose of the group—task accomplishment and member satisfaction.

A modified group-leader approach was defended by proposing that

[8] R. Lippitt and R. K. White, "An Experimental Study of Leadership and Group Life," in *Readings in Social Psychology*, 3rd ed. by E. E. Maccoby, T. M. Newcomb, and E. L. Hartley (New York: Holt, Rinehart & Winston, Inc., 1958).

individual differences among members, the need for total group stability, and specialization of tasks forces its application in practice. The full group leader concept is operative only in the laboratory or as an ideal.

The dual purpose of the group led us to consider the two dimensions of leadership: the initiating and directing dimension and the consideration dimension. These dimensions are not opposites and must both be incorporated even though the nature of the group may call for emphasis of one over the other. The advantages and disadvantages of emphasizing one of these dimensions were outlined and the likely personality of such leaders was described.

Fourteen possible functions of the formal leader were suggested. Some are much more important than others. Depending on the group, some will be fulfilled more than others but all are possible roles the formal leader may fill or be called upon to fill.

Finally, the authoritarian, democratic, and laissez-faire leaders were described. The democratic style is most effective but there are situations in which group members prefer to operate under one of the other two.

17

THE LEADER AS MANAGER

What has research shown to be the important behaviors in leadership? Why is the first-line supervisor essential to implementing organizational policy? What problems does participation solve? What claims does Likert make for System 4 management? How can the four-factor theory of leadership be used to predict worker performance? Why not change the group to fit the leader? Is leadership style the key to effectiveness?

In a lecture delivered in 1968, Chris Argyris, a long-time student of the relationship between individual and organization, made some predictions about future organizations. He stated:

> The functions of leadership will also be expanded. As in the case of the structures, varying patterns of leadership will be developed for use under specific conditions. An executive, guided by a set of decision rules, will know when to be directive and controlling; when to create conditions of psychological success; when to focus primarily on organizational demands and when to concentrate on individual growth; when to openly manipulate; and when to behave autocratically.[1]

[1] Chris Argyris, "Understanding and Increasing Organizational Effectiveness" (Commercial letter, Canadian Imperial Bank of Commerce, Toronto, October 1968).

I am not sure how far into the future Argyris was predicting but I feel that much of it is here with us now. The seeds have already been sown through books such as this one and others dealing with different aspects of organizational and industrial psychology and the psychology of work. The increasing amount of research and the concern for research as well as the number of management courses and seminars given all across the country shrink the gap between now and future.

Unfortunately (it could be fortunate but in practice is not), a major finding in investigation of leadership styles is that supervisors imitate the style of their own supervision. Even when junior or middle managers are given an extensive training course which concentrates on developing modern management styles, it has been found that the effects soon give way to imitation of the management style to which they are subjected. It has been well documented that a pressure technique designed to "smarten people up" and originating from the top managers of a large organization quickly percolates to the lowest level of supervisor.[2]

The organizations which will survive and grow in the next few decades are those willing to cast off old-fashioned techniques and adopt new styles of leadership, with their implications for new psychological contracts and communication patterns.

So far we have discussed a lot of social psychological findings and principles; now it is time to roll up our sleeves and see their implications for running an effective organization.

MANAGEMENT SKILLS AND CLIMATE

Once researchers realized that the trait approach to leadership was fruitless, they began studying leadership *behaviors* rather than people who were leaders. To do this it was no longer necessary to use the traditional church-military hierarchical model. Leadership behaviors could be studied in any group and soon led to studies in the industrial and business organization which we can use to guide us toward effective management. The results of some of these studies have been referred to in the last chapter; now we go on to apply them, and others, to a knowledge of management skills.

Building on work done at the Survey Research Center (University of Michigan), Mann[3] defined three skills required of the supervisor or manager. First, *human relations skill*, which involves the ability to work with

[2] R. H. Guest, *Organizational Change: The Effect of Successful Leadership* (Homewood, Ill.: The Dorsey Press, Inc., and Richard D. Irwin, Inc., 1962).

[3] F. C. Mann, "Toward an Understanding of the Leadership Role in Formal Organization," in *Leadership and Productivity,* eds. R. Dubin et al. (San Francisco: Chandler Publishing Co., 1965).

and to judge people, including a knowledge of the principles of behavior, understanding of human interaction, and an awareness of human motivational problems. Second, *technical skills,* which include ability to employ techniques, methods, and equipment required to carry out specific tasks. Third, *administrative skill,* which refers to the ability to understand and work for organizational goals rather than to work merely for immediate group goals. Under this third skill would come planning and organizing work, making appropriate task assignments to group members, inspecting, following up, and coordinating the work of subordinates.

Rensis Likert, whose work has been mentioned,[4] also described five conditions which must be present to ensure effective supervisory behavior. First, *supportive relations,* which implies that the whole organizational climate as well as the behavior of the supervisor has to be seen by the worker as maintaining his personal worth and importance and supporting his values. Second, *group emphasis* in supervision, meaning that each worker must be part of an effective group which has high performance goals, group loyalty, and effective interaction. Third, *high performance goals,* meaning that the supervisor must not only be employee-centered but must also have "contagious enthusiasm" regarding the importance of achieving high performance goals. Fourth, *technical knowledge* which the supervisor must have to deal competently with work problems faced by his group, or the ability to see that technical knowledge is provided by others. Fifth, *coordinating, scheduling, and planning,* essentially the linking-pin function we described in Chapter 7. This means the group leader must present views, goals, values, and decisions of his group to the groups where he is linking pin and bring back views and decisions of other groups to his own.

As can be seen, the skills and climate which are the necessary context for effective leadership acts are controllable. That is to say, they can be taught to competent leaders and leader candidates (the skills) and can be developed within the organization (the climate). It is no longer necessary to rely on selecting and promoting people who have some combination of mysterious leadership traits. Effective leadership acts can be called for by intelligent management and that control over managerial environment is within the reach of those who know how to produce it.

THE SUPERVISOR—KEY TO SUCCESS

Unless basic work groups are high-producing and low-costing, all the machinations, knowledge, and fancy footwork at upper and middle management levels mean nothing. Until the men and women who dig the ditch,

[4] R. Likert, *New Patterns of Management* (New York: McGraw-Hill Book Company, 1961).

fill out the report, unload the boxcar, assemble the parts, write the letter, teach the children, type the policy, package the meat, or sell the shoes do so effectively, all the management skills in the world will not make the organization an effective one. But how is this basic unit to be made effective? We must start with the person responsible for the unit—the first-line supervisor. If he fails, the whole managerial pyramid is valueless.

Research done by Mosel [5] underlines this fact. We know from our earlier study of perception, motivation, psychological contracts, attitudes, and group dynamics that any incentive designed by management will work only if perceived by the employee as likely to follow when the behavior to be motivated is produced. If the worker does not perceive the incentive as likely to follow his efforts, the behavior may not be produced. Thus the best laid plans of managers depend for their effectiveness on how the workers perceive these plans.

Mosel obtained the subjective estimates of 900 employees as to whether five regular work incentives would be received under specified conditions. The five were as follows:

1. Promotion in next eighteen months if most outstanding producer in section.
2. Dismissal in next eighteen months if worst producer in section.
3. Receipt of cash award for sustained superior performance if warranted.
4. Having suggestion adopted in Suggestion Awards Program.
5. Supervisor writing recommendation for cash award for sustained superior performance if warranted.

There was a wide spread in the estimated probability of receiving them but they were most often estimated by employees as "uncertain" except for the final item dealing with supervisory support. (The greatest uncertainty was about having a suggestion accepted; see Chapter 7.)

Mosel found that the rates of perceived probability were unrelated to the employees' age, sex, salary, marital status, or education. What he did find, though, was that *"the probability of a supervisor's writing a recommendation for a cash award has an effect upon the probabilities of the four incentive events"* (italics in original). In other words, when supervisory supportiveness was high, expected probability of receiving the incentive was high; and when supervisory supportiveness was low, expectation of receiving the incentive was low. Expectation of dismissal (item number 2) varied, showing that low confidence in the supervisor made very little difference on this item.

[5] J. N. Mosel, "Incentives, Supervision, and Probability," in *Personnel Administration*, XXV (January-February 1962), 9–14.

Mosel's findings are important; they demonstrate that the first-line supervisor has considerable influence over the motivating force of the formal incentive systems set up by management. It is as if the confidence an employee has in his immediate supervisor generalizes to his confidence in the whole management system. The implication is that formal incentive systems may fail because of the leadership role taken by first-line supervisors.

A number of researchers have shown that close supervision as against general supervision is related to low-producing work units as against high-producing units. Likert, for example,[6] has shown that there is a great difference in productivity when first-line supervisors are close as against general supervisors. The high-producing supervisors make very clear to their subordinates exactly what they must do and why, then give them freedom to do it the way they can work best. The distinction between general and close supervision is "the difference between getting a janitor to keep the floors clean, as contrasted with sweeping routinely every one half hour with a twenty-inch broom ten strokes to the minute" (Estes, 1960).

An experimental verification of the effects of close supervision was made by Day and Hamblin.[7] Their subjects were 96 girls aged 17 to 19 years doing assembly work in the lab. Close supervision yielded lower productivity plus aggressive feelings toward the supervisor and co-workers. When punitive supervision was employed (making frequent sarcastic and critical remarks to the girls as they worked), they also found lowered productivity and verbal aggression (but not toward co-workers). The amount of aggressiveness under close supervision was greater in those girls who had the lowest self-esteem.

As suggested earlier in the book, rising levels of workers' education, increase in work technology, and changing attitudes toward self-expression all tend to make close supervision a procedure of limited value today. Coupled with this, it is associated with low productivity.

LEADERSHIP AND PARTICIPATION

Perhaps the greatest controversy about leadership styles today is concerned with participative or participatory leadership and its cousin, participative democracy. Certainly, in areas of university administration one tends to find the students and young faculty members overtly or covertly aligned against the deans, department heads, and other representatives of "the establishment" in trying to determine the amount of participation that should be present in daily decision making.

[6] Likert, *New Patterns of Management*.
[7] R. C. Day and R. L. Hamblin, "Some Effects of Close and Punitive Styles of Supervision," *American Journal of Sociology*, LXIX (1964), 499–510.

Researchers whose work supports the effectiveness of p
management and decision making are regarded as extremists of
relations school" by hardheaded, experienced managers and b,
tional structuralists who claim there is a gap between the research findings
and the practical realities of running a complex organization. However,
psychologists, students, managers, organizational researchers, and the lot
are the same as any other people we have been describing in this book.
Once they have a perceptual set, a well-developed attitude, and a supportable theory, their adaptation level makes anyone else's ideas become the
work of "the enemy." Both sides could profit from holding their breath,
blanking stereotypical counterarguments, and listening to what the other
side has to say.

Among the strongest voices in favor of participation have been Douglas McGregor (of theory X and theory Y fame) and Rensis Likert (about
whose current ideas we shall say more in the next section). Participative
leadership is a natural development from a democratic leadership style. It
calls for freedom and independence for the individual yet allows the formal
leader an active and important role of exhortation, rewarding, motivating,
suggesting, and encouraging the group's members. The participative leader
must not give up his leadership role or else the group becomes ineffective.
Nor can he be employee-centered to the extent that the task is neglected
or he will soon find himself a wet nurse for incompetent members, merely
encouraging their incompetence or satisfying his own needs for nurturance.
His interest in subordinates must always be modified by his interest in getting the job done through effective individuals.

Participative management is based on group decisions, mutual discussion of common problems, and shared responsibilities. Evidence has
been presented that total participation is better than participation through
a representative, and participation through a representative is better than
no participation at all in planning and implementing changed techniques
in an industrial setting.[8] This has been supported by further practical
studies—as that of Robert Guest [9]—in which it is shown that a large complex organization can shift to more participative forms of management
without alteration of its formal structure and thereby achieve enviable
increases in effectiveness.

Guest's report points out the necessity of linking all organizational
units to the top unit in the hierarchy. This supports Likert's contention
that participation is possible even in the largest organization. He lays out
the steps required for success in such a program. First, the necessary climate

[8] L. Coch and J. R. P. French, "Overcoming Resistance to Change," *Human
Relations,* I (1948), 512–532.
[9] R. H. Guest, *Organizational Change: The Effect of Successful Leadership*
(Homewood, Ill.: The Dorsey Press, Inc., & Richard D. Irwin, Inc., 1962).

must be developed so that people understand the necessity of reaching decisions or taking action as a group. Second, this requires that all members have an awareness of the problems; this, in turn, presupposes effective linking communication nets. Third, there must be discussion but this has value only when it leads to agreement and decision for action. Fourth, members must commit themselves to the specific decisions. Fifth, everyone involved in the problem or everyone who will be affected by decisions must be allowed to participate. Finally, there must be follow-up and feedback on the decisions. All of this presupposes a democratic leadership style from the very top down to the very bottom of the hierarchy and it also presupposes effective linking-pin functions throughout the entire organization.

Now the proponents of participative management point out some cautions about its introduction and use. It cannot be introduced overnight. The first step—development of the correct climate—is essential and may take considerable time. Actual results in terms of improved performance depend on the size of the organization, the number of levels in the hierarchy, the number of specialized groups, the complexity of technical operations, and the level of insecurity and personal hostility at the outset of change.[10] Also, the trappings and techniques of participative management, without a full commitment on the part of senior management, is easily perceived as a "put-up job" by subordinates with a subsequent lack of cooperation. Proponents of participation urge moving into it slowly and cautiously while warning that things may get worse before they get better and that it is a difficult process to reverse once started.

Further cautions about participation are that certain white-collar employees and government workers may experience lower satisfaction when given a higher degree of independence in decision making. Although this has been attributed to their feeling that if they were good enough to be independent they should get promotions and higher wages, it could also support the caution of moving into participative management without first developing the climate for it.

There has also been a warning [11] that authoritarians and persons who have no strong need for independence are unfavorably affected by participation; this must be taken into consideration before launching a new participative management program. The same studies also confirm the negative reaction to participation which follows from encouraging pseudo-participation. It is *psychological* participation which has important effects; the worker perceives and feels that he is personally involved regardless of

[10] Likert, *New Patterns of Management.*
[11] F. C. Mann and F. W. Neff, "Involvement and Participation in Change," in *Psychology in Administration,* ed. T. W. Costello and S. S. Zalkind (Englewood Cliffs, N.J.: Prentice-Hall, Inc., 1963).

the degree of actual participation. Yet attempts to dupe the workers into psychological participation without real participation bring rapid negative reactions. Finally, we are reminded that, to be motivationally effective, participation must be directly related to the objective of the participation and that a general sharing of unrelated problems will not predispose workers to accept a specific change that will affect them and about which they have not been consulted.

A difficulty which can develop under participative schemes is that top management, by helping the people on the shop floor and front office, are putting undesirable pressures on foremen and middle management. This may result in supervisors becoming passive and dependent and the company losing their talent and dynamism. However, such problems can be overcome—for example, by putting much of the decision making, policy making, and operating responsibility into their hands.[32]

Even such impressive changes wrought through participative management as described by Marrow and his associates [13] have been criticized because of the experimental difficulties of knowing the cause-effect relationships involved—that is, was the participation responsible for the change? The researchers might reply, of course, that in spite of technical-experimental criticisms, the end results are impressive.

SYSTEM 4 MANAGEMENT

Drawing on his own experience and research and that of his associates at the Institute for Social Research in Michigan, Rensis Likert has refined his earlier theories and those of others into a management approach called *System 4*.[14] He argues that the system is based on extensive and verifiable information from rigorous, quantitative research which can be replicated.

Experienced managers, he finds, consistently describe work units (departments, divisions, organizations) that they know well quite differently when they are very high producing and very low producing units. The descriptions are similar regardless of whether the work units are described by managers in Production, Sales, Financial, office, and so forth, and regardless of whether they are staff or line.

The descriptions are quite extensive but all are placed on a scale entitled System 1, System 2, System 3, and System 4. In basic terms, System 1

[12] James E. Richard, "A President's Experience with Democratic Management," quoted in *Organizational Behavior and Administration*, rev. ed., ed. Paul R. Lawrence and John A. Seiler (Homewood, Ill.: Richard D. Irwin, Inc., and The Dorsey Press, Inc., 1965).

[13] Alfred J. Marrow et al., *Management by Participation* (New York: Harper & Row, Publishers, 1967).

[14] Rensis Likert, *The Human Organization* (New York: McGraw-Hill Book Company, 1967).

is exploitative-authoritative; System 2 is benevolent-authoritative; System 3 is consultative; and System 4 is participative. A few examples from the descriptions used are "to what extent are subordinates involved in decisions related to their work?" (System 1: "not at all"; System 4: "are involved fully in all decisions related to their work"). "Extent to which the review and control functions are concentrated" (System 1: "highly concentrated in top management"; System 4: "quite widespread responsibility for review and control, . . ."). "Extent to which there is an informal organization present and supporting or opposing goals of formal organizations" (System 1: "informal organization present and opposing goals of formal organization"; System 4: "informal and formal organization are one and the same; . . .").

With very few exceptions, managers describe the high-producing units toward System 4 and low-producing units toward System 1. It also appears as an inconsistency that managers tend to describe their own organizations as being less toward System 4 than they say they desire them to be. Some low-producing managers even feel that they should use more of a System 1 management until high productivity has been achieved and only then move toward a System 4 management! Such managers are not likely to achieve high productivity in their units, says Likert.

The argument is that if a manager has a well-organized plan of operation, high performance goals, and high technical competence (in himself or his assistants) and then applies a System 4 management as against a System 1 or 2 style the results will be quite different. His organization will display greater group loyalty, higher performance goals, cooperation, and peer assistance, experience less pressure, hold more favorable attitudes toward management, and have higher motivation to produce. If it is a sales organization it will have a higher sales volume, lower sales costs, higher quality business, and more earnings by salesmen.

Any shift toward System 4 management must come from the top. When top management is committed to System 2 it is difficult for any submanager to learn System 4 and use it. It is emphasized that System 4 is a style which must be *learned* by managers who propose to institute it and that its successful introduction is gradual, taking perhaps a few years.

THE FOUR-FACTOR THEORY OF LEADERSHIP

Bowers and Seashore,[15] having reviewed the major research programs and findings on leadership from 1950 to the mid sixties, concluded that all

---

[15] D. G. Bowers and S. E. Seashore, "Predicting Organizational Effectiveness with a Four-Factor Theory of Leadership," *Administrative Science Quarterly*, XI, No. 2 (1966), 238–263.

had a great deal in common although they tended to use different terms and broke leadership behaviors down into different descriptive units. They found that four dimensions emerged from all these studies which could be considered as comprising the basic structure of leadership. These are:

1. *Support:* This is any type of behavior which makes a group member have a feeling of personal worth and importance.
2. *Interaction facilitation:* This is behavior which encourages mutual affect and close relationship among group members.
3. *Goal emphasis:* This is stimulation of enthusiasm for goal achievement and excellence of performance.
4. *Work facilitation:* This is behavior which aids goal achievement by such things as scheduling, coordinating, planning, and providing resources such as tools, materials, and technical know-how.

These divisions could be subdivided further according to the particular situation being studied. They could be collapsed to reflect the dual purposes of the group—membership satisfaction (1 and 2) and goal achievement (3 and 4).

The authors point out that all of these are behaviors which can be provided by any group member to other group members; this means leadership can be exercised by a formally designated leader or through mutual support of members or lie in some combination of formal and informal leadership. Also, we may find one or more aspects emphasized by the formal leader and another or other aspects emphasized by other members. Yet there are sound theoretical and practical reasons for having a formally acknowledged leader to set the pattern of mutual leadership for subordinates to supply one another.

Their findings are that, if a manager wants to increase the extent of his subordinates' support for one another, he must increase his own support *and* his own emphasis on goals. If he wants to increase the extent to which they will emphasize goals to one another, he must increase his own facilitation of interaction *and* his emphasis on goals. If he increases his facilitation of work, he will increase the extent to which his subordinates increase facilitation of work. If he increases his facilitation of interaction, his subordinates will increase their own facilitation of interaction.

We see clearly that the manager is norm-setter. Each of the factors of leadership present and possible to all group members can be increased by the manager and substantially improved. This means he is truly the leader and that, inasmuch as acts of leadership take place within his group, they follow his lead and example. We have said before that leadership style is related to the style of supervision to which the leader himself is subjected. Now if leadership is a function of the group and all members are potential leaders the same principle is in effect. Members carry out leadership acts to the extent that their formal leader does so. As the manager fulfills more of all four types of leadership behaviors, both separately and in combination, there will be an increasing number of leadership behaviors displayed by group members. In other words, the model is not one of simple leader-to-peer leadership but, rather, different *aspects of performance* are associated with different leadership characteristics.

Bowers and Seashore have worked out predictors for worker satisfaction with company, fellow workers, job, income, and manager; and with staff-clientele maturity, business costs, advanced underwriting (their major study was in insurance), and business volume. These predictions were made on the basis of the leadership behavior (or combined behaviors) displayed in the group. In five out of the twelve predictions, *peer goal emphasis* (the third leadership factor as displayed by group members to their peers) was the best predictor either by itself or as an additive to another predictor.

THE CONTINGENCY MODEL

One of the most interesting and potentially useful theories of leadership effectiveness to have been advanced is Fiedler's contingency model.[16] Fiedler has been doing research on leadership effectiveness for many years and has come to a rather different conclusion than some of the other researchers we have mentioned. The main difference is that he feels *the job should be fitted to the manager* rather than the manager being retrained or readjusted to different supervisory styles than those to which he is accustomed. In this way the organization can make use of the management talent it already has available for surely, says Fiedler, it is easier to change almost anything in the job situation than to change a man's personality and his leadership style. Why not change the shape of the hole rather than try to change the shape of the peg?

Between the two extreme leadership styles (tell workers what to do and how vs. share responsibilities and involve all in participation) there are many shades of styles with evidence to support almost any one of them. Through a relatively simple technique, Fiedler identifies the management style of individuals and the atmosphere of groups, then predicts what styles go with which groups.

Leadership style is identified by the way a man describes favorably or unfavorably his *least-preferred co-worker* (LPC), the person with whom he works least well—whether it is someone he works with now or someone he knew in the past. Those who describe their LPC relatively favorably tend to be permissive, human-relations-oriented, and considerate managers

[16] Fred E. Fiedler, *A Theory of Leadership Effectiveness* (New York: McGraw-Hill Book Company, 1967).

(high-LPC leaders). Those who describe their LPC unfavorably tend to be managing, task-oriented, and less concerned with human relations (low-LPC leaders). The one is effective in some types of group, the other in different types of groups.

Groups can also be described in terms of three dimensions. First, *leader-membership relations* which indicates the degree to which group members trust and like a leader and are willing to follow his guidance. The trusted leader does not need special rank or power to get things done. This first dimension can be measured by a simple group atmosphere scale, rather similar to the LPC scale. Second, the *task structure* is an important dimension. It is measurable in terms of the degree to which the group task is spelled out step by step and can be done according to a detailed set of standard operating procedures, or in terms of how much the task must be left nebulous and unstructured. The vaguer the task, the more difficult to exert leadership pressures for accomplishing it. When the task is clear, authority can be supported and a worker can be disciplined for lack of performance. The third dimension is that of *position power*. This refers to the power inherent in the leadership position apart from the personal power of the individual leader—for example, the power to fire, hire, and promote.

Now the leadership style (high- or low-LPC) can be cast in a table with the three dimensions of the group as in Figure 17-1. Using this chart, Fiedler has found that the contingency model can predict the best leadership pattern for many different types of work groups (survey teams, open-hearth shops, heavy machinery plants, meat departments, service stations, farm cooperatives, sales display teams, tank crews, bomber crews, pilot training groups, military combat crews, basketball teams, bowling teams, supermarket grocery departments, research labs, and others).

The vertical axis of the graph indicates the best leadership style for the particular work group situation as shown by correlation of the leader's LPC score and his group's performance. It can be seen that the best leadership style depends on how favorable the particular situation is for the leader. In those situations in which it is very favorable or very unfavorable to achieve the task by group effort, the task-centered, low-LPC leader works best. Where the situation is intermediate in difficulty, a permissive, nondirective, high-LPC leader is more successful.

Fiedler points out that his model complies well with our common experience of work groups. We do not expect nor want the trusted leader in the unambiguous situation to ask our advice—we want him to get on with his formal leadership job. Also, the disliked chairman of the volunteer group facing an ambiguous task will accomplish nothing if he asks the group what they should do. On the other hand, the liked and respected leader of a creative planning or research group has to be permissive to

FIGURE 17-1

EFFECTIVE LEADERSHIP STYLE VARIES WITH THE SITUATION

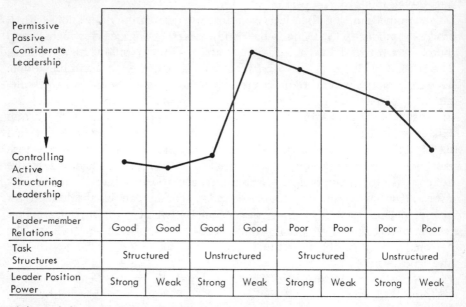

Leader–member Relations	Good	Good	Good	Good	Poor	Poor	Poor	Poor
Task Structures	Structured		Unstructured		Structured		Unstructured	
Leader Position Power	Strong	Weak	Strong	Weak	Strong	Weak	Strong	Weak

Adapted from F. E. Fiedler, "Engineer the Job to Fit the Manager," *Harvard Business Review*, XLIII, No. 5 (1965), 115–122.

get maximum support from all members; a directive leader would cut off the potential ideas and participation of group members.

Many work groups are not of one stable type, though. They change as the task at hand changes. The contingency model takes this into account. When the highly structured routine gives way to crisis and the task becomes ambiguous, the manager must change from directive to permissive until the operation becomes routinized again. The director of research or planning must be permissive and member-oriented to bring the best out of the group but, when the plan is complete and has become a structured work program, the director describes the task of each in detail and how it must be done and permits no deviations to any individual group member.

The advantages of Fiedler's approach are numerous. Existing talent can be utilized by changing the group to fit the manager. Needed technical and professional people can be hired regardless of their individual leadership styles. Rather than retraining managers, work groups can be readjusted. The three group dimensions can be altered to fit the key man. First, position power can be changed either by giving the leader subordinates of nearly the same rank as himself, or by giving him subordinates two or three ranks below himself. He can be given sole authority for the group task or he can be required to have unanimous group approval on decisions. Communication patterns can be structured either to reinforce or weaken his power position. Second, the task structure can be changed. The task can be made precise to the detail or it can be outlined only as a general problem. Third, the leader-member relations can be adjusted by changing group composition in the direction of similar backgrounds, attitudes, and beliefs, or by introducing men of different cultural, linguistic, and training background.

By adjusting these three dimensions a work group could, theoretically, be categorized under any one of the eight situations to make it optimal to meet the style of the formal leader. Although the emphasis in the contingency model is engineering the job to fit the manager, an awareness of his own style and the type of situation in which he is likely to be successful will be of great benefit to the manager. It will also warn him of those changing situations in which he should try to adjust his style to the group.

CONCLUSION

All theories outlined in this chapter are of value to the manager. It is not merely a question of choosing one over the others. Their emphasis may be different—Likert's theories require retraining of personnel; Fiedler's theories require readjusting work groups. Once the manager understands the implications of both theories in the larger context of social psychology, he can see the value of using both approaches.

Writers and theorists on leadership often present excellent evidence to support their theories. The described changes in productivity, morale, and other measures of effectiveness as the result of using *their* leadership approach are very impressive.

However, we must not be seduced into thinking that it is leadership style alone which produces effectiveness. Leadership is extremely important, but so are other things. Many have been discussed in this book (motivation, aspiration, job attitudes, the peculiar dynamics of a given group, etc.) and many other things have not been discussed or have only been mentioned (education, technical skills, task demands, the cultural-economic context in which the organization operates). These are all factors which influence effectiveness directly and leadership can only modify their relationship to effectiveness, some more than others.

SUMMARY

Building on the previous chapter, which described leadership roles in the context of group dynamics, we have gone on to consider the role of manager as leader. Mann describes the three basic managerial skills as human relations, technical, and administrative. The climate in which effective management is to be exercised has also been described (by Likert) as one with supportive relations, group emphasis, high performance goals, technical knowledge, and good coordination, scheduling, and planning relative to other groups.

To underline the importance of the first-line supervisor in any complex organization, Mosel's study was referred to. It was demonstrated that the formal incentives of management were effective only when the supervisor was supportive and effective. Some studies of close and punitive supervision as against general supervision were mentioned, with the evidence strongly favoring general supervision for higher productivity and other measures of effectiveness.

The argument for participative management was outlined, and we referred to a number of proponents and their supportive research. Some of the dangers, cautions, and opposing arguments were also mentioned.

This brought us directly into a consideration of System 4 management advocated by Likert, one of the leading proponents of participation. He makes a strong argument with supportive evidence that System 4 is far superior to Systems 1 and 2, and even to System 3. This type of management style must be learned and introduced slowly to the ongoing organization.

Next, the four-factor theory of leadership of Bowers and Seashore was discussed. Building on the group-as-leader approach to leadership, they conclude there are four basic acts of leadership: support, interaction facilitation, goal emphasis, and work facilitation. The way that the formal leader carries out these acts and the emphasis he puts on combinations of them directly influences the way in which group members themselves carry out the four leadership acts.

Fiedler's contingency model was the final major theory mentioned. His approach is to engineer the job to fit the manager. Depending on whether the managerial style is high-LPC (permissive, member-oriented, etc.) or low-LPC (task-oriented, authoritarian, etc.), the manager will be most effective in some types of groups and not in others. The groups can be described in terms of three dimensions: leader position power, task structure, and leader-member relations. These can be adjusted to make the group optimal for the leadership style of the manager.

Finally, it was noted that other things besides leadership are required for effectiveness and that the approach to understanding leadership should be two-pronged—training managers and adjusting groups to existing managers.

THE MANAGER AS TEACHER

How can the manager use the Law of Effect to produce desired be-
havior in his subordinates? Why is the responsibility of the manager as
teacher unavoidable? What learning concepts can be readily applied to
daily management? Having produced desired behavior, how can it be
maintained? How can we remove the barriers to improvement of a subor-
dinate's performance? How do subordinates use their manager as a model?

In the experimenter's lab [1] four students were seated at a table, screened
from one another, each with a signal light in front of him. They were involved in a ten-minute discussion of a case. Two students had been told
that their signal lights would flash whenever they said something insightful; two were told that their lights would flash whenever they said something lacking in psychological insight. Through these controls the experimenter was effectively squelching or increasing the degree of participation
of the group's members.

In another lab the experimenter [2] was instructing students to "say all

[1] W. F. Oakes, A. E. Droge, and B. August, "Reinforcement Effects on
Participation in Group Discussion," *Psychological Reports*, VII (1960), 503–514.
[2] J. Greenspoon, "The Reinforcing Effect of Two Spoken Words on the
Frequency of Two Responses," *American Journal of Psychology*, LXVIII (1955),
409–416.

the words you can think of." Whenever a student said a plural word, the experimenter said, "Mm hmm"; when he said a singular word, the experimenter said and did nothing. Within a few minutes the ratio of plural words to singular words spoken by the subject increased significantly.

Now let us consider a meeting of one division of an organization. The manager is in the chair and he is asking for suggestions. After the first suggestion, he says, "Okay, John. Now let's have some more ideas." Another man speaks up on the issue and the manager says, "Bill, that's excellent. Well thought out and well presented. Anyone else have any comments on Bill's suggestion?" If the manager keeps up this line (ignoring John and congratulating Bill) every time each of them tries to make a contribution, what will happen?

According to the Law of Effect, operative in all these examples, John's contributions will decline and Bill's contributions will increase.

This fundamental principle of learning has been known for centuries to people who trained animals, and to anyone else astute enough to observe it. But only in this century was it clearly formulated in what we call the Law of Effect. Basically, the law says that behavior associated with satisfaction or rewards (psychologists prefer to call it *reinforcement*) has a likelihood of being repeated in the future. What is rewarding to one person, we know, may not be rewarding to another person, or not *as* rewarding to another person, but there are many easily identified and readily employed reinforcers.

Reinforcement works whether or not the person being reinforced (or, indeed, the person providing the reinforcement) is aware of it. Social approval is commonly used to reinforce behaviors without either party being aware of it. In laboratory experiments involving the reinforcement of subjects with encouraging nods, "mm hmm," or "that's good" when they employ singular pronouns (like "I," "me") while composing sentences or telling a story, and reinforcing another group only when they use plural pronouns (like "we," "us") or not reinforcing the use of any pronouns, the difference in pronoun use in each group is considerable even in a brief time measurement.

Many other forms of social approval are available to the manager to encourage the desired and prevent the undesired behaviors of his subordinates. The kind word, the obvious interest, the willingness to listen and hear another person out, sincere reassurance to the anxious, and the smile of appreciation, thanks, or congratulation. Properly and sincerely used, these are all effective reinforcers. They can be used to produce and increase behavior which contributes to effectiveness—and they do not cost the organization or the manager a cent!

If you tend to consider the subordinates in your unit as dumbheads, lazy, lacking in initiative and imagination, it is time you stopped, examined your conscience, and tried to discover what type of reinforcement you are unconsciously using to prevent effectiveness in the group. Even retarded and severely disturbed children who have never spoken a word in their lives or have never been able to interact effectively with other children or adults, are taught to speak and interact through refined application of the Law of Effect.

But we must examine a few things in more detail before being able to make best use of this basic principle of learning.

MANAGING AND TEACHING

Many teachers are managers in educational and other types of organizations but few managers consider themselves as teachers. Actually, everyone both teaches and learns from others as part of day-to-day interaction although some are better at teaching than others. There are a number of reasons why it is necessary for the effective manager to be a good teacher.

First, the whole nature of work and of the relationship between the worker, on the one hand, and his organization and his manager, on the other hand, is changing and will continue to do so. Effective organization holds out to civilization the promise of goods, services, and the satisfaction of other personal needs. In spite of some rather bad cancer spots at various places on the globe; and in spite of our modern equivalent of placard-carrying prophets of doom who see mankind starving, suffocating in environmental pollution, or blowing himself to nuclear smithereens; and even in spite of ample evidence of the presence of greed, stupidity, and apathy; history affirms that the human race has never had it so good and that the unrealized potential for mankind is only beginning. All this means that man's advance up the need hierarchy will continue. Witness the growth in adult education programs; the increasing demand for higher levels of formal education in high school, technical school, and university; the number of educational and semieducational publications sold each year; the wakening interest in the environment by amateur astronomers, microscope hunters, rock hounds, and naturalists of every sort. To satisfy higher level needs, people want to know more and more about the world around them. A big piece of that world is the world in which they work. They will continue to want to know more about it and to be able to use it for their personal growth. The best teacher for this job is the manager.

Second, truly effective organization requires the use of the talents of all members. Many have talents of which they are not even aware and others have talents which are only partly used. The effective manager must know how to recognize and develop these.

Another important reason is to take the pressure off the manager himself. If he has trained his subordinates well, he can delegate to them for his benefit as well as for their own growth, and through both means can build a better work unit.

We have seen that leadership style tends to be patterned on the style of leadership to which one is himself subjected, and that leadership acts of group members depend on leadership acts of the formal supervisor, so the manager is already a teacher whether he knows it or not.

THE PSYCHOLOGY OF LEARNING

A specialty of North American psychologists is the study of learning. Many of the demonstrated principles of learning have found their way into classrooms and teachers' colleges and finally into the treatment of retarded children and therapy for those with behavior disorders. Only now are managers beginning to glimpse the significance of learning principles for effective organization. Specifically, learning psychology has many useful findings to offer to the supervisor trying to mold an effective work team.

As mentioned in the first part of this book, human behaviors are of two types. First, those built-in or programmed into the person as a biological organism. Second, those learned or acquired in the process of interacting with our social and physical environment. The distinction is a crude one for the second kinds of behaviors are often founded on the first, yet it is a useful division for our purposes. Our major interest, of course, is the second type of behavior.

Because these habits or learned behavior patterns, are flexible and changeable, the manager who understands how they are formed is in a position to influence the shape they are likely to take. The effective manager uses learning principles often without knowing he is using them, and the ineffective manager unknowingly uses them to shape subordinate behavior in the wrong direction. This latter point may be more important than any other. It is easy to reinforce poor behaviors and develop ineffective habits in our children, students, and subordinates without being aware of it. The manager in the example quoted above may be reinforcing Bill's contribution of half-baked and puerile ideas at the same time as he is reinforcing John to say nothing.

THE BASIC CONCEPTS

There are two forms of learning, according to many psychologists. The first is classical or Pavlovian (named after Ivan Pavlov, the great Russian physiologist) and its main concern is with conditioning reflexes or responses of the autonomic nervous system. Our concern is mainly with the second form, instrumental or operant learning, so called because it is "instrumental" to the person or organism or it "operates" on his environment.

A basic concept in learning theory is that of *drive*, which has been mentioned in Chapter 5. For many learning theorists drive and motivation are fairly synonymous terms. You will recall a distinction was made between the primary or physiological drives and the secondary or learned drives. Naturally, it is these latter which are more important to us here. Anxiety (or the need to reduce it) is one of the most important secondary drives. So also are needs for recognition, information, status, achievement, feelings of satisfaction, and interest in one's work.

A second basic concept is that of *stimulus* or *cue*, which is the occasion for the person to carry out a behavior. The stimulus may be something outside the person or something internal, such as a memory. Some stimuli are simple, such as the lunch whistle which is the occasion for a worker to take a break from work. Others are much more subtle, like the tone of the manager's voice or the furrows on his brow or a slight shake of the head from a fellow worker. Socially perceptive persons pick these cues up readily although they are lost on those not skilled in social nuances. Some stimuli may not be consciously observable and may remain unidentified although they still are the occasion for a response.

The result of a stimulus is a *response*. It may be any activity. It becomes paired with the stimulus so that when the stimulus occurs the response is likely to follow. Like stimulus, it can be either obvious, such as picking up the phone when it rings (stimulus), or subtle, like looking busy when the top brass is around. Because social behavior is highly complex, it is often difficult to isolate which stimulus goes with what response.

The reinforcer, we have seen, can be anything which serves to increase or maintain the strength or rate of responding. It would be impossible to enumerate all the things which could serve as reinforcers. Although management tends to rely on its formal incentive system as its reinforcers, we have seen throughout this book that many other things could be reinforcing effective or ineffective behavior. A major part of management's job is to find out what these reinforcers are. The next section of this book will be devoted in large part to such questions.

Now to return to the Law of Effect. We see that the person must be in a drive state (he must want or need something, like social approval); there must be a stimulus or cue (the perception of an opportunity to express an opinion), a response (an expression of one's opinion), and a reinforcement (the approval of others of what has been said) before the likelihood of the response taking place again in the future is increased.

MORE LAWS

To better understand the Law of Effect, there are a few other things we might watch in the learning psychologist's laboratory. The study of *generalization* and *discrimination* are among these. In Pavlov's early research on conditioning dogs to salivate, he found that if he sounded a tuning fork immediately prior to putting some powdered meat into a dog's mouth and repeated pairing the sound of the tuning fork (stimulus) with the puff of meat powder into the mouth the dog soon produced saliva (response) whenever he heard the tuning fork, regardless of whether or not he got the meat powder. Further, Pavlov found the dog would generalize the sound of the stimulus to other similar stimuli, such as sounding the note on the piano rather than the tuning fork. Generalization implies, then, that stimuli similar to the original stimulus will also produce responses but the less similarity, the less power they have to produce the same response. Getting a nod from the chairman accompanied by the words, "Any comment on that, John?" may be a straightforward stimulus calling for a response. But when the chairman turns to John and merely nods without saying the words, the stimulus generalization may or may not be sufficient to produce a response from John.

Now let us say that a manager regularly employs social reinforcement whenever a subordinate makes suggestions or voices opinions. He may soon find that people are making all kinds of foolish suggestions and expressing useless opinions. The same could be true of the production supervisor who reinforces output and gets high output but poor quality; or who reinforces good quality and gets it along with low output. The problem may be that from the manager's desire to hear good suggestions the employee is generalizing to any type of suggestion at all and is failing to discriminate that only the useful opinion is reinforced. Thus generalization without discrimination can produce inappropriate behaviors.

Discrimination learning is part of daily living. Just as the little child learns to discriminate between water and a soft drink because one is more rewarding than the other, so the worker can learn the difference between good work and shoddy work, between valuable ideas and worthless opinions, because they are rewarded differentially by his supervisor. Indeed, this is a major role of the manager as teacher—differentially rewarding good and better ideas or performances which will contribute to group effectiveness and carefully avoiding the reinforcement of useless and harmful contributions to the group's purposes.

There are limits to a person's ability to discriminate even though fine discriminations can be learned. Pavlov found his dogs could discriminate between a metronome beating at 96 beats per minute as against one beating at 100 beats a minute. However, when a finer discrimination was required, not only did the dog fail to discriminate but his total behavior broke down: he became neurotic and carried out inappropriate, even bizarre behaviors. The manager who requires too fine a discrimination between a good and a poor idea or performance could, then, find the behavior of the subordinate erratic and unpredictable. A supervisor should always be certain to spell out or otherwise indicate clearly what performance is expected and what is not expected. When poor performance is rewarded on one occasion and criticized on another, the person will become confused, anxious, and may stop contributing completely.

When positive performance is forthcoming from subordinates, it is nice to be able to recognize it and reinforce it. But what does one do when the only performance shown is mediocre at best? Is it then necessary to wait patiently for the subordinate to display a rare flash of brilliance and then reinforce it? No. B. F. Skinner, the champion of operant conditioning theorists, and his followers have demonstrated how easy it is to condition pigeons, rats, dogs, children, and adults to carry out a complex series of behaviors through a procedure called *reinforcing successive approximations*. Take, for instance, teaching a pigeon to walk along a platform in a figure eight pattern before receiving a piece of grain. If we wait for him to do this himself and then reward him, we might wait forever. First, we wait for the pigeon to make a spontaneous turn to the right, then give him his reward. After this occurs several times the pigeon is continuing right turns quite nicely. Now we stop rewarding him and wait until he not only turns right but also moves in a half circle to the right before starting to reward him again. When he has learned this well, we stop the rewards again until he starts to add to this half circle a spontaneous slight turn to the left, and so forth, and so forth until a figure eight is walked at the end of which he can depress a key to receive a piece of grain. This process is sometimes referred to as "shaping" or "shaping up" a response. The simplicity with which it works to train a dog to do tricks or to change the pattern of behavior of a baby is really amazing for the new trick can be learned in a matter of minutes.

Now the employee is hardly the same subject as a rat or pigeon in a Skinner box, but the identical principles of learning are applicable. The greatest difference in the real life situation is the lack of a controlled environment; there are too many unknown and uncontrollable stimuli and reinforcements available to the subject which may be shaping up and maintaining behavior patterns contrary to the desired ones. Nonetheless, from time to time the manager may find himself in situations where he has control over the major reinforcers and where contaminating stimuli and reinforcers are minimized—for example, in some types of formal meetings, when he is working supervisor of a retail sales group, and in certain types of military teams. In such situations he may be able to shape behaviors and maintain them, although it involves more work than the psychologist shaping a pigeon in the lab.

MAINTAINING DESIRED BEHAVIOR

Learned patterns of behavior may continue as habits over long periods of time. However, when reinforcement ceases, a shaped behavior pattern may soon cease. In the lab we call this the *extinction* of learning. We extinguish learned behaviors by stopping our reinforcement of them. If we wish the subject to relearn extinguished behavior, we start reinforcing again and usually find that learning takes place more quickly. Notice that extinction refers to behaviors and not to "forgetting" things.

However, we observe that many behavior patterns continue without apparent reinforcement. The fisherman may stand and cast all day into the stream without landing a trout and his "casting behavior" is not extinguished. Equally, the slot machine addict may pump silver dollar after silver dollar into the one-armed bandit without getting a payoff. Skinner has been able to explain and demonstrate this continuous behavior by describing different *schedules of reinforcement.*

When a response is reinforced each time it is made, it is extinguished soon after reinforcement ceases. However, when a response is reinforced only sometimes or only after it has been performed a certain number of times, it is more difficult to extinguish. Thus we can have interval schedules and ratio schedules of reinforcement. *Interval schedules* are reinforcements "by the clock," provided at set times. Coffee breaks, lunch breaks, four-thirty whistles, and paydays are forms of reinforcement on interval schedules. Probably, they are not particularly effective, though. One thing we notice about reinforcement at fixed intervals is that performance tends to fall off immediately after reinforcement is given. There is usually a noticeably slow warm-up period immediately after coffee break or lunch break and possibly even the day after payday. Experimenters find that *variable interval* reinforcement—giving the reinforcement at random rather than set times—results in smoother behavior patterns. Thus a pigeon reinforced every time he performs while learning his trick will have his reinforcers gradually extended to variable intervals of, for example, one minute, three minutes, five minutes, two minutes, four minutes, and so on, whereupon we find his performance superior to what it is when he is rewarded each time or rewarded on some fixed interval schedule. Our stream fisherman is reinforced on this type of schedule; we witness that his behavior is smooth and continuous and that it is highly resistant to extinction once he has been shaped up.

Ratio schedules are similar except that the reinforcement follows after a certain number of work units have been performed. Piecework is designed this way, as are certain types of commissioned sales work (although selling may involve both interval and ratio reinforcement). As with interval schedules, *variable ratio* reinforcement is superior to fixed ratio reinforcement both in terms of better performance rates and greater difficulty of extinction. The slot machine payoff is a variable ratio one and we certainly see how successful it is at keeping its players working.

In the psychology lab we find that human beings respond to these various schedules in a manner very similar to rats and pigeons. In the office, factory, boardroom, or store, the manager finds himself in a different ball game than the experimental psychologist. Contaminating factors such as group-imposed norms, ostracization of rate busters, and control of reinforcers by the highly routinized system rather than by the individual supervisor or manager makes the application of learning principles much more difficult.

One of the biggest problems the manager faces is how to extinguish those undesirable work behaviors which continue at a high rate and are very resistant to extinction because they are reinforced on effective combinations of variable ratio and interval schedules by fellow workers, by the workers' own sense of satisfaction, or by the system itself. Instructors in the university face a similar problem. The awarding of grades in a highly systematized manner maintains undesirable habits in the student—memorizing rather than understanding, recognizing rather than composing clear ideas, and cramming for exams rather than studying throughout the term.

Yet the principles are available for our use and all we must do to see their effectiveness is look at the chain smoker, the fingernail biter, or the heavy drinker. Although his mouth feels fetid, his fingers look so disgraceful that he keeps his hands in his pockets or his head feels so badly the next morning—still, all it requires to keep him going year after year is that occasional cigarette that really feels good, the anxiety-satisfying nibble, or the pleasant glow which is the first sign of one too many. Indeed, with time and practice the reinforcement schedule of the smoker, nail biter, or drinker is extended more and more so that it takes less frequent and less proportionate rewards to keep him going.

As I mentioned before, the principles and the information are available. The psychologist is reluctant to come out of his lab to the manager's situation. Therefore, the manager must use his ingenuity and wit to bring the principles of the psychologist to his office, factory, or work team. There may be situations for some managers in which the application of these principles is straightforward; for most, such situations will be limited; for all willing to think and work at it, there will be some. The end result will be improved effectiveness.

IMPROVING PERFORMANCE

As well as through the techniques described, there are a number of other methods available for improving the learning and modifying the behavior of subordinates. *Knowledge of results* is one of the most important. Many learned habits require active and conscious participation. Feedback on how he is progressing toward an objective is important in such learning, both as a reinforcement to continue and as a corrective to adjust and improve behavior patterns. These are situations in which the manager has a very definite role to play.

Imagine a man trying to target-shoot without ever knowing whether he hits the target. Or imagine him trying to improve his shooting if he got feedback on his hits and misses only once a year (as we sometimes do with appraisal programs). Although vast experimental evidence supports it, it requires little imagination to see that the best feedback is when knowledge of results is immediate and concise.

It defies both common sense and experimental evidence, yet probably millions of workers throughout the world never get *any* feedback on their performance from their organization or its official representatives; and those who get good and constant feedback are the exception rather than the rule. Even classroom teachers get goose eggs on this point; *monthly* examination results may be returned two weeks after the performance. School classroom techniques would not produce many sharpshooters, and typical management techniques would not produce any. It is sad to think of all the managers at the world's bars having their after-work drink and bemoaning how hopeless their subordinates are!

What a difference it would make if the manager, besides giving immediate social reinforcement when appropriate, were to call the subordinate aside every now and then and say, "John, you may have noticed that I've been encouraging you to do X over the past few months. I want you to know that I'm pleased with your performance. I want to point out one thing to you, however. Instead of doing X with a y, try doing it with a z. You'll see that it makes a difference. Keep up the good work, and I'll keep up the feedback and try to steer you in the right direction."

In the higher, as against the simple, forms of learning the role of *understanding* is important. In ideal learning the principles of how to do things and do them well are discovered by the learner himself. The "new math" taught in our schools tries to utilize this principle. Often, it means slower but more effective learning than under direct teaching forms. We still have a lot to find out about this technique but managers could probably make use of it by ensuring that they provide the climate for new learning and new discovery to take place among their subordinates.

The teaching of creativity to subordinates is a good example of moving in this direction. Some theorists have noted that children tend to be rather creative and spontaneous until they have become regimented by the school system and other cultural demands, and that teaching creativity in adults involves teaching them to be child-like again, in some sense. When problem solutions are always settled by fiat from above and the exercise of personal creativity is not called for from the subordinate, the very climate of work inhibits creativity. Also, when conformity and working within the framework of his superiors' preconceptions are demanded, and when the only ideas reinforced are those of immediate functional utility, there is little opportunity for him to stretch his talents. Failing to understand and motivate creative people is probably one of the major flaws built into the formal organizational structure as closely defined work positions leave little room for creativity. It has been suggested that effective managers and supervisors are in necessary conflict with highly creative subordinates because the supervisor's job involves effecting company policies. I do not believe this conflict is necessary. I can think of one instance of an internationally acknowledged creative person who has grown creative in an organization where his talent was recognized early. His manager looks in the other direction even when the man disappears completely from the office for a month at a time. This is feasible because the truly creative person is motivated from within more than by the formal controls of the organization. A great challenge for the creative manager is trying to find ways to reward and accommodate creative subordinates in his unit.

Teaching and improving creativity bears some relationship to *job enlargement,* advocated by many contemporary theorists of work as a very important next step for the modern organization. One of these theorists, Herzberg,[3] outlines a number of steps for the process. First, the job must allow enough achievement possibilities for the employee to learn from his achievements more about his occupation or job then he knew previously. Such achievements must be recognized by management as the reinforcement in the first stage of learning. Second, more complex tasks must become available for the worker to help him understand relationships with other aspects of the group work. Third, the task must be open-ended in the sense that it allows for growth and the possibility of creativity. Fourth, the worker must get formal advancement both as a reinforcement and as the means of providing higher level task complexity. Advancement does not have to include promotion in rank. Finally, the job must provide intrinsic interests and give the worker some feedback of a sense of personal value. Perhaps very few jobs can provide all these things simultaneously, but the presence of some of these components is necessary to wean the worker from hygiene seeking toward motivator seeking.

Much of the above discussion leads us to acknowledge the value of active participation in the learning process on the part of the learner. Again, there is ample research evidence to show the superiority of active as against passive forms of learning both verbal material and complex behavior patterns. We employ such techniques in formal training sessions— role playing, case study, in-basket games, human relations training, and simulation and field exercises. There is no reason why the manager could not employ regular active participation, making his work group a constant informal training session. They will learn better and he can lead his group more easily toward greater effectiveness.

[3] Frederick Herzberg, *Work and the Nature of Man* (Cleveland: World Publishing Company, 1966).

LEARNING BY IMITATION

More than once we have mentioned that a man's supervisory style follows the style of leadership to which he is subjected. We recognize, of course, the behavior patterns of parents in their children and have ample evidence from laboratory experiments of the influence of a "model" for learning complex behaviors. Following along the lines of Dollard and Miller, the personality theorists mentioned in Chapter 4, Bandura and his associates [4] have demonstrated how much learning takes place through the imitation of a model.

The manager himself is an important model both for job attitudes and behavior patterns in his subordinates. In Chapter 12 we talked about the power he exercises because subordinates identify with him. Later, we talked about the contagious enthusiasm he must have for the job and how leadership behaviors carried out by group members are related to leadership behaviors carried out by the formal leader.

No one is ever going to become an effective manager through a Walter Mitty–type dream or by simple manipulation of reinforcement contingencies. Above all, he must be a pace-setter whose enthusiasm for the task, drive to achieve, flexibility in correcting his own behaviors, experimental search for greater effectiveness, and optimism about future outcomes are things his subordinates are happy to imitate.

CAUTIONS

Research in learning has been perhaps the most productive area of research in psychology for more than a generation. Although the theorists and researchers are divided on many issues, the findings on which they express basic agreement would fill many volumes. As with personality theory, motivation, and other aspects of social psychology, this chapter touches the surface of learning principles. Because it is not possible to go into all details here, a few cautions must be pointed out to the manager willing to experiment.

First, human beings are not rats. Although the same principles of learning apply to both, the human is a highly complex social animal. There are many personal and individual variables operative at any time to influence the way he learns.

Second, punitive or negative social reinforcers are not as effective for good learning as positive reinforcers. They may have some immediate effect in changing behavior but this effect rolls off rapidly when punitive reinforcement continues and the learner's performance may deteriorate to a low level.

[4] A. Bandura & R. H. Walters, *Social Learning and Personality Development* (New York: Holt, Rinehart & Winston, Inc., 1963).

Third, teaching creativity and high-level performance to persons with years of practice at poor work habits is bound to be a long uphill struggle. Good teachers must be patient.

Fourth, do not be a manipulator of people in the sense that you use people as impersonal objects or as means to achieve your own personal goals. The manipulator is soon caught out and his reinforcements will be resisted as people cease to cooperate and even go out of their way to frustrate him. A teacher is not a manipulator. He is a person who uses his skill and knowledge to bring out the best in others, helps them maximize their potential, and gives them a sense of self-value and personal worth. He respects his students and they respect him.

Finally, remember that the employee is also capable of shaping up the manager. A colleague of mine, a specialist in behavior modification, loves to recount incidents when even his undergraduate students have deliberately and successfully set out to change his pattern of classroom behavior without his knowledge. It is possible for the subordinate, either wittingly or unwittingly, to reinforce ineffectiveness in a supervisor. Flattery as a social reinforcer is not always effective because people are often sensitive to or suspicious of attempts to influence them with this technique. But other forms of what the social psychologist calls *ingratiation* are more subtle. Ingratiating oneself to ensure good treatment from the supervisor can be done by carrying out behaviors the supervisor likes to see (even if they are valueless to goal achievement) or by making statements supporting ideas, attitudes, or values which the manager is recognized as holding.

CONCLUSION

Whether or not either he or his subordinates are aware of it, the effective manager probably shapes and maintains effective performance in his subordinates, and the ineffective manager shapes and maintains foolishness, irrelevant behaviors, and activities which hinder goal achievement and membership satisfaction.

In Chapter 5 we pointed out the manager's potential role in raising aspiration levels of his subordinates. He can do this by example and by rewarding successive approximations to high achievement. A case was also made for managers to teach workers to be motivator seekers and not to be dependent on hygiene seeking. The manager has great possibilities for leading employees up the need hierarchy to greater personal development and fuller use of talent and creativity. Not only would this make better people of the subordinates but it would lead to greater organizational effectiveness. Now might be a good time to glance back at some of the major points made in Chapter 5 and try to understand them in light of learning principles.

Let there be no doubt that the manager is a teacher. Simply look at the list of learning principles he uses or should be using in daily situations:

stimulus control
reinforcement
requiring discrimination
feedback and knowledge of results
requiring active participation and practice
imitation
providing climate for understanding and insight
extinction of poor work habits

There is no room in the thinking of managers for short-sighted attitudes like, "We have high-priced staff people to do this. What are they running all these training programs for if I have to be a teacher?" Such an attitude is wasteful and inefficient on many counts. First, the manager is already a teacher whether he wants to be or not. My point is that he should become a *good* teacher. Second, it takes little more, if any, time to be an effective teacher while interacting with subordinates as one would do regularly anyhow. Third, the formal training program can rarely accomplish the highly specific training requirements peculiar to each management unit. If he has a specific objective, the manager should become his own active unit teacher.

Early in this chapter, I mentioned the growing need of people to find out more about the world around them. Finding out about the job is an important part of this. Curiosity, the need to know and understand, and the need to cope with one's environment are among man's major motives. They apply equally well to knowing about his world of work as about desire for other forms of knowledge. Evidence of seeking to satisfy these needs to understand one's organization and occupation may be good indicators of personal growth and psychological health.

Once again the psychological principles are available. It is up to the manager to put them to best use in his peculiar work situation.

SUMMARY

A few short examples of social reinforcement were presented to show how behavior can be modified by application of the Law of Effect. This is the basic law of learning and it states that rewarded behavior has a likelihood of being repeated.

We all teach and we all learn in the course of a normal day's activities. But the manager fills a teacher role which is more important than that of most people—both because of his responsibility to his subordinates and because he wishes to achieve effectiveness in his unit.

The psychology of learning and some of its basic concepts were explained. Drive, stimulus, response, and reinforcement are key concepts in understanding how learning takes place.

Discrimination and generalization were described and reinforcement through successive approximations was presented as the technique for ensuring desired behaviors.

Desired behaviors are maintained by rewarding according to various schedules of reinforcement. (Undesired behaviors are also maintained this way.) Variable interval and variable ratio schedules are the most effective.

A number of methods for improving performance were discussed. Knowledge of results or feedback is one very important method. The role of understanding was stated and steps toward job enlargement were suggested.

Imitation and modeling play a large part in the learning of subordinates and was given special brief mention.

A number of cautions were outlined for the manager to heed while applying learning principles to improve his group's performance.

5

THE SCIENCE OF ORGANIZATIONAL BEHAVIOR

Having been introduced to social psychology, its principles, and its application, the reader is now invited not merely to pick up and use the findings of social scientists but to actually become a scientist while still maintaining his management role. Each management problem is unique and the application of findings from another problem does not always bring a solution. Then there are the problems which have no precedent in the research literature. Are they to be neglected? Not if the manager is truly up to date and scientific.

First, Chapter 19 examines what the manager needs to do to be effective and tries to reduce the answers to concepts which can be used by the scientist. The next chapter provides the tools of research in a simple way. "Science" itself overawes many practical-minded managers but in this chapter it can be seen in its essentials, stripped of many of its mysteries and easily applied to management.

The concluding chapter of the book leaves the student with a model or framework which he can use to examine his unique organizational problems as they arise. The model is flexible enough to use for the most simple or the most complex problem encountered in trying to build an organization of optimal effectiveness.

19

EFFECTIVE
MANAGEMENT

This chapter outlines some of the things a manager must do to maintain and increase his effectiveness. What is the prime cause of managers "going to seed"? What is required to be a sensitive diagnostician? What is so bad about working for a living? Is power always resented? Why do some people make better managers than others? Is theory Y the only alternative to theory X—what about theory Z?

One of the more effective managers I once worked for had scarcely heard of social psychology. He finished high school and started university —but abandoned it after a few months and had never taken any further formal courses. After about ten years in the organization, he had reached a lower-middle management position with responsibility for a sizeable operation and supervision of forty to fifty people.

He was well liked by his subordinates and would always go to bat for them; he was a good socializer with his men and held a couple of parties annually at which his wife was a good hostess; he had an enjoyable sense of humor, listened to and appreciated rather than told jokes; he got along well with other managers and supervisors at similar or lower levels than himself; he recognized and rewarded hard work and talent; he kept work output and group morale higher than most if not all other units; he was flexible enough to bend the rules for a good reason; he was always available for a personal chat or to hear out a problem, whether or not it concerned the job; he even made the rounds frequently to shoot the bull with everyone under his supervision; his office was often the focus of social activity during slack periods and of informal group decision-making activity during busy periods, for he would call in any other knowledgeable persons handy to help decide a tough one; he lost his temper every now and then, threw slackers out of his office when he knew they had work to do, and loudly chewed out those who goofed off or pulled stupid boners; his experience was broad and his technical knowledge was high but he always respected and welcomed an opinion at variance with his own.

In many ways he probably typified good junior and middle managers everywhere. He had his problems, too, of course. He arrived much earlier than the others each morning; left quite late, carrying unfinished work with him; tended to panic during novel situations; could not cope well with crisis; broke into a cold sweat and snapped to military attention when the direct line from the general manager buzzed; was supportive of disruptive cliques; tended to do work himself rather than delegate it; and suffered from ulcers and other physical complaints.

Over the years since, I have followed his career from a distance through inquiring of mutual acquaintances or of the occasional member of that organization I come across. At first, his new appointments seemed to be at the same level and then, gradually, they seemed to involve less responsibility and even "dirty" positions. The last I heard he was assistant manager of a ten-person operation! What happened to this man who seemed to have such promise?

Perhaps all of us with a few years' work experience have seen similar declines. As a management trainee one of the objective lessons I recall—which was, in retrospect, an excellent part of the training program whether intended as such or not—was to spend three full days *alone* in a back office (one almost needed a map to find it) being instructed in absolutely nothing, just "spending some time with" a man who had been acting director for close on to a year almost twenty years previously. He had his own private secretary in his unpartitioned office. She had once been the senior "girl" in the pool, next in line for a supervisory position. Now in her early sixties she was an obese, pasty-faced old maid who, each morning, took out a suitcase-sized makeup case, sat it in front of her typewriter, and proceeded to apply makeup and beauty treatments all day long, stopping only for lunch break and to sip a cup of coffee brought by a clerk in the neighboring office. My "trainer" invariably arrived very late, took prolonged lunch hours, and left early. Nothing of an "active" nature ever crossed his desk —only old policy files (he sent me to the archives, which I did not know existed until this time, to get old cases and decisions he had been involved in). Invariably, these files had multiple volumes and I never saw anything on his desk which was not historical. I felt "spooked" after my three days, as had my buddies before me.

Now what has happened to people like these? In those days we used to pass it off as a decline in ability (as if it were equivalent to tuberculosis or some debilitating disease) or to the supposition that "he must have made an enemy at some time who is now 'up there.'"

Although it is plausible that such men have "gone to seed" or made an enemy in the organization, it is more plausible according to scientific thinking that, stretched to the limit of their potential (in itself a positive thing), they have failed to keep (or be kept) up to date with the demands of contemporary organization. It makes more sense to the social psychologist interested in management theory and application to consider them as men who have not kept pace with demands. All professions are changing and regardless of whether one is an engineer, medical doctor, schoolteacher, electrician, pipe fitter, or manager, he *must keep up to date*. In some professions (e.g., psychology) it is a matter of daily survival to keep up to date. In others (like management) the changes are slow enough to be insidious. These days anyone who thinks he can reach a management position and then just glide the rest of the way to retirement is going to glide into a position like my trainer, the former acting director.

People who may have taken on a supervisory position because of their experience, skill, or knowledge in some area of specialty, but who are not willing to devote some energy to the study of their new profession of management are those who fulfill the Peter Principle—they have reached their level of incompetence. Although they may start out well in their new responsibility and even maintain a high level of output over several years, there is no standing still and they must either go forward or backward.

THE DIAGNOSTICIAN

Particularly in the last section on leadership, some directions were suggested for the self-development of managers and the types of skills they could make good use of. The next few chapters are devoted to helping the manager become scientific in his search for effectiveness. Throughout this book a great deal of emphasis has been put on explaining principles the manager can bring into his daily work. It has been mentioned that he must become a diagnostician.

Diagnosis involves analyzing and identifying events in such a way that causes can be assigned to them. Often, diagnosis is used in the negative sense of being able to recognize diseases or sickness from their symptoms. In the organizational sense the manager must do this. But diagnosis also involves assigning causes to positive events—higher morale, more efficiency, less complaints from the public who are served by the organization, and so on. My personal opinion is that concentrating on finding causes of positive events and encouraging and strengthening them will produce more long-run effectiveness than diagnosing negative events and performing emergency surgery.

What must the diagnostician be? First, he must have a high skill level. This can come from studying books and taking courses in both behavioral and nonbehavioral aspects of management. It can come from experience and experimentation. And it can come from being competent in the specialization area in which he exercises management (e.g., education, hospital administration, architecture, banking). Second, the diagnostician must be a sensitive observer. This can come from high skill level and practice. But it also comes from open-minded willingness to perceive cause-effect chains and from actively seeking them.

Sensitivity to human behavior, as mentioned earlier, does not come merely from books on psychology. What about sensitivity training (or T grouping or encounter groups)? These have their strong proponents among highly respected theorists. A number of learning principles favor group training for good learning to take place. Also, there are proponents of sensitivity training as a means of bringing out the human and social potential in people.

However, sensitivity training has yet to show that it is of long-term value. Participants are more often than not highly responsive during and immediately after sessions, but follow-up testing shows little change in their attitudes and personality. One of the problems is of "reentry" from the training session to find the world has not changed even though the participant himself wants to change. The same is also true of many other types of training sessions.

More research and more sophisticated types of T grouping may help the manager of the future, and we should regard them open-mindedly.

The manager as a sensitive diagnostician can use many different signs and symptoms to help him understand, measure, and predict what is taking place. As as illustration, the level of complaint that he hears from subordinates and fellow members may provide clues to the group and organizational health. Maslow [1] has written up this point with keen wit in a discussion "On Low Grumbles, High Grumbles, and Metagrumbles." He suggests that the level of complaint is an indicator of the motivational level at which people live and could be a measure of organizational health, given a large enough sample. Thus complaints about cold, fatigue, poor shelter, and danger to health are indicators of an organization functioning at a very

[1] A. H. Maslow, *Eupsychian Management* (Homewood, Ill.: Richard D. Irwin, Inc., and The Dorsey Press, Inc., 1965).

low level under poor management conditions. Also low level would be complaints about threatened security needs, such as fear of being laid off arbitrarily and having to put up with indignities to keep one's job. These complaints at the physiological, security, and social levels of the need hierarchy are called low grumbles and reflect poor management and ineffective organization. High-level complaints reflect self-esteem, dignity, self-respect, and autonomy needs. As high grumbles they would reflect a more effective organization. Metagrumbles would reflect self-actualizing values: complaints which reflect a need for perfection, justice, beauty, truth; inefficiencies; and so on. From this Maslow expresses his opinion that grumbles will always be present in the organization but that management should not consider this as a sign of discouragement. Rather, the level of grumble should be moving to higher stages of metagrumble as an indication of the organization's health and growth.

The main thing is for the good diagnostician to recognize change for good or for bad, to isolate the reinforcers which maintain improvement or deterioration, and to develop conditions or apply medicines which will bring improvement. Early in this book we spoke about fears of hopelessness in the face of rapid-pace social change and work demands. I find this sense of powerlessness quite common among today's university students. However, I attribute it to their lower level experience of life and lack of application of their book-learned knowledge. Certainly, managers are in an enviable position to *do something* positive in the face of fear or powerlessness. Much more so than the average subordinate.

IS WORK EVIL?

When we examined psychological contracts we looked at some common management myths and the possibility of putting them into effect through self-fulfilling prophecies. The whole concept of work and particularly of labor have certain connotations in our language. *Labor* is the more biological term referring to the production of essential and consumable products (farm laborers). It is also related to the concept of *pain* (as in childbirth). *Work* is more satisfying and given social recognition (a work of art).

Perhaps because we have built a certain amount of monotony and pain into work (factory work, assembly line work), it has taken on a negative rather than a positive social meaning (see earlier references to negative attitudes toward many blue-collar jobs). In countries like Spain where there is still a considerable amount of individual craftsmanship there seems to be a pride of work among manual workers like shoemakers, dressmakers, and iron workers and an attempt to put personal creativity into their products (works of art). Of course, one still finds in Madrid the corner shoemaker who will make a pair of shoes and most women still have their own dressmakers for coats, suits, blouses, or even undergarments. Although some factory-made objects such as cars and appliances do not seem as well put together as their North American counterparts and some construction work would not meet North American standards, in the few Spanish factories I have visited the manual workers and tradesmen seemed to display a favorable attitude toward their jobs. My personal observations are supported by the extremely low turnover rates in spite of the high demand for skilled and semiskilled workers. My Spanish colleagues tell me that these low turnover rates apply equally to white-collar and managerial personnel.

My feelings are that we still look down on work as the unfortunate lot of that 99.99 percent who are not born rich. Not only theory X, but also McGregor's theory Y seems to me to operate on this implicit assumption. The difference is that in theory Y we try to make work more palatable by glossing over the evil through the incidental satisfaction of social needs. Why should we be reluctant to work? Why should we consider it as our unfortunate lot? Men, women, and children have worked from the beginning of time—not because it is our *lot*, but because it is something we are capable of doing to shape the environment around us rather than be dependent upon it.

One of the challenges to managers today is to make workers aware of this reality. I realize that it is easier when managing professionals and technicians—such as in school systems, hospitals, or architectural firms—and that the challenge will increase as one supervises lower level workers, but I think it is something for which the manager of the future must strive. I have interviewed a lot of waiters, cooks, farmers, and skilled factory workers and I know that they can take great pride in their jobs and in the way they do them, and that they can also have great aspirations for the future. Among miners and diamond drillers, I have seen fierce pride in their jobs and contempt for those who could not meet high standards of output. I knew a cement finisher who was truly famous for the speed and quality of his work, and a roofer who was known so widely as "The Pro" (he was a "professional" in his work) that most of his intimates did not know his real first name and few other than his mother called him anything but "Pro" to his face.

Rather than accept negative attitudes toward work, the manager will find it more profitable to teach directly and through example that work is personally and socially valuable. This may be impossible if you are supervising assembly workers in a bubble gum factory or a cheap-skate manufacturer of shoddy goods or manager of a "clip joint," but I assume that those who take management seriously have a serious job to do. Ensuring that all subordinates have the opportunity to feel important, needed, successful, and useful and that they have the opportunity for growth and improvement through their job is part of the manager's responsibility.

Negative attitudes toward work or the projection of negativism through hostility directed at the boss is not something with which we are born. Also, it is highly unlikely that young people join the workforce each year carrying such negative attitudes with them. My experience is that young people taking their first "real" job do so with enthusiasm, readiness to learn, and willingness to devote fair time and energy for fair return in money and experience. Whatever happens to sour them over the years must come from a frustration of their ideals, a barrier to reaching their level of aspiration, their socialization in the normative attitudes of senior group members, being turned off by supervisors and company policies, and so on. It is within the power of managers to exercise hygienic control over many of these conditions. Effective management means ensuring a growth climate for the growing, preventing the newcomer from deteriorating, and "rescuing" senior people who have gone sour. The last task is the most difficult, especially when company policy and the nature of the job obstruct the manager's teaching function.

Although little has been said in this book about individual differences among people, the facts are that some workers are "tougher" than others, need less guidance, and can grow healthy under adverse circumstances. Others are "weaker" and languish without help even in a benign climate. Like tomato plants in the back garden, it is sometimes difficult to know what makes some flourish while others wilt. Sensitivity to such individual differences also contributes to management effectiveness.

As Maslow asserts, work can actually make well people grow toward self-actualization! "Given fairly o.k. people to begin with, in a fairly good organization, then work tends to improve the people. This tends to improve the industry, which in turn tends to improve the people involved, and so it goes." [2] There is no need to regard work as a necessary evil, then, whether one tends to do so because of the influence of the so-called Protestant ethic, or as a modern-day reaction against the Protestant ethic. (In some ways the ethic encourages working hard while in other ways it considers work as an evil to put up with for the sake of personal salvation.) Work is probably at least neutral, and more likely good. It can certainly be used for the good of individual, group, and society in spite of the tendency to regard it as somehow associated with suffering and evil. Let the manager keep it in correct perspective so that his subordinates might follow suit.

[2] Maslow, *Eupsychian Management.*

MANAGEMENT AND POWER

Earlier, I mentioned that youth rejects the concept of *in loco parentis* (anyone assuming a parent role toward him) and is likely to reject it even more in the future. Probably, young people and older people have always resented such attitudes in others but have been more willing to put up with them than is the young person of today. Yet here is a paradox I have found so often while counseling young people in their personal and vocational problems—that they despise parents for their inability to give straight-forward advice or guidance or for being democratic when they should be authoritarian. (E.g. Son asks father: "What do you think of the university program I have selected?" Father responds: "If that's what you're interested in, fine, go ahead; I'll pay the shot.")

The generation gap has always been with us from my reading of history and literature, yet the thing which magnifies it in our day is youth's outspoken sensitivity to adult "bull." So often the young person falls between two chairs as he meets either the uncritical acceptance of dogmatic democracy or the selfish application of autocracy. Actually, both are easily recognized by the young person as selfish—the first based on fear of error, criticism, or loss of love and the second on naked self-interest or lack of sensitivity and understanding.

What youth seeks is the same as elders seek, except that young people are more outspoken and critical. They want the truth. As Tennessee Williams wrote in his play *Cat on a Hot Tin Roof,* no one accepts "damned mendacity."

The objective requirements of any given management situation may call for autocratic use of power. But those whose authority is solely reward, coercive, and legitimate power without expert and referent power may be self-seekers who neurotically need to exercise command. People who seek management positions because they need control over others should not be given authority in an ideal situation. When they are given power, they may use it badly because the objective demands of the group situation are likely to be buried under their personal need satisfaction. Managers who struggle for and need power (to be distinguished from those with high need for achievement) should be regarded suspiciously when they are applicants for higher positions.

Here we come back to the leader as father figure again. The ideal father accepts his leadership role as part of his life vocation. He considers himself as "father" to the extent that his self-concept and his job or duty are inseparable. As such, he is recognized by all as acting for the family, with their support. Culturally, he is the member of the family group most qualified for the position and he accepts the responsibility entailed while receiving the support of the family members. Probably, he gains no particular satisfaction out of bossing family members around but he is able to say "No" or be stern because he has the knowledge others lack about the total situation and long-term goals. His faith and devotion to the total group enable him to withstand temporary unpopularity and tears of offended members.

Related to this is the pleasure he gets in seeing his children grow. Just as the father marks out another niche on the kitchen doorpost as his son grows, the good manager takes pride in seeing his subordinates accepting more responsibility, being creative, and even leaving the group to take on leadership elsewhere. Indeed, the good father or manager is able to take second place when another group member is more capable of exercising the leadership role under a given set of demands.

The type of parent I refer to is not the one who assumes that his position gives him automatic authority in decisions but the one who is respected even when he administers pain and hurt since everyone recognizes the legitimacy of his responsibility. He is not governed by selfish needs and fears of being disliked but by his need to achieve truth, justice, opportunity for all, and the best means of reaching the objective, while ensuring that no one is trampled on.

As the family has confidence in this type of father, so the group has trust in this type of leader. No one resents such a father-leader and people can be supportive of him even when he errs.

On the other hand, phony fathers—or those who take the role without the qualifications, rights, or responsibilities—will receive contempt for their usurpation.

MANAGEMENT GROWTH AND INDIVIDUAL DIFFERENCES

Still talking about the ideal manager (who probably finds life difficult outside of the reasonably healthy organization, or one he can be instrumental in improving), it is worth mentioning a few words about the possibility his job holds out for personal growth. Personal growth will reflect on the health of his own group which, in turn, will reflect on organizational growth.

The great American myth that all people are both equal in opportunity and ability is simply not true. Ideally, we know there are situations in which any member can carry out leadership acts, and when they do not exist the good manager will create such situations to help his subordinates grow. Yet the truth of individual differences is that some people are superior to others in a given skill or capacity—whether it be to play basketball or violin or chess, to sketch animals, to do carpentry, or to fill a managerial role. In Chapter 13 the pecking order of chickens was mentioned. The superior chicken chooses a superior diet, among other things. When that diet is given to inferior chickens, they improve greatly, but they never reach the level of the superior chickens. The same is true of human skills. I had a friend who slaved at the violin and constantly strove for technical competence, but he could never reach the standard of another friend who played with detached casualness but had "the knack of the thing." With study, practice, and just plain sweat, great improvements can be made in management skill. But there will always be those to whom it comes more easily than others. I can think of a number of individual students I have had who desperately wanted to be good managers but whose chances of success I felt were so low that I was obliged to counsel them away from management as a vocation.

Part of our Christian ethic keeps us from being pushy, or makes us undersell ourselves even when we are capable. This can happen especially to "the nice guy" who might take on a responsible position if it were thrust upon him and provided he were asked at least twice but who otherwise might feel uncomfortable about "going after" a promotion. I have a feeling that a lot of talent is lost in our big organizations because of this ethic since some of these people are the very ones who would take on a management position with the sense of responsibility called for by a leadership vocation. Indeed, if some form of leadership is not thrust upon them, some of these people may even feel frustrated in the organization. The manager should watch for individuals like these.

Earlier research by Fiedler showed that effective leaders maintained a certain "psychological distance" from their subordinates.[3] These psychologically distant leaders considered themselves professional managers, had power "up the line," and gave a good deal of freedom and responsibility "down the line." They felt their subordinates should be ready for promotion within a few years. The psychologically close manager was a contrast. He saw his job in terms of smooth interpersonal relations, informal ties with those around him, and did not push the promotion of his subordinates as rapidly. Using company income as a measure of effectiveness, it was found the psychologically distant manager was more effective provided he was both endorsed by his own superior and supported by his assistants. The study was done in consumer co-ops.

Many a new young manager (or university professor) has later regretted that he insisted on all staff (or students) addressing him by his first name. Although this may symbolize his democratic intentions, its psychological closeness puts cultural restraints on his objectivity. One can be equally democratic and more objective when a level of psychological

[3] F. E. Fiedler, "The Leader's Psychological Distance and Group Effectiveness," in *Group Dynamics,* 2nd ed., ed. D. Cartwright and A. Zander (Chicago: Row Peterson, 1960).

distance is symbolized by the fact that he is addressed in a formal mode by his subordinates. This is not to be *elitist* and one is more likely to be respected than scorned for it in most types of organizations.

Dogmatic democracy is as often accepted as *the way* to be a leader as is unthinking authoritarianism. Both are wrong. By now we should know that almost any leadership situation, certainly normal management, requires ability to apply the two extremes and anything in between when called for. Because a manager displays a high degree of directiveness does not mean he is undemocratic—his work situation may call for it.

Coming back to individual differences, one would be sadly mistaken to assume that all subordinates are "good guys" with infinite potential. In the average organization the vast majority *are* good guys and all will be found to have unrealized potential. But the effective manager can distinguish the growing from the nongrowing subordinates and can nourish them according to their capacities as well as have the patience to try to pull the ungrowing into the stream of personal development. To think otherwise is to misinterpret McGregor.[4] "He sees most human beings as having real capacity for growth and development . . . as genuine assets in helping him fulfil his own responsibilities. . . . He does not feel that people in general are stupid, lazy, irresponsible, dishonest, or antagonistic. He is aware there are such individuals, but he expects to encounter them only rarely. In short, he holds to theory 'Y'" (page 140). Seeing most human beings like this does not blind the effective manager to the fact that *some* people are s.o.b.'s and it is wise to recognize them as such and treat them accordingly.

THEORY Z MANAGEMENT

By now I hope the reader is thoroughly suspicious of any management absolutes. Openness to new ideas, willingness to experiment, and courage to proceed are probably as close to absolute rules as he is likely to find. No one should be deceived by catchy ideas such as "theory Y" or "new patterns in management" (the title of Likert's book) into thinking that at last the major problems of management have been resolved—"how-to-do-it" style.

I am not going to say any more about changing management in a changing society but I feel it is paramount to think of effective management as *functional*, geared to the needs of the group. Management is not a thing existing by itself; it is a function of the organization. As the organization changes, evolves, shifts its purposes, takes on new personnel,

[4] D. McGregor, *The Human Side of Enterprise* (New York: McGraw-Hill Book Company, 1960).

matures, the management function will change. This is why theory X management *might have been* effective at one time in North America and may be effective today in some parts of the globe or under unusual circumstances. Theory Y management is more effective today but may not be at some future time and place because the organization may take on new forms. Theory Z management calls for the recognition that management style must adjust to the needs of the organization at whatever state of evolution it has reached.

Suspicion of absolutes is the key to theory Z management. Objective awareness of the demands of the unique group and organization, even of the unique individual, are the ideal. As an ideal it may rarely, if ever, be reached. Yet, like justice and beauty, we seek it while knowing we can achieve only its imperfect form. Recognizing its existence as a possibility and being willing to work for it is what counts.

SUMMARY

Those who choose law, medicine, dentistry, nursing, diplomatic service, religious life, law enforcement, psychology, and many other professions as their vocation are always "preached at" a little bit by their senior colleagues in the process of learning their social role. In one sense this chapter does that very thing for those who choose management as a profession. It is not a "don't do" type of preaching but a "do" type. People entering the professions have before them a future of higher income and the opportunity to taste the sweeter fruits of life. At the same time they take on a higher level of duties than the average citizen. The one who wants the benefits and privileges without the hard work and burden of responsibility is destined to personal and professional failure. Because of the nature of their work, the doctor, lawyer, nurse, and schoolteacher are less likely to forget this simple truth than is the manager.

Through a couple of anecdotes, it was pointed out that the manager must keep up to date with the demands of the contemporary organization. Just imagine what happens to the doctor or dentist who reads and studies nothing after finishing his internship!

The manager as diagnostician, sensitive to cause-effect relationships and knowing how to piece them out, was next mentioned. He is equally sensitive to individual and group behavior. As a good diagnostician, he is capable of using a wide range of signs to discover both what is right and what is wrong, treating the wrong and supporting the right. Low grumbles, high grumbles, and metagrumbles are an example of the types of signs he can use.

The myth of work as evil was attacked and it was claimed that work is at least neutral and offers the potential for healthy individuals to achieve greater personal development.

The manager's power was discussed. Seeking after power to satisfy personal and neurotic needs is easily recognized as phoniness. A careful analogy between the father of the family and the manager's role—careful because the world has its share of inadequate fathers—was drawn. The analogy must be a cautious one between effective manager and *ideal* father.

Personal growth of the manager becomes evident in the growth of his subordinates, for the effective manager is concerned with developing those under his charge as he is with developing himself. There are limits to personal growth. All men are not born equal in a biological sense nor do they receive equal opportunities from their environments. Individual differences in growth potential must be recognized although the reaching of full potential is an ideal, never quite reached in anyone. The good manager recognizes individual differences in potential as well as he recognizes that there are some s.o.b.'s who must be treated precisely as that.

Theory Z management involves objectivity, recognition that the organization changes in a changing world, and that so do people and group demands. Willingness to try to cope with this reality is part of theory Z. Theory Y and dogmatic acceptance of democratic leadership are to be kept in their proper perspective—effective at the moment but not enshrined for eternity.

The next two chapters give some direction for putting theory Z into effect.

20

THE MANAGER-SCIENTIST

This chapter outlines scientific methodology as a management technique. What do managers and scientists have in common? Why must theory underlie practice? Why hypothesize? How can we gather "hard" data with little or no extra effort? Can a manager set up a scientifically controlled experiment with people? What is the difference between an S-R study and an R-R study? What are the essential features of a psychological experiment? What is the problem of experimenter bias? Are there limits to experimentation?

A delightful anecdote was told by Francis Bacon (1561–1626) about how a group of early fifteenth-century monks disputed for thirteen days about how many teeth there are in a horse's mouth. They dug through all the ancient books and chronicles and references to all the learned writings. On the fourteenth day a young friar suggested to them in all humility that the problem might be solved by opening a horse's mouth and counting the teeth. At this the senior monks were furious, "flew upon him and smote him hip and thigh, and cast him out forthwith." They declared him an impertinent upstart with no understanding of how such weighty matters were to be resolved by reference back to tradition and the statements of great men. Returning to the dispute, they argued many more days before finally declaring that the matter could not be resolved due to a lack of appropriate information.

The story strikes us as ludicrous, of course, but it is not all that far from what we sometimes witness among the "learned graybeards" in the contemporary organization. Even in the supposed "councils of the wise" (in university committees composed of senior academics) one may witness pompous foolishness. Looks of shocked amazement or pious utterances like "We've never done it that way before" are just as likely to greet the bold young manager as they did the bold young monk.

Taylor's "scientific management" was based on his nineteenth-century industrial research although many contemporary managers still employ his techniques almost one hundred years later. True scientific management does not consist merely of utilizing a bag of tricks based on the findings of industrial and personnel researchers. Rather, it consists of the day-to-day application of the tools of social science. These tools are no more immutable things than are any other tools and would bear as much resemblance to Taylor's techniques as would the contemporary carpenter's hammer to a medieval one. Indeed, just as the contemporary carpenter and the medieval carpenter perform rather different tasks with quite different materials, so do today's industrial plants differ from Taylor's. Hardboard, skill saws, and electric drills would be as strange to the ancient carpenter as would copy machines, filing systems, computers, and modern assembly lines to Taylor. The future will see the tools change as surely as the hammer will give way to new techniques and styles. But, just as the basic principle is to get two pieces of material to stick together, so we can outline a few basic principles of science.

The *first* thing any scientist does (whether astronomer, zoologist, or anything in between) is to *make observations* of his subject matter. For the manager this is people, their behavior, and its results. The *second* thing is tied in closely with the first. It is *measurement*. One measures star movement, another muscle movement, another weighs chemicals, another measures particle speed, another social attitudes. The manager measures productivity, progress to a goal, ability, worker satisfaction, and many other variables associated with input-waste-output in terms of people, money, and materials. The *third* thing the scientist does is to *predict* on the basis of his observations and measurements: Will the star be eclipsed? Will the substances form a compound? Will the attitudes be consistent? Will productivity go up? Will scrap loss go down? Will the time to goal achievement be reduced? The *fourth* step completes the cycle; the scientist now observes to see whether his predictions are accurate, measures their degree of accuracy, and refines his predictions. Thus does science advance in an ever more refined cycle as illustrated in Figure 20-1.

FIGURE 20-1

THE CYCLE OF SCIENCE

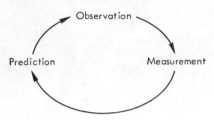

These basic steps are so simple that it has been proposed that every human being who functions normally operates on the basis of scientific principles. The baby in his highchair is given a new toy. He *observes* it. He reaches out, grasps it, lifts it, and having thus *measured* its size, weight, and hardness, he *predicts* that it might be edible. He brings it to his mouth, bites it, sucks it, observes that it is inedible, and rejects the hypothesis of his prediction. He proceeds to examine (observe and measure) it more closely and formulates new predictions (hypotheses) about it. And so forth.

The manager observes that the work carried out by one of his subordinates is of good quality. He starts to make mental notes (measurement) of the reports which come across his desk for signature from this worker each day and carries out more extensive observations and measurements of the worker's related behaviors. After some time he has gathered enough data to make a prediction that the subordinate's work would continue to be good even if he did not check it through completely each time. He calls the worker in and tells him he is pleased with his work and will delegate signing authority to him on his own reports; they will now be submitted only to be initialed. He can now carry out further observations and measurements by checking through only every tenth report to see whether his predictions are good. If they are borne out over time, he may decide to delegate more to this particular subordinate.

If the baby and the manager and everyone in between employs the scientific method, what is the difference between them and the man in the white coat who smells like a chemistry set? Essentially, this: The scientist employs *more refined methods* of observation, measurement, and prediction. He has his microscopes, telescopes, test tubes, calipers, and formulae, of course, but these are just the hardware and specialties of his peculiar trade. The refined methods can be employed by anyone and it is these we shall now proceed to examine. There is no reason why the modern manager cannot employ some of these more refined methods in the course of his daily observation, measurement, and prediction to improve on his own managerial performance.

THEORY AND PRACTICE

Occasionally, one hears the criticism that the "the professors and university people" are so involved in their theories that they have little to offer those who are busily engaged in practical affairs. By now I hope you have learned enough theories of motivation, theories of attitudes, theory of exchange, and so forth to react with skepticism to such adverse comments. It is unfortunate that we tend to regard things labeled "theoretical" as vague, fanciful, and arbitrary.

The vagueness of the word *theory* is perhaps due to its rather wide range of dictionary meanings. The notions of speculation, supposition, and conjecture are usually implied. For our purposes good dictionary meanings are: belief, policy, or procedure proposed or followed as a basis for action; and a body of generalizations derived from experience or practice in some field. For psychologists the idea of theory often involves some coherent set of hypothetical, clearly defined, and predictive principles which can be used as a frame of reference to examine some aspect of behavior. Thus a theory of attitudes hypothesizes a relationship between some clearly defined aspects of behavior (cognitions and feelings) and makes predictions about that relationship (a change in evaluative elements produces a change in cognitive elements). It is only when we have a coherent theory that we can deduce principles, formulate hypotheses, and check out the validity of our predictions.

As theory must be based on data, it involves us in observation and measurement. We might say that theorizing involves a process of abstracting, or leaving out the details, of the things we observe, and tying these abstractions together into some sort of relationship. In Lieberman's study, referred to in Chapter 15, for example, the researcher took the abstract concepts of role and of job attitudes, put them into a relationship, and predicted that if role changed there would follow a change in job attitudes. His subsequent measurements confirmed this. In the same manner, but informally, the manager who calls together his subordinates for a discussion of a problem may observe that some workers participate enthusiastically in the discussion and comment among themselves that "we should get together like this more often." Subsequently, he may think he observes more cohesiveness and cooperativeness in his group so he theorizes (consciously or nonconsciously) that there is a relationship between the abstract ideas of problem discussion meetings and cooperativeness. He may go a step further and predict that more meetings would produce more cooperativeness and then decide to try out his theory.

The theory might be quite a simple one about the relationship between an employee's experience in meeting the public and his effectiveness as a salesman, or it might be a highly complex one which posits a primary relationship between organizational effectiveness and the observable interaction of the organization's members.

The whole scientific procedure is based on the assumption that events and phenomena do not occur merely by chance but, rather, that things are linked together in cause-effect sequences. For the manager it may appear that good days and bad days are completely random, or related as much to his horoscope as to anything else. One of the major purposes of this book is to give the manager clues so that with practiced observation he may be able to discover the causes which underlie the varying effects of good days and bad days. Being able to predict good days and bad days in terms of cause-effect, he is then in a position to do something about it and not merely be the victim of circumstances.

Horoscopes and various forms of superstition are, as is science, attempts to establish some regularity in the relationship between events. Perhaps the most important difference for us, though, is that science works. Not that we are able to make unerring predictions about human behavior in every case, but it allows us the opportunity to control events and make ever better future predictions—which horoscopes do not offer us.

When we discover regularities in the relationship between events, we call them *laws*. Fortunately, the world is lawful, not as chaotic as it sometimes appears. When we lay down our pencil, it stays on the desk; when we touch fire to paper, it burns. Human behavior is quite lawful also. When I buzz my secretary, she comes into my office; when I tell someone I can see him at three o'clock, he arrives for his appointment; when I hire a man to do my firm's accounting, he does it. There are exceptions, of course. Occasionally, the pencil rolls off the desk or the paper refuses to burn; or the secretary does not respond; or the man is late for his appointment; or the accountant is an embezzler. But these I regard as exceptions to the law of regularity and the more I come to know about the event, the more clearly I theorize about the cause-effect relationship, and the better am I able to predict even the exceptions. With the experience of refined observations and measurements, I come to predict that my secretary responds when I buzz her—except when I buzz her between two forty-five and three p.m. when she is off to coffee break with the switchboard operator.

Human behavior is astonishingly lawful and predictable. All normal people (in North America!) stop at red lights, almost all employees arrive at work on time, the paycheck almost always arrives at the end of the month, and nearly all healthy males go to work each day or wish they did. Countless events take place with amazing regularity throughout our waking day to demonstrate the lawfulness and predictability of human behavior.

Indeed, breakfast food manufacturers. depend on it! Even the rate of exceptions to these laws is quite predictable, if we need to be convinced.

What good management is all about is being able to make good predictions—even of the exceptions. However, it is best to hold our optimism in check for the unique individual interacting with other unique individuals sometimes prevents these laws of regularity from coinciding with what people do right now. Psychologists have reconciled themselves to being content with *probabilistic* laws (laws that are correct with degrees of probability above chance) and managers would be well advised to follow suit.

As many of us know from experiences we would rather not recall, it is often easier to disprove a theory than it is to prove one. To take advantage of this safer side, the scientist usually sets up the theory under investigation from the negative point of view. If, for instance, he thinks that B follows from A, he may set out to show that C, D, or even X have just as good a chance of following from A as does B. This is known as the *null hypothesis.* When the scientist makes the measurements following his predictions, and when he demonstrates that C, D, or X do *not* follow from A in the same way that B does he is *rejecting the null hypothesis* and favoring a relationship of cause-effect between A and B. Thus one might speculate about the relationship between staff turnover and higher pay in other organizations and form a theory, based largely on exit interviews, that the main reason people quit the firm is for higher pay elsewhere. But there are other possible reasons for quitting the firm: greater promotional opportunity, greater job security, greater challenge elsewhere, and so on. The null hypothesis should be formulated this way: There is no greater chance of an employee leaving for higher pay than there is of him leaving for greater promotional opportunity, job security, challenge, and so on. Unless the laws of probability allow for the rejection of the null hypothesis, the conclusion about the theory must remain as the famous verdict in Scottish law: not proven. The implication would remain that there is as good a chance of people resigning for other reasons as there is that they resign for better pay.

Back in the fourteenth century a philosopher by the name of William of Ockham stated a rule that "it is vain to do with more what can be done with less." This has become known as *Ockham's Razor* and it describes a principle of theory-making and lawmaking which scientists consider quite important. It is the *principle of parsimony* and it means that we should not have more theories or laws than are necessary. If we start formulating separate theories about the behavior of everyone under our management, we may find that these theories begin to conflict and become confusing so that we do not know which one is best. As this would reduce our ability to predict, we use Ockham's Razor to cut away superfluous theories.

An example of parsimony employed in this book is the perception-interaction theory; it has been used to explain not only how we see our social world, but also communication, psychological contracts, and other aspects of behavior. The exchange theory is another example for we use it in trying to understand much of group dynamics.

GATHERING DATA

Throughout the course of his waking life, any individual is constantly observing and gathering data. He stores some, rejects some, acts on some. The problem with ordinary data gathering, though, as against scientific data gathering is that our day-to-day observations of behavior are frequently unreliable, sometimes being colored by our attitudes and values. Also, the samples of behavior we observe are often limited and "biased," not representative of typical behavior and hence not a good basis for the generalizations we want to make. Finally, many facets of behavior are not always readily observable, such as personality, motivation, attitude systems, skill potential, and knowledge.

It is possible for us, then, to draw erroneous conclusions from our observation of human behavior. Indeed, we may even hold contradictory theories simultaneously and, where one does not seem to fit, we are content to use its opposite. If this sounds far-fetched, what about the manager who in the course of a week or so can expound the following "theories" and "laws" about behavior without realizing that he is contradicting himself:

Never too old to learn.	You can't teach an old dog new tricks.
Clothes make the man.	You can't make a silk purse out of a sow's ear.
East is east and west is west and never the twain shall meet.	We're all brothers under the skin.
Repeat a lie often enough and people will believe it.	The truth always comes out.
These young kids haven't got enough sense to keep their mouths shut until they find out what the business is all about.	What we need around here are some new ideas.

These are certainly not signs of scientific management!

Data gathering by the scientist-manager can be done in a number of ways. The first is naturalistic observation. This is a technique used by many scientists—such as astronomers, zoologists, and psychologists. Its major disadvantage is that we usually have to wait for the behavior to occur. The atronomer interested in comets, meteorites, or novae has to wait for them to happen. Similarly, the manager interested in creativity among his subordinates often has to wait for it and then try to discover what brought it about. Also, having witnessed the event once, there is no assurance it will ever occur again.

Often enough, if we want data about what people think, what their attitudes are, what is their motivation or reason for carrying out certain behaviors, or what they think their potential is, the easiest way to get that data is to *ask* them. We must never get so deep into the woods of scientific methodology that we cannot see the forest for the trees. Some purists in certain branches of psychology are fearful of gathering data in such a simple way. Although this second method of gathering data is immensely useful and practical a note of caution is not without foundation. What if Taylor had asked his famous "little Pennsylvania Dutchman" how much pig iron he could load on a car in a day and was content with the answer? The answer would have been a bad one for the man had absolutely no idea how much he could load using Taylor's methods. We also saw what happened when the Hawthorne researchers asked the relay assembly girls how the lights affected production.

We all know instances when insecure workers will lie to cover up a fear, but more important are those situations in which the verbal answer of the worker is wrong because he has forgotten, has made an error, or simply does not know. As an example, I recall working on the Canada-United States border one summer as an immigration officer. On some occasions we were supposed to keep a tally of the number of cars and passengers that we checked through. When business was brisk we could easily lose tally and sometimes we would simply forget—yet it was necessary to turn in *some* figure for our tally at the end of the day. We would "guesstimate" it, of course, but heaven help the departmental statisticians who depend on the accuracy of such numbers! Here, as with so many similar instances, it is not a question of the worker being unwilling or uncooperative but, rather, of his not fully understanding the significance of what he is asked to report.

In spite of these problems, there are still many situations in which the simplest way to get the best information is to ask or carry out an interview. Many techniques we have discussed rely on asking: attitude surveys, personality tests, intelligence tests, sociometric measurements, and the like. Also, the manager must not forget that there is a wealth of information available to him in personnel records. To answer some of the theoretical questions that crop up, all he must do is go through the personnel files (or have the personnel people do it for him) and do a bit of statistical analysis. This gold mine of information often gathers cobwebs in organizations which should be using it. Some organizations have a discouragingly long application form, for example, which is never looked at again after the applicant is hired. Other worker records, production records, and so on can often be used for reasons above and beyond the purposes for which they were originally gathered. Cafeteria records, pay office records, local division reports, and many others can prove useful even though they have been gathered by verbal report and may contain biases.

However, the major distinction in terms of data gathering between the scientist and the nonscientist is the use of the experimental method. Scientists have developed the experiment into a sophisticated technique to enable more precise measurements and accurate predictions to result from their observations. It is this method of gathering information that we must examine.

THE EXPERIMENTAL METHOD

The major advantages of the experiment over other means of gathering data is that it provides maximum *control* and accurate *measurement*.

Control over the situation in which we wish to take our measurements provides a number of advantages which naturalistic observation and verbal reports do not. We have experimental control when we can produce the identical situation over and over again. This means that we do not have to depend on a single observation from which to form or test our theory. By replicating the experiment, we can refine our predictions of a cause-effect relationship from "sometimes" and "usually" to "ninety-five times out of a hundred" or "nine hundred ninety-nine times out of one thousand," and so on. (Statistical techniques make it quite unnecessary to replicate an experiment one hundred times to predict a probability of ninety-five out of one hundred.) Repetition also means that the identical observations can be made by an independent observer whose measurements may not be as biased as our own (see a later section on experimental bias). All sciences demand repeatability so that an event is open to all qualified observers. Private and nonrepeatable measurements cannot be considered part of a scientific law. Take the studies by Sherif and the autokinetic effect referred to in Chapter 14. Although his original studies were carried out in the 1930s, we can easily replicate them today and find almost identical results.

The scientist also wishes to control the experimental situation in such a way that the effects he is observing are sure to be related to the causes he thinks they are related to and not to some other set of unknown causes. Observing that productivity goes up after introducing a new work procedure, is the manager justified in concluding that the new procedure and the rise of productivity are cause-effect? Or could the rise be due to some other "contaminating" factor such as the novelty of the procedure? Or to the fact that the manager-scientist is so keenly interested in his experiment and watches it so closely (everyone knows he is watching it and wants to help him make it succeed) that this affects the way his subordinates work? Many such pitfalls await the novice experimenter.

The experimenter can use different forms of measurement: *nominal measurements* (the terms "unit number three" or "B division" would simply distinguish one unit from another); *ordinal measurements* ("first," "more than," "sixth," "ranking on a scale from one to seven," etc., which all put the things to be measured into some equivalent of a numerical order); and *ratio measurements* ("3.502," "5⅛," "−.05," etc., all numbers counted from a zero point and having equal intervals). Nominal data, basically only descriptive, is of the most limited value. Ordinal measurements are limited because many mathematical functions cannot be performed with them. All mathematical functions can be performed with ratio measurements so, when possible, the experimenter wants to get this third type of data.

The major measurements made by the psychologist are of stimulus (S) and response (R). The stimulus is to cause as the response is to effect. This is why experimental psychologists like to break down behavior into stimulus-response units. (Some are referred to as *S-R* psychologists.) A *stimulus* is considered anything which initiates activity in the person. It could be the sound of the lunch whistle, the opening of the elevator door, a stop light, a letter from a customer, a new company policy, a memo from upstairs, the sight of a group of people lounging around the water fountain, or any other thing or event which comes first in a psychological relationship. A *response* is the consequent event or thing which is brought about by the stimulus. As the S is the cause, the R is the effect, or the thing that the person does as a result of the S. Responses could be getting up and going to the cafeteria, walking into the elevator, stepping on the brakes, sending a telex to headquarters, issuing instructions to subordinates, preparing a report, losing one's temper, or any other behavior following the receipt of some stimulus.

Following from the above and using the common symbols for stimulus and response, our first psychological law would be: *If S, then R.* Keep in mind that a causal relationship between S and R *need not* specify what philosophers call the "necessary or sufficient" causes of the effect (if the cause is present, the effect *must* follow). For social psychologists the effect often has many different "contributory" conditions (this cause contributes to this effect).

A second important law is: *If R, then R.* This R-R law is a bit different from the S-R law. What the law does is to state a regularity between response measurements. For example, if R_1 is high, then R_2 will be high. Take the example of need for achievement: men who are measured high on an achievement need test (R_1) can be expected to be moderate risk takers (R_2) which can be observed and measured in various forms of their behavior. Equally, we might be able to predict that if R_1 is low R_2 will be low. So if job skill as measured by skill tests is low (R_1) then output (R_2) will be low.

Although our R-R law allows us to predict, it is not a causal law like the S-R law. People who score high on a supervisor's skill test (R_1) might make good supervisors (R_2). This would be an R-R law. However, to change a person's supervisory knowledge and skill, he might be exposed to a course in supervisory training which would then be the S to the R of good supervisory behavior. Indeed, the more such training courses (S) he is exposed to, the better his skill as a supervisor may become (R). This would be an S-R law. All psychological laws, whether S-R or R-R, are not perfect laws but are probabilistic, as has been mentioned.

To find out more about the statistics used by psychologists to make predictions of relationship, the student should take a look at the chapter on statistics in almost any introductory psychology textbook, or examine them in more detail in a book on statistics.

THE PSYCHOLOGICAL EXPERIMENT

In the traditional experiment the investigator varies or manipulates one or more variables (called the independent variable) and measures another or other variables called the dependent variables. The *independent variable* is so named because the experimenter can control or vary it. Often, it is a stimulus which can be manipulated but also it may be something like age, sex, size of the group, experience of the worker, composition of the group according to numerous factors, and so on. Usually, we want only one independent variable in an experiment; otherwise, we will not be certain which variable was causal. This is a big problem in social psychology; we have seen in our consideration of group dynamics how closely one factor can be related to others.

Studies are experiments only when the investigator controls the variable in the sense of deliberately manipulating it. Studies which measure differences already in existence or which happen to occur are not experimental, even though they may be precise and extremely valuable to the scientist-manager.

The *dependent variable* is the response which the investigator measures. It is the variable which he hypothesized was dependent upon his manipulation of the independent variable.

In between the manipulation of the independent variable and the measurement of the dependent variable are all those other factors and conditions which must be controlled or held constant if the measurements are to be precise. In some types of psychological experiment, this calls for elaborate environmental controls which are available only by developing laboratory conditions. Most managers do not have the opportunity or time to carry out such experimentation. But one thing they can often do quite easily and which is frequently sufficient for holding conditions constant is to make use of a set of control and experimental conditions. For many studies the *control conditions* will simply be normal conditions. Measurements are made of responses in the control situation without any variables being manipulated. For example, if the experiment involved granting new delegated authority to first-line supervisors and the dependent variable was to be the measurement of productivity and morale, measurements of productivity and morale would be taken before the study commenced or would be taken of equivalent groups in which such delegation would not be made. These would be measurements under control conditions. The *experimental condition* would be one wherein the measurement of dependent variables was made after the manipulation of the independent variable (after the delegation of authority).

As can be seen from the above, it is often necessary to employ more than one group of people in an experiment. When this is done we refer to one as the *control group* (not subjected to a stimulus or independent variable manipulation) and to the other as an *experimental group* (exposed to the stimulus or to the manipulation). In fact, we could say that the basic psychological experiment is quite simple; it involves the experimental group exposed to the independent variable (assumed to be causal) while a control group is not. The groups are then compared in terms of dependent variables (the assumed effect). If there is a statistical difference in the measurement of the dependent variables in the two groups, an S-R relationship is inferred between the two variables.

Some psychologists, in setting up their control and experimental groups (depending on the experiment itself), will make use of "split-litters" of rats to ensure that the rats in the control group are twinned with those in the experimental group; others will attempt to set up "co-twin" groups with one of each twins in the control and experimental groups. These are attempts to control for differences in heredity and background experiences of the experimental subjects. Social psychologists do not usually take such precautions (it would severely hamper their research and put all the world's twins in the employ of psychologists), but often they do make use of matched groups in their investigations.

In *matched groups* each member of the experimental group should be equated to a member of the control group. For example, let us say we were investigating the effects of a new work flow chart which we had predicted would reduce errors in customer service. We introduce the work flow chart to group A but not to group B and measure the difference in errors. The difference is not significant. However, further investigation reveals that the average work experience on this type of job is eight months for group *A* while it is three years and six months for group *B*. As the groups were not matched, contaminating factors such as experience, company loyalty, and cohesiveness could be interfering with the measurement. Age, experience, sex, marital status, education, and other relevant factors may be important when matching groups for control or experimental conditions. Optimally, for each member of the experimental group there should be a member of the control group with the same characteristics.

Sometimes we can use the same group of people for both control and experimental conditions if we have a good *base line* measurement before we start to manipulate the independent variable. Thus we have a good set of measurements of the group's performance over a sufficient period of time before the independent variable is manipulated or before any reinforcements are changed. Such a base line should take into consideration the day-to-day fluctuations, the result of both known and unknown factors. Thus if we introduced a new procedure one day and compared productivity to what it was the day before, the results might be contaminated because of the confusion created by the new procedure. If we compared productivity on a normal weekday with that of a Friday afternoon before a long weekend, the results might give us a distorted picture of the effect of manipulating the independent variable.

Concise measurement of independent and dependent variables provides the researcher with one of his major problems. At times we have to become a bit like Humpty Dumpty in *Alice in Wonderland* and define our terms so they mean what we want them to mean. For example, if we are experimenting with group cohesiveness, we may decide to set an arbitrary point at which we say a group is cohesive (see Chapter 11) and below which point of measurement we say it is noncohesive. Or we may specify that a particular type of psychological contract is in operation if *a*, *b*, and *c* are present and measurable and if *x*, *y*, and *z* are absent. Or we may say that a worker's job attitude is positive if he responds positively to $\frac{n}{x}$ of the items on our attitude questionnaire. Whenever we can reduce the behaviors we are examining to precise measurements like this, it helps to make accurate predictions, allows our experiments to be replicated, and lets any outsider know exactly what we are talking about.

AN S-R EXPERIMENT

Many great experimental psychologists have stated that it is impossible to lay down a set of rules that would make someone a good experimenter. (Many managers have said the same thing: that it is impossible to draw up a set of rules that would guarantee that one would be a good manager.) Good experimentation (like good management) is learned primarily by observing good experimenters and practicing under the guidance of those who have experience. It is learned by doing and taught by contagion.

To get you started on the way, we shall look here at the steps involved in an experiment with which you are already familiar. We shall say that we want to test out Van Zelst's findings (Chapter 11) for their applicability in our management setting. Recall that Van Zelst allowed workers to express first, second, and third choice preferences for a work partner and then, as far as possible, paired those mutually chosen, combining pairs into groups when larger teams were required. Turnover, labor costs, and material costs were then measured and found to be significantly lower than they were before the change.

The theory here is that cohesive groups will be effective groups. We are conjecturing about the relationship between two abstract concepts—group cohesiveness and group effectiveness.

The hypothesis to be tested is that if we change our subgroups to ensure that cohesiveness exists, it should improve effectiveness in terms of morale and productivity. The null hypothesis is that it does not make any difference whether we change the subgroups or not; their effectiveness will remain about the same.

In this experiment the independent variable is the formation of subgroups on the basis of sociometric choice. The structure of the subgroups is the event being manipulated.

The dependent variable is effectiveness in terms of morale and productivity. We shall measure morale in terms of staff turnover and productivity in terms of labor cost per unit and material cost per unit (or whatever cost index is convenient and, hopefully, gathered as information by someone else).

Variables which we will have to try to hold constant or take into account when making the measurement of our dependent variable are mainly those other factors beyond our control which may influence effectiveness upward or downward—for example, the introduction of new machinery or procedures, moving to new facilities, a labor dispute, and new task demands. If such factors cannot be ruled out, an attempt must then be made to determine (perhaps by comparison with other units in the organization) how much they would influence the dependent variable upward or downward.

As for control or experimental conditions, it would probably be difficult to have separate control and experimental groups; the word would soon spread to the control group that a new procedure was introduced in the experimental group. This could bring about complications by making the groups compete with one another, discourage the control group and lower their morale, and so on. As did Van Zelst, we could get a good long base line of premanipulation measurements before actually starting our experiment. He used a nine-month preexperimental measurement. We might do even better by turning to personnel records and monthly reports on cost indices (making sure that no extraordinary events like cutbacks due to recessions have distorted the data).

Now, using the group at hand for its own control, we begin the manipulation. We do not inform the group that they are the subjects of an experiment but simply that a new policy is going to be introduced wherein, as far as possible, people are going to be allowed to choose with whom they wish to work as partners or fellow group workers. With anonymity assured, they are each given a standard form asking them to designate in order the three other members of the total group with whom they would most like to work. They are to fill it out privately, sign it, and return it in an envelope. The groups will then be rearranged with, as much as possible, no major disruption of the office, sales force, hospital, school district, or whatever.

The dependent variables will be observed and data analyzed as they become available. (Van Zelst measured them over a period of twenty months.) If the measurements remain about the same, our theory ends up in the wastebin like many others and we assume that Van Zelst's situation must have been quite different from ours. If our measurements of effectiveness decline, then we have an aborted experiment on hand and we must get out of it as quickly and gracefully as is possible. If effectiveness improves, we may feel a bit smug, pass on our results to our fellow managers, make out a nice little report for the people upstairs, give our subordinates a little pat on the back, tell them what has taken place over the past months, and become interested in trying further research.

We should be cautious about the early data from our manipulations. Remember the Hawthorne studies and the manipulation of the lighting. The "Hawthorne effect" may distort our data upward because of the novelty of the first few weeks after the sociometric choice or the desire of the workers to please. Or the data may be distorted downward because people have to learn new roles, resolve new friend-employee role conflicts, and learn new tasks.

As no one can predict what the outcome will be in your particular situation, good luck if you decide to try it! You should reread Chapter 11 particularly the sections on morale and productivity. There will probably be some change and the odds are that it will bring improvement rather than deterioration. Serious decline in productivity is not likely as long as major disruptions are not forced on your group. Slight declines in productivity or no increases may be offset by increases in morale and declining resignations as well as improvements in your own managerial and research abilities.

AN *R-R* STUDY

The experiment described above can be done by many managers with out moving from their desks and without more than a few minutes' expenditure of time. Now we want to look at something similar which is not of an *S-R* or experimental nature but of an *R-R* or correlational nature.

For this example, we shall use a similar theory: that effective groups will be cohesive groups. The hypothesis will be slightly different for nothing is to be manipulated. It is this: If we measure the effectiveness of existing groups and then measure their cohesiveness, we shall find that the higher the effectiveness, the higher the cohesiveness.

As nothing is to be manipulated, we merely proceed to make our two measurements. Effectiveness is R_1 and it will be measured in terms of morale and productivity as in our *S-R* experiment. Cohesiveness is R_2 and it will be measured by means of a cohesiveness index as explained in Chapter 11. To get this, we must distribute a questionnaire similar to that in our experiment. But now, instead of manipulating groups, we determine the number of mutual choices in each existing group and divide by the number of possible mutual choices. The higher the index number we get, the higher the level of group cohesiveness. The next step is a statistical correlation between R_1 and R_2. The null hypothesis is that the cohesiveness index has no relationship to the level of productivity. If the null hypothesis is rejected, we can then assume that a relationship does exist.

If the null hypothesis is rejected, we might also notice the fundamental difference between the *S-R* and *R-R* studies is that in the experiment we were trying to isolate a cause-effect relationship whereas in our *R-R* research *there are no grounds for assuming a cause-effect relationship.* This is one of the dangerous traps into which the novice statistician stumbles. For example, it might be easy to demonstrate that the increase in the number of churches in a city correlates with the increase of crime in that city or with the increase in visits to psychiatrists. This does not mean that churches spawn crime and behavior disorders. Indeed, we might just as easily find that the nation's suicide rate is increasing at the same rate as the number of cavities in people's teeth is decreasing, but we are not likely to predict that when everyone has perfect teeth they will all commit suicide.

A point for caution in our *R-R* study (and sometimes in the *S-R* study) in trying to formulate causal hypotheses when a relationship is discovered, is that both measurements may be following from some third variable and that any conjectured cause between R_1 and R_2 may be spurious. Thus the higher the position in the organization, the more favorable the attitude to the company may be, but rather than being causally related, these two measurements may be related to a third causal factor: level of education.

However, if the R-R study has established a relationship, we may be tempted to try a bit of experimentation to determine cause-effect.

One assumption made in this R-R study is that a number of comparable groups are available for measurement. Here we get into the procedure of matched groups, already referred to. If there are only three distinct groups under our management and they are not really comparable in terms of productivity, then this R-R study is not for us. However, if there are a dozen or more comparable groups under his management (possibly even less), it might be an interesting study for the new manager-scientist to cut his teeth on.

EXPERIMENTER BIAS

One of the most famous, thorough, and amusing books in the history of psychological experiments is about a horse. His name was "Clever Hans." [1] Around the turn of this century an eminent committee of experts testified that Clever Hans was apparently solving problems of mathematics and musical harmony with great skill and grace by tapping out the answers with his hoof without any assistance from his master. (The master received no recompense for this great feat and it seemed that Mr. von Osten, the owner, was quite unaware how Clever Hans solved the weighty problems. Eventually, the researcher found that the horse was able to discriminate the minute head and eye movements of those who asked the questions and as he approached the correct number of taps with his hoof he picked up their cue as to when he was supposed to stop tapping. An amazingly perceptive horse! He would have made an excellent politician!

The story is told here because it demonstrates one of the great pitfalls for researchers in social psychology. There is a tendency for us to make our own experimental subjects and our own statistical analyses reach the conclusions that we want them to reach. Human subjects appear to make use of some extremely subtle cues like Clever Hans did to make the experimenters' expectations come true. One of my colleagues at the University of Manitoba (Professor John Adair) had a group of his students carry out experiments on perception with undergraduate subjects in which experimenters who expected the subjects to be successful found them so while experimenters who expected them to be failures found them failures. Then the experiment was done over with other groups of subjects, but this time there were no experimenters, only the tape recordings of the first experiment. Once again, the prophesied perception of success or failure was found. This illustrates how subtle we must be in picking up social cues to tell us what is expected from us.

[1] O. Pfungst, Clever Hans (The Horse of Mr. von Osten): A Contribution to Experimental, Animal, and Human Psychology (New York: Holt, Rinehart & Winston, Inc., 1965).

Our main concern here is that, having set up his experiment or R-R study, the manager-scientist may proceed to make his hypothesis supportable simply by the strength of his conviction that the expected results will come. His subordinate-subjects somehow pick up subtle cues from him that now productivity is supposed to go up, that morale is to increase, that absenteeism is to decline, or whatever dependent variable he wishes changed, and they subtly proceed to ensure his success.

In much social psychological research it is necessary to conceal the true purpose of the study from the subjects until after all manipulations and measurements are completed. Most responses being measured are verbal or otherwise under the voluntary control of those involved. If they feel they are being tested or must make good impressions or if they would like to be cooperative, or if the data collection stimulates an interest which did not previously exist, the very fact of measurement may distort the results. Experimenters find, however, that it is best to give the subjects *some* plausible explanation of what is going on even though this means temporarily deceiving them.

LIMITATIONS OF EXPERIMENTS

Although the S-R experiment seems to provide a great advantage over the R-R study, it does have a number of disadvantages. The first disadvantage stems from the fact that it is not always possible to use the absolute size of the scores on the measurement of the dependent variable to tell us about how much of this variable we can expect to find in other situations. In other words, we do not always know how much manipulation of independent variables produces how much measurement of dependent variables. On the other hand, the R-R study tells us that if we have R_1 we can expect to find R_2 with some level of confidence.

The problem stems from the necessity of using ordinal measurements (rather than ratio measurements) of our dependent variables. We do not have an absolute lower limit and an absolute upper limit to our measurements but only gradations, for which the intervals are in a sense arbitrary. Thus, in a study of job attitudes, I may find that a manipulation of independent variable x produces a change in job attitudes from a base line of 2.55 on my attitude scale to a point at 5.10 on the scale. But I cannot then say that positive job attitudes have doubled because of my manipulation of x. As the numbers are not absolute, a change of job attitude in another group from 3.15 on the attitude scale to 5.85 as a result of manipulation of independent variable y might represent twice as much change as does 2.55 to 5.10 as a result of manipulation of independent variable x (or it may be the other way around). As I do not know whether x or y has a stronger relationship to the dependent variable, I do not know which one would be better to use.

Another disadvantage of the experiment is that, when no significant differences are found between the experimental conditions (the level of confidence is not sufficient to reject the null hypothesis), it cannot be automatically concluded that the hypothesis is false. There may be a relationship between independent and dependent variable not found by the experiment. The failure to prove the relationship may be because of insufficent manipulation of the independent variable or some other experimental condition. As social psychology is such a rapidly developing field, there is little agreement at the present moment about what all the relevant variables are or how they should be defined. Most of today's experimental social psychologists deal with relationships that have not been investigated previously. As a consequence, there have been a number of incidents in which an expected relationship which failed to materialize in one experiment was demonstrated in another experiment because of a variation in the strength or manipulation of the independent variable or a better control of some interfering variable.

As well, the expected relationship may not appear because the dependent variable has not been defined and measured precisely enough. Measurements like "positive job attitude" may be too crude to show anything but gross differences in the dependent variable. The most obvious difficulties come, perhaps, from the lack of control over the experimental situation; too many other factors may be influencing the dependent variable as well as the one being manipulated. Until methods are discovered for holding such contaminating variables under control, it may not be possible to demonstrate an S-R relationship.

A final limitation on experimentation is quite bothersome. It is that reasons of economics, legality, responsibility, and plain morality often prevent us from manipulating variables we would like to manipulate. The hypothesis we would like to test over the next six months may be too costly; or the risk of disturbing a reasonably well-functioning unit may be too great; or it may put the union on our neck.

Nonetheless, a great feeling of satisfaction is in store for the manager-scientist who can pull off a neat and unambiguous experiment, no matter how simple it may be. It is something like washing out your first fleck of gold dust when you are panning for gold or scoring your first goal in hockey in a real game or breaking par after years of trying.

CONCLUSION

The Western Electric program (Hawthorne studies), referred to so often in this book, first demonstrated the possibilities of research on social behavior at the plant level. This interest was stirred up again in World War II through the studies of morale and motivation in American soldiers particularly. Stouffer's book *The American Soldier*[2] has become a classic demonstration of how social psychology can be put to work to solve problems of human beings interacting outside of the laboratory. We have come a long way from the rather mechanistic approach of Taylor, the great pioneer researcher of the 1880s.

Two factors hamper social psychological research in contemporary management problems. First, because there is so much work and research to be done at the theoretical level in a relatively new and interesting field, the vast majority of researchers are concerned with basic theoretical problems. Given the nature of social psychology in the present day, this is as it should be. Second, too few trained social psychologists have personal contact, experience, or understanding of the social psychological problems faced by the manager in his day-to-day work.

If Mohammed will not go to the mountain, then the mountain should go to Mohammed. That is to say, if for the moment social psychologists are preoccupied to the extent that they neglect management problems, let managers assume the secondary role of social psychologists. You managers are as likely to have your theories, hypotheses, and conjectures about social interaction of your groups as you are to find answers to your problems in the research of social psychologists. Why not test out a few of these hypotheses, starting with the most simple ones? Seek the advice of local psychologists (social or any other type of psychologist can help you). The possibilities of advancing the field of knowledge and of improving your own understanding and management style, are immense.

Take up the challenge both for personal benefit and to make your organizational world a better place for all to live and work.

SUMMARY

Too many things done by the manager each day relative to social behaviors succeed or fail on the basis of luck. Too often we rely on that great teacher, experience, and persist in our errors year after year.

The ordinary tools of social living enable us to predict the world around us. All we need do is hone these tools to a fine edge to make the better predictions we all want. Increase in scientific knowledge, as with any other knowledge, comes with improvement of the cycle of observe-measure-predict-observe-measure. The scientist is a scientist mainly because he has developed this technique more fully than the layman.

Instead of relying on wise old sayings and housewives' tales, we should be sharpening our observation of social behavior. This is one of the

[2] S. A. Stouffer et al., *The American Soldier Vol. I: Adjustment During Army Life* and Stouffer et al., *The American Soldier Vol. II: Combat and its Aftermath* (Princeton, N.J.: Princeton University Press, 1949).

major purposes of this book. First, we must formulate clear hypotheses and gather data which will either support or reject them. To prevent this support or rejection being based on our personal biases and feelings, we must use the scientific method.

Naturalistic observation and interviewing (or asking questions) are good methods of data gathering but the most refined is the experimental method. In this technique a definite cause-effect relationship can be pinpointed. By manipulating the stimulus and measuring the responses, the S-R investigator is able to check out causal relationships between independent and dependent variables. The first experimental law of psychology is: *If S, then R.*

The second method, although not experimental, is eminently practical for the manager-scientist. Through it he can determine a predictable ratio between measurable responses. This leads to formulation of the second law: *If R, then R.*

The traditional psychological experiment calls for manipulation of the independent variable, holding all other variables constant and measuring the dependent variable. To hold all things constant usually requires a control and experimental group although the control group may be used for the experimental group if a good base line is established. If this is not possible, matched groups are then called for to prevent misinterpretation. One essential of the experiment is that it is objective. This means it can be replicated by any other competent and interested investigator.

An example of an S-R and an R-R study with some of their advantages and pitfalls was outlined. Both are based on our earlier discussion of cohesiveness and productivity.

The difficult problem of experimenter bias was dealt with briefly. One immediately sees its relationship to the self-fulfilling prophecy described in Chapter 3. Although it is a very subtle phenomenon, one of the first steps in controlling it is to ensure that experimental subjects do not know the true hypothesis of the study.

Finally, the limitations of the social psychological experiment were reviewed. A number stem from the necessity of using ordinal data in our statistical analysis. Others are the result of not being able to reject the hypothesis of the failed experiment and of the frustration of not always being able to check out our hypotheses experimentally for financial or ethical reasons.

The conclusion of the chapter put the challenge of becoming a manager-scientist squarely before the manager.

21

A RESEARCH MODEL
FOR THE EFFECTIVE
ORGANIZATION

This chapter concentrates on developing a model which the manager can employ both to test out the current effectiveness of his organization or some part of it, and to use for general research and theory development. What is meant by "effectiveness" and how can it be measured? How can the manager fit his important questions and problems into a simple model? How can the model be applied to solve management problems?

With the introduction to applied social psychology and a summary of scientific methodology tucked under his hat, the modern manager is in a far better position to be effective than the generation of managers before him. He has a grasp of the basic principles of psychology with some insight into how man ticks as an individual and how groups of men interact to accomplish their goals. Now he can observe the dynamics of the group more objectively and can pinpoint some of its weaknesses and strengths.

He knows what sort of objectives he should strive for in teaching his men effectiveness.

Yet one of the most discouraging aspects of teaching is to see one's brightest students, those who in the classroom appear to grasp the material quickest and understand it easiest, unable to see past the ends of their noses when faced with a "real life" situation. Given an instance in which one might expect that they put their "book learning" into practice, they seem to forget everything the textbook said and fall back on their primitive pre-education instincts. One hears rather amazing commentaries about this phenomenon. Several times I have had my ears pricked by senior management people advising fresh university recruits that "now you have finished with university, so forget about those textbooks because your real learning is about to commence." This is probably the attitude of the hardened pragmatist who feels there is no school like the school of hard knocks.

Also frequently heard are the comments of those who lack a university education: "Good grief, is this what a university education does to them?" In practice, this appears a not unjustified comment. Often, the new recruit to the organization seems "all thumbs" in an intellectual sense. He does not know how to deal with the public, interpret obvious company policy, or cooperate with the work team.

Why is there such a gap between the textbook and its application? Is it necessarily so? I am convinced that it is not. However, there are a number of reasons for this gap. First, many textbooks the student is confronted with are written in a strictly theoretical-research approach. In fact, the "best" textbooks are presented in this manner; this gives the textbook writer high status among his colleagues. Second, many university instructors emulate the textbook authors in attempting to maintain a level of "purity"; they use a research-based approach which would forbid them to introduce practical problems in other than a casual manner. I have heard colleagues imply the application of their works to practical problems "would be a possibility," while remaining more interested in its theoretical applications. A third, obvious reason for the gap is that the young graduate is often completely naïve about what day-to-day life in the organization is all about. He is more accustomed to mingling with peers whose major life problems do not extend beyond the next set of examinations than with "mature" people trying to cut a niche for themselves and their families in the modern rat race. A fourth, unfortunate reason is that many graduates lack the intellectual flexibility to make the connection between the textbook and the real life problem.

I am reminded of a rather pathetic case history I read when I was a student of clinical psychology. The source of the case and much of the detail escapes me now but, in summary, it seems that a man had built himself a successful manufacturing business over the years through hard work and driving ambition. He had sent his son away to college; the boy had graduated from engineering school and returned to work at the father's factory. There he began to suffer from a gradual psychological breakdown which first became apparent from the bizarre and fantastic "inventions" he began drafting up. When his father became aware of this, *he assumed it was the result of all the reading and studying the boy had been doing over the past several years at college and that he would soon get over it if left alone.*

My point is that the graduate or the person who has been taking courses or doing reading in management is sometimes rather smugly regarded as unrealistic and impractical; he is thought to need some time before he "gets his feet back on the ground." This is an unfortunate attitude. Yet the problem we are facing in this chapter is a real one. How do we bridge the gap between theory and practice?

The natural sciences (physics, chemistry, biology, geology, etc.) have had fewer problems bridging the gap and the payoff from them to many organizations has been great as a result. The social sciences have had more difficulty. Perhaps this is because they deal with less tangible subjects than rock layers or chemical compounds, perhaps it is partly because of the social scientists themselves, and perhaps it is mainly because many great leaders of industry, business, government, the church, and the military have demonstrated their ability to be successful and effective without the aid of formal training in the social sciences. There are few great natural scientists without formal scientific training.

Having pondered this problem over the past several years, I have come up with the following proposal: it is my suggestion for a model of organizational effectiveness. By use of this model, the manager-scientist can apply what he knows to the unique organizational problem he faces. The model should help him both to isolate critical variables in the management process and to research questions which arise.

To the outsider it sometimes appears a question of luck or accident whether the organization serves him well or not. In spite of the uniqueness of each organization, variables can be isolated which would distinguish the effective from the noneffective organization. Yet attempts to discover the common important factors for all organizations have not been notably successful. There are a number of reasons for this, including the problems of trying to measure ongoing processes in the highly complex organization, but one of the most important reasons for failure is probably due to the unique combination of factors which operate in each organization at any given time in its history and development.

This uniqueness is enough to discourage the serious researcher and to make the manager fall back on his "gut feelings." Both are in error.

EFFECTIVENESS

The first step in building our model is to attempt a definition of effectiveness. McGregor [1] described the well-functioning, effective group somewhat as follows:

1. The atmosphere tends to be informal, comfortable, and relaxed.
2. There is a good deal of discussion in which nearly everyone participates, but the discussion remains relevant to the task.
3. The objectives are well understood and accepted by all members of the group. Initially, there is free discussion of the objective but it eventually is formulated in such a way that they could all commit themselves to it.
4. The members listen to one another. Every idea is given a hearing. No one is afraid of being considered foolish by putting forward even extreme ideas.
5. There is disagreement for disagreements are not overridden. The reasons for disagreement are examined and there is an attempt to resolve them rather than suppress them.
6. Most decisions are reached by some form of consensus in which there is a general agreement and willingness to accept the decision. Formal voting with a simple majority is held suspect as the basis for best action.
7. Criticism is frequent and frank but comfortable and shows little evidence of personal attack.
8. Members feel free to express their feelings as well as their ideas not only on the problem to be solved but on the very operation of the group. NO GROUPTHINK
9. Assignments to members are clear and are accepted.
10. The group chairman does not dominate nor is there evidence of a power struggle while the group is involved in achieving its task. The issue is not *who* controls but *how* to get the job done.
11. The group is self-conscious about its own operation.

Although this description is still valid, we need something more exact and more easily measurable. Most commonly, effectiveness is defined in terms of the degree of goal achievement observed in the organization. As we refer to the *degree* of goal achievement, this allows us to refer to grades or levels of effectiveness and not simply effectiveness as against noneffectiveness.

The next step is to determine what is meant by *goals*. Two types of organizational goals have been distinguished.[2] There are the *official* goals,

[1] D. McGregor, *The Human Side of Enterprise* (New York: McGraw-Hill Book Company, 1960).

[2] Charles Perrow, "Goals in Complex Organizations," *American Sociological Review*, XXVI (1961), 855.

the general purposes of the organization, as put forth in its charter, annual reports, public statements by key executives, and other authoritative pronouncements. There are also the *operative* goals, which point to the things the organization is trying to do through its operating policies, regardless of the nature of its official goals. For example, the statutes of the college of which I was dean were drawn up in the 1860s and stated quite clearly that one of the major purposes was the training of the clergy. This is an official goal which is still in effect in indirect ways, but the operative goals are to provide a good university education to all students who attend the college now, regardless of denominational background and vocational aspirations.

Obviously, the manager is mainly interested in the operative goals although other members of the organization may have a strong interest in the official goals. This way of looking at goals helps us focus on effectiveness from the viewpoint of the major decision makers who are involved in what the organization is actually trying to accomplish.

After surveying the available research literature, Price [3] came to the conclusion that five variables are positively related to effectiveness. These are:

1. productivity
2. morale
3. conformity
4. adaptiveness
5. institutionalization

He also concluded that productivity is more closely related to effectiveness than are the other four variables. Thus an organization with a high degree of productivity and a low degree of morale is assumed to be an organization with a high degree of effectiveness.

Productivity is defined as the ratio of output to input and is similar to the term *efficiency*. High productivity, then, is high output as a result of low input. The input may be in money, machinery, man-hours, skilled as against unskilled personnel, and so on. The output may be in goods, services, ideas, numbers, financial figures, and so on. In general, we might say that productivity is measured in terms of some *quantity of output*.

Morale is defined in terms of the degree to which the needs of the individual are satisfied. If a high number of needs of a high number of individuals in the group are highly satisfied, morale is then high. If a high number of needs of a high number of individuals remain unsatisfied, morale is then low. Satisfaction, for our purposes, refers to the fulfillment of needs

[3] James L. Price, *Organizational Effectiveness* (Homewood, Ill.: Richard D. Irwin, Inc., 1968).

along the entire range of Maslow's need hierarchy. In practical terms, satisfaction for the individual worker is usually made up of a mixture of monetary rewards, fulfillment of social needs, and a sense of purpose or accomplishment in his task. If one or more of these is negative (e.g., relatively low pay), the others must be satisfied to a higher degree to balance out and keep the individual satisfied. As we know from Chapter 11, satisfaction is more than a function of the *amount* of rewards received. The amount may satisfy one person but not another, and this is true not only of monetary rewards. Also, we know that individual personalities vary in respect to their various need strengths; some, for example, are more dependent on social need satisfaction. Finally, we must remember our discussion of *comparison levels* and *distributive justice* which underlines that the important thing about rewards is the perception of their fittingness rather than their objective amount. Morale, then, is measurable in terms of attitudes and perceptions of the group members rather than in terms of the organization's policies.

Conformity, in the sense that it is related to effectiveness, refers to whether or not the behavior of persons within the organization and the behavior of the organization as a unit complies to the ideology set up as its norms and rules. First, this would mean an ideology to which they could adhere. The ideology could consist of principles which are part of organizational policy—citizen participation, community service, racial equality, and improvement of the individual. In those organizations which definitely want to bring about a change in the person, it is relatively easy to observe such norms and see whether or not they are achieved as goals—for example, in hospitals, police forces, school systems, prisons, military training units, and so on. We could observe, for instance, whether or not those discharged from prison were rehabilitated or convicted of further crimes; were they trained to the principles of the prison organization? In other organizations conformity to principles may not be as apparent but such phrases as customer satisfaction, superior quality produce, guaranteed workmanship, and specializing in service are their mottos and public goals. The conformity we refer to indicates a lack of deviation from these normative goals. For it to be useable as a measurement of effectiveness, the ideology must be clearly stated and unambiguous. If it is clear and unambiguous, it can provide a unifying purpose to the organization and its members in seeking their goals.

Adaptiveness as a measure of effectiveness refers to the degree of flexibility of the organization. If it is highly adaptive, it can respond quickly to changing situations. This is more important in some types of organizations than in others—for example, clothing manufacturers, electronics industries, and military equipment suppliers. Often, we forget how important it is in social organizations, as in the Boy Scouts, religious institutions, and school systems. In fact, any type of organization can suffer from "bureaucratic ossification" and a ritualism of its procedures. Many things could be used to measure adaptiveness—for example, autonomy to make decisions, training programs, new hardware, procedural reorganization, opening of new markets, diversification, and so on.

Institutionalization is the last of Price's five measures related to effectiveness. In this context institutionalization refers to the degree of support an organization receives from its environment: community and general public support; government support; support of professional societies and trade unions; and so on. This type of support would involve the conformity of nonmembers of the organization to its norms and their acceptance of its ideology and goals. Take, for example, a program introduced a few years ago in the province of Manitoba to retrain people in "defensive driving." The wide range of community support for the agency's professed norms and purposes indicated a high degree of institutionalization. Any form of positive attitudes of acceptance by nonmembers would indicate institutionalization (and a lack of such attitudes or negative attitudes would indicate noninstitutionalization). We might think of such things as customer loyalty, support of alumni, successful recruitment programs, lengthy lists of job applicants during normal economic conditions, and positive public image as indicators of the degree of institutionalization.

These five indicators of effectiveness can be more or less standardized even when one wants to compare the effectiveness of other different organizations. It must always be remembered, as discussed in Chapter 20, that the scientist deals in things which can be observed and measured. When we speak of effectiveness, then, we refer always to something which can be measured according to some *quantitative* degree of productivity, morale, conformity, adaptiveness, and institutionalization. If this simple point is overlooked, we cease to be scientific and are right back to the "guess" and the "gut" feeling (although we will probably always have these with us).

THE MODEL OF EFFECTIVENESS

The trick in any type of model-building is to have a few clearly defined basic ideas. The initial model must be as simple as possible. It can always be made more complicated later. As we saw in our chapter on scientific method, we must have a clear idea of what our dependent variable is. The dependent variable remains the same, once defined, for it is the thing we really want to know about and we have set up techniques for measuring how much of it we have. Figure 21-1 shows this first step.

All this illustrates is that we know what our basic dependent variable is to be but we do not know what independent variables or events influence its measurement. With Figure 21-2 we go a small but important step further.

FIGURE 21-1

THE BASIC MODEL

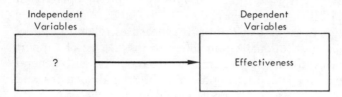

What we have done is to indicate that we are in a position to define what we mean by effectiveness through measurements or indices of five observable events. These could be treated individually or they could be weighted to form a total index of effectiveness, or used collectively and separately at the same time.

We have started with this model by examining the measurements which we ultimately wish to know for only when we know whether or not the organization is effective can we do something about it. But now it is necessary to work backward through the model by asking questions about how effectiveness is likely to be achieved.

FIGURE 21-2

THE DEPENDENT VARIABLES DEFINED

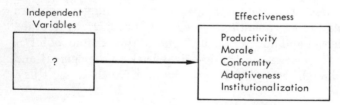

As indicated elsewhere, effectiveness is not merely a question of luck, and the basic unit of an organization of people accomplishing something well is the individual. In other words, we do not have effective organizations without effective individuals. The antecedents of our dependent variable must be sought, then, on the level of the individual. But we have seen that the individual makes sense only in the context of the social group. Therefore, we must equally examine antecedents of effectiveness on the social level. This brings us to complicate the model further, as in Figure 21-3.

The next, obvious, thing the manager-scientist is going to ask is how to measure individual and group effectiveness. This is not too difficult for group effectiveness; we can use measurements similar to those we used

FIGURE 21-3

LOWER LEVEL EFFECT ON
ORGANIZATIONAL EFFECTIVENESS

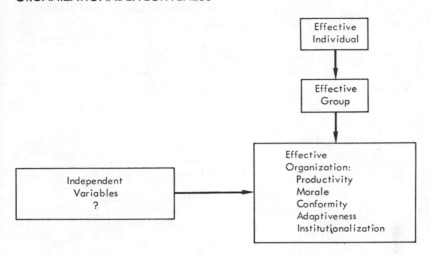

for the general organization except at a different level. In other words, we can set up a measurement standard for group productivity depending on what the group has as its assigned tasks. Group morale can often be measured more simply than organizational morale. Conformity of the group to organizational norms, the amount of deviation, and the unity of purpose it displays give us a third possible measurement. Group adaptiveness is measurable similarly to the way we would measure organizational adaptiveness but, again, at a different level. Institutionalization may not always be measurable on the group level, depending on the group and the organization of which it is a part.

For individual effectiveness, there are usually many measurements and measuring devices available according to the individual role in the organization. Once again, we could have productivity or personal output as a gauge. We could also use a measurement of creative output for most jobs. Personal loyalty or commitment to the job and the organization could be rated in terms of degree. Personal development, level of responsibility and maturity, conformity (or deviation) to organizational rules, policies, and norms can be rated. The degree of influence on fellow workers or non-organization persons may also be measurable. Most of these things are measured in some form in many personnel and supervisory rating schemes. Other specific measurements of individual worker effectiveness may be employed because of the peculiar circumstances of the job or the uniqueness of the organization. What must be kept in mind is that these are suggestions or examples of observable behaviors which could be used to rate individual effectiveness. Within each organization the manager-scientist must determine what his particular organization really wants to measure.

We are talking about effectiveness on three different levels simultaneously. In the same manner that the antecedents of effective organization are important to the organizational scientist, he must be equally interested in the antecedents of group and individual effectiveness. This is particularly true for the middle management and lower management investigator. The model must be elaborated a step further as in Figure 21-4.

FIGURE 21-4

THREE LEVELS OF EFFECTIVENESS

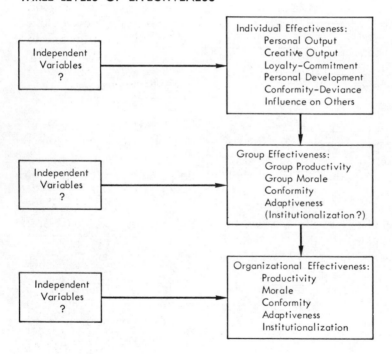

So far our attention has been concentrated on the things we want to find in our organization, our group, and our individual—our dependent variables. That is as it should be; only with a clear picture of what we want can we seek the best means of achieving it.

Filling in the independent variables at the level of the individual is not a great problem. Personnel research and selection has concentrated on them from the beginning. Depending on the job involved, some are rather obvious matters of health, age, sex, educational background, ability to communicate, physical strength, specific training, and so on. Others are obvious but more in the line of human engineering such as conditions of the physical environment, quality of equipment employed, location of the physical plant in the community, hours of work, noise factors, assembly line units, internal communication mechanisms, quality of supplies, and physical partition of offices and sections. There are also less obvious variables, often taken into consideration by personnel departments depending on the job involved. These could be personality factors, personal stability, intelligence, creativity, self-esteem, and so on. To outline *all* of these possible independent variables would be as difficult as it would be useless. Unique jobs call for unique combinations of them.

What must be stated about these independent variables on the level of the individual, though, is that ritualism often becomes a substitute for scientific investigation. Outdated personnel forms often contain a good deal of useless information and a lack of relevant information. I once did a study in a large commercial organization in which it was proposed to make use of personnel assessment forms, the completion of which was part of company policy. They turned out to be absolutely useless and without standardization. It is all too often taken for granted in the personnel office that a candidate with qualification X is the best man to do job Y effectively. A good example of this is a recent report by Noe.[4] In this study the researcher found that those supervisors who performed poorly on the tests used were rated high by their own supervisors.

Sometimes Personnel makes intentionally biased judgments (although the reasons why are sometimes buried in long-forgotten policy) and sometimes they make them unknowingly. (I once did some research on personnel assessment in which it was found that, unknown to the assessors, women were invariably assessed differently than men although this was not the intent.)

What must also be recalled is that any investigation of the relationship between the independent variables and the dependent variables must be controlled scientifically. This means that, as far as possible, contaminating factors must be held constant. These factors, we said in the last chapter, are called the intervening variables. So, for instance, if we want to measure the relationship between educational background (independent variable) and personal output (dependent variable) of people doing complex assembly work, we would have to hold such things as age, motor coordination, and work experience (intervening variables) constant.

This last example leads us directly to our next point, for by now we know that the individual cannot be considered outside of his social context. The norm for personal output may be different in one work group than in another. Isolating the important independent variables at the social

---

[4] W. K. Noe, "A Pilot Study of the Validity of Ratings Done on First-Line Supervisors," *Studies in Personnel Psychology*, II, No. 1 (April 1970).

group level is a bit more difficult than at the individual level. However, much information is available from the work of social psychologists both in practical and theoretical setting. A great deal of this information has been referred to in the text—for example, norms, style of leadership, communication patterns, cohesiveness, level of participation in decision making, and so on.

Relevant variables can probably be squeezed into three general categories. First, there is the *structure* of the group. This could include its size (can five men really do the job better than four men? how much better?); cohesiveness (are groups of friends more productive than groups of nonfriends?); communication patterns; status relationships among members; power relationships; style of the group leader; level of participation in decision making; and norms.

Second, there are *task demands* made on the group. These could include the complexity of the task, the degree of perfection on completion to be satisfactory (tolerance for error or incompleteness), and the time limits imposed (speed vs. quality). Also, how much autonomy do they have in designing the task? How much does the task depend on human factors as against automated or machine-produced factors? How is the work proportioned to individual members relative to their competence?

Third, there are *environmental factors*. These could be the social environment in the sense of the group's relationship to other groups in the organization; it could also refer to the group's relationship to nongroup persons—is it a group which serves the public directly? The environmental factors could also refer to the physical location of the group either in the sense of the space it occupies (first floor as against fifth floor; spacious as against cramped quarters) or in the sense of the community environment (in a downtown location; in the suburbs; in a small town; close to sports and recreation facilities).

Once again, the examination of a relationship of any of these factors to group effectiveness would require holding possible contaminating factors constant when comparing groups—if the effects of group size were being examined, the groups compared would have to have the same task demands and environmental factors.

Isolating organizational level independent variables is not as easily done as at the individual and group levels. The main reason is the relatively smaller amount of research available. Nonetheless, the body of completed research is increasing. Also, the astute manager-scientist should have enough practical experience to form theories of which organizational level factors are related to effectiveness in his particular organization.

A number of the group level factors are also relevant at the organizational level. Certainly, some structural variables such as size, participation, communication patterns, leadership styles, and specialized divisions are also relevant at the organizational level. The same is true of environmental variables. Task variables in terms of the degree of automation, amount of centralized control, degree of sophistication required (a hospital as against a warehouse), company policy, and system of sanctions may be quite relevant to effectiveness on this level. There are also other possible variables such as the salary and other reward systems, level of professionalization (a university as against an assembly plant), competition as against monopoly, current economic conditions in society, availability of labor, political environment, and present personnel of the organization which might bear a direct relationship to effectiveness.

Again, intervening variables must not be overlooked. If questioning the relationship of centralized control as against decentralized control to effectiveness, the comparison would have to be made with control of, for example, the economic environment and the labor market.

THE COMPLEX MODEL

Now we are ready to complicate the model a bit further, thus making it a bit more realistic a picture of what we face with our "real life" organization. Figure 21-5 sketches in these relationships.

FIGURE 21-5

THE COMPLEX MODEL OF
ORGANIZATIONAL EFFECTIVENESS

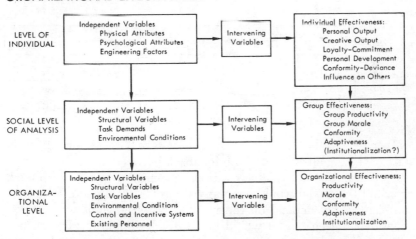

In the complex model we see that variables influencing effectiveness at the organizational level are influenced directly and indirectly by variables at the level of the individual and the group. The effective organization is built of effective individuals who work effectively in groups. For example, the control and incentive systems instituted by the organization depend on its individual members (e.g., they differ in a university as against in a military unit) as well as on the degree of autonomy granted to groups and divisions within the organization.

Unfortunately, it is necessary to take our completed model a step further. This is because, on closer examination, the model in Figure 21-5 could be considered a static picture of the organization while we know that the organization is an ongoing process, always pulsing, changing, growing, like a live thing. Thus we know, for example, that the institution of better control and incentive policies at the organizational level may make available new personnel at the individual and group level—the effective organization attracts more effective individuals. But we also know that a change on the horizontal level may produce changes at the same level: a higher output at the group level may produce new group motivation; increased creative output at the individual level may produce new individual needs. Indeed, a change at any point in the model may produce a change upward, downward, backward, or forward at any other point. Thus we must end up with a maximum complexity as in Figure 21-6.

FIGURE 21-6

MAXIMUM EXTENT OF INFLUENCE AMONG VARIABLES

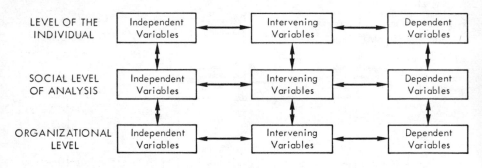

In other words, the complete model must take into account the dynamic state of the organization and the feedback between and across levels. This does not mean that all possible relationships must always be examined. Whether or not the model would have any value for examination of a particular problem would depend on the number of variables it were necessary to consider in each box. It would be relatively simple to fill each box with a litany of possible variables even when considering a simple problem. This would not be too valuable a procedure for the investigator.

The more fruitful approach would be to allow for the uniqueness of the organizational problem being investigated by limiting the boxes to only those variables relevant to the question. As we said earlier, the trick in using models is to start off with the most simple analysis of the problem and to complicate it only if it becomes valuable or necessary to do so. One does not complicate the model beyond what is required to provide a solution.

AN EXAMPLE OF THE APPLICATION
OF THE MODEL

For the sake of illustration, we will next look at a question of effectiveness as related to the type of leadership one finds in the organization. Starting off with some empirical data from Fiedler which has been discussed in Chapter 17, we might describe the variables in the contingency model of leadership in a simple form as in Figure 21-7.

FIGURE 21-7

**APPLICATION OF MODEL TO
FIEDLER'S FINDINGS ON LEADERSHIP**

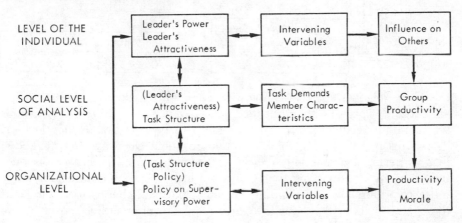

Here the three variables isolated by Fiedler (leader attractiveness, task structure, leader power) are described by the three levels of independent variable. Attractiveness has to be considered in terms of the attitudes of the group members toward the individual leader; task structure can be described on its own; the leader's position power is determined by organizational policy toward autonomy for its supervisors. Now if one holds constant the task demands (amount of time to complete the task, degree of perfection called for, etc.) and the characteristics of the group members, one can investigate group effectiveness when the independent variables are manipulated.

In turn, the total effect on productivity and morale in the organization could be measured.

If the researcher is then satisfied with his findings, he need not elaborate the model further. However, if further questions arise in his investigation in which other relationships are queried, the model can then be made more complicated as in the hypothetical application illustrated in Figure 21-8.

FIGURE 21-8

HYPOTHETICAL APPLICATION OF MODEL TO LEADERSHIP QUESTIONS

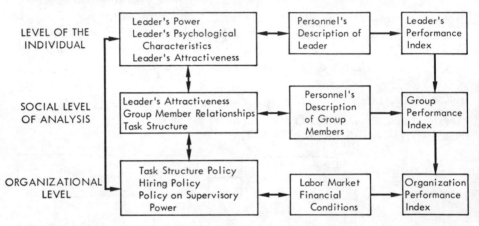

The relationships to be investigated in this hypothetical application are certainly not exhaustive but representative of some interesting questions which might relate supervisory leadership to organizational effectiveness.

Thus one may wish to find out more about the way that attractive leaders perform so that they can be distinguished from nonattractive ones before hiring or promoting them. This might be done by establishing some index of performance and finding out what personal characteristics related to attractiveness bring about the performance level or individual effectiveness. In such a study the attractiveness of the leader may become the constant and the personal characteristics such as age, education, personality factors, and so on may become the independent variables.

The type of individual hired into an organization or promoted within it might depend on company hiring policies; thus the organizational level independent variable is linked with the individual level. The organizational level independent variables are, in turn, related to current conditions in the society within which the organization operates. These could be economic or political or other cultural and social conditions. The policy of the organization would also be related to the availability of personnel with the required characteristics and whether such individuals were willing to work for the organization.

Other relationships have also been added in Figure 21-8. One might investigate the relationship between the characteristics of the leader and the characteristics of the group members for some relationships may be more benevolent than others (a young leader of older group members may not contribute toward leader attractiveness). One can see a potential circular relationship here between leader attractiveness, leader characteristics, group member characteristics, and the attitude of members toward the leader.

Also, the links between organizational effectiveness and organizational policy might be investigated; also, those between the personal effectiveness of the individual leader and group effectiveness (the leader may have the characteristics required but lack "contagious enthusiasm" which Likert says is needed in a leader). Group effectiveness, in turn, is linked to organizational effectiveness.

In such a manner it might be possible for the organizational researcher to extend existing findings so they could be applied to problems of his unique organization. If there were interesting findings, he might be tempted to extend the model even further in an attempt to clarify the picture of his particular organization and its effectiveness.

SPECULATIVE APPLICATIONS OF THE MODEL

The example of leadership considered above is a relatively easy one; Fiedler has already done the work for us and it is just a matter of fitting it into the model. Now we turn to a consideration of a few problems that could conceivably arise in any organization. Here the manager-scientist sees that certain organizational events are going to occur so he wishes to find out their influence on effectiveness; or he wishes to introduce a change because he thinks it will bring greater effectiveness but he wants to be sure.

The first hypothetical example involves the introduction of a new Performance Appraisal Policy. Let us assume that senior management is considering the idea that a performance appraisal program be initiated whereby all employees will be given feedback at certain intervals. The gathering of data for appraisal will commence now and the first appraisal will take place in six months. There will be another appraisal six months later, and thereafter annually. The employee will then have the opportunity for a measurement of his performance growth in the organization.

A hardheaded senior manager disagrees with the proposed policy. It will cost money, he says. It will consume working time; it will accomplish nothing for the company. As far as he is concerned, it is just another harebrained, frilly idea dreamed up by someone in the personnel office who has nothing better to do with his time. The policy is accepted in spite of his objections but all the senior managers are going to watch the development of the program carefully and will ax it if it appears superfluous or, at least, they will cease supporting it and the program may dwindle away.

Figure 21-9 shows how the model of effectiveness might be applied to discovering what performance appraisal does to effectiveness in this company. Independent variables are introduced at the organizational and individual level (the group level is not important in this particular problem, at least not at the moment). In order to be sure that any change which takes place is not due to other factors, there should be a control group (Figure 21-9b). Intervening variables which might influence individual change (age, sex, rank or position in the organization, number of years in the organization) should be held constant in experimental and control groups. Measurements of change in performance at the individual level and change in effectiveness at the organizational level must be made by taking the present measurement and comparing it with later measurements. This must be done with both groups.

FIGURE 21-9(a)

HYPOTHETICAL PROBLEM ON
INDIVIDUAL-ORGANIZATIONAL LEVELS

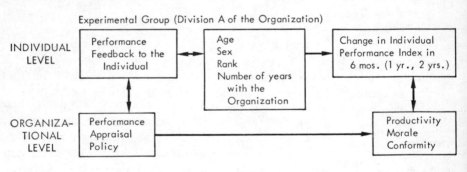

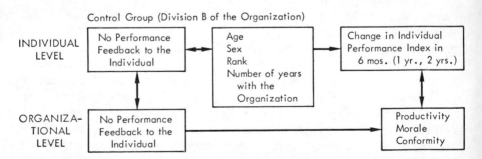

This bit of important research could be done by the manager-scientist with relatively little effort. The independent variables at organizational and individual level are introduced by the company. He must assure that a control group within the company (or a comparable group outside it, which is more difficult) is available. He should obtain current performance ratings of the persons in both groups, afterward getting the performance index which is part of the appraisal program. Measurements of organizational effectiveness should be periodically available to him. Information to control his intervening variables should be available from personnel records. In six months' time he will be able to do a statistical analysis (or get someone else to do it for him) and have his first data. Follow-up data, as it becomes available, will soon give an indication of the value of the program. The hardheaded objector to the program's introduction can then be either supported or converted by the facts rather than by "gut feelings."

The next hypothetical example deals with a question on the group organizational level (once again, it would be possible to extend or complicate it to include the individual level). Here the problem is posed whether a cutback in personnel is likely to change effectiveness at the organizational level. If it does produce change downward, how much of a change? The question may arise because of environmental factors at the organizational level (markets, general economic conditions, financial problems) or simply because someone feels it is time to "trim off some fat." Before the cutback is introduced, measurement of dependent variables must be made at both levels so that a base line is available for comparison. Reduction in group size and task demands must be equivalent when groups are to be compared. Depending on the nature of the changes, it may be necessary to use a control group although it may be possible to use the pre-change base line as a comparison. Intervening variables (fluctuating market conditions, introduction of new equipment and automation, change of location of plant) must be held constant at organizational level or taken into consideration over the period of time during which measurements are made. These variables are outlined in Figure 21-10.

FIGURE 21-10

HYPOTHETICAL PROBLEM ON
SOCIAL-ORGANIZATIONAL LEVELS

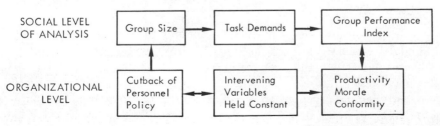

Now measurements made over an interval of time should give some indication of how the cutback influenced effectiveness of the various groups and of the total organization.

In both the speculative examples in Figures 21-9 and 21-10 it can be seen that the problem posed is reduced to the minimum information required to answer the immediate question. It would be relatively easy to extend the models depending on the time, resources, cooperation, and information available to the researcher.

CONCLUSION

We have presented here speculative examples of how the general model of effectiveness may be used. Each unique organizational problem may be dealt with according to its particular characteristics. In this way the model provides flexibility.

One factor not taken directly into account by the model but which must not be lost sight of in its use is that an organization is a process. One past problem has come about because of the tendency to think of organizations in terms of structure and the consequent design of static models or the use of static descriptions. The model proposed in this chapter is not intended as static; its feedback loops allow for ongoing interaction and changing sets of relationships.

It used to be a popular game, taken seriously by everyone, to ask "great men," leaders of the world's successful organizations, the key to their success as outstanding leaders of industry, government, or commercial enterprise. Equally seriously, they would tend to respond with a bit of ambiguous folk philosophy, often leaning toward theology, which would then become the guideline for their admirers. Some researchers, and certainly many practical managers, have not progressed much farther today. In retrospect, it can be seen that the simple naming of variables, whether based on experience, observation, or analysis of questionnaires, becomes a random and piecemeal exercise with questionable results. The investigation of what is happening in the organization must be done in an orderly fashion. The complexity of the contemporary organization does not allow for crystal ball gazing nor can it rely on charismatic leadership.

SUMMARY

An attempt has been made in this chapter to provide a simple schematic model which could form the basis for investigation of factors related to effectiveness within the organization. The model proposed can be used to examine organizational dynamics at the level of the individual, the group, and the total organization. It is flexible enough to be used to examine single questions which do not immediately affect all three levels; yet it can be used to examine the most highly complex problems which plague the modern manager.

The model does a number of things:

1. It allows for the measurement of organizational variables.
2. It allows for the uniqueness of each organization.
3. It is not so complex as to be valueless.
4. It is not so simple that it loses predictive ability.

It is stressed throughout the chapter how important it is to specify the dependent variables and effectiveness is proposed as consisting of five measurable variables: productivity, morale, conformity, adaptiveness, and institutionalization. At the individual and group levels, the measurement of effectiveness will vary depending on the unique demands of the job; however, a number of suggestions have been made to measure productivity, creativity, commitment, personal development, conformity, and influence on others, at the level of the individual. On the group level, the variables are probably similar to those at the organizational level.

Measurement of the independent variables must also be accurate. Some broad general categories have been suggested such as structural, environmental, and task variables at the group level; and these plus control systems and political and economic factors at the organizational level. At the individual level the general categories of physical characteristics, psychological characteristics, and engineering factors have been suggested as guides to a possibly lengthy litany.

Illustrations of simple and complex models have been provided, both of a hypothetical nature and from the research literature on leadership. Now the manager should set up a model according to the specific organizational problems he needs to pursue, employing the general principles of scientific investigation outlined earlier in the text. By using what he has learned about individuals and groups, their needs and dynamics, he should be prepared to make the world of his organization more understandable to himself and to his fellows, allowing for prediction of events and for improvement of the organization as a unit and of its members as human beings.

BIBLIOGRAPHY

ARGYRIS, CHRIS, *Personality and Organization*. New York: Harper & Row, Publishers, 1957.

———, "Individual Actualization in Complex Oranizations," *Mental Hygiene*, XLIV (1960), 226–337.

ASCH, S. E., "Studies of Independence and Conformity: A Minority of One Against a Unanimous Majority," *Psychological Monograph*, LXX, No. 9 (1956).

BALES, ROBERT F., "Some Uniformities of Behavior in Small Social Systems," in *Readings in Social Psychology*, eds. S. E. Swanson, T. M. Newcomb, and E. L. Hartley. New York: Henry Holt, 1952.

———, "The Equilibrium Problem in Small Groups," in *Working Papers in the Theory of Action*, eds. T. Parsons et al. New York: The Free Press, 1953.

BANDURA, A. and R. H. WALTERS, *Social Learning and Personality Development*. New York: Holt, Rinehart & Winston, Inc., 1963.

BASS, B. M., *Organizational Psychology*. Boston: Allyn & Bacon, Inc., 1965.

BAUMHART, R. C., S. J., "How Ethical are Businessmen?", *Harvard Business Review*, XXXIX, No. 4 (July-August 1961), 6–31.

BLAUNER, R., "Work Satisfaction and Industrial Trends in Modern Society," in *Labour and Trade Unionism*, eds. W. Galenson and S. M. Lipset. New York: John Wiley & Sons, Inc., 1960.

BORDEN, GEORGE A. et al., *Speech Behavior and Human Interaction*. Englewood Cliffs, N.J.: Prentice-Hall, Inc., 1969.

BOWERS, D. G. and S. E. SEASHORE, "Predicting Organizational Effectiveness With a Four-Factor Theory of Leadership," *Administrative Science Quarterly*, XI, No. 2 (1966), 238–263.

CAMPBELL, R. E., "The Prestige of Industries," *Journal of Applied Psychology*, XLIV (1960), 1–5.

COCH, L. and J. R. P. FRENCH, "Overcoming Resistance to Change," *Human Relations*, I (1948), 512–532.

CRUTCHFIELD, R. S., "Conformity and Character," *American Psychologist*, X (1955), 191–198.

DAHLE, T. L., "Transmitting Information to Employees: A Study of Five Methods," *Personnel*, XXXI (1954), 243–246.

DAVIS, M., "Community Attitudes Towards Fluoridation," *Public Opinion Quarterly*, XXIII (1959), 474–482.

DAY, R. C. and R. L. HAMBLIN, "Some Effects of Close and Punitive Styles of Supervision," *American Journal of Sociology*, LXIX (1964), 499–510.

DEARBORN, DEWITT C. and HERBERT A. SIMON, "Selective Perception: A Note on the Departmental Identifications of Executives," *Sociometry*, XXI (1958), 140–144.

ERLICH, J., J. W. RINEHART, and C. HOWELL, "The Study of Role Conflict: Explorations in Methodology," *Sociometry*, XXV (1962), 85–97.

EMERSON, R. M., "Power-dependence Relations," *American Sociological Review*, XXVII (1962), 31–41.

ETZIONI, A., *A Comparative Analysis of Complex Organizations*. New York: The Free Press, 1961.

FESTINGER, L., *A Theory of Cognitive Dissonance*. New York: Harper & Row, Publishers, 1957.

FIEDLER, F. E., "The Leader's Psychological Distance and Group Effectiveness," *Group Dynamics*, 2nd ed., eds. D. Cartwright and A. Zander. Chicago: Row Peterson, 1960.

——, "Engineer the Job to Fit the Manager," *Harvard Business Review*, XLIII, No. 5 (1965), 115–122.

——, *A Theory of Leadership Effectiveness*. New York: McGraw-Hill Book Company, 1967.

FRENCH, J. R. P., Jr. and B. H. RAVEN, "The Bases of Social Power," in *Studies in Social Power*, ed. D. Cartwright. Ann Arbor, Mich.: The University of Michigan Press, 1959.

FRENCH, J. R. P., JR. and R. Snyder, "Leadership and Interpersonal Power," in *Studies in Social Power*, ed. D. Cartwright. Ann Arbor, Mich.: The University of Michigan Press, 1959.

——, H. W. MORRISON, and G. LEVINGER, "Coercive Power and Forces Affecting Conformity," *Journal of Abnormal and Social Psychology*, LXI (1960), 93–101.

FROMM, ERICH, *The Sane Society*. New York: Holt, Rinehart & Winston, Inc., 1955.

GIBB, C. A., "An Interactional View of the Emergence of Leadership," in *Leadership*, ed. C. A. Gibb. Baltimore: Penguin Books, Inc., 1969.

GOFFMAN, ERVING, *The Presentation of Self in Everyday Life*. Garden City, N.Y.: Anchor Books, 1959.

GOODE, W. J., "A Theory of Role Strain," *American Sociological Review*, XXV (1960), 403–496.

GREENSPOON, J., "The Reinforcing Effect of Two Spoken Words on the Frequency of Two Responses," *American Journal of Psychology*, LXVIII (1955), 409–416.

GROSS, N., W. S. MASON, and A. W. McEACHERN, *Explorations in Role Analysis*. New York: John Wiley & Sons, Inc., 1958.

GUEST, R. H., *Organizational Change: The Effect of Successful Leadership*. Homewood, Ill.: The Dorsey Press, Inc., and Richard D. Irwin, Inc., 1962.

HAIMAN, F. S., "The Specialization of Roles and Functions in a Group," *Quarterly Journal of Speech*, XLIII (1957), 165–167.

HAIRE, M., "Role Perceptions in Labour Management Relations: An Experimental Approach," *Industrial and Labour Relations Review*, VIII (1955), 204–216.

—— and W. F. GRUNES, "Perceptual Defenses: Processes Protecting an Original Perception of Another Personality," *Human Relations*, No. 3 (1950), 403–412.

HERZBERG, FREDERICK, *Work and the Nature of Man*. Cleveland: World Publishing Company, 1966.

_____ et al., *The Motivation to Work*. New York: John Wiley & Sons, Inc., 1959.

HOLLANDER, E. P., "Conformity, Status, and Idiosyncrasy Credit," *Psychological Review*, LXV (1958), 117–127.

HOVLAND, C. I. and I. L. JANIS, eds., *Personality and Persuasibility*. New Haven, Conn.: Yale University Press, 1959.

HUXLEY, ALDOUS, *The Devils of Loudon*. London: Chatto & Windus, Ltd., 1961.

JANIS, I. L. and S. FESHBACH, "Effects of Fear Arousing Communications," *Journal of Abnormal and Social Psychology*, XLVIII (1953), 78–92.

JENNINGS, HELEN H., *Leadership and Isolation*, 2nd ed. New York: Longmans, Green & Co., Ltd., 1950.

JOURARD, S. M., *The Transparent Self*. Princeton, N.J.: Van Nostrand Co., Inc., 1964.

JURGENSEN, C. E., "What Job Applicants Look For in a Company," *Personnel Psychology*, I, No. 4 (1948), 443–445.

KAHN, R. L., "Human Relations on the Shop Floor," in *Human Relations and Modern Management*, ed. E. M. Hugh-Jones. Amsterdam: North Holland Publishing Co., 1958.

KATZ, D., "The Functional Approach to the Study of Attitude Change," *Public Opinion Quarterly*, No. 24 (1960), 163–204.

KELLY, JOE, *Organizational Behavior*. Homewood, Ill.: Richard D. Irwin, Inc., and The Dorsey Press, Inc., 1969.

KELMAN, H. C., "Processes of Opinion Change," *Public Opinion Quarterly*, XXV (1961), 57–78.

KRECH, D., R. S. CRUTCHFIELD, and E. L. BALLACHEY, *Individual in Society*. New York: McGraw-Hill Book Company, 1962.

LAWLESS, D. J., "Employee Attitudes Toward Self and Job According to Time at Work and Status Achievement" (unpublished Ph.D. thesis, University of London, 1969).

LEWIN, KURT, *Field Theory in Social Science; Selected Theoretical Papers*, ed. D. Cartwright. New York: Harper & Row, Publishers, 1951.

_____, "Group Decision and Social Change," in eds. E. Maccoby, T. M. Newcomb, and E. L. Hartley. *Readings in Social Psychology*, 3rd ed., New York: Holt, Rinehart & Winston, Inc., 1958.

LEWIN, K., R. LIPPITT, and R. K. WHITE, "An Experimental Study of Leadership and Group Life," in *Readings in Social Psychology*, 3rd ed. by E. Maccoby, T. M. Newcomb, and E. L. Hartley. New York: Holt, Rinehart & Winston, Inc., 1958.

LIEBERMAN, S., "The Effects of Changes in Roles on the Attitudes of the Occupants," *Human Relations*, IX (1956), 385–402.

LIKERT, RENSIS, *New Patterns of Management*. New York: McGraw-Hill Book Company, 1961.

_____, *The Human Organization*. New York: McGraw-Hill Book Company, 1967.

LIPSET, S. N. and R. BENDIX, *Social Mobility in Industrial Society*. Berkeley: University of California Press, 1959.

MAIER, NORMAN R. F., *Psychology in Industry*, 3rd ed. Boston: Houghton Mifflin Company, 1965.

MANN, F. C., "Toward an Understanding of the Leadership Role in Formal Organization," in *Leadership and Productivity*, eds. R. Dubin et al. San Francisco: Chandler Publishing Co., 1965.

————, and F. W. NEFF, "Involvement and Participation in Change," in *Psychology in Administration*, ed. T. W. Costello and S. S. Zalkind. Englewood Cliffs, N.J.: Prentice-Hall, Inc., 1963.

MARROW, ALFRED J. et al., *Management by Participation*. New York: Harper & Row, Publishers, 1967.

MASLOW, A. H., "A Theory of Human Motivation," *Psychological Review*, L (1943), 370–373.

————, *Motivation and Personality*. New York: Harper & Row, Publishers, 1954.

————, *Eupsychian Management*. Homewood, Ill.: Richard D. Irwin, Inc., and The Dorsey Press, Inc., 1965.

McCLELLAND, DAVID C., *The Achieving Society*. Princeton, N.J.: D. Van Nostrand Co., Inc., 1961.

————, "Business Drive and National Achievement," *Harvard Business Review*, XL (July-August 1962), 99–112.

McGREGOR, D., *The Human Side of Enterprise*. New York: McGraw-Hill Book Company, 1960.

MEREI, F., "Group Leadership and Institutionalization," *Human Relations*, II (1949), 23–39.

MILLS, C. WRIGHT, "Labour Leaders and the Power Elite," in *Industrial Conflict*, eds. A. Kornhauser, R. Dubin, and A. M. Ross. New York: McGraw-Hill Book Company, 1954.

MORENO, J. L., *Who Shall Survive?*, 2nd ed. Beacon, N.Y.: Beacon House Inc., 1953.

MORSE, N. C., *Satisfactions in the White-collar Job*. Ann Arbor, Mich.: Institute for Social Research, The University of Michigan, 1953.

MOSEL, J. N., "Incentives, Supervision and Probability," in *Personnel Administration*, XXV (January-February 1962), 9–14.

MURRAY, EDWARD J., *Motivation and Emotion*. Englewood Cliffs, N.J.: Prentice-Hall, Inc., 1964.

NEWCOMB, T. M., *Personality and Social Change: Attitude Formation in a Student Community*. New York: Dryden Press, 1943.

NOE, W. K., "A Pilot Study of the Validity of Ratings Done on First-Line Supervisors," *Studies in Personnel Psychology*, II, No. 1 (April 1970).

OAKES, W. F., A. E. DROGE, and B. AUGUST, "Reinforcement Effects on Participation in Group Discussion," *Psychological Reports*, VII (1960), 503–514.

PARKINSON, C. NORTHCOTE, *Parkinson's Law: Or the Pursuit of Progress*. London: John Murray, 1958.

PERROW, CHARLES, "Goals in Complex Organizations," *American Sociological Review*, XXVI (1961), 855.

PFUNGST, O., *Clever Hans (The Horse of Mr. von Osten): A Contribution to Experimental, Animal and Human Psychology*. New York: Holt, Rinehart & Winston, Inc., 1965.

PIGORS, PAUL and CHARLES A. MYERS, *Personnel Administration: A Point of View and a Method.* New York: McGraw-Hill Book Company, 1956.

PORTER, L. W. and E. E. LAWLER, "Properties of Organizational Structure in Relation to Job Attitude and Job Behavior," *Psychological Bulletin,* LXIV (1965), 23–51.

PRICE, JAMES L., *Organizational Effectiveness.* Homewood, Ill.: Richard D. Irwin, Inc., 1968.

READ, W. H., "Upward Communication in Industrial Hierarchies," *Human Relations,* XV, No. 1 (1962), 3–15.

RICHARD, JAMES E., "A President's Experience with Democratic Management," quoted in *Organizational Behavior and Administration,* rev. ed., by Paul R. Lawrence and John A. Seiler: Homewood, Ill.: Richard D. Irwin, Inc., and The Dorsey Press, Inc., 1965.

ROETHLISBERGER, F. J. and W. J. DICKSON, *Management and the Worker.* Cambridge, Mass.: Harvard University Press, 1939.

ROKEACH, M., *The Open and Closed Mind.* New York: Basic Books, Inc., Publishers, 1960.

ROSENBERG, M. J., "A Structural Theory of Attitude Dynamics," *Public Opinion Quarterly,* XXIV (1960), 319–340.

_____, "An Analysis of Affective-Cognitive Consistency," in *Attitude Organization and Change,* eds. C. I. Hovland and M. J. Rosenberg. New Haven, Conn.: Yale University Press, 1960.

RYCHLAK, JOSEPH F., *A Philosophy of Science for Personality Theory.* Boston: Houghton Mifflin Company, 1968.

SECORD, T. S. and C. W. BACKMAN, *Social Psychology.* New York: McGraw-Hill Book Company, 1964.

SHERIF, M., "A Study of Some Social Factors in Perception," *Archives of Psychology,* No. 187 (1935).

SHULL, F. A. JR., and D. C. MILLER, "Role-Conflict Behavior in Administration," a paper read at the American Sociological Association, New York, 1960; quoted in *Social Psychology* by T. F. Secord and C. W. Backman. New York: McGraw-Hill Book Company, 1964.

SMITH, P. C., "The Prediction of Individual Differences in Susceptibility to Industrial Monotony," *Journal of Applied Psychology,* XXXIX (1955), 322–329.

SMITH, HENRY CLAY, *Psychology of Industrial Behavior,* 2nd ed. New York: McGraw-Hill Book Company, 1964.

STEPHENSON, WILLIAM, *The Play Theory of Mass Communication.* Chicago: University of Chicago Press, 1967.

STOGDILL, R. M., "Personal Factors Associated with Leadership: A Survey of the Literature," *Journal of Psychology,* XXV (1948), 35–71.

STOUFFER, S. A., et al., *The American Soldier Vol I: Adjustment During Army Life* and Stouffer et al., *The American Soldier Vol. II: Combat and its Aftermath.* Princeton, N.J.: Princeton University Press, 1949.

STRICKLAND, L. H., *Surveillance and Trust,* J. Personality, 1958, XXVI, pp. 200–215.

TAYLOR, F. W., *The Principles of Scientific Management*. New York: Harper & Bros., 1911.

TOFFLER, ALVIN, *Future Shock*. (New York, Random House, 1970.)

VAN ZELST, R. H., "An Interpersonal Relations Technique for Industry," *Personnel*, American Management Association, July 1952, pp. 68–77.

WALKER, C. R., "The Problem of the Repetitive Job," *Harvard Business Review*, No. 28 (1950), pp. 54–58.

_____, and R. H. GUEST, *The Man on the Assembly Line*. Cambridge, Mass.: Harvard University Press, 1952.

WEBER, MAX, *The Theory of Social and Economic Organization*. New York: Oxford University Press, Inc., 1947.

WHYTE, W. F., *Streetcorner Society*. Chicago: University of Chicago Press, 1943.

_____, *Human Relations in the Restaurant Industry*. New York: McGraw-Hill Book Company, 1948.

_____, *Money and Motivation: An Analysis of Incentives in Industry*. New York: Harper & Row, Publishers. 1955.

WOODWARD, J., *Industrial Organization*. London: Oxford University Press, Inc., 1965.

INDEX

Bandura, A., 344
Bargaining, 219, 294
Base line, 376
Basic initiating rank, 225
Bass, Bernard M., 23, 121, 122
Batching, 24
Baumhart, R. C., 294
Belittling, 72
Belongingness, need for, 85
Bendix, R., 254
Bias, experimenter, 380-81
Blauner, R., 26, 157, 252
Blind spot (social), 37
Bloc, power, 242
Blue collar workers, 252-53
Body type, 42
Bonus schemes, 150
Boomerang effect, 194
Borden, G. A., 304
Boredom, overcoming, 23-25 (*See also* Monotony)
Bowers, D. G., 326
Brain, in perception, 31
Brainwashing, 166, 193-94, 198
Brennan, 23
Bribery, 249, 295
Bulletin board, value for communication, 137
Bureaucracy, 109-12
  non-bureaucracy, 112-13
  Weber's definition, 110
Burke, Edmund, 295

Cabal, 209
Campbell, R. E., 25
Cantril, Hadley, 35
Carnegie, Dale, 166
Castration complex, 72
Catatonic, 72-73
Catholics, as achievers, 254
Cattell, Raymond B., 58
Cause, 39-40
  effect, 368-69, 379
  of social event, 39-40
Central communication position, 138-39
Centralization of power, 240-41, 397 (*See also* Decentralization)
Cerebrotonia, 60
Challenge of complexity, 163
Challenging work, 157, 343
Change
  effects of, 18-21, 353
  management of, 11-13
  in personality, 39
  social, 11-13, 355
  in work, 335
Choice, reasons for
  in conflict situation, 291-94
  of others, 211-13, 253
  and proximity, 217

Circle pattern of communication, 138-39, 315
Clerical workers, 22
Climate (work), 357
  for participation, 324
  for self-development, 157
Cliques, 209, 256
Close-mindedness, 179-81
Clusters, attitude, 168
Coacting groups, 117
Coalition, power of, 238, 242
Coch, L., 228, 323
Code names, 140
Cognitive
  component of attitude, 167
  dissonance, 170-73
  economics, 38-41, 42-44, 50
  system, 35
    and attitude change, 184
  theory of motivation, 79-80
  world of managers, 12
Cohesiveness, 210-11, 376, 379
  and comparison level, 222
  group, 25
  and morale, 226-28
  and norms, 273, 290, 367
Commitment
  to change, 197-98
  and person choice, 220
Committees, and role strain, 122-23, 289
Communication, 9, 125-43
  convincing, 190-93
  not listening, 137-38
  one-way vs. two-way, 138
  patterns, 138-39, 331
  receivers of, 141
  solutions, 134-37
Communication problems, 127-34
  and status, 132, 257
Communicator characteristics, 189-90
Communist managers, 64
Comparison level, 390
  for alternatives, 221
  in exchange theory, 215
Competition, 150
  between groups, 118
  as motivating, 92-94
Complainers, 98, 354-55
Complex man theory, 159-63
Complexes, personality, 55, 73
Complexity
  of decisions, 18-19
  of task, 343, 396
    and communication, 139
    and organizational type, 116-17
Compliance, 187
Compromise, 221-22, 292-93
Confidence, information in, 290
Conflict
  between groups, 118-19
  preventing, 289

Factor analysis, 57-58
Failure, influence on aspiration, 89-92
Fear-arousing communication, 192-93
Feedback (*See* Knowledge of results)
Feshbach, S., 192
Festinger, L., 170, 172
Fiedler, Fred E., 328-31, 360, 399, 401
Field observation, 216-17
Field theory, 56-57
Fixation, 73
Flat organizations, 121
Flexibility, in managers, 161-62
Food presentation, and attitude change, 194
Ford, Henry, 158
Ford, model T, 112
Form, Wm. H., 256
Free will, 80
French, J. R. P., 228, 233, 239, 270, 323
Freud, Sigmund, 52-54, 57, 59, 61, 80, 217
Fringe benefits, 99, 154
Fromm, E., 17
Frustration
  from lack of communication, 138
  of workers, 153
Functional disorders, definition of, 73
Futility, sense of, 19
Future Shock, 19

Gamblers, managers as, 64
Games, and competition, 93-94, 296
Generalization, 337-38
Genital character, 61
Genius, definition of, 73
Gibb, C. A., 309
Goals, 320, 388-89
  definition, 83
  emphasis on, 327
  high performance, 320
Godwin, William, 183
Goethe, 155
Goffman, Erving, 140
Goode, W. J., 294
Grapevine, communication via the, 137
Greenspoon, J., 333
Gross, N., 287, 291, 293, 294
Group, 396
  as agent of change, 197
  coacting, 117
  control group, 375
  dual purpose of, 107-09, 327
    and leadership, 309-10
  dynamics (definition), 206
    study of, 9
  effective, 388-91
  formal and informal, 106-07
  influence, 197
    on aspiration, 90
    on attitudes, 179
    on morale, 226-27
    on norms, 271-72
    on persuasibility, 199

Group (*cont.*)
  leadership, 303-07
  matched group, 375, 380
  size of, 120-22, 396
    and satisfaction, 121
  therapy, definition, 73
  types of team, 228
Grumbling, 354-55
Grunes, W. F., 26, 48
Guest, R. H., 22, 319, 323
Gut experience, 20, 391

Haiman, F. S., 307
Haire, M., 26, 30-32, 48
Hallucinogens, 20
Halo effect, 40
Hamblin, R. L., 322
Hawthorne studies, 145, 151, 152, 153,
    227, 371, 378, 382
Health
  and leadership, 302
  and worker status, 253
Heart attack, rates of, 70
Hedonism, 80-81, 89, 148, 152
Heredity, and personality, 58-59
Herzberg, F., 16, 96, 343
  motivation-hygiene theory, 96-99
High-credibility, 189, 195
Hippocrates, 60
Hobbes, Thomas, 231, 240-41
Hollander, E. P., 277
Homans, George, 217
Honeymoon, for managers, 291
Hostility, as communication barrier, 135-36
Hovland, C. I., 186, 189, 190, 195
Howell, C., 294
Human relations skills, 319-20
Huxley, Aldous, 198
Hypnosis, 170, 198
Hypothesis, 367
  null hypothesis, 369, 377, 379, 382
Hypothetical construct, 166
Hysteria, 68

IBM, 25
Id, 53-54
Identification, 187
  as a defense mechanism, 73
  as power source, 234, 344
Idiosyncrasy credits, 277
Idiot, definition, 73
Imbecile, definition, 73
Imitation, 344, 346
Implicit personality theory, 40
Impressing by signs, 126
Incentives, 156, 321-22
  and competition, 92-94
  definition, 83
  economic, 148-51
  group vs. individual, 153
  money as, 94-96, 154

417

Power (*cont.*)
  majority vote, 241
  manager, 358-59
  nature of, 230-32
  and norms, 276-77
  process, 236
  reacting to, 239-40
  structure, 231, 241-42
  types of, 233-35
Powerlessness, 20, 355
Preconscious, 74
Predictability, 368-69, 372
  basis of social interaction, 15
  and choice of persons, 218
Prediction, 365-67
  by attitude, 166-67
  by norms, 281-82
  in role conflict, 292-94
Prejudice, 169, 178
  definition, 168
  in hiring, 295, 309
Price, James L., 389, 391
Primacy-recency question, 192
Prisoners of war, resistance to propaganda, 191
Probability, 369
Productivity
  decline of, 150
  definition, 389
  and environment, 145
  high and low, 322, 325-26, 331, 372
  and morale, 227-28
Projection, 54, 90
  by managers, 47
Projective test, 74
Promotion, 290, 321, 324, 343, 360
  and expectation, 92
  and role conflict, 288
Propaganda, Chinese, 191
Proximity and choice, 217-19
Psyche, 74
Psychegroup, 216
Psychiatry, definition, 6
Psychoanalysis, 52-54
Psychological contract, 144-64, 370
  nature of, 146-48
  types of, 148-63
Psychological distance, 238-39, 296, 360-61
Psychological tests (*See* Tests, psychological)
Psychologists
  categories of, 6
  organizational, 7
Psychology
  applied, 6
  definition, 5
  experimental, 6
Psychoneurosis (*See* Neurosis)
Psychopath, 66
Psychosis, 20, 65 *passim*, 309
Psychosomatic disorders, 69-70

Quixote, 29-30, 32, 49

Racial groups, 43-44
Ratebusters, 161, 274
Rational-economic theory, 148-51
Rationalization, 54, 250
Raven, B. H., 233
Read, W. H., 132
Recognition
  as a motivator, 97
  as satisfying, 253
Recognition threshold, 36-37
Regression, 74-75
Reinforcement (*See also* Reward), 334, 336-40, 342, 344-45, 355
Repetitious jobs, 21
Repression, 53
Research Center for Group Dynamics, 57
Research reports, amount of, 4-5
Resources, and power, 232-33
Response, 337-39, 373-82
Responsibility
  manager's awareness of, 294-95
  as a motivator, 97, 325
  and satisfaction, 157, 253
Rest periods, 24
Retarded workers, 23
Retirement, 24, 296-97
Reward (*See also* Reinforcement)
  definition, 83
Richard, James E., 325
  in exchange theory, 214
Rinehart, J. W., 294
Rites of passage, 291
Rogers, Carl, 56, 74, 80, 156
Roethlisberger, F. J., 145
Rokeach, M. J., 179-80
Role, 280-98
  effect of change, 284-85
  clash of, 286-87
  expectations, 281-85
  male, 295-97
  nature of, 280-82
  obligations, 282
  strain and conflict, 272, 285-94
    built in, 287-89
    choice in, 291-94
    reduction of, 289-91
Role price, 294
Rorschach ink blots, 71
Rosenberg, M. J., 168-69
Rotation, work, 24
Rousseau, 152
Rychlak, Joseph, 59

Safety, and competition for safety records, 93-94 (*See also* Security)
Salary
  as a hygiene factor, 97, 99
  as just, 247
Sampling, in person choice, 218-19